THE GOODFELLOW CATALOG OF WONDERFUL THINGS

Traditional & Contemporary Crafts

CHRISTOPHER WEILLS

A BERKLEY WINDHOVER BOOK
published by
BERKLEY PUBLISHING CORPORATION

Standard Book Number: 425-03402-X

Berkley Windhover Books
Berkley Publishing Corporation
200 Madison Avenue
New York, New York 10016

Printed in the United States of America.
Berkley Windhover Edition, October 1977.

Table of Contents

Senior Editors
  Christopher Weills
  Bill Netzer

Art Director
  Sharon Stein

Editors
  Bette London
  Linda Morrison
  Margaret Webster
  Avril Angevine
  Arlene Noble
  Jon Stewart

Editorial Assistants
  Susan Clark
  Gene Ulansky
  Molly Lyne
  Mary Neff
  Barbara Wilms

Design
  Sharon Stein Studio
  Berkeley, California

Production Staff
  Anne Morrison
  Joan Powell
  Tom Farmer
  Avril Angevine
  Susan Melim

Staff Photographers
  Bill Netzer
  Bob Knickerbocker

Phototypesetters
  Mori
  Susan Clark
  Lisa Papa

Acknowledgments

This book is the cumulative product of many people's energies and assistance. A few deserve special mention. Bob Scheer's considerable generosity and encouragement made the book possible. His commitment also included the conversion of his garage into the living / working space for the Catalog. And in the last hectic days, he sustained an exhausted but dogged staff with gourmet repasts. Ida Scheer graciously shared her life and apartment with the Goodfellow staff, whose labors spilled over from the adjoining garage. Mark Switzer believed in Goodfellow and helped unhesitatingly. Mr. John Pillsbury, our bank manager, permitted the dream to flourish. Sy Rubin of Berkley Windhover saw our vision when others didn't.

Other friends to thank are Tim Baker (Berkeley Printing Center), Connie Field and Steve Talbot, James Meyer, Francy Balcomb, Narda Zacchino, Harvey and Pat Cohen, Dugald Stermer, Cricket Ahrens, Tuck and Susan Weills, Anne Weills and Dan Siegel, Penny, Paul and Elizabeth Matson, Kenly Weills and Rudy Petschek, Christopher Scheer, Tom Stein, Vincent Creek, Bill Northwood, Steve Wasserman, Eric Foor, Barbara Kinsbury and Bitsy Lyne, Susan Lyne, Warren and Denise Hinckle, Larry Bensky, Clark Photo Graphic of San Francisco, Arnie Passman, Buzz Wilms, Robert Chartoff, Brenda Walker, Russell Bass, Gerry and Joan Lubenow, Peter and Abbey Johnson, Shelia Grant, Jonathan Siegel, Judy Scott and Don Stillman, Nancy Bleck, Cora Gregory, Richard Lethridge, John Kohn, Linda Morse and Peter Cohen, Dick Fine, Ray Nitta, Kate Beckett, Cheryl French, Howie Stein, Billy Moore, Marica Meyer, Patric Mayers, Robin Freeman, Beverly Hoesing, Frederick and Nicki Stein, Geoffrey Stein, Chere Mah, David and Nancy Siegel, Nikki Arai, Vicki Steinheimer, Arthur Blaustein, Ellen and Buzz Murphy, Christopher and Julia Fries, Ernie Waugh, John Kreidler, George Zender, and most especially John and Audrey Weills.

This Catalog is different. Unlike ordinary mail-order-house catalogs, The Goodfellow Catalog of Wonderful Things is designed for *direct orders*. You send your orders directly to the craftspeople who make the items you choose.

The Goodfellow Catalog of Wonderful Things was conceived as a sort of meeting ground between crafts producers and consumers. All of the products in this book are handmade. Each is a unique work of art, crafted with special care—and with all the wonderful idiosyncrasies that only individually created items can have.

The name and address of each craftsperson appears in italics on the page where his or her write-up occurs. Each participant has provided his or her own product information and biographical sketch, touching on his or her work, attitudes, interests and/or lifestyle. The result is a personal glimpse of each craftsperson—much like a photograph which catches an individual in mid-step.

Unfortunately the Catalog cannot show everything these craftspeople make. What we have tried to offer is a portion of their best work. Most of our artisans have their own brochures and welcome inquiries regarding custom work.

The Catalog has made every effort to insure the reliability of the craftspeople here and their ability to fill all custom orders. The responsibility for a satisfactory transaction, however, rests between you and your craftsperson. Most items will be delivered by United Parcel Service in four to eight weeks; but because of the many exceptions, we suggest you request a delivery date and carrier information when submitting your order.

It is important that your orders be accurate. In most cases, the Catalog provides all of the information necessary for placing complete orders: sizes, materials, designs, colors, dimensions, weights and so forth. Be sure to clearly state your preferences, including second choices where appropriate. In some cases, shipping costs and arrangements will have to be worked out between you and your craftsperson. Special-order costs will also be a matter for individual discussion.

Orders to craftspersons in your own state will be subject to state sales taxes, and state and local tax regulations should be consulted and followed by both buyers and sellers.

A word about prices. This was best expressed in the first edition of the Catalog and still holds true: "Needless to say, the economy has lately been subject to almost daily explosions and implosions. Consequently, some degree of price fluctuation is apt to exist. The gold and silver used in the making of jewelry, for instance, is subject to price changes at any given moment. We trust the changes will be slight, and hope they don't occur at all." It's worth mentioning that a few of our craftspeople wrote in to *lower* prices on items they can now produce more efficiently.

We have tried to insure the accuracy of prices and information given for products, but where there is any question we suggest that you consult the individual artisan.

At the end of the book you will find two alphabetical indexes. The first lists the names of the craftspeople and, in some cases, their stores and workshops. The second is a product and craft index. This will be particularly useful since, for aesthetic reasons, we have arranged the Catalog as a random array of wonderful things.

In addition there is an extensive reference section covering major crafts organizations; fairs and periodicals; book reviews; state arts councils; and schools with instruction in crafts.

We are already dreaming of Goodfellow Three. Production, in fact, should begin sometime in Spring 1978. We look forward to hearing from all our readers, and we welcome any inquiries and suggestions. Write to us at The Goodfellow Catalog of Wonderful Things, P.O. Box 4520, Berkeley, California 94704.

Finally, we hope that both buyers and browsers alike will enjoy reading this book for the human story it tells. Until only recently, a person without a craft was considered a person without character. It is still true that the spirit of individual craftsmanship is one of independence and self-reliance—values that our New World heritage was built upon. To these qualities our craftspeople add imagination, elbow grease, humor, love of nature, talent, perseverance and more. We hope that you will be as delighted and inspired as we have been to know them through these pages.

The Goodfellow Editors
May 1977

The Human Touch

The great "Crafts Revolution" proclaimed by *Time* magazine back in the late 1960s has today conquered America.

No longer confined to the rural enclaves of Appalachia or the Ozarks (where crafts have always thrived), nor to the urban counterculture that gave rise to *Time*'s enthusiasm, the mystique of things handmade is now deeply rooted in every ethnic group, income level and geographical area of the nation.

Consider these statistics, gathered a few years ago by Lou Harris Associates:

• Nearly 90 percent of America's adult population believes that arts and crafts improve the quality of their lives.

• Two out of every five adults—or about 52 million of us—currently engage in woodworking, weaving, pottery, ceramics or some other craft as either a hobby or a profession. Another 26 million Americans say they wish they did.

• Nearly half of all adult Americans, or 71 million, attend at least one crafts or other arts show every year. Believe it or not, that's a few million more than make it to one or more spectator sports events each year.

As proof that they're serious, these same Americans are willing to put their money where there mouth is. About two-thirds of all adult Americans would be willing to pay an extra $5 each year in taxes—if they could be assured that the money would be spent directly on support of arts and crafts. Nearly half the population would put up $25 a year, and over a third would willingly pay $50 a year.

Yet, despite this overwhelming public enthusiasm, government support for arts and crafts accounts for less than *two ten-thousandths* of one percent of the annual national budget.

Happily, the American people seem to have identified themselves with values and priorities that may be decades ahead of those of the powers-that-be. For the great crafts awareness that has emerged in America over the past decade is truly a forward-looking phenomenon—not, as some see it, the last grasp of a cold, beleaguered present at the romanticized values of yesteryear.

No, the lesson of the Crafts Revolution

is not a yearning for simplicity, or for romanticism, or even for the old Calvinistic virtues inherent in things made of blood and sweat. It is, I think, that Americans want and demand a sense of *quality* in their lives and in the things around them. And they want a sense that man—humanity—somehow is imbued in the threads and dyes of the clothes they wear, the jewelry they adorn themselves with, the utilitarian and nonutilitarian objects they live by and with. It is, it seems, a longing to know that the things we touch with our hands have been "man"ufactured by other hands—and that, because of this, those things have genuine human value.

It is particularly appropriate that such values should pervade America as it enters the first decade of its third century. In the colonial and post-revolutionary era, crafts were not a way of life, but *the* way of life. In our second century, the gods of Technology, Mass Production, Industry and Consumerism hurled the nation wildly into the twentieth century, during which—within one generation—we have collectively experienced untold prosperity, tragic poverty, two World Wars and very little real peace.

No wonder that we enter our third century with trepidation and an uncertain search for new values. But the signs that exist are hopeful. The growing recognition that individuals should play a part in the world they live in, should again learn a measure of self-sufficiency together with interdependence, should look for and value the human touch in objects they live with—these signs, we think, portend a healthy, vital future.

Alone, the appreciation for arts and crafts will not save the world, not even a small piece of it. But it's an indication—and a powerful one—that more and more people every day are learning that quality and humanness can still have a place in the world, that the individual matters and that the work we do—if we truly invest our hearts, minds and hands—can improve the quality of life for everyone.

The Goodfellow Catalog of Wonderful Things is, we hope, a testament to this belief. It is at once a celebration and an acknowledgment that American crafts today represent a strong and irrepressible force to improve the quality of life for tomorrow.

This catalog has been a long time aborning, some four years since conception. When Christopher Weills,

my erstwhile cohort in publishing and long-time comrade-in-almost-everything, came to me with the idea for a monthly crafts newsletter and eventual catalog, my inclination was to dismiss it as yet another pipe dream. But Christopher, as everyone who knows him soon learns, is a master of pipe dreams.

Some months later, he astonished me by asking if I might write and edit some copy for the first issue of the small, occasional newsletter he was publishing. Reluctantly, I accepted and soon found myself unpaid editor of The Goodfellow Newsletter, as Christopher set about the job of immersing himself in the world of craftspeople.

There, in the midst of the final years of Vietnam, the gathering storm of Watergate and the sad, bitter last gasps of the "counterculture," Christopher discovered that the Crafts Revolution was healthier than it had ever been in the headiest days of flower power. It had not only survived the cynicism and bitterness of Vietnam, Watergate and drugs, but was fast becoming a force entrenched in the salad of American lifestyles. It was activist, aggressive, self-sustaining, positive and—most important—intensely human.

As the Newsletter grew, so did our awareness that crafts represented something much more than a romantic hobby or a cottage-industry livelihood for dropouts. In the rural areas traditionally known for crafts we found an amazing spurt of growth as young people again took up the tools of their parents and grandparents. In 1974 more than 70 craft organizations, representing some 5,000 craftspeople, registered in Appalachia alone. Similar figures appeared in the Ozarks, in Alaska among the Eskimos and Aleuts, in New England, in the Southwest among Native Americans and Chicanos, in the Deep South among the rural blacks.

In the cities and suburbs crafts fairs and sidewalk artisans attracted ever greater attention, finally becoming a political issue in some areas due to competition with retail stores.

And in the bookstores, entire walls were suddenly devoted to crafts books and periodicals, as publishers released hundreds of new titles each year.

The editorship of the Newsletter eventually passed into more competent—and reliable—hands, as I returned to full-time journalistic pursuits. But, Christopher, the master pipe dreamer, was a man possessed. With the help of parents, friends, a bank manager and Master Charge he attended hundreds of crafts fairs, met and corresponded with thousands of craftspeople, organized and publicized one of the biggest crafts events in Northern California—all the while collecting and sifting material for what he hoped would be the finest representative gallery of craftspeople and their work ever put between the covers of a book.

In 1974 he published, with his own money, the first Goodfellow Catalog of Wonderful Things. It ran little more than a hundred pages and featured half that many craftspeople. And while it was a beautiful and useful book, it sold barely enough copies to cover the printing bill, what with no distributor or advertising.

And so it was back to the drawing boards, all the while cranking out the Newsletter and keeping in constant touch with craftspeople all over the country.

And for the next 2½ years, from a small garage-office-home in Berkeley, and with the unflagging support of friends and family, this issue of the Goodfellow slowly grew and took shape.

The following pages, then, are in a real sense symbolic of the world they portray. For they represent a "thing," an object filled with human vision and devotion, a tangible, visible statement asserting that quality and humanity can make life more harmonious, more joyful, more peaceful . . . and lots more lively.

As was said in the first Goodfellow Catalog: "Crafts are tools for people, made by special people who make special tools for special people. That's a simple and a wonderful thing. This is a catalog of such things."

Let me add: This catalog is itself a tool, a special tool made by a special person, and we hope that you will find it a wonderful thing.

Jon Stewart

Wonderful Things

Teddy Bears—These fuzzy fellows, these cute furry guys, these bears are 100% shearling sheepskin stuffed with polyester fiberfill. They are available in black, white or spice brown. Each bear is 18'' tall. All 24 parts are sewn together by machine using heavy nylon thread. Then the bear is stuffed and the back sewn up by hand with linen thread. Bears are equipped with ears, paws, tail and eyes. The eyes are two-color split cowhide, sewn on with linen thread. The ears and tail are tug-resistant. $30 each, shipping not included.

Jeremiah Sullivan—Jeremiah was born thirty-one years ago in a small hospital in West Los Angeles. It was a converted nursing home soon to become a vacant lot and eventually one of the earliest Taco Gato eateries.

Jerry, as he has come to be called, has assumed a low profile from the start. Little was heard from him until his development of the Teddy Dog, which after many failures, finally became the Teddy Bear. Assuming another low profile, Jerry, as he is still known to many, hasn't done much since. Down but not out? The lull before the storm? Only time will tell.

But for the moment, these few stuffed bearzie-wearzies are all that can be seen of Jeremiah Sullivan. A man who failed to arrive when nothing much was happening. Surely if not a great fellow, at least a good fellow.

Jeremiah Sullivan, 1660 Butte Street, Richmond, California 94804.

Morning Light Quilt—Machine-pieced and quilted with hand-sewn finishing. Between twenty and forty different fabrics in a variety of weights and textures are used. Measures 92'' by 69''. Available in shades of blue. Other colors possibly available upon request. Write for information on additional quilt sizes/designs. $410 postpaid.

Soft, Quilted Pouch—Can be used as a clutch purse or to hold some special treasure. Pieced and quilted using cottons and blends in a variety of weights and textures. Measures

about 8'' by 10'' closed. Available in shades of blue, brown, green and burgundy/rose—all with complementary prints. State first and second color choices and if pieced or quilted surface should be exterior. $14 postpaid.

Portfolio—Calligraphy and drawing supplies as well as personal, school and business papers/books fit comfortably in this soft, quilted portfolio. Constructed mostly of denims and chambrays, the portfolio has a large interior pouch for books and papers plus smaller pockets for pens, brushes, etc. Closed, measures approximately 12½'' by 15½''. Available in shades of blue only. $28.75 postpaid.

Morning Light Studio—People often ask, ''How did you become a quilter?'' It's not an easy question to answer because, to me, the question translates as, ''How is it that you are what you are today?'' Who knows why I'm me?! I do know that as a child I was probably influenced by my mother, who was a seamstress and quilt maker, and by my sister, who was a painter and graphic artist.

I prefer to call myself a ''textile artist,'' and described my work as ''pieced textiles''—the terms ''quilter'' and ''patchwork and quilting'' seem to have too narrow a connotation. My craft is self-taught, and I work exclusively in the genre of string quilts, i.e., any pieced design made up of narrow strips, or strings, of fabric.

The two major concerns in my work are monochromatic color, with subtle differences in tone and texture; and light-dark compositions, with either sharp contrasts or gradational transitions.

Marie Lyman, c/o Morning Light Studio, 1234 Northwest Twenty-fourth Avenue, Portland, Oregon 97210.

Leather Backpacks—These packs are made from the finest leather. Originally designed as day-packs, their durability permits a wide range of uses. Every care has been taken to insure the finest craftsmanship. I use two kinds of leather for the packs: top-grain cowhide, which has a finely grained surface and a fur-like quality on the inside (opposite page, left); and chrome-tanned latigo, one of the strongest of the 3-oz. leathers, which allows carving and design work on the surface (below). The straps are made of oak-tanned leather with adjustable sheepskin pads. All buckles are solid brass, and I use steel zippers and nylon thread for durability. Specify size: small (opposite page, right), 12'' deep, 8'' across the back, 22'' front and sides; or large (opposite page, left and below), 14'' deep, 10'' back, 24'' front and sides. Choose top-grain cowhide or chrome-tanned latigo leather. Colors available are: yellow, bright tan, light brown, dark brown, maroon or cordovan. Please give your height and weight. All packs are waterproofed and come with care instructions. Small packs $63, with design $78. Large packs $75, with design $93. Postpaid.

Vaca Muerte Leather Company—It took me twenty-seven years to learn that I loved creativity and needed to make things with my hands. Learning, growing, failure, success, challenge, the satisfaction of working with my hands and mind and being fully responsible for the quality of craftsmanship is something I will never give up.

I began to make backpacks for the same reason that I started to make other things out of leather: to produce a quality product for a reasonable price, out of a material that I enjoy working with. It took a while.

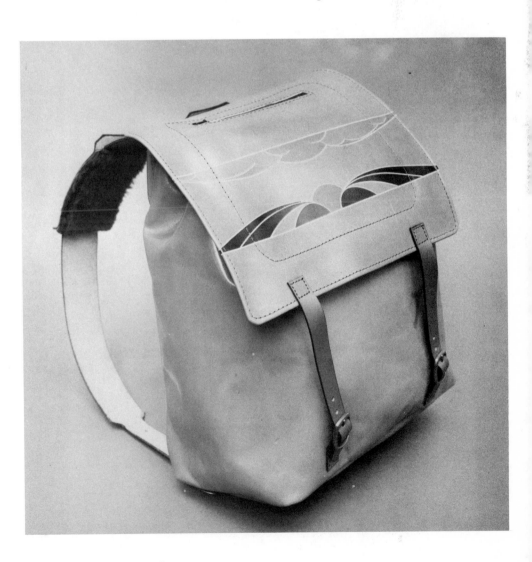

*John Beuttler,
c/o Vaca Muerte
Leather Company,
1360 Neilson Street,
Berkeley,
California 94702.*

Ceramic Kitchenware—All the items pictured here are glazed in smoke blue, smoke green, smoke white, gloss brown and ash green. They are also available glazed in these colors on their interior surfaces only. The exterior is then left unglazed, exposing the rich color and texture of the clay. The sugar dish is 3½'' wide by 4½'' high. The creamer is 3'' wide by 5'' high. The cream and sugar set weighs 2 lbs. and costs $10. The French onion soup bowl is 4¼'' wide by 3½'' high. It weighs 14 oz. and costs $5. Set of three cannisters: large cannister is 5½'' wide by 9½'' high and weighs 6 lbs. 3 oz.; medium cannister is 5'' wide by 8'' high and weighs 3 lbs. 14 oz.; small cannister is 5'' wide by 6½'' high and weighs 2 lbs. 13 oz. The set costs $33. The pitcher is 4'' wide by 9'' high. It weighs 3 lbs. 6 oz. and costs $19.

Klockhollow Pottery—Klockhollow Pottery was established in 1969 and has been run principally by Bill Klock, who also teaches pottery in Plattsburgh. In 1976, David Farrell, another potter, joined Bill Klock in an attempt to make the pottery a full-time endeavor. Since that time, Dave and Bill have been working in partnership producing an extensive line of repeat ''standardware.''

The pottery is located in a rural area on thirty-eight acres of woodland. It is accessible from all points, and shares an adjacent stream and the privacy of the oak, maple and birch.

Bill Klock and David Farrell, c/o Klockhollow Pottery, R.D. 1, Box 313, Morrisonville, New York 12962.

Handmade Musical Instruments—Constructed of fine-quality musical instrument woods. Sound boards of cedar or spruce, backs and sides of walnut, maple or other hardwood; necks of Honduras mahogany or maple, steel-reinforced when necessary; fingerboards and bridges of ebony or rosewood; vielle friction pegs of ebony or maple. Six-string guitar (steel strings), $650 postpaid. Six-string star motif guitar (steel strings), $800 postpaid. Five-string vielle with carved top, fretless or optional tied nylon movable frets, $400 postpaid.

Sacred Fire Frogs Delight Handmade Musical Instruments—I've been making instruments for a number of years. A year and a half ago I attended a session of Earthworks School of Guitar Construction and Design, and I've been concentrating mainly on guitars since that time. I am also a member of the Guild of American Luthiers. The materials I use are chosen for their acoustical qualities, strength and beauty. I focus a lot of energy on the sculptural aspects of instrument building, believing that an instrument should look as magical as it sounds. I always bear in mind that sculpting the wood means sculpting the tone as well. I'm open to and interested in custom work and crazy inventions to try and capture the cosmic sound. Music is magic and definitely one of the paths up the mountain.

Fred Carlson, Sacred Fire Frogs Delight Handmade Musical Instruments, c/o The New Hamburger, Plainfield, Vermont 05667.

9

Windsor Chairs—These Windsor chairs are handmade in the traditional manner. The turned and bent parts are oak, shaped with drawknife, plane and spokeshave. The seats are of pine, carved with chisels and an inshave. The turning is done by eye and hand on a power lathe; the spindles and bent parts are shaped with a spokeshave and block plane. The bent parts are boiled in a tank over a wood fire and then bent onto wooden molds. The chairs are finished by hand-rubbing with oil—please specify natural or dark walnut when ordering.

Tom McFadden—From the age of four or five I have had an interest in tools and wood, nurtured by two grandfathers, one an M.D., the other a carpenter and farmer. With apprehension and encouragement from my wife, I quit my clerical job and became a furniture maker. I moved out to Marin County late in 1965, and up to Mendocino County in 1973.

A desire for freedom and especially for variety in my life led me into the "back to the land" movement. My partner Peggy and I have twenty acres here and raise most all our food on it. Right now we have thirty thousand board feet of logs on the ground in our woods and are planning to have it milled up so we can add on to our house and barn, and build a workshop.

My life is very full and I like it that way. In my work I am free to design and build the very best that I can. I have the time; the money usually seems to be available. I have a variety of choices and can challenge myself. My lifestyle affords me a feeling of connection to the earth, and working with my hands is completely integral to it.

Tom McFadden, Star Route 6200, Philo, California 95466.

Comb back chair, $225
Bow back chair, $190
Side chair, $120
Shipping not included.

11

Forged Ladles—Pictured are a small iron ladle with traditional twisted handle and a large copper ladle with a forged leaf handle. Available with variations in size, material and handle. The small ladles are formed from 3'' disks; the large ladles, from 3½'' disks. The handles are approximately 8'' to 9'' long. These vary because I forge them with a hammer and anvil, as our great-grandfathers did, and no two are the same. Small iron ladle with either handle, $12.50. Large iron ladle with either handle, $15. Small copper ladle with either handle, $17.50. Large copper ladle with either handle, $20. Shipping not included.

Gene Fleming—The whole process is a one-man operation done in my shop in a nice old redwood barn, surrounded by beautiful mountains and vineyards. My main tools are the coal fire in the Buffalo forge, hammer, anvil, vise, and my head and hands. I intend my ladles to be used by your grandchildren and their children's children.

I like doing custom work. I have made iron gates, railings, fireplace pokers, snake door handles, dragon door knockers, castle-like hinges for heavy redwood doors, a brass violin-player doorpull for a music studio and more.

I have been developing my skills as a blacksmith and general metalworker for eight years. I'm twenty-eight and have a wife and a one-and-a-half-year-old daughter (who has her own 55-lb. anvil).

Gene Fleming, P.O. Box 427, Geyserville, California 95441.

Leather Briefcases—My naked-grain, oil-finished cowhide briefcases are machine-stitched with nylon thread. They are 16'' wide by 13'' high by 3'' deep. They have three large compartments and two envelope-size compartments. Special features include metal zipper compartment, locking zipper and metal-reinforced handle. The case is dark rust with multicolored appliqued laminations of leather incorporated into handles; each side is different. Totally indestructable. Shipping weight 3 lbs. $140 postpaid.

Moods—I am a full-time, self-taught studio artist. I have been working out of my studio/craft gallery since 1972.

Joseph Michael Sedeski, c/o Moods, 91 South Main Street, Wilkes-Barre, Pennsylvania 18701.

Boundwoven Rugs—Taking ideas from the Scandinavians as well as others, I try to create carpets which people can enjoy and use for years. With this in mind I pick the best yarns available and weave my carpets with three layers of wool around a linen core or warp. This results in a rug about ¼'' thick that both lies well and wears well. In the same way, I choose the colors and patterns to wear well aesthetically. The designs are inspired by interlocking geometric patterns and color preferences found in cultures all over the world.

Surprisingly, the results are unique and not predictable. They link the traditional world with the contemporary one. The rug pictured is 34'' by 8', and woven in white, black and warm grays. Several rugs of the same colors can be combined for a large room. Inkle-woven bands accent the selvedge edges. I can weave up to a width of nearly 5''. My carpets sell for $40 a running foot for the 34'' width, and $45 a running foot for a 56'' width. A 30% deposit is required for commissioned work.

Nina Holland—My lifestyle—well, it *is* predictable. I don't live in a tree house or in the desert. In fact, I enjoy indoor plumbing and eat bread from the supermarket. Yes, you guessed it, I'm over thirty—in fact, over forty.

I borrowed the idea of cleaning rugs in the snow from the Scandinavians. My debt to these people doesn't end there, because I appreciate their tradition of weaving and I use the fine wool and linen yarns which they produce.

I do write a bit, and teach a bit, because I enjoy it, and because it helps support my ten-year addiction to the craft of weaving.

Nina Holland, 37 Draper Avenue, Plattsburgh, New York 12901.

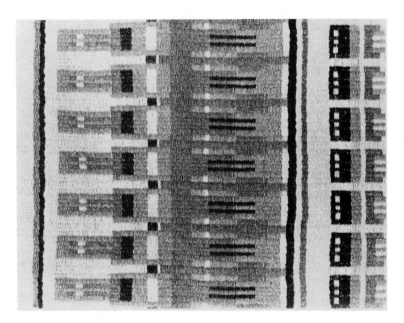

Stoneware Jars—My small corked stoneware jars measure approximately 5'' by 3¼''. They are fired to cone 10 in a reduction atmosphere. Glazes available are shiny light blue, shiny reddish to chocolate brown, matte speckled yellow-brown, shiny gray-green celadon, matte pinkish white and matte or shiny speckled blue, made from the ash of my very own apple trees. Each jar has its own word— ''fireflies,'' ''grandeur,'' ''luck,'' ''mouse turds,'' ''dignity,'' ''bugs'' and ''slugs'' are a few from over one hundred. $6.50 each, postpaid.

Great Farm Pottery—These small stoneware jars are my tribute to Japanese discipline, and I have happily made thousands of them. My first pottery teacher had been in charge of Shoji Hamada's visit to San Jose State College a number of years ago, and he filled me with veneration for Japanese tradition and discipline.

The words on these jars—a modernization—often serve as therapy for me. They reflect what I'm reading, thinking, seeing, doing. That they appeal to others bears witness to some universal flow between us all.

I work here on the Great Farm—all five and a half acres of it—sixteen miles from the Canadian border in a part of northern New York state which has sometimes been called the Siberia of North America. Lots of quiet, beautiful vistas and clean air and water. I like it.

Anne Burnham, c/o Great Farm Pottery, R.F.D. #1, North Lawrence, New York 12967.

Necklace and Earrings—The circular domes are reticulated sterling silver. Each is heated to desired texture and color. The beads are pre-Columbian style; each is unique. The chain is crocheted of fine silver wire. Its whiteness contrasts with the grays of the domes and beads, which have subtle hints of color. The necklace, 18" long, is $27; earrings, 2" long, are $9. Add $1.25 shipping charge per order.

Beverly Cameron—I have been making jewelry for nine years. Unfortunately, it has not usually been possible to do it full-time. One of my problems is the tendency to make one-of-a-kind pieces. It's great for the soul but hasn't done much for my wallet. Custom orders are more than welcome. They give me the enjoyment of designing for both function and personality.

All my work is of original design, and covers a wide range of techniques. Each piece meets high standards of aesthetics and craftsmanship. I consider myself both an artist and a craftsperson. I have a B.F.A. in sculpture, and although most of my creative urge is satisfied through making jewelry, occasionally I need to carry through an idea in "pure" sculpture.

San Francisco has been my home for eight years. Like many craftspeople I feel drawn to a more natural lifestyle, but the city also has its charms. I have been active in the women's movement, doing such things as co-publishing a book of women's artwork, being a founding member of the San Francisco Women's Art Center and coordinating its first show, "Craftswoman as Artist." I also helped start a women's warehouse space where I now have my studio, teach classes and do my art and craft work full-time.

Beverly Cameron, 2325 Third Street, San Francisco, California 94107.

Country Store Hanging Lamp—The standard lamp used in the churches and meeting halls of yesteryear. Brass lamp has iron shade and brass hanging yoke. Oil-burning model lifts out of the center hanging ring for easy refueling. The electrified model comes with concealed wires and 12' transparent cord. Height: 28''. Diameter: 15''. $62, with brass shade, $77, shipping not included.

Rustic-Roll Wall Lamp—Rustic elegance. Large brass reflector radiates as only solid brass can do. Oil reservoir holds over one quart of fuel. Also comes in electric model. Height: 20'', width: 9''. $52, shipping not included.

Brass Parlor Chandelier—This elegant dining light comes with concealed wires and a 12' transparent cord, $119. The oil-burning model has a unique center filling basin for easy refueling of all three reservoirs, $119, shipping not included. Optional glass student shade, $12. Aladdin© burners, $15, shipping not included.

Brass Wall Lamp—Lamp is all brass. The oil-burning model unscrews from the wall bracket for easy refueling. The electric model has concealed wires and easy-to-mount bracket. Height: 23''. $47.25, shipping not included. Optional glass student shade (shown), with mounting spider, comes in dark green, opal white or amber yellow. $12, shipping not included. All wall-mounted lamps can be special-ordered in double and triple configurations.

Carriage Trade of Tahoe—In the olden days the name carriage trade applied not only to wagon builders and fixers, but also to the ''jack of all, master of none'' craftsmen who traveled the country roads by horse-drawn carriage, selling, building, fixing or working at whatever they could. That is exactly what I do at Carriage Trade of Tahoe. Making custom and production leather kits, brass lamps, oak furnishings, beds, and rebuilding antique carriages and sleighs is my only form of income. After three years, the business now owns me exclusively.

Bob Stokes, c/o Carriage Trade of Tahoe, P.O. Box 2011, Olympic Valley, California 95730.

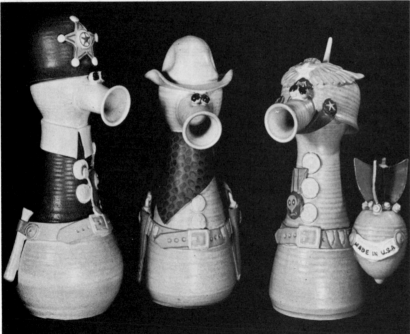

Children's Banks—Wheel-thrown stoneware. Available in six styles: Grenadier, Opera Buff, Soldier, Cop, Cowboy and Bomber Pilot. Each bank is hand-painted. Access to the banks is in the bottom. Banks are 8'' to 10'' tall. Catalog available for 75 cents. $25, shipping not included.

Stone Street Stoneware—I learned how to make pottery while attending college in New York State. Most of my current work is the result of five years of development. I have always enjoyed the silly things in life, and I guess that these banks reflect that. Aside from working in clay I'm not much good at doing very meaningful things—such as writing biographical sketches. I'd rather draw a biographical sketch . . . .

Garry Sherman, c/o Stone Street Stoneware, 410 Stone Street, Oneida, New York 13421.

Biographical sketch →

20

Fantasy Hats—Hats have special magic. They hide your thoughts and ward off evil spirits. My hats are hand-crocheted; no two are alike. The colors available in wool/acrylic are almost unlimited. In raffia they are more limited: red, yellow, light blue, dark blue, light green, dark green and brown. Rainbows are available if you're a gypsy soul like me. Almost all hats weigh less than 1 lb. and are about 6'' tall in the crown. They are not fragile. They can be crushed and pushed back into shape with no difficulty. When ordering, send measurement of widest part of head. Specify color preference; yarn or raffia; and the kind of trim desired (hand-woven band, flower, beads or all three). Also, please enclose a description of your basic personality. (I try to make each hat to suit the person wearing it.) For 9'' narrow brim: wool $15, raffia $25. For 15'' broad brim: wool $20, raffia $30. Add $1 shipping charge.

Christina Larkin—I love hats and always wear them. One day I saw a friend coil-weaving a basket with raffia, and it occurred to me to try crocheting a hat with raffia. The first one was lumpy and rather strange, but I saw the possibilities. I tightened up my loops and added color.

Each hat I make I like better than the hats I've made before.
Christina Larkin, P.O. Box 38485, Hollywood, California 90038.

Canoes—I build canoes using white cedar ribs 2½'' wide. Planking is red cedar fastened to the ribs with brass cinch nails. Inwhales, stems, gunwhales, thwarts and seat frames are ash, as are the decks. The seats are hand-woven cane, and the canoe is covered with canvas and painted gray or light blue. The canoe is 16' long, 30'' wide, 12'' deep and weighs 15 lbs. $650. Crating and shipping costs are high, so you'd best pick it up. If you can't, write me and I'll get the least expensive and most reliable shipping information to you.

Robert Zimmerman—Seeing a J. Henry Rushton canoe first prompted me to start building canoes, and I have followed as closely as possible the methods of construction that great nineteenth-century craftsman used.

Although it is possible to buy a canoe built of materials other than wood, none match its excellence. A wooden canoe is in its element; it retains the spirit of the wood and the forest from which it was made.

The canoe should be thought of in terms of the same frailties possessed by our own bodies: a broken rib or torn skin are serious injuries which take time to mend. There is so much enjoyment to be found in the quiet places of water that I see no real need for the ''white water'' variety of canoeing. I build canoes for those quiet places.

Robert Zimmerman, c/o Wykeham Rise, Washington, Connecticut 06793.

Tool Chest—These tool and instrument chests are designed for those who really care about their equipment, whether for woodworking tools, photograhy equipment or drafting tools. The main body of the chest is made of Baltic birch, a durable laminate with 19 layers per inch of high-grade birch, dovetailed for maximum strength, equipped with nickel-plated hardware and sealed with a penetrating oil finish, hand-waxed and hand-rubbed to let the light color and beauty of the birch show through. A walnut finish is also available. Custom designs for chests are welcomed. Shown here is Number 200, with two drawers each 1-15/16" high, height of interior compartment 6" with tray, overall dimensions 11¾" wide, 24" long, 9¾" high, shipping weight 28 lbs. $125, shipping not included.

Steve Doriss—I have been professional involved in woodworking for three years, deriving my total income from furniture making, cabinetmaking and carpentry. I have worked as a free-lance craftsman and have been the project supervisor of a small furniture shop.

Early in 1976 I invested my savings and three months in developing a line of chests and making the prototypes. My chests represent a lot of careful thought as well as my feelings toward the unique beauty of wood, the relationship a craftsperson has with his tools and the necessity of maintaining quality in craftsmanship.

Steve Doriss, P.O. Box 1635, Fort Bragg, California 95437.

Soy, Vinegar or Oil Cruet—Perfect finger control by vacuum pressure. Eliminates drip. Great for wok cooking! Capacity approximately one cup. Includes saucer. Glazes available: transparent green, rust red, sky blue and white, white "luster" and deep black. Shipping weight about 2 lbs. $6.25, shipping not included.

Los Reyes Pottery—The workshop specializes in hand-formed stoneware pottery for use in the kitchen and at the table. Our work is sold directly from our shop adjacent to the Point Reyes National Seashore, as well as at fairs and by mail order. To our great satisfaction we find that much of our ware is sold to local folks to fill their domestic needs.

Harvey and Terumi Young, c/o Los Reyes Pottery, P.O. Box 311, Point Reyes Station, California 94956.

Oil Lamp—The oil lamp casts delicate shadows in a dark room, and burns up to 24 hours between fillings. Complete instructions included. Specify cut pattern (slits or round spiral) and color (off-white or rust gold). Measures 3'' to 3½'' in diameter, 5½'' to 6'' high. $20 postpaid.

Mushroom Jar—The corked mushroom jar can be used for herbs, spices, bobby pins, paper clips, vitamin pills, bassoon reeds or whatever. It is not recommended for liquids. Colors vary; specify a general preference for earthy red, greenish black or creamy white. Measures 3'' to 3½'' in diameter, 1½'' to 3'' high. $5 postpaid. Both the oil lamps and the mushroom jars are made of a red stoneware clay, and fired to approximately 1,300°C. There is no lead in any of the glazes.

Black Silver Mud Stone—I live and work on an old farm in Southwest Washington, with everything an isolated rural life entails—gardening, plumbing, wiring, auto geriatrics, raising animals, baking, canning, carpentry, building kilns and making pots.

I work alone, and find my inspiration in the various rhythms of being—daily cycles of eating and resting; seasonal cycles of planting, growing and harvesting. I make pots I enjoy living with. I want my pots to work well, to be a pleasure to both the eye and the hand. I want my pots to reflect some of the energy and magic that occurs in the forming process. This energy makes a hand-crafted pot alive and part of the communication between me, the potter, and you, the user.

Elaine Myers, c/o Black Silver Mud Stone, Eden Valley Road, Rosburg, Washington 98643.

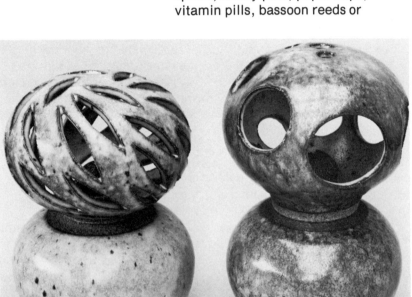

27

Rubber Stamps—The Alphabeasts set contains all twenty-six of the popular letters, each in the shape of an animal beginning with that letter (A for Alligator, D for Dragon, U for Unicorn . . .). The Numbirds set contains all ten numerals (zero through nine), each in the shape of a bird, plus three additional stamps (Worm, Egg and Feather) from which the mathematical signs can be made. Both sets are original designs by Bloomberg and are mounted on fine maple blocks, individually stamped with the image on top and hand-rubbed with linseed oil to protect and seal the wood. Each set comes in a pine carrying case, with a stamp pad and bottle of ink in a choice of seven colors (black, brown, red, orange, purple, blue and green). The complete Alphabeasts set sells for $56; the set of Numbirds for $28.50. Individual stamp blocks from either set can be purchased separately for $3.50 each. Catalog available for $1.

All Night Media—In the fall of 1975, All Night Media consisted of two individuals, a handful of media equipment and a one-room studio. Today, in the brief span of less than two years, All Night Media consists of two individuals, a two-room studio and three hundred and eighty-seven rubber stamps.

During that time, Robert Bloomberg and Marilyn Freund, co-founders and sole occupants of All Night Media, have devoted themselves ''to delivering meaningful art to the people, through the medium of rubber stamps, thereby eliminating fuel-consuming, air-polluting trips to inconveniently located art galleries and museums which are never open when you really need them, anyway.''

''Now anyone can become an artist,'' says Bloomberg, who is one, ''and in the privacy of their own home, without complicated mechanical devices or messy creams.''

''With rubber stamps,'' points out Freund, ''the only skill required is the ability to move one's arms up and down.''

When not moving their arms up and down, All Night Media spends most of its time in the production of film, video and media events, such as the world's first Video Scavenger Hunt. When asked about the connection between these media pursuits and rubber stamps, Bloomberg replies, ''The repetition of images. I used to repeat myself a lot as a child.''

Robert Bloomberg and Marilyn Freund, c/o All Night Media, P.O. Box 227, Forest Knolls, California 94933.

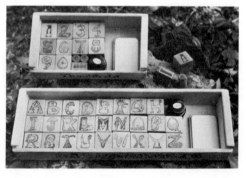

Glass Wine Cups—Available in red, blue or clear glass, these cups are 4'' high and 4½'' long, with a 6-oz. capacity. They weigh ¾ lb. each, and are $30 each plus $1.10 shipping charge.

Soda Fountain Glasses—The glasses are 7½'' tall and have an 8-oz. capacity. Shapes and handles vary subtly. They weigh ½ lb. Glass straws, $2. Glasses, $18 each plus $1.10 shipping charge.

Pitcher and Glasses—Crystal pitcher holds 48 oz., weighs 2 lbs., and is 8'' tall. Glasses hold 8 oz., weigh ½ lb., and are 3'' tall. Colors available: crystal with blue lip, crystal with green lip, white with blue lip, white with green lip. Pitcher $30 each, glasses $12 each, postpaid.

Lorenz Studios—I find my work extremely demanding, but I receive great pleasure from it. Performing in my studio, I give each piece a personal touch and I'm constantly dancing, dancing with that molten glob of matter, pulling, pinching, blowing, making it whatever I want. There is no greater experience than to create an extension of yourself.

Larry Livolsi, c/o Lorenz Studios, R.D. 3, Morrow Hill Road, Canandaigua, New York 14424.

Sweater-jackets—My sweater-jackets have a woven front and back in wool, handspun or cotton. The sleeves and sides are crocheted in wool. The jackets have buttons or zippers and are very warm. When ordering, please specify colors or natural (white, gray or black) handspun. I also need these measurements: back and front widths, desired length from neck to waist (or lower), waist size, arm length, and arm width at wrist and shoulder. Packaged weight 1½ lbs. Woman's jacket, $75; man's jacket, $85, shipping not included.

Sheila Gamble—I was born in San Francisco and grew up there. I graduated from San Francisco State College with a B.A. in French and an elementary school teaching credential. While teaching in San Francisco, I began weaving. I gave up teaching full-time and pursued everything about weaving/fiberwork, following it to Canada and then to Alaska in 1972.

Since then I have been working with fibers as both a sculptural medium/art form and a working craft of life. I enjoy making beautiful, useful things. I presently live and work by the ocean near San Francisco where I can balance my inside work with my love of nature and organic/environmental forms.

Sheila Gamble, 18 Shelter Cove, Pacifica, California 94044.

Brass Disk Necklace—Made with either five columns of beads with brass circles or eleven jingly brass disks hanging from the bottom of a pendant. The pendant is suspended from a bar of beaten brass. Available in the following color combinations: dark blue, turquoise, and red; turquoise, red and black; turquoise and jade green; carnelian red and rust; dark blue, red and green; dark blue, turquoise and rust. The first color listed is predominant. The necklace is 24'' long. Celtic-type pins are also available in these two pendant styles. Necklace $35 postpaid; pin $25 postpaid.

Wings of Horus Necklace—This necklace consists of a pair of pierced and engraved brass wings with a carnelian set in the center. All of the beads are shades of carnelian red and rust with brass spacers. Delicate beaten brass feathers hang from the tail. Each of these necklaces is different and made to order. Length 21''. $75 postpaid.

Carri Gicker—I have been studying jewelry for nearly ten years. It still fascinates me and keeps me going, for there are always new styles and techniques to explore.

I have been very much influenced by the folk styles of Norway, Eastern Europe, Central America and Japan. All these elements are combined in my jewelry. I'm also very interested in Egyptian jewelry. I make almost all of the metal components of my necklaces, including chains and clasps.

Carri Gicker, 84 Jones Bar Road, Nevada City, California 95959.

Pewter Dining Ware—These serving pieces are made in lead-free pewter from life-castings of real asparargus. They weigh from 4 to 14 oz. and are 94% tin and 6% copper. They have an exceptionally high finish for pewter and are often mistaken for silver. Each is hand-finished. Pieces come gift-boxed. Relish spoon, $12; salad spoon and salad fork (sold only as set), $30; jam spoon, $7.50; two-tine fork, $12. All prices postpaid.

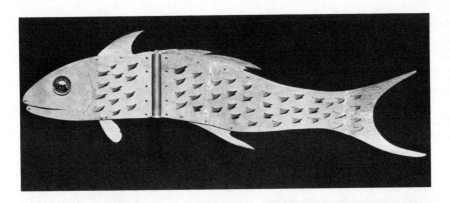

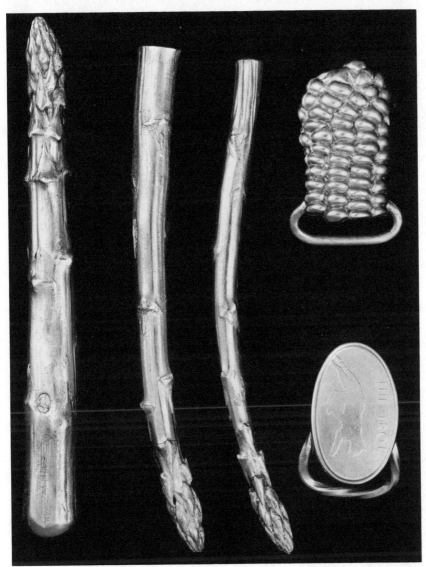

Solid Pewter Belt Buckles—All 1¼''
belt width, 2 to 3 oz. each, 92% tin,
5% copper, 2% antimony, 1% lead.
The Moose (my hallmark), $8.50;
The Trot (motion study of a cat),
$8.50; Sweet Corn, $8.50 (in 24k un-
lacquered gold plate, $12). Also
available: 24k gold over pewter Music
Buckle with an excerpt from Chopin's
Prelude in E minor.

Plain Asparagus Castings—Skinny,
$10; medium, $15; giant, $20.

Weathervanes—Each one is
handmade and is a commissioned
piece made for a specific location.
They are functional vanes designed
for years of maintenance-free
operation and, properly mounted, will
withstand high winds. Cardinal
points, arrows and other decorative
pieces can be fabricated to
specifications. Brass, copper, nickel-
silver patina or bright, hammered
finish. Shown here: fish weathervane,
26'' copper vane with green glass
eyes, raised scales and cardinal
points, $185. In brass, $80.

Walter White—I am inspired by the
wind and driven to play music. My
real love is the wind itself, so I lean
toward flexible wind pieces; I like the
way they lift my eyes to the sky. I am
not a jeweler. I work in metal as a
form of 3-D sketching. Quick ideas
yield decorative objects—more solid
thoughts yield wind toys. My general
direction is toward the larger, human
scale. Asparagus and the wind!

*Walter White, c/o Roth/Sindell,
11046 Santa Monica Boulevard, Los
Angeles, California 90025.*

Portrait Dolls—Martha Washington, our favorite doll, is graceful and elegant. The head, arms and legs are made in our own satin-creme bisque porcelain. Fully dressed, she is 19'' down to her period-style shoes, which complement her petticoat, pantaloons and dress with lace fichu. Our dress designs are developed from researching the costumes of the period. We have deviated slightly with Martha's costume, in that we offer her dressed with pantaloons, which were not in vogue in her day. Donna feels that they add to Mrs. Washington's comfort. We wish the name of Denbi Doll to be synonymous with classic porcelain dolls of the highest quality craftsmanship and we have registered the name as our trademark. We sign, date and number each doll issued, and maintain a register of the collectors' numbers. Martha Washington doll $59.50 postpaid. Cindy doll $43 postpaid. Doll stand 95 cents.

Denbi Dolls—Donna and I have been married twenty years, during which time we have been busy rearing a family of four sons. Donna has always been involved in art, particularly painting and sculpture. I have spent many years in the ceramics industry and now, to our great joy, we are working together full-time doing something we both love and take pride in. We are positive about our future in the craft and apart from an occasional incidental financial hindrance, we enjoy each day!

We started about two years ago with the idea of providing an American source for high-quality portrait dolls. We have developed our own techniques for modeling, molding, firing and finishing as we strive to provide the best-looking doll with the highest-quality materials. We have developed our own ''satin-creme'' porcelain to have an ''antique'' looking complexion and a smooth silky texture after the vitrefying firing of the porcelain. Doll enthusiasts refer to the texture as ''bisque.'' We use a higher maturing temperature than the ''biscuit'' firing operation common in the pottery industry.

Ronald and Donna Brookes, c/o Denbi Dolls, Box 2292, North Canton, Ohio 44720.

Baby Quilts—Cover a little one with our one-of-a-kind quilts. Center design shows Fat Cats and Friends up to their tricks. Designs vary. Warm calico prints form the pieced border, with overall machine quilting for strength. Poly-filled and machine-washable, 36'' by 48''. $65 postpaid.

Fat Cats and Friends—For young children and the young at heart. Hand-silk-screened and hand-painted animals of 100% cotton muslin, backed with bright calico prints and filled with polyester fiberfill. Safe, lovable, washable, nonallergenic. Striped cat $10.50, big cats $15.50, little cat $8, standing cat $11.50, nasty dog (not shown) $13.50. All prices postpaid.

Patricia Berrini—I have been professionally involved in crafts since 1969, when I began work towards an M.F.A. in ceramics. After completing my degree, I taught ceramics at a small college in Vermont. I ''retired'' in January 1975 to have my first child. When she was two months old, I made her several toys, which became prototypes for the present ten Fat Cats and Friends.

Fat Cats and Friends is a cottage industry with a designer, painter and marketer (me), a silk-screener, a quilter and four well-paid women who help with the sewing now that we have grown so.

Although I would love to run a fine crafts store, we are so rural that there is virtually no retail market. For that reason, we sell wholesale and, recently, mail-order.

Patricia Berrini, c/o Fat Cats and Friends, R.D. 1, Norwood, New York 13668.

Textiles—The rainbow, one of the most beautiful and inspiring natural phenomena known to man, is here woven into a variety of articles to wear or to use in your home. The weave is a variation of an old American Indian weaving pattern. The yarns are 100% wool (with cotton warp), a mixture of natural-color Greek sheep's wool and American and Scandinavian color-fast dyed yarns. All items are dry-cleanable. Pillows have an inner muslin lining stuffed with polyester filling. They are either light gray/white or charcoal gray/white with a rainbow band. Small, 14'' by 14'', $25. Large, 17'' by 20'', $35. Purses, with colorful corduroy lining and a small extra pocket, come in light gray/white, charcoal gray/white, or orange/white (all with rainbow band), and have rainbow shoulder strap. About 13'' by 14'', $40. Rugs have wide bands of color on a light gray background, 3' by 5', $145; 3' by 6', $160. Belts have a double-round buckle and fit waist sizes 24'' to 38'', $9.

Orchard House—After several years of trying to find my way in the world through academic pursuits, I have returned finally to what I love best to do—working with my hands. My heart is equally divided between my weaving and loom-building. My workshop is next to my home, an old farmhouse in an apple orchard near Sebastopol.

I learned to weave in Sweden, and perhaps because of that training and my own Scandinavian heritage, I find that my weaving focuses on the traditional and functional. I like to use the things I make, to have them be a part of my everyday life—to walk on my rugs, wear my fabrics, carry my purses. It makes a special occasion of every moment.

Corinne Anderson, c/o Orchard House, 7740 Atkinson Road, Sebastopol, California 95472.

Triangle Dinner Gong—Made of iron with macrame hanger, the triangle is tempered to a cherry red and gives a brilliant ring. Finished with either clear lacquer (a natural blue steel) or flat black. Please specify which you prefer. The triangle is 11'' high and weighs 3 lbs. $14.

Split End Wavy Kitchen Pot Rack—The rack measures 34'' tip to tip; the hook area extends 22''. The ends are shaped into hearts (shown), horns or vines. I will custom-make the rack any length, adjusting the cost accordingly. Weight 12 lbs. $38.

John Graney—I opened my business last winter, operating my shop out of a converted barn on our property. I was apprenticed for about one year with a local blacksmith. After drifting around in college and straight jobs, I finally settled into my present lifestyle in the country.

Never before have I found such a challenging and personally rewarding occupation. This is it for me. The old smiths I meet enjoy showing me the tricks of the trade, and I am encouraged by their reception.

About my work—I cut no corners. I use my hammer, anvil and forge to the fullest; I was taught along traditional lines. I use recycled materials, salvaged iron when possible. I'm involved in making my own coal by charcoaling wood in mud mounds. I also make my own tools for shop and home—tongs, knives, whatever.

I prefer custom work. My favorite preoccupation is firescreens. Please write for a catalog of the forty items I make and sell.

John Graney, Route 2, Box 63A, Blue River, Wisconsin 53518.

Dear Hearts and Gentle People Stocking Dolls—My grandmas and grandpas are hand-stitched and stuffed with cotton. Their clothes are sewn from old clothing and lace. Hair is of natural fibers in old people shades. Each doll has a unique personality. Children seem to naturally treat them with the respect that old people deserve. Each gentleperson is humbly signed with a heart on its bottom by their creator, who has one also. Small: 9'', 10 oz. packed, $12.50. Medium: 20'', 15 oz. packed, $23; with grandbaby, $28. Life-size: 10 lbs. packed, $200.

Cathy Learned—I live with my daughter Jill and our cat Ninzy. Besides Jill, my very favorite things include orange blossoms, rain, music, walking, hot air balloons and rosy cheeks.

Cathy Learned, 909 Laurel Street, #1, Santa Cruz, California 95060.

Aprons—Made from calico prints and solids of any color desired. The aprons have a patchwork-quilted bib and pockets on the apron front. Small, medium, large; short or tall. $25 postpaid.

Magic Corner Quilts—I am working toward the time that my craft can be my principal form of income. I have been making quilts for four years and began by selling them out of my restaurant in Elk, California. The more I got into working with fabric the more artistic possibilities I realized and am still realizing.

I do my sewing at home and sell by word of mouth. I enjoy making objects that are functional as well as aesthetic. Another thing that makes me feel good about patchwork is that my family can relate to it through the things I make for them. Somehow more formal art forms are harder to share.

In the area where I live, which is pretty rural, it is very hard to make a living. Making quilts feels very much in keeping with my lifestyle here. I have always been involved with art on some level. I find quilt-making the most satisfying of all.

Shanti Benoit, c/o Magic Corner Quilts, Box 122, Elk, California 95432.

Quilts—The quilt pictured is for a double bed, hand-quilted from cotton prints. Quilts are also available in corduroy or other material of your choice. Indicate general color scheme, choose muted or bright colors. Also indicate whether the quilt should be tied, quilted by hand or machine-quilted. (Hand-quilting takes a considerable amount of time and will, therefore, cost more.) All quilts are one-of-a-kind items. Double bed, $250 to $500. Single bed, $200 to $400. Crib, $75. All prices postpaid.

Potholders—Made from cotton prints and blends, stuffed with cotton batting. Each one is individually designed. State color preference. $5.50 postpaid.

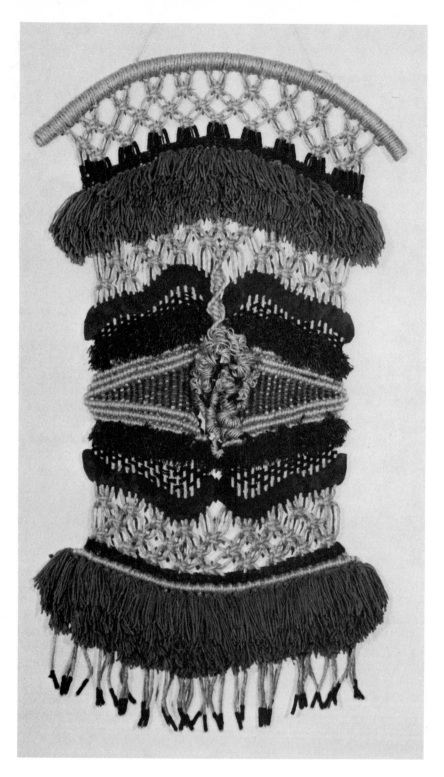

Nancy Robb Dunst—I used to be a psychologist but changed careers about two years ago when I realized I could give more to people on a visual level than on a verbal one. Most of my wall hangings have a Southwestern or primitive style to them, and I usually use a combination of jute, yarn, suede, feathers and shells. I have a studio and showroom in Scottsdale, but do most of my work at my home studio.

I have had many funny reactions to my change in careers, but I think the funniest one was from my family doctor, who has known me for about ten years. I went to see him because I had a sore throat, and while he was preparing a penicillin shot he asked where I was counseling now. When I told him I had given it up to become an artist, he immediately wanted to check me for hepatitis and V.D.!

Nancy Robb Dunst, c/o Earthline Designs, 4225 North Thirty-sixth Street #14, Phoenix, Arizona 85018.

Wall Hangings—The ''Classic'' has a contemporary African appeal. It is a jute knotting with three different colors of yarn fringe, weaving and suede inserts. It can be ordered in rust, gold, gray, brown or cream. All have a black accent. For specific colors, please send color swatches. Orders require a 30% deposit. Weight 10 lbs., 2½' by 5', $200.

Hand-built Ceramics—These hand-built designs are made of high-fire porcelain and stoneware clays with red-iron oxide stain. Intricate linear detail on all items. Fish Teapot, 8½'' by 8'' by 3½'', $85. Birdhouse Teapot, 12½'' by 12'' by 4½'', $85. Bird Head/Tree Jewelry Box, 7'' by 9'' by 3'', $150. Fish Salt and Pepper Shakers, $35. Shipping not included.

Suzanne Adan—I place a great deal of emphasis on detail of the clay and on illogical and nonsensical combination of images in my work. I enjoy combining and incorporating animal images with trees, leaves, logs and columns, brick buildings, picket fences, fish, birds—like the teapot with the tree-limb handle and a bird's-head spout.

My interest in collecting toys and dolls has heavily influenced my ceramic pieces. I exhibit my work regularly at the Candy Store Art Gallery in Folsom, California.

Suzanne Adan, 3977 Rosemary Circle, Sacramento, California 95821.

Homespun Yarn—Our yarns represent many long hours spent in transforming the raw wool into yarn. Following our ancestors' methods, we sort, tease, card, spin, wash, dye and block the wool. When ordering, specify whether yarn should be thick, thin or bulky compared to regular knitting worsted; how many plys and how much texture; and natural or synethetic dye source. Sample prices: one-ply natural white yarn $1.30 per oz.; two-ply "in the grease" natural $1.20 per oz.; one-ply natural black $2.25 per oz.; one-ply "onion skin" $2.25 per oz.; and CIBA synthetic-dyed one-ply yarn $1.55 per oz. Sample card $1 (refundable).

Carol Graham—Five years ago, my husband Jim and I left the rush of Southern California to seek a simpler lifestyle. We've settled on a farm in Northern Idaho. We have an organic garden and raise dairy goats.

Joanne Thompson—By the time my husband and I moved to the cold country I was a fanatic about wearing only natural fibers. When I saw Carol spin on her Ashford wheel, I succumbed to the magic of spinning and got myself a wheel.

Carol Graham and Joanne Thompson, c/o North Idaho Homespun, Route 1, Box 459, Bonners Ferry, Idaho 83805.

44

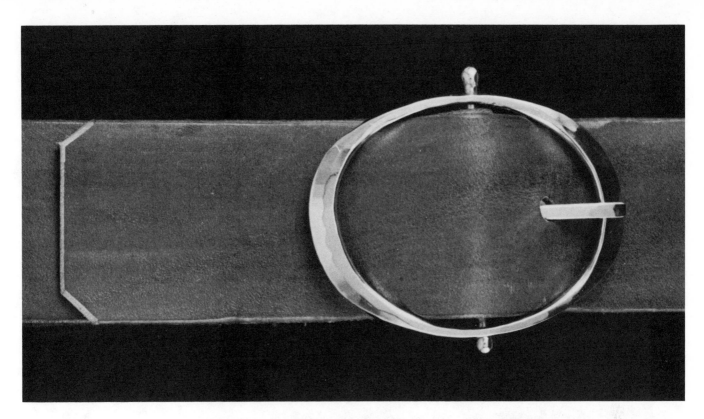

Hand-forged Belt Buckle—What's holding up your pants these days? We offer you a hand-forged buckle in either solid sterling silver or solid bronze, designed by Southwestern silversmith Allan Reynolds. Mounted on a natural, oiled strap leather belt sized to your personal measurements. Small (1¼'' by 2'') $17.50 in bronze, $30 in sterling. Large (2'' by 3'') $20 in bronze, $37.50 in sterling, all prices postpaid.

Allan Reynolds—My wife and I work together as silversmiths. We operate our business as a family partnership. We have been professional silversmiths for four years and feel completely dedicated. Not only that, but we just have a great time doing it! There really is a feeling of life in using one's hands to create objects that have beauty and sensitivity.

Allan Reynolds, 1111 West Sanford, Arlington, Texas 76012.

Woven Fireplace Brooms—These brooms are made of fine quality broomcorn and have hardwood handles. We use broomcorn, a type of sorghum, weave the broom with jute on a nineteenth-century broomwinder and sew them flat or round with red cotton twine. The round brooms stand on their own. They are about 37'' long and weigh 1½ lbs. The three styles shown (left to right) are: Shaker Flat Broom, $8; Colonial Wisp Broom, $8; Early American Round Broom, $8.

Feather Dusters—The peacock feather dusters are made of peacock eye tail feathers and hardwood handles. Although you might think they are only decorative, they are highly functional dusters. The eye tail feathers contain a natural oil that repels dust and dirt, so they remain good-looking after much use. They are 26'' long and weigh 1 lb. $12. The turkey duster is the traditional duster of Early America. It is excellent for all your heavy dusting. It is 21'' long and weighs 1 lb. $7.

Bellows—Our newest product, developed with Ken Kushner, will help keep your fires cheery and warm. The bellows are made of cherry, oak, black walnut or birch. They are hinged with leather and the nozzles are made of brass. Designed leather appliques are available for the front of the bellows. When ordering please specify style and wood choice. Top left, modern bellows, 21'' long, 5 lbs., $38. Top right, heart-shaped bellows, 15'' long, 4 lbs., $35. Bottom left, large traditional bellows, 19'' long, 4 lbs., $36. Bottom right, small traditional bellows, 15'' long, 3 lbs., $32.

High Point Crafts—We work out of our house and, weather permitting, out of our yard in Tully, New York. That's me with my lady, Jane, and our dog, Bilbo, in the picture making brooms one sunny spring day. We learned the craft of broommaking about four and a half years ago, at an Outdoor Education Center that taught Early American crafts. We began making brooms as a part-time business, but soon realized that we could put more energy into the brooms and have a successful business on our hands. The past four years have been spent getting our business together and enjoying our lives as craftspeople.

Since we began, we have worked hard to make better and better quality brooms and are proud of the product we sell today. From brooms we have branched out to feather dusters and bellows. All of our products are highly functional. It is important to us that people realize they can use our products, which will maintain their good looks through years of use.

Joe Panzarella and Jane Byrne-Panzarella, c/o High Point Crafts, R.D. #2, Sky High Road, Tully, New York 13159.

Unicycle Clown—A toy for anyone who likes to run fast, fast, fast. The clown is 12'' high and is steered by a handle 18'' to 36'' high. The handle can be ordered in three lengths: short, for ages 2 to 4; medium, for ages 5 to 8; long, for ages 9 up. When pushed, the clown's arms swing wildly and his legs pump rapidly. Unpainted $20; hand-painted $30 postpaid.

Circus Cannon—Definitely not a war toy, but rather a circus toy that shoots ''dashing daredevils'' made from round wooden clothespins. The cannon is adjustable for elevation, and its maximum range is about 5'. It shoots very gently and the daredevils are quite blunt. Cannon is 4'' wide, 8'' long and 4½'' high. Unpainted cannon with 6 daredevils, $7. Hand-painted cannon with six painted daredevils, $13. Extra sets of six daredevils: plain, 50 cents; hand-painted $2. All prices postpaid.

Squeeze Acrobat—A portable toy of universal appeal and ancient origins. Suitable for children from 5 up. Made in a variety of personages, moods and colors. When ordering, describe in general terms the sort of person you would like. Acrobat is 6'' to 9'' tall; stand is 9'' tall. Unpainted acrobat $7, painted acrobat $15, stand $1.50, postpaid.

The Merry Toymakers—We Merry Toymakers are just three people, striving to make the best toys we can. We make our toys at home, using a large variety of hand and power tools, many of which we make to suit our needs. We are surely among the happiest people on earth, and we mean to stay that way and not grow into a factory.

Jack Dohany and Elaine Shelton, c/o The Merry Toymakers, 430 North Third Street, San Jose, California 95112.

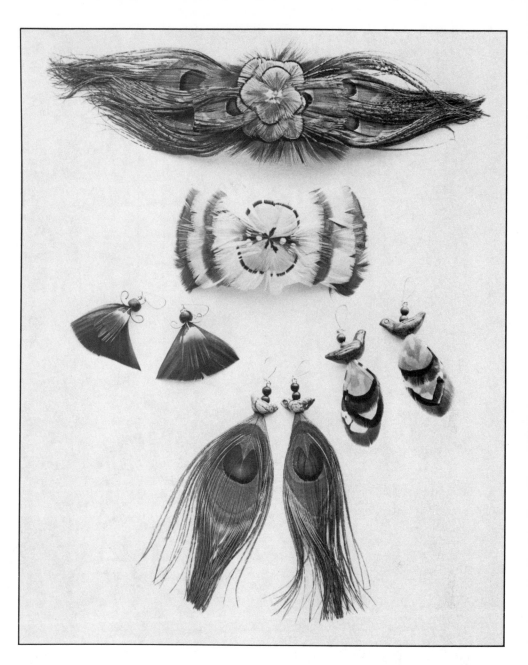

Rectangular barrettes
(or combs), $6.50.
Brass wire with bead
earrings, $2.50.
Ceramic bird
earrings, $4.50.

Feather Jewelry—I make my jewelry with feathers from peacocks, turkeys, maribu geese, guinea fowl and five types of pheasant (reeves, Chinese ring neck, silver, Lady Amherst and golden pheasant). I use red, yellow, pale blue, iridescent blue, green, brown, black, mustard and white feathers; all colors are natural. With the exception of the earrings, the jewelry is made by gluing the feathers individually on leather. Although it seems fragile, this jewelry is actually quite durable since the feathers can be steamed if they get wet or mussed up, and restored to their former splendor.

Kathleen P. Scullion—I have been a feather jeweler for two years. I enjoy the idea of having my own business. It makes me feel very independent, as if I have a lot of control over my life. My main interests are painting and writing. I enjoy doing the jewelry and find that the colors of the feathers inspire me in my art. I was formerly a journalist in South Africa and find jewelry making to be an interesting, though less eventful, occupation.

Kathleen P. Scullion, 2008 Francisco Street, Berkeley, California 94709.

Colonial Style Furniture—We work mostly in pine, cherry, oak, walnut and mahogany. All surfaces are hand-planed, and joinery is typical of the best country furniture. Most pieces are held together with wedges and wooden pegs, or hand-forged nails. Finished with hand-rubbed varnish; some pieces are distressed to simulate wear and tear. These pieces look old, but are my designs just as I would have made them had I lived 200 years ago. All one-of-a-kind pieces. Windsor Chair $300. Double bed $850. Hutch, 72'' wide by 87'' high by 18'' deep, $1,500. Carved chest, 24'' wide by 24'' high by 18'' deep, $400. Catalog $2.

Peter Kramer—Since I was quite young I have gone to restorations and museums and studied pieces of furniture I would love to have owned. However, I could neither find them in antique shops nor afford them if I had. That's what got me started designing and making my own pieces.

Each is inspired by the imagined story of life in Cloven Mill, a fictional early eighteenth-century village I have invented. Cloven Mill was a bustling community of settlers who lived simply, and their furnishings reflected this lifestyle. Early colonial furniture could withstand the harshness of the environment and still show the flavor of the colonists' feelings. I try to capture this quality in all my work.

Peter Kramer, Washington, Virginia 22747.

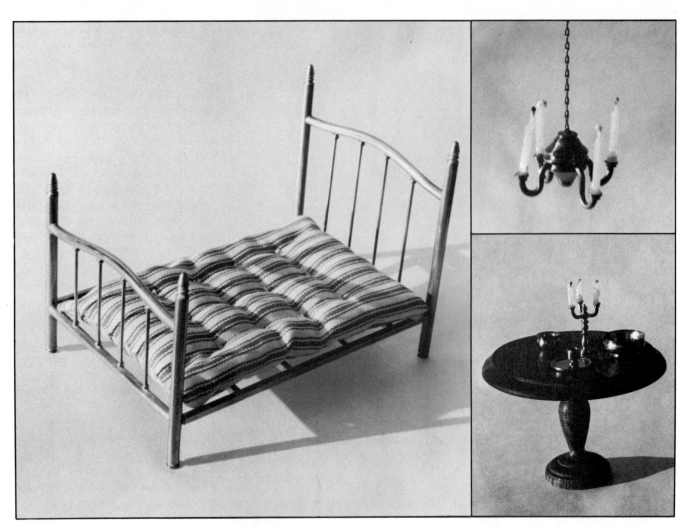

Doll Furniture—We make doll furniture scaled 1'' to the foot. Brass items are machined brass, not brass-plated steel. We strive to create quality miniatures that sell for a reasonable price. We make three different brass beds, 4'' wide, 4½'' high and 6'' long. The beds have individually tooled posts and ornaments and bass wood bed slats. In addition, we make candlesticks and candelabra (with real candles), brass bowls and spittoons. We make other doll furniture and can custom-build miniatures from your pictures or drawings. Beds, $17.50 each; candlesticks, $3 each, $5.50/pair; candelabra, $16; bowl, $8; spittoon, $6.

Dollworks—We are a partnership of two. Shelley is a photographer turned designer-craftsperson who has supported herself by making and peddling jewelry in Stockholm and Berlin. Lee is a reformed technocrat who has abandoned computers in favor of a more creative trade.

For the past six months we have been operating out of the basement of our house in Berkeley. We ultimately intend to move our workshop to the country and live by making miniatures.

Lee Ackerson, c/o Dollworks, 1031A Hearst Street, Berkeley, California 94710.

Wooden Rocking Horse—The horse itself is sturdily made of alder wood; the rocker and support are maple. It has wooden pegs, rather than screws or nails. Tack is oak-tanned saddle leather; rivets and buckles are solid brass. The tail is made of genuine horsehair. The horse comes disassembled for storage or shipping. Assembly takes about 10 minutes. The assembled horse is 23'' wide by 56'' long (at rocker) by 45'' high. It weighs 40 lbs. and is sturdy enough to support an adult. It does not shoot projectiles or make noise, in keeping with my feeling that there are too many things that do. I hope that it reflects the two elements at the heart of any good toy: love and magic. Crated weight 80 lbs. $600 includes crating but not shipping. $75 deposit required with order.

Dick Showalter—I live in a tiny village fifty miles from Eugene, Oregon. I am thirty-three years old, a dropped-out marine biologist and self-taught woodworker. I was one of thirty craftspeople to receive a 1974 National Endowment for the Arts Craftsmen fellowship award.

I make many of my own tools. I also cut and cure my own lumber and make my own doweling, not in the spirit of anachronism, but to enable me to control as completely as possible the character of my finished work.

Dick Showalter, McKenzie Bridge, Oregon 97401.

Pottery—This type of pottery is made in the style of the American Indians: without the use of the potter's wheel. After firing, the pottery is decorated with a dilution of acrylic paints. Colors and design are chosen for each piece, in an effort to create harmony with each individual form. There are no glazes used, so the red clay remains close to its original color. Pictured are a black two-spout vessel, 7'' wide by 11'' tall, $35; a light red-brown bowl with black design, 3½'' high by 9'' wide, $28; and a vase with a brown, beige, red and black design, 8'' wide by 7¾'' high, $40.

Almut Hellman—I am German-born, thirty-four years old, and have resided in San Francisco for the last ten years. I am a photographer, and have been involved in several photographic exhibits. I am interested in all phases of pottery and have pursued my interest in this art form on a free-lance basis for the last year.

Almut Hellman, 1751 Union Street, San Francisco, California 94123.

Traveling Rucksack—An example of a custom order, the rucksack is made of chrome-tanned boot leather, hand-sewn and laced, with marine brass fittings and lock, top handle detachable. Interior document pocket. $625 postpaid. Also available in water buffalo with ivory closing, dark brown, $550 postpaid.

Ensemble Briefcase—For those who live out of their bags, a truly large luggage-weight case for heavy loads, fitted with three main compartments and in integral back-mounted case with flap for the pigskin secretary included. Silver name plate. English top-grain leather fully lined with pigskin, steel-reinforced handle hardware and heavy-duty hand-sewn luggage handle. Middle compartment fitted for eyeglasses case on one end and pens on the other. Twin locks with keys and security strap with brass buckle. Size: 22'' by 13'' by 5½''. $600 postpaid.

Pony Express Saddle Co. Ltd.—We are leathersmiths committed to traditional methods and European design of the last century. Apprenticed in Copenhagen, Denmark, we recently moved to Mill Valley, California, where we make our home and do limited production handwork and custom orders. We feel we are introducing a new world of top-drawer leather products expressed in functional design.

We operate our business as an unincorporated company of two principals in partnership. After all, we *are* married! We employ no apprentices or help, as many of our methods are largely forgotten and take years to perfect. We maintain top quality by doing it ourselves. Under the old European system of guilds, we have been considered master journeymen in leather. Some of our work is in the hands of European royalty.

Vincent and Elsa Takeuchi, c/o Pony Express Saddle Co. Ltd., 761 Edgewood Avenue, Mill Valley, California 94941.

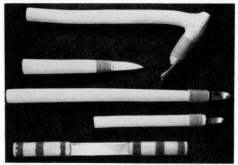

Wood Carving Tools—Based on Northwest Coast Indian designs. Blades made from tool steel, handles made from red alder. Each piece is unique. From top to bottom: elbow adze with gouge-type blade, 14'' long, $45; straight knife, 10'' long, $30; crooked knife, designed for two hands, 18'' long, $35; crooked knife, one-hand design, 10'' long, $30; draw knife, flexible blade, 14'' long, $40.

Beaver Crest Carving—This is an example of my work, done in yellow cedar. Although this is a one-of-a-kind piece and cannot be reproduced exactly, I would like to make facsimiles to order. $450.

Carved Spoons—Made of red alder. I carve the wood while it is still green, using my own tools based on Indian designs. The spoons can be made to any size; 8'' and 10'' sizes shown. Prices (from top): $65, $40, $60 and $45, shipping not included.

Murray Green—This Canadian woodcarver spends part of his year in California and part in British Columbia. He has been an apprentice to the Haida Indians north of Vancouver, and has taught classes on how to make tools based on Indian designs in both Vancouver and San Francisco.

   He has the honor of being the only non-Indian carver exhibited in the Centennial Museum in Vancouver. His tools and wood carvings have been exhibited in the Craft and Folk Art Museum in Los Angeles and the San Francisco Museum of Modern Art. Murray Green is interested in commission carving work including replicas.

   Murray Green, c/o 3394 Blair Drive, Hollywood, California 90068.

Mohair Scarves—Hand-woven neck scarves, made of a combination of mohair/nylon and brushed wool/viscose yarns in a variety of colors—the mohair yarns in solid colors and the brushed wool in subtle, variegated shades. When ordering scarves, please indicate tones rather than specific colors: solid (reds, pinks, yellows, browns, greens, blues, black, white); tweed (two-color combinations of the same colors); vertical stripe (white with rainbow stripes, or any solid-color background with harmonizing color stripes); plaid (indicate basic color or two-color scheme desired and three to four other colors will be harmonized). After they are woven, the scarves are brushed to raise the long nap, resulting in a soft, thick, luxurious product. Scarves are available in two sizes: small, 5'' to 6'' by 2 yards; and large, 10'' by 2 yards. Shipping weight 3 lbs. Small scarves (solid tweed or stripe) $18, large scarves in solid or tweed, $18, stripe, $20, or plaid, $22. Shipping not included.

Phantasmagoria—In 1974 my husband and I opened a small store to sell used and new books on natural lifestyles and new-age topics, and our own crafts. Jonathan works in stained glass, while I work with yarns, fabrics, colors and textures.

My in-store workshop pleases me, for I believe many crafts, including weaving, need to be demystified. Consumers need to understand what actually goes into craftwork. The only way to understand why a handcrafted article is twice as expensive as its manufactured counterpart is to make it yourself, or to watch the work in progress.

Karen Fayth, c/o Phantasmagoria, 311 South Eleventh Street, Tacoma, Washington 98402.

Salt-glazed Teapots—They are 7'' to 8'' tall. The glaze is light-brown body with blue and off-white decoration. Weight 2½ lbs. $30 each, shipping not included.

The Independence Clay Works — I live sixty-four hundred feet up on the side of Mt. Blitzen in what remains of an old mining town. My wife Julie and I have two teenaged boys, Ben and Greg. We raise a few goats, pigs, rabbits, chickens, ducks and geese. I am continually surprised at how nice my life is.

Dennis Parks, c/o The Independence Clay Works, Main and Gold Streets, Tuscarora, Nevada 89834.

60

Wooden Tongue Drums—The drum is probably the earliest and most universal type of instrument known to man. Used in whatever form—be it initiatory rites, magic, dance, religious ceremony, war, rock concert or symphonic orchestra—the hypnotic effects of rhythmic drumming and the primal urgings associated with it are known to all cultures and peoples. These particular drums are patterned after the Aztec "teponaztli" and the Mayan "tunkul." The present design, tongue proportions and resonant chamber have been carefully worked out to produce a fine-quality musical instrument that sounds, looks and feels nice. The woods used for the drum bodies are ponderosa pine and luan Philippine mahogany; the nodes are inlaid with maple. The drums pictured here are small "talking" drums, 3½" by 7¼" by 18". Large bass drums (5½" by 9¼" by 28") available by special order. Prices vary according to the wood used for the tongues. Hawaiian koa $50; California redwood $40; Douglas fir $40; black walnut $50, postpaid.

Ray Nitta—I am a teacher, street artist, runner and student of life. I am a co-director of the Center for Open Learning and Teaching, and teach a workshop on musical instrument-making there.

Ray Nitta, 2520 Shattuck Avenue, Berkeley, California 94703.

Tureen and Bowl Set—The set has 11 pieces. Each one is formed and glazed by traditional hand techniques. It is dishwasher-safe and ovenproof. Tureen is 8½'' in diameter, 10'' high and holds 5 to 6 quarts. Each bowl is 7'' in diameter, 3'' high and holds 2 cups. The ladle is 10½'' long. Total weight is 16 lbs. Set can be glazed in white with blue decoration or brown. The glazes are lead-free. $100, shipping not included.

Wine Set—The stoneware wine set has 8 pieces. Decanter has a corked stopper, holds 2 quarts and stands 14'' high. Each goblet is 5'' high and holds 1 cup. Total weight: 6 lbs. It can be glazed in white with blue decoration, brown, brown and white, blue and white, or black and white. Lead-free glazes. Dishwasher-safe. $60. Shipping not included.

Colander—Stoneware colander is formed and glazed by traditional hand techniques. It has a rawhide loop for hanging. It is 9'' in diameter, 6½'' high and weighs 2 lbs. Can be glazed in white with blue decoration, brown, brown and white, blue and white, or black and white. Glazes are lead-free. Dishwasher-safe. $22, shipping not included.

Casseroles—The stoneware casseroles come in two sizes. The 3-quart casserole is 9'' in diameter, approximately 8'' high and weighs 4 lbs. The 1½-quart casserole is 6'' in diameter, 6½'' high and weighs 2½ lbs. They can be glazed in white with blue decoration, brown, brown and white, blue and white, or black and white. The glazes are lead-free. The casseroles are dishwasher-safe and can be used in the oven. The 3-quart casserole is $35, shipping not included. The 1½-quart casserole is $25, shipping not included.

Oatmeal Mountain Pottery—We have been full-time potters for six years and work primarily in functional stoneware. We live and work in an old candy factory on the South Side of Pittsburgh.

It's not only important to make a pot that's aesthetically pleasing, it must also be comfortable to use day in and day out. We hope we can make pieces that people can live with and that can be a part of their daily lives.

The more we do, the more we want to do. Creativity feeds itself.

Ken and Jane Barber, c/o Oatmeal Mountain Pottery, 2338 Sarah Street, Pittsburgh, Pennsylvania 15203.

Recipe File and Coin Bank—Made in the form of a rural mailbox, natural finished pine with two coats of satin varnish. The file is 6¾'' wide, 14½'' deep and 7¼'' high. The lower drawer contains 25 index guides (appetizers, bread, etc.) plus 25 blank cards. The upper drawer is for clippings, pencils, whatever. At the rear of the file is a coin slot with a collecting box inside. The flag is of red cardboard and has a clip to hold recipe cards. There are green felt corners on the bottom of the file. Packaged weight 7 lbs. $36, shipping not included.

Harold Carlson—For forty years I have been a self-employed home builder and designer. Almost two years ago, three important things happened almost within days of each other. The I.R.S. seized my house, Saigon fell and I quit building. I had refused to pay any personal income tax as a protest against the U.S. involvement in Vietnam.

A month before the axe fell I had homesteaded four acres to the rear of my property, changed my lifestyle and begun anew. My land is wooded, beautiful and has a live stream. This summer I plan to build a sawmill powered by a water wheel of my design.

I work as an individual but often have a helper, or farm out work such as varnishing, sanding, etc.

My tools are excellent and my 12'' surface planer is the envy of my friends. It has earned me many a pie or loaf of bread.

From log to finished product, right here on Stevens Creek, is my aim.

Harold Carlson, c/o Stevens Creek Workshops, P.O. Box 177, Blue River, Oregon 97413.

Hand-woven Bags—Made of all-wool yarns. Each bag has three colors, incorporating various designs similar to the one pictured. The bag shown has a string color background with the pattern in navy and white. It is about 12'' by 12''; fully lined and with an adjustable shoulder strap. Shipping weight 1 lb. $40.

Nao Riggs—I have been designing and producing needlework pillows, hand-woven bags and wall hangings for the last five years. I work at home and do all of the work myself. I sell mostly to small shops and individuals.
  Nao Riggs, 1544 Taylor Street, San Francisco, California 94133.

Belt Buckle—The buckle is cast from my original modeling in clay. It measures 3½'' across and is a limited edition. Silver $97 postpaid, brass or bronze $37 postpaid.

Earrings—Each earring is made of two pieces, one silver and one brass. Both pieces are hand-cut and etched. They are 1'' long. $16 postpaid.

Village Artworks—I'm a former commercial artist and am happier now as a new craftsperson. I've been sort of easing into it slowly for the last seven years, trying to learn enough to make a living doing work of my own. For the last two years, I've been pretty much able to do just that. I really like it—being my own boss, doing my own designs and talking to other craftspeople and crafts fans at fairs. I'm still amazed that I can actually make metal do what I want it to. I do a lot of etching on my pieces because I still love sketching and it makes my pieces unique and personal.

Sally Lyon, c/o Village Artworks, 8 West Main Street, Wappingers Falls, New York 12590.

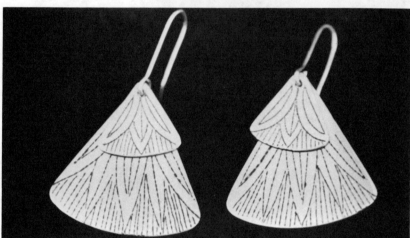

Pipes—Rare woods from around the world, hand-crafted into an excellent smoking pipe. Rosewood or ironwood bowl, patchwork stem of rare woods. Each pipe comes with a redwood or walnut base holder. Pipe is finished with natural oil, and is 5½'' long with 2''-high bowl piece. Shipping weight 3 lbs. $20.

Headless Enterprises—Many life changes have led me to woodcrafting. I find it enjoyable work. I have been living in Northern California for the past few years. I'm planning to move a little further north in the near future to settle down on some land.

Besides making pipes with the exotic woods, I make cutting and serving trays, backgammon boards and numerous types of wood and silver boxes. I keep in mind that there are a lot of wood products available to the public. The exotic woods I use, however, are very seldom seen: rosewoods from Asia and Africa, ironwoods from Africa and South America, hardwoods from Africa, South and North America and Asia.

Chet Malin, c/o Headless Enterprises, P.O. Box 768, Guerneville, California 95446.

Feather Hatbands—Since the days of ancient Greece, people have said, "Put a feather in your cap"—and that is precisely what I do. A hat is an expression of your character and spirit, not merely an article of clothing. A special hatband can make any hat uniquely yours. These adjustable hatbands are made of pheasant feathers on a leather backing; some have shell centers. Hatbands tie with leather thongs so they can be moved from one hat to another. Bands are 1½" wide and 22" to 26" long. Send head or hat measurement. If this information is not available, I will send 23" for female and 25" for male. Colors available are green/blue/blonde; beige/black; mixed browns; red/brown. $15.

Ninette Larson—"One is immediately taken with the iridescent quality of the self—how its colors are ever-changing and remain never the same. It is like a feather caught in the wind." This is my favorite quote. I find the spirit of freedom in every feather. It is this spirit, as well as the ever-changing iridescent colors, that attracted me, and continues to attract me, to feathers. I began as a weaver incorporating feathers into my work. I became so interested in them that now I work exclusively with feathers.

Ninette Larson, 1427 Bancroft Way, Berkeley, California 94702.

Raku Pottery—These boxes are fired using the ancient Japanese technique of raku. This process produces brilliant gold and copper lusters with rich variations in color and texture. The boxes are hand-built, and all glazes are lead-free and completely safe for table use. Three types of boxes are available. Low: 4¼'' wide by 6'' long by 2'' high, $25. Medium: 4'' wide by 5¾'' long by 3¼'' high, $25. High (shown here): 4'' wide by 5'' high by 4'' long, $25. All postpaid. Specify gold or copper luster glaze.

Tim Ballingham—For the past ten years I have had the delightful opportunity of working with clay. My primary interest is in form and I think of each of my works as a sculptural object. Every small box is a tiny sculpture demanding creativity and sensitivity in its fabrication.

I find much joy in creating and in so doing learn a great deal about myself. With this learning comes a better understanding of my relationship to all people. This joy I have for my work is there to be shared with all who will look.

Tim Ballingham, Route #2, Westmoreland, Kansas 66549.

Gorgets—The gorget (French for collar) has been a traditional form of throat ornament and protection for centuries, from early man to knights in armor. Each earthenware gorget is hand-painted, signed and shaped to comfortably suspend around the neck from a crocheted necklace. The clasp is made of fine silver. Rounded shape is available in black on white, black on rust, and lustrous raku-fired gold. Each measures 6'' by 3''. $25 postpaid. Pointed shape comes in same colors and measures 6'' by 5''. $25 postpaid.

Pamela Ballingham—I have operated a well-equipped ceramic studio for three years, but formally began business with my husband Tim two years ago. This past year we traveled nineteen thousand miles establishing store and gallery outlets and spent much time in perfecting our record-keeping and packaging techniques, and in general professionalizing our approach. My sole income is derived from my craft, and I contribute half of our combined income.

Myself? I derive meaning from work done independently, done with perfection and done with a sense of contribution to beauty and spirit.

Pamela Ballingham, Route #2, Westmoreland, Kansas 66549.

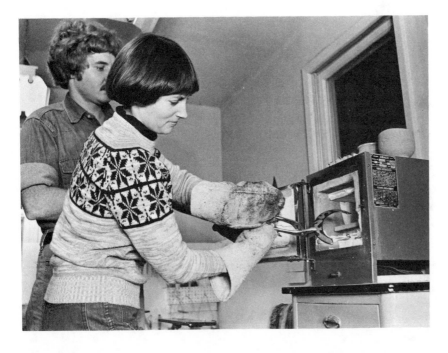

Roman Chain—The necklace is constructed of loops of gold wire that are individually soldered and then woven together. The catch is made of lathe-turned ivory with gold fittings. Only yellow 18k gold is used. The choker shown is ¼'' in diameter and 15'' long. $900 postpaid.

Necklace—The necklace is made of vermeil (silver-gilt) and hand-carved elephant ivory. The metal is forged, formed and carved sterling silver in a fabricated linkage system, electroplated with 24k gold. It is approximately choker length. Vermeil $750; yellow, green or rose gold $1,800.

Vincent Street Studios—A partnership formed by Margery Beth Rose and Janice C. Whitcraft. Both have been professionally involved in crafts for several years. Both received M.F.A. degrees from Rochester Institute of Technology, majoring in metalsmithing and jewelry.

Margery Beth Rose and Janice C. Whitcraft, c/o Vincent Street Studios, 125 Vincent Street, Syracuse, New York 13210.

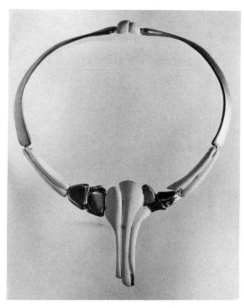

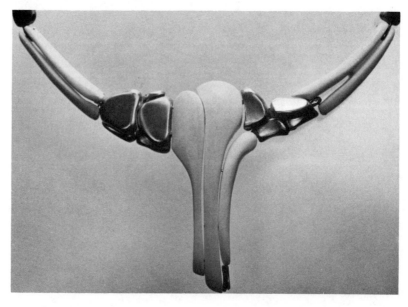

Ladderback Rocker—With a five-slat back and no arms, this rocker is ideal for sewing, knitting and baby-rocking. Cornshuck seat, 42'' tall, with 31''-long rockers. $97.50, shipping not included.

Stanton Woodcraft—Our nonprofit, community-owned enterprise is devoted to the development of the workers and the community. C. Lynn Frazer is the manager of the woodcraft shop, which produces solid Appalachian hardwood furniture and decorator items of the highest quality, all competitively priced.

Stanton Woodcraft, Airport Road, P.O. Box 516, Stanton, Kentucky 40380.

Hand-spun Yarns—The fleece is hand-washed and hand-carded with the greatest of care, to insure that the integrity of the fibers is maintained. We use only very carefully selected fleece. Where color is desired, CIBA dyes are used, and the formula is carefully recorded for future orders. Yarns may be spun to your specification. Simply submit a color sample, along with your design requirement. The standard yarns (singles, two-, three- and four-ply yarns), $1.45 per oz. Add 5 cents per oz. for natural dark fleece. Add 5 cents per oz. for CIBA dyed colors. Add 10 cents per oz. for color-blended heathers. $5 prepayment on all orders. Samples are $1. Prices do not include shipping.

Newstalgia Yarns—I have been an active participant in the world of crafts for as long as I can remember. I think it is the satisfaction of creating something beautiful or useful, born out of inspiration and coaxed to completion by a disciplined devotion to quality, that keeps me fascinated. The feeling of independence from the clutches of the super-mechanized, mass-produced items ever available for the consumer's convenience and for the destruction of aesthetics, has strongly reinforced my interest in crafts for many years.

The ultimate logic is that working the magic fiber (wool) through the various processes—sorting, cleaning, dyeing, teasing, carding—through the spinning wheel, skeining, setting the twist, is a pure and simple joy for me. Making quality yarns combines the basics of spinning with the many, many hours of experimentation with dyeing, blending and designing with the pleasure of creating yarns for that super-special project.

With a few years of spinning behind me, I still have the same feeling about this, the most sensual of crafts—the test is in the touching.

Carole A. Scott, c/o Newstalgia Yarns, P.O. Box 6053, Richmond Beach, Washington 98160.

Doll Houses—Each Roseybug doll
house has hand-cut cedar shingles
and shake roof. Exteriors are trimmed
in hardwood, with set-in stained-glass
windows. Outside doors are paneled
mahogany with brass decorative
doorknob. Inside doors are paneled
hardwood—usually painted white.
The inside is completely finished,
including wallpaper, baseboards and
moldings. The Crooked Doll House
shown here has a stone chimney
which extends inside to the stone
fireplace with walnut mantel. The
stones are California jade, quartz and
others. The floor in this house is
mahogany. Outside trim is oak and
walnut. The door is redwood outside
with birch veneer on the inside. Room
size is 12½'' by 12'' with 9'' and 10''
ceiling height. $225, shipping not
included. Houses are not available in
great quantity or in kits. Options
include: stairs, parquet floors,
electric lights, stone chimney, stone
fireplace with hardwood mantel, and
stone foundation. Prices vary with
number of rooms and options desired.
Quotes upon request. Hand-crafted
miniature accessories also available.
All doll houses and accessories are 1''
to 1' scale.

Roseybug Miniatures—My workshop
is the downstairs area of our
two-room cabin, built in a natural
hilltop clearing on our fifty-acre
parcel in Ukiah, California. On warm
days I work outdoors in the cool shade
of the fir trees. We have no
electricity, so most everything is cut,
carved and sewn by hand.
Occasionally I go to the city to use my
power tools and sewing machine.
   Our water is carried from a spring,
our light is kerosene and our heat
comes from a woodburner. But we do
have a gas stove and refrigerator!
   I work from 7:30 in the morning
until 4:00 or 5:00 in the evening. At
noon I take a break and either walk or
ride my horse to pick up the mail a
mile away—or just enjoy the
surrounding countryside and gather
my thoughts. In the evening I sew
miniature quilts and other doll house
accessories. Bedtime comes early,
but so does the new day.

*Linda Rosenberg, c/o
Roseybug Miniatures,
9050 Orr Springs Road,
Ukiah, California 95482.*

...my theme: the celebration of Woman as mother, sister, harlequin, clown, priestess; Woman joyous, contemplative, mysterious, but always strong.

1. Red Haired Woman, $950
2. Day Dream, $950
3. Studio Portrait, $375
4. Night Scene, $800
5. The Flapper, $800

Wall Hangings—My wall hangings are representational paintings created with fabrics of many textures and colors; embellished with hand and machine embroideries, beads, feathers, acrylic painting and three-dimensional sculpture. All hang free from a pole except when otherwise specified.

Evelyn Brenner—My theme is the celebration of Woman. I love women of all occupations, ages, times and locations. When I work I become part of them and when I'm done I hate to say goodbye.

I have been professionally involved in crafts for approximately twenty years and have sold my pottery throughout the U.S., Latin America and Europe. Three years ago I became intrigued with textures, cloths, embroideries, etc., and created my first wall hanging. I have had a solo show, was featured in the Vicrtex display window, won several prizes at group shows and have happily sold both through craft shows and privately. I have a fully equipped studio in which I work eight to nine hours a day.

My canvas and palette are cloth, beads, feathers, clay and thread. I bring together these tactilely exciting materials to create a new whole. My intention is to unite a contemporary painting style with the folk art tradition. I approach each wall hanging as I would a painting, with its disciplines of space and color. Each area of a work must speak for itself. Ideally, the finished work should unite quality of craftsmanship with beauty of conception.

Evelyn Brenner, 665 East Seventh Street, New York, New York 11218.

Stoneware Teapot—This 6-cup pot has double reed handles that serve to steady the pot while tea is being poured and also create a unique design. The pot can be prewarmed with hot water or kept warm on top of the stove with an asbestos or metal flame diffuser. Colors: gold, turquoise, white, denim blue. Shipping weight 4½ lbs. $20, shipping not included.

Ceremonial Vessels—Created to satisfy some fantasy of yours. Some are for storage of anything from jewels to cookies; some are goblets, wine vessels or vases. They are primarily unglazed stoneware with carved, stamped or slip decoration and occasional bits of real gold. They can be glazed or even lined with velvet. Prices range from $40 up. If you send me a description of what you want and your price range, I'll work up an idea and send you plans and an estimate.

Sharon Jones—My work is strongly influenced by the pottery of Korea, China, Japan, Africa and, of course, the wonderful pre-Columbian pottery of the Americas. My love for the pottery, textiles, basketry, clothing and architecture of these peoples has led me to travel to Japan, Guatemala, Mexico and the North American Southwest to meet artisans, and has left me in complete awe of their work.

Like most craftspeople, my medium inspires me tremendously. I like to play large areas of bare clay against the softness of glazed surfaces and against even the glow of metallic lusters. My designs evolve from using the pots myself; I am continually improving on them functionally. My ceremonial vessels' primary function is visual and tactile pleasure. They satisfy my flamboyant bent.

I live in the Sierra Foothills of my native California, where I work alone in a studio outside of town, modestly supporting myself with my craft.

Sharon Jones, 126 Orchard Street, Nevada City, California 95959.

Walking Sticks—Canes, walking sticks and staffs are made of white oak, hard maple, ash, hickory, walnut or zebrawood. The designs carved into them vary, but all include flowers of some kind, leaves and a butterfly, or they can be carved to your specific design. Length suggestions: for a cane, which is about 1-1/8'' in diameter, measure one you are already comfortable with; for walking sticks, measure from the top of your elbow and add 2'' (sticks are 1¼'' in diameter); a staff (1½'' in diameter) should be equal to your height. Each $65, or $85 made of zebrawood.

Robert Simola—When my wife has reached the top of a mountain and I am fifteen minutes behind her, I find a walking stick very useful for leaning on while I stop and admire the view. It is also excellent as a sword for fighting invisible foes and as a support when walking on wobbly rocks over a stream or while going up and down hills.

Robert Simola, 512 East Fourth Street, Ontario, California 91764.

Crazy Quilt Purses—These purses are made in my own original crazy-quilting style, with hand embroidery, an interior pocket, gingham lining and button closing. They do not sag and are machine-washable. Fabrics are heavy cottons and blends. I can use your fabrics if you wish. Specify predominant colors desired. Large purse, 10'' by 12'' with 33'' shoulder strap, $35 postpaid. Small purse, 8'' by 10'' with 25'' shoulder strap, $30 postpaid.

The Quilt Patch—I started the Quilt Patch in Tacoma, Washington nearly five years ago, to design and market quality quilted items. My studio is now in my home in the California desert. In the course of designing, I developed a technique of crazy quilting that is the subject of my book, *The Contemporary Crazy Quilt Project Book* (Crown, 1977). Although I also use traditional quilting techniques, my most popular work is that done in my own contemporary crazy-quilting style. My creative works range from glasses cases to king-size quilts, and include one-of-a-kind items. I welcome inquiries.

Dixie Haywood, c/o The Quilt Patch, 43623 North Twenty-fourth Street West, Lancaster, California 93534.

Jewelry—Over twenty designs are available which feature Alaskan themes. Hand-engraved sterling silver contrasts sharply with dark backgrounds of polished ebony or rosewood. Mother-of-pearl inlay is often used, as shown here in the log cabin's smoke and the owl's eyes. Pendants are $40, bolo ties (not shown), $50 postpaid. Size: 2¼'' by 1¾''.

Jay and Barbara Greene—Our goal in moving to Alaska four years ago was to become more self-sufficient and to disassociate ourselves from many of the conventional bonds of modern society. We have built a log home and workshop in the small fishing community of Halibut Cove on Kachemak Bay. There are no roads here, so our supplies arrive by boat or float plane. We provide our own electrical power from a Jacobs wind generator.

We make our living as full-time metalsmiths. Until now our work has been available only through four fine-arts galleries in Alaska.

Jay and Barbara Greene, Halibut Cove, Alaska 99603.

Wooden Tubs—I make deep wooden bathtubs in several styles. They can be installed like a regular tub, or sunken Japanese fashion. This tub is about 30'' wide by 54'' long by 25'' deep, in cedar and mahogany. A variety of woods and finishes are appropriate. Tubs may be left plain or lined with epoxy or fiberglass. All are laminated with epoxy glue and treated with a nontoxic wood stabilizer. A colleague of mine can carve designs, if you wish. Costs vary, depending on this and that. This one is $1,000.

Mirrors, Cat's Cradle—These mirrors are handmade from maple or birch, and no two are exactly alike. If you'd like a spot of color, you may have a ring of red, yellow, blue or gold (see middle mirror). They're carefully finished and guaranteed. For 6'' to 7'' diameter, $12. For 9'' to 10'', $18. For 11'' to 12'', $22, shipping not included. The Bag-in-a-Box is a magazine rack, doll's bed or cat's cradle. The frame is birch. The 9-oz. marine-quality Army duck is easily removed for washing. It's 16¾'' wide by 11'' high by 14'' deep. With sanded, unfinished frame, $12. Varnished, $14.

Morgan Bay Crafts—This is a little family business. Mark does the woodwork. Margret sews. Rob and Andrew help around. We have a little shop by a salt marsh at the head of a pretty bay. We're fortunate to be able to study with a teacher and make a living at something so enjoyable.

Mark Baldwin, c/o Morgan Bay Crafts, Surry, Maine 04684.

Jewelry—Wrapped and twisted sterling silver bracelet and choker may be purchased separately. Bracelet, 5¾'', $24. Choker, 14'' long, $72. Sterling silver bracelet inlaid with 2 copper circles and 10 sections of abalone, set with hand-carved tusk ivory, is available in a limited edition of 50, numbered, signed and dated. About 5¾'', $180. Sterling silver earrings in hand-formed holloware style, with black onyx beads, 2'' long, $60. Except for the wrapped and twisted bracelet and choker, the jewelry items are one-of-a-kind pieces and cannot be reproduced exactly, but will be made in a manner similar to the ones pictured on this page. Shipping not included.

Thundercrafts—My business has developed slowly over the past five years. I came to Vermont from a job as assistant art director for a Scorcese film in Hollywood. Once here, there was no work available. A friend had a torch and we taught ourselves to use it, starting out with a brazing rod and making belt buckles and sculptures, hitching down to Boston and selling store to store. While slowly accruing tools, information and experience, I learned to solder and began using silver. I experimented with styles, techniques and materials, going from fabrication to etching to inlay, overlay, gold, ivory, ebony, abalone, etc. I've been in galleries and have done many commissions.

Ishwara Futral, c/o Thundercrafts, West Barnet, Vermont 05870.

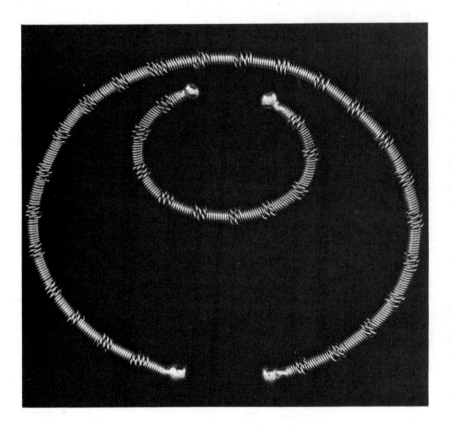

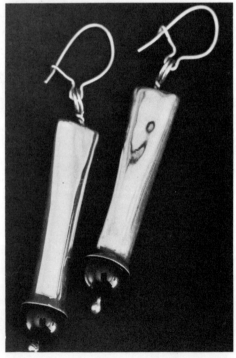

Bicycle Frames—Silk Hope frame sets are built to the cyclist's individual measurements. Standard materials used are Reynolds 531 butted tubing with Campagnolo cable guide and fork ends. Vagner flat top crowns are complemented with Prugnat long point and DuBois lug sets. Saddle lug clamps and brake bridges are reinforced. Low temperature silver brazing alloys are used throughout, excluding the joining of fork ends with bronze. For those not initiated, these are some of the finest materials. Frame sets are etched, primed, sealed and painted using acrylic enamel with catalytic hardener to color selection. Frame sets can be equipped as complete cycles to individual specifications. A $50 deposit is required with each order. Frame and fork set $270. Additional fittings and many options are extra. Shipping charge $10.

Silk Hope, Ltd.—I am the single employee of Silk Hope, Ltd., a corporation chartered in 1974. My work is completely devoted to the manufacture of cycle frames, repairs and special work such as construction of cycles for the handicapped. I have worked professionally with bicycles since completing high school in 1971 at North Carolina School of the Arts, where I majored in visual arts—sculpture, ceramics, painting and art history.

Silk Hope, as a one-person operation, has a low volume of work. Frames are finished at a maximum of one per week.

Since the shop is located in my home, there is a joint lifestyle—hand-dug well, gardens, wood heat, country setting. It's a good location for both living and working.

McLean Fonvielle, c/o Silk Hope, Ltd., P.O. Box 82, Saxapahaw, North Carolina 27340.

Fire Tools—A three-piece set with hooks; each piece is hand-forged from a ½''-diameter iron rod and is approximately 36'' long when finished. After forging, each piece is finished with beeswax to enhance the natural black color of forged iron. $55, shipping not included.

Copper and Iron Ladle—Hand-forged iron handle with hand-sunk and planished copper bowl. Overall length is about 16'' with a 4''-diameter bowl. The bowl is bright polished copper and the handle is the deep black of forged iron. The ladle weighs 1½ lbs. packed. $24, shipping not included.

Meat Fork—Hand-forged iron fork. A delicate-looking yet substantial fork, approximately 15'' long. As with all other forged iron articles, the color is a rich black. It weighs 1 lb. packed. $20, shipping not included.

Woodstock Forge—What feelings would make anyone want to hammer on white-hot iron? It is the kind of question you ask yourself on a hot, humid day as you stand in front of a roaring soft-coal fire.

A lot of it has to do with the respect you feel for a craft tradition that reaches back through the ages. Deeper feelings emerge from the respect that you feel for the anonymous knights of the anvil, who asked only to be allowed to do their work well.

Blacksmithing is now my only form of employment and it is providing about half our family's income. My wife Peggy provides the other half by teaching hand weaving and driving a school bus. In reality, she is my partner. She helps me with the work as much as possible, but more importantly, she is constantly giving me gentle encouragement to change and grow.

I am a fugitive from the American industrial system—a former tool and die maker. There is no room for feelings or personal growth in that system. Working within my craft is really a way to learn about myself.

David A. Osier, c/o Woodstock Forge, R.R. 2, Woodstock, Connecticut 06281.

Desert Sand Tapestry—Designed by Carole Rae, this tapestry is 28'' by 54''. It is hand-woven with hand-spun rust and brown wools and has a soft white angora-textured background. Packaged weight 10 lbs. $460.

Hand-woven Pillows—These pillows are 16'' by 20''. They are all wool with hand-spun yarns and have polyester-filled liners. Available in 3 color combinations. Natural: beige, camel and white; medium tones: brown, rust and light gray; dark tones: chocolate brown, maroon and green. For special colors submit color samples. Shipping weight 5 lbs., $55 each. Custom pillows are $60 each.

Carole Rae Fiber Center—My concepts in weaving have evolved from my experiences living on a Northern California wilderness preserve and weaving with the natives in Guatemala.

During the Renaissance, tapestries were used to cover cold expanses of wall. It's the same today. Weavings have more appeal than flat paintings. And the most tactile weavings are the most appealing.

Carole Rae, c/o Carole Rae Fiber Center, 101 Kansas Street, Suite 380, San Francisco, California 94103.

Baker's Dough Ornaments—We make Christmas tree ornaments from baker's dough—flour, water, salt and food coloring, covered with varathane plastic for preservation. The ornaments are about 4'' by 5'', and they will be shipped in gift boxes with acetate lids, ready for gift-giving. Some of our most popular designs are: Santa face, angel, Victorian house and pie. $5 each.

Amato Design Company—We own and operate Amato Design as a partnership. We have been doing baker's dough ornaments for four years now. We also design wallpaper, gift paper, and greeting cards, and do free-lance illustration and design work.

Most of all, we enjoy being together, creating and traveling. Last but not least, we have a dog who can say ''hamburger.'' Can you beat that?

Linda and John Amato, c/o Amato Design Company, 2621 Laguna Street #4, San Francisco, California 94123.

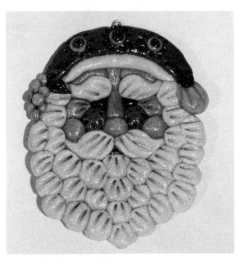

Looms—We build hand-crafted, jack-type looms of solid oak, cherry or walnut. They are available in 40'' or 54'' weaving widths with either 4 or 8 harnesses, and are equipped with your choice of 8, 10 or 12 dent reed, 750 (40'') or 1000 (54'') round wire heddles and tie-up sticks. The large shed has even tension of top and bottom ends. The substantial and well-balanced beater can pack the heaviest rug material. Shown, 40'' 8-harness oak loom, $710. Brochure, 50 cents.

Fireside Looms—My wife Rachel, when our daughter Andrea was born, divided her time between loom and bassinette, finding fulfillment in both. She took classes in natural dyeing and wool spinning, and from then on, weaving became a full-time love. When she asked me to make some accessories for her loom, I began to understand the relationship between weaving and woodworking, and my absorption with the total process began to equal hers.

Searching for a more complete knowledge of this basic art, we lived for a year in Spain, where weaving is a part of the culture. We learned the fundamentals of loom construction in Granada from master weaver Nicholas Perez. I am now building about forty-four looms a year, tending chickens and livestock, sawmilling, volunteering at Wildgarden School and trying to be a human being as well.

Rachel and Gary Sweatt, c/o Fireside Looms, Box 11, Deadwood, Oregon 97430.

Funky Flying Fantasies—These flights of aerodynamic fantasy evoke memories of old-fashioned toys in their design and traditional construction. All planes shown are original creations hand-crafted from selected woods without the use of nails or screws. All joints are reinforced with hardwood dowels for extra strength. The smooth satin finish is water- and alcohol-resistant. Each plane has a propeller that turns. The Seaplane and Biplane with pants (pants are wheel covers) have functional wheels. These funky flying fantasies make unique gifts for pilots of all ages. Tri-motor Biplane, $100. Flying Boats, $55. Biplane with Pants, $70. Shipping not included.

Robert Winland—I was raised in the small town of Lovell, Wyoming. After graduating from the University of Wyoming, I moved to the Cincinnati area and have worked as an art teacher and craftsperson since then. Currently I teach half-time and devote the remainder to expanding ''Cowboy Bob's Flying Circus.''

I have always been interested in antique toys, airplanes and cars. in my work I try to capture a whimsical feeling while maintaining a high level of craftsmanship and attention to detail. I strive to make works of art that are also fun to play with and look at. I believe that the ability to play is one of the things that defines our humanity. It is important to the well-being of people of all ages. It gives me a great deal of pleasure to see people interact with my creations.

Robert Winland, 118 North Seventh Street, Hamilton, Ohio 45011.

Man's Tailored Vest—Made of the finest soft garment cowhide. The bound pockets and buttonholes set off the well-fitting design of this comfortable vest. Colors are golden natural, medium brown or dark brown; indicate first and second choices. Sizes 34 to 44, with machine-stitched bound pockets, $55; with hand-laced pockets, $75. Add $3 for sizes 42 and 44. Special orders taken.

Woman's Deerskin Vest—You will love the soft, supple feel of this fitted vest. It has a hand-braided front closure, and comes in a golden natural tone. Hand-washable in nondetergent soap. Sizes: petite (6 to 8), small (8 to 10), medium (10 to 12) and large (12 to 14). With suede side out (shown), $47.50. With smooth deerskin side out, $57.50.

Windy Mountain—After eighteen years of sewing with fabric, I decided to try my hand at leather work. I explored stores and boutiques all over, searching for ideas and inspiration, but found only basic, overused styles. In 1974 I became a partner in a leather shop in the Sierra Foothills. I sold my bedroom set for $600 and invested the money in deerskin and garment cowhide.

I had never attempted leather construction and was pretty apprehensive. But the only way to find out was to dive in headfirst. One year of partnership in the shop taught me a great deal about business as well as leather. My partner knew something about soft leather and was a good guide, as were the many books I scoured on the subject. Most of my knowledge came from good old trial and error, though.

Quality and good fit are my most important objectives. Each piece of leather is hand-picked, or hand-tanned by a friend. But a piece of leather is only as good as the pattern, grade of thread and knowledge used to make it into a long-lasting, comfortable garment. My heart is in my work, as you will see and feel if you decide to own one of my vests.

Windy Mountain, General Delivery, Big Fork, Montana 55991.

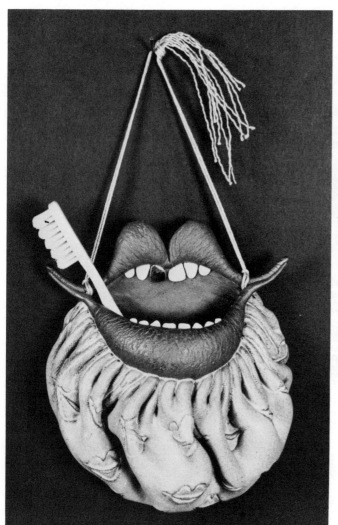

Teapot and Teacups—These can be purchased separately. The teapot is cone 6 stoneware, and comes in shiny royal blue or shiny cream-rust. Some people find this piece obscene, some find it amusing—but don't serve tea in it when your parents come to visit! It measures 9'' by 11'' by 6'' and weighs 2 lbs. 13 oz. (8 lbs. packed). $65, shipping not included. The pouch teacups are fun to drink out of—the liquid makes little lapping sounds as it catches on the folds of the clay. They are cone 9 porcelain, and come in the following colors: light blue glossy glaze with yellow coils around the handles and brown tiger stripes on handles; or warm beige glossy glaze with gold luster on coils around handles. Each teacup is 4'' by 5½'' by 4½'' and weighs 13 oz. (4 lbs. packed). $18 each, shipping not included.

Mouth Pouch—I suggest that you use it as a toothbrush holder. Dentists love them for their offices, and I'm told that when children keep their toothbrushes in the pouch, they suddenly start loving to brush their teeth! Stoneware cone 6, with low-fire gold luster on one tooth. Made from hand-gathered slab; lips are press-moulded and teeth are individually inset in white clay and separately painted. Colors are shiny royal blue, gold semi-matte and lavender-gray matte. The pouch is 5½'' wide by 6½'' high by 3'' deep and weighs 5 lbs. packed. $24.

Heart Pins—All pins have a gold-luster border and are made of cone 9 porcelain with feathers added. A flower decal comes on either pale lavender or antique beige background; solid luster colors available are rose, purple, orange, dark red, dark blue, turquoise, aqua, emerald green or solid gold. The pins are 1¾'' by 1¾.'' $15.

Kathy Jeffers—I enjoy working in clay because I love the sensuality of the material itself and because it affords me endless possibilities for playing and experimenting with new creative ideas. I find many things about our world quite bizarre and nonsensical; on the other hand, there is much loveliness to be found. I also feel that most people take themselves and others too seriously. I hope that my work is a direct reflection of these feelings.

I am of the opinion that "clay is what clay does" and do not feel that pottery has to be earthy and functional in order to remain true to itself. I've been working in clay for nine years, and for four years it has been my sole means of making a living. I have recently started doing sculpture, and my goal is to be a professional illustrator using clay as my medium.

Kathy Jeffers, c/o Downtown Potters' Hall, 115 Mercer Street, New York, New York 10012.

Batik Paintings—These batiks include several techniques incorporated with the traditional wax-resist dye-bath method. Each piece is individually drawn. Styles range from graphic to a painterly look. A 1½'' border of the final dye bath color is left to frame the picture. The batiks are colorfast, and a slight amount of wax is left in the material to promote durability. Sizes are up to the buyer. The present range is 10'' by 10'' to 30'' by 40''. Any colors can be used, and orders should specify predominantly warm or cool colors, or an even distribution of both. Prices range from $20 to $180. Shown here: Floral painting, 26'' by 28'', $80; Sunset I, 26'' by 28'', $90. Framing instructions included. Add $2 per batik shipping charge.

Diane Rittberg—I have been seriously involved with art since 1967, and after experiencing many media, I have found batik the most exciting. It is a most important part of my life. Prior to settling in California, I lived in several parts of the country, following the art programs in colleges at each locale.

Diane Rittberg, 8577 Edgebrook Drive, Garden Grove, California 92644.

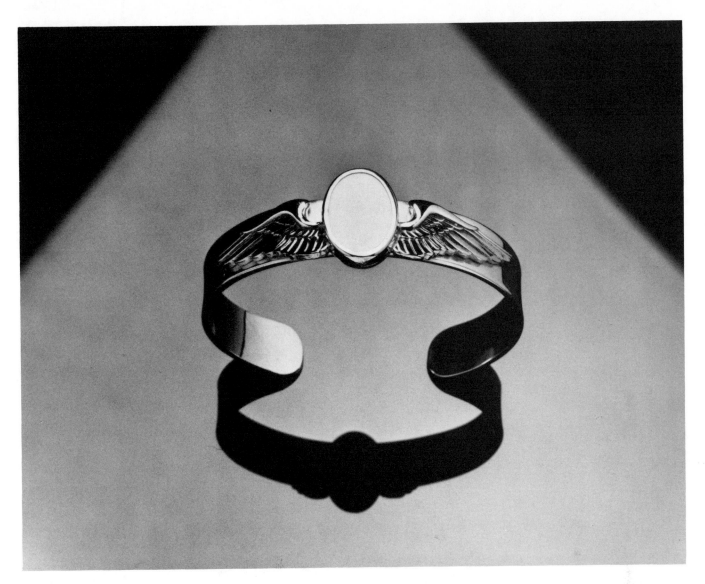

Wing Bracelet—The bracelet is made of sterling silver and is ½'' wide. The white material in the center setting is elephant ivory. When ordering, please remember to state who will be wearing the bracelet (a man with a medium wrist, a woman with an extra-small wrist, etc.). A polishing cloth and a few paragraphs on the care of the bracelet are included. $125.

Ellen Dimsdale—My work is done in the back of my San Francisco shop. Except for one or two art fairs a year, this is the only place I sell my work. My business has always been a one-person operation, and entry into this catalog represents my first effort to expand. I produce pieces for sale in the shop, special-order pieces for my customers and occasionally a piece for myself which is not for sale—one that I might enter in a show. At this point I feel that jewelry design is my lifework. I feel really good about getting so much satisfaction from this work, and I'm trying to share this satisfaction by training a woman to fabricate so she will have a skill to support herself . . . or just express herself.

Ellen Dimsdale, c/o Benoy, 3550 Twenty-second Street, San Francisco, California 94114.

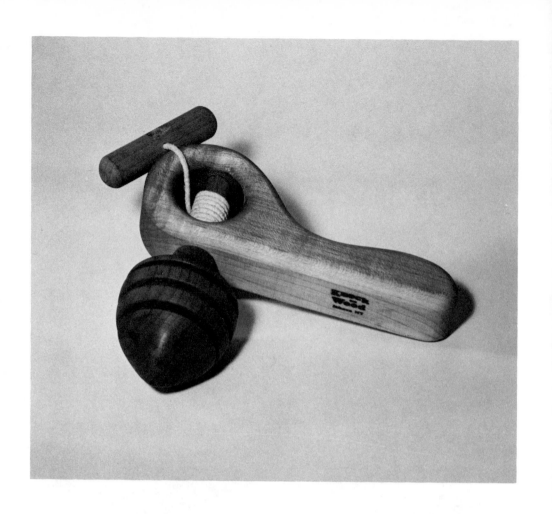

98

Solitaire—This is a peg-jumping game in which the object is to leave only one peg. The board is mahogany; the pieces, birch. Approximately 10'' in diameter. Instructions and 34 pegs included. $15 postpaid.

Tic-Tac-Toe—Made of hard maple with walnut cover over hidden storage compartment for marbles. Approximately 4½'' square with oil finish. Extra marble included. $10 postpaid.

Hand-turned Drop Spindle Top— Made of black cherry with a maple handle, approximately 7½'' long. All edges and corners rounded for safety. Nontoxic, mineral oil finish. Suitable for children three years and up; adults too. Spins for a good long time. $12.50 postpaid.

Knock on Wood—I have been doing woodworking full-time for three years now, making my entire living (such as it is) by it. I was originally destined to be an English teacher, but when the money ran out on my graduate school fellowship, I looked around for what I could do and discovered woodworking. I am far happier now, spending my days amidst the lovely clutter of wood shavings and works-in-progress.
David Hoffman, c/o Knock on Wood, 1601 Trumansburg Road, Ithaca, New York 14850.

Handmade Paper—Paper is available in laid, antique laid and woven screens in a variety of sizes: 8½'' by 11'', 17'' by 27'', 18'' by 24'', 32'' by 42''. Special sizes, many colors and personalized watermark services are available. The paper is fabricated using 100% pure cotton rag and linter fibers with buffering and sizing agents included to insure their permanence. We also provide Hollander services for pulp to be used by the individual in his own studio. We will quote prices for this service over the telephone. Price list for papers available on request. Our basis for pricing is $.005 per square inch (18'' by 24'' sheet, $2.00).

The Farnsworth & Serpa Handmade Paper Mill—This firm was born out of the desire to work with fine, high-quality paper that would stand the tests of time.

Don Farnsworth was educated in the art school manner and worked professionally as a lithographer and an art conservator until taking up paper making. Bob Serpa was a literature student, teacher, printer, idealist and property manager until joining forces with Don to establish the Mill.

The Farnsworth & Serpa Handmade Paper Mill houses two Hollander beaters, hydraulic presses, vats and a variety of European paper molds, and it is located in a 4500-square-foot building.

Farnsworth & Serpa Handmade Paper Mill, 1333 Wood Street, Oakland, California 94607.

Stained-glass Windows—Custom-designed stained-glass windows may be enjoyed in front of existing windows or fully installed. We make panels ranging from 12'' by 24'' to 24'' by 60''. These panels cost between $200 and $500, including handmade hardwood frames, usually of oak or mahogany. We use German hand-blown glass, which comes in hundreds of transparent, milky translucent and traditional opalescent colors. Most of our time is spent working with architects, designers and individuals. Prices on custom work run $40 to $90 per square foot (firm quotes made). Estimated shipping weight of a flat leaded panel is 5 lbs. per square foot. Crating costs run about $15. Shown here, Heron on Rocks. Framed dimensions: 28'' wide by 52'' high, hardwood-framed. $395, shipping not included.

Lien Studio—We take great pride in the simplicity of our designs and the fine craftsmanship of our work. Our products represent our attempt to satisfy what we feel is necessary in stained glass—windows that complement, rather than overpower, architecture and decor; windows that let light into your room and are also beautiful to look at.

Michael Lien and Joan Machiz, c/o Lien Studio, 3212 Palomares Avenue, Lafayette, California 94549.

Leathercraft—These leather items are made of garment-weight top-grain cowhide, soft and lightweight. All pieces are hand-cut and machine-sewn. Leather baseball caps have an adjustable strap in the back—one size fits all. "Bicyclist's Cap," pale yellow crown, gold deerskin wings, $24. "Zap Cap," rust red cowhide, gold deerskin lightning, $20. "D-Duck Cap," cream goatskin crown, rust bill with detail stitching, big brown eyes, $20. Backgammon board, two tones, with or without snakeskin. Felt-backed, comes with pouch for pieces (pieces not supplied). Roll to store. Measures 20" by 24", $60. Tennis racket covers all have zipper closure and are plastic-lined against moisture. Styles available: Monogrammed, Stars and Stripes, Lotus Blossom, Diagonal Stripes, $18. Pun'kin bag has pleats that expand to a soft pumpkin shape. Zipper close with adjustable strap for shoulder or hand carrying. Choice of golden tan, dark brown or strawberry rust, 9" by 9", $20. All prices plus shipping charge.

Designs by D—Coming from a family of designers—grandfather an architect, mother an artist, father a furniture designer—my fascination with working with my hands was bound to lead to leathercraft. Having acquired the skill of sewing leather, I've been working at it ever since. Designing soft leather bags and accessories has brightened my craft world with beautiful things.

Diane May, c/o Designs by D, 350 Francisco #1, San Francisco, California 94133.

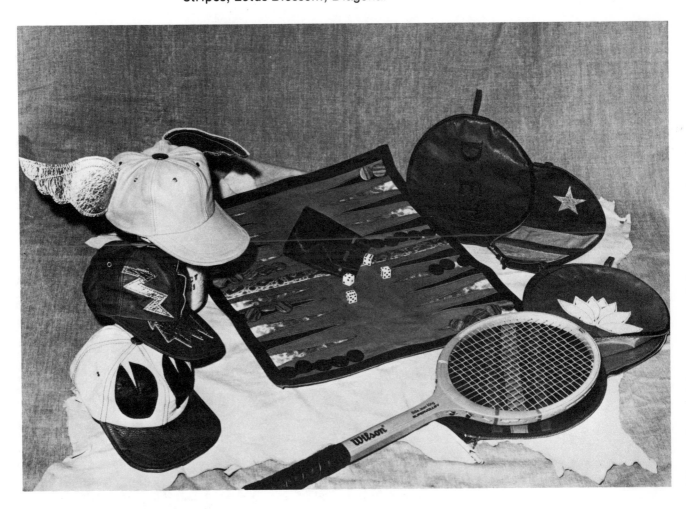

Soft Sculpture Doll House—The house is made of pinwale corduroy with roof and door of wide-wale corduroy, with quilted fabric lining. The roof unsnaps from the front to provide access to the inside. The stuffed handle has a machine-appliqued sky scene. The door has a brass button knob and loop closure; the window, a hand-painted flower-box trim or eyelet lace curtains. The doll house is carried by its handle like a purse. It's stuffed with a tree, green fuzzy grass, doll, bed, quilt and horse. Please give first, second and third color choice for house, and specify preference for appliqued sun, moon, cloud, stars or rainbow. Choose hair, eye and skin color for doll. A red corduroy barn is also available. Its contents include tree, grass, cow, pig, two sheep and four horses. Shipping weight 1 lb. All machine washable. $30, shipping not included.

Suzanne Sullivan—The idea for my doll house came to me drifting off to sleep one day after doing a lot of sewing and working out designs for a wooden dollhouse. My grandmother taught me to sew when I was five and my grandfather, who was a carpenter, used to make wooden doll houses for me. I like to think they inspired me.

Suzanne Sullivan, Box 307, Cotati, California 94928.

Circadian Woodworks—We grew out of a need to provide a textile arts school with a loom capable of reliable performance in traditional and experimental weaving situations. These looms are a hand-crafted expression of function, durability and aesthetics. Mechanical reliability and structural integrity are balanced with a respect for wood and attention to detail on the part of the woodworker.

Circadian Woodworks, 120 Main Street, Colusa, California 95932.

Maple Looms—We make finely crafted floor looms and matching benches. Both looms and benches are made of Eastern (rock) maple treated to a hand-rubbed Danish oil and wax finish. The loom has a 47'' weaving width and comes in four- and eight-harness models. It utilizes a heavy-duty rachet and pawl system combined with a cable friction brake for precise warp adjustment. It also features easy beam and beater lift-off and a 90° beater lock for sleying ease. Four-harness loom $610. Eight-harness loom $795; shipping weight about 200 lbs. Crating fee $40. Bench $99. The loom price includes a reed, 600 steel heddles and tie-up cord. A deposit of ⅓ purchase price secures an order with the balance due upon notice of completion. Catalog available. Custom orders invited.

Leather Bags—Our bags are designed to be functional as well as beautiful. The combination of hard and soft leather makes them light, comfortable and durable. The soft leather is a heavyweight garment leather, both strong and washable. The hard leather is oak-tanned, which is used in American saddlery, and will not lose its body. The shoulder strap is made of braided saddle leather and plaited garment leather, and is made so that it acts as a drawstring, allowing the bag to open wide and shut flat with a harness button closure. Tassles on the strap are optional. Every bag has an inside pocket. Our belt pouches are hard leather stitched to soft, and are great for hiking or bicycling, carrying checkbooks, passports, glasses, film or small cameras. The soft leather is available in yellow, light or dark brown, navy blue, orange or rust. Flap designs available are oak tree, sea or mountain scene, linear abstract, Spanish tooling, and red, yellow, tan or blue rose. Inlaid tapestry designs are $2 extra. Please indicate your choice of size, shape, soft leather color and design. The large size comes in a round or square shape, 8'' wide by 10'' deep, $35. The medium size comes with round or pointed shape, 7'' wide by 9'' deep, $33. Belt pouch, 5'' by 8'', $12.50. Shipping not included. Catalog 25 cents.

Mystic Rose—Linda and I met in 1971 in Barcelona, Spain, while I was making and selling leather goods. I learned my craft there and brought my skills back to California. When we began working together here, our combined energies and talents provided all the elements we needed for a creative and enjoyable business. It provides us with a creative outlet and allows us ample time to play in the world and discover who we are.

John Jorza and Linda Mals, c/o Mystic Rose, 326 O'Connor Street, Menlo Park, California 94025.

Man's Vest—A loosely fitting, loom-shaped vest hand-woven with the finest wool and mohair yarns. Fastenings of wood, ceramic or shell are chosen to enhance each individual garment. The vest is available in tweeds of browns, reds, greens, golds or blues. All sizes; give suit size or chest measurement when ordering. $55.

Woman's Vest—A loosely fitting, loom-shaped vest hand-woven in combinations of wool, mohair and alpaca. Each garment is slightly different, an individual and unique work of art. Available in naturals or black and white. All sizes; give chest measurement when ordering. $50.

Joyce Teis—I learned to weave in the mountains of Tennessee and have great respect for the traditional heritage of my craft.

I share my life with my husband Dan, a painter, and our six children. I share my studio with Patches, our calico cat, who chases my shuttle, tumbles on the treadles and inspects every thread between lap naps.

For ten years I designed theater, opera and ballet costumes. Now I prefer the more subtle excitement of creating my own textures for the traditional, simple garments I weave—tunics, tabards and vests.

Joyce Teis, 729 Bent Lane, Newark, Delaware 19711.

Eagle Skull Oil Lamp—This lamp is solid sterling silver and weighs 13½ troy ounces. It is 5'' wide by 1½'' high, and will burn vegetable oil or kerosene 2 to 3 hours before it must be refilled. Wire wicks will be included. The lamp is a sculpted reproduction of the golden eagle, that creature which flies highest and closest to the sun; the Principle of Wisdom; the most exalted state of Scorpio. The skull represents the ''ultimate vessel''—holding the fuel and source of light. $500 postpaid.

Unicorn—This sculpture is sterling silver with opal eyes. It stands about 2'' high. The Unicorn represents purity of purpose—that part of one's being that, in the face of all deviations and distractions, holds true to its own course in life by following the spiral path of the ephemeral horn. $125 postpaid.

Christalene—I am an artist using the lost-wax method of metal casting to give substance and tangible form to alchemical concepts and ideas. Each of my pieces represents alchemical images of psychic growth and the transformation of ''self'' into a more exalted being. All pieces are individually hand-crafted. In the lost-wax technique, a wax form is first carved and created. It is surrounded by earth, destroyed in fire, gestated in empty space and reborn in water so that the pattern in wax is transformed into a thing of durability and beauty.

I have been professionally involved in lost-wax casting of precious metals here in Topanga Canyon for the past six years. Many of my jewelry pieces are of limited editions or are one of a kind. I work in both 14k gold and sterling silver. Wherever possible my pieces are carved completely in the round—no backs or incomplete sides.

Christalene, P.O. Box 282, Topanga, California 90290.

Planters—These unique planters are made in two pieces, the bottom piece, or pedestal, being a water receptacle. The inside bottom of each pedestal is glazed so that the planters will not leave a ring when set on wood. We suggest that you use a wick to draw any excess water from the pedestal to the soil. This will help to safeguard against overwatering. Wicks for this purpose can be found in almost all plant stores. Planters come in the following sizes: small, 6'' to 7'' in diameter, 6'' to 7½'' high, $10; medium, 8'' to 9'' in diameter, 7½'' to 9'' high, $13; large, 9½'' to 11'' in diameter, 9½'' to 11'' high, $15. All postpaid.

The planters are available in the following colors: opaque white with either green or blue banding; Heidi pumpkin, a natural orange-brown with yellow highlights; and Mangrove gold, a rich yellow-gold with gray-green highlights. The pots themselves are a natural red clay body fired to stoneware temperatures.

Flying Elbows Pottery—Flying Elbows Pottery has been in existence for two years. The business is owned and operated by myself and is located in a garage compound behind my house where the studio and gas kiln are situated.

I have been involved with production pottery for several years and enjoy the company of other production potters, especially here in Northern California. I am constantly delighted with the high amounts of energy coming from craftsmen in this area. There is a great exchange of information. Building a kiln always results in a party.

There is a special joy in being able to create your own business and watch it grow. Every day I wake is another day I do not have to punch a clock, fight traffic or sell myself out in any way. It is only now that I can truly understand what freedom is really all about. I am a free man. My life belongs to me.

With luck I will be able to move further into the country in a couple of years. Working for yourself is a rotten way to make a living, but it beats working for someone else.

Robert Edwin Atkinson, c/o Flying Elbows Pottery, P.O. Box 3004, Chico, California 95926.

Drums—Like traditional craftspeople, most of the wood I use in my drums is local, growing here in rural Northern California. I choose the wood while the tree is standing; the bark of the tree reveals its grain patterns. The tree is felled and cut into slabs, which dry for a year or more and then are cut into staves. The staves are assembled and bent over a wood fire, and the final shape is achieved with a spokeshave and scraper, as coopers have been doing for centuries. Left to right, small oak log drum, $100; ceramic belly dance drum, $46.25; a two-headed log drum, $100 (unfinished); back row, left to right, tuneable oak conga drum, $250; small oak log drum, $100; and a walnut stave drum, $60 (unfinished). All prices postpaid.

Ralph Pisciotta—Ten years ago I started playing and making drums. I researched the traditional techniques of coopering, woodcarving and hide curing. After five years of study, drum making became my principal source of income. A local taxidermist, with thirty years of experience, cures the hides I use for my drums, and I make my ceramic drums with the help of a local potter.

I think hand-crafted things will help revive an aesthetic lacking in our culture. The craftsperson, once an inherent part of each community, has been replaced by machines. But machined products lack a certain inspirational quality. Wouldn't we savor our soup more if we ate it from a hand-carved bowl? Would we still be rushing through our lives if every door we passed through was made of solid wood? The things we touch in our daily lives should remind us to maintain beauty in what we are and what we do.

Ralph Pisciotta, Box 1060, Willits, California 95490.

Batik Dolls—All my dolls are made from batik dyes on unbleached muslin and are fiber-filled. Russian and Samurai dolls are backed with cord-less corduroy in a complementary solid color. Russian and Samurai dolls come in four sizes: 6½'', $8; 8½'', $10; 10½'', $12; and 12½'', $15. The Top Hat men are backed with suede (small) or upholstery material (large). The Top Hat man stands either 15'' tall, $25; or 24'' tall, $50.

Maureen Rosenblum—From the time that I was three or four years old, my days were spent playing with my dolls, cutouts and coloring books. When the time came to earn a living, I decided to become a: kindergarten teacher; caseworker in an elementary school; teaching assistant in a college speech course; creative dramatics teacher; antique store manager; salesperson in a coffee, tea and spice store; switchboard operator; assistant director of a neighborhood center; salesperson in a Christmas trim-the-tree shop; and children's zoo attendant.

What I found was that there was much less reality in the real world than in my own world of dolls and cutouts. After twenty-five years, I've come back to myself and, once again, spend my days playing with dolls.

I work in my basement studio with my radio tuned to a classical station. I wax and dye while my dog tries to get me to chase her, finally gives up and lies down to sleep at my feet with a sigh.

Maureen Rosenblum, 3016 West Michigan, Milwaukee, Wisconsin 53208.

Stationery—Assorted patterns and colors are included in each set. Made of rice paper on card stock. Cards and envelopes measure 6¼'' by 4½''. Set of 10, $6.

Clay Hang-ups—Baker's clay ornaments made from flour, salt, water and color, and coated with lacquer to insure durability. Each ornament is hand-formed, which gives it an individual personality and yet preserves the high quality and design of the basic master. The colors are varied and are all bright, shiny and lasting. The ornaments are 3'' to 4'' high and about 2 oz. They make wonderful Christmas ornaments and are also fun in children's rooms or in little nooks anywhere.

From left top: giraffe $4, mouse $4, rocking horse $4, soldier $5, clown $5, Big Bird $4, camel $5, Santa $5, teddy bear $4, goose $4, Raggedy Andy $5, Raggedy Ann $5. Add 15 cents per ornament for shipping. Minimum order $20.

Dough Delights—John and Julee Ash have been making Dough Delights for five years. Julee is also a designer of interiors and fabric things, and John is a medical illustrator.

John and Julee Ash, c/o Dough Delights, 1705 Bryden Lane, Santa Rosa, California 95404.

Weed Shirts—Long-sleeved, loose-fitting shirts of all-cotton unbleached muslin, embroidered in color or white-on-white with weeds—Queen Anne's lace, clover, daisy, plantain, dandelion or stylized vines. Women's and men's sizes small, medium and large, $20 each.

Noisy Crow Quilts—A descendant of British cabinetmakers, I have been involved in fine arts since infancy. About five years ago I switched from watercolor and pastels to needlework as a personal protest against the engulfing tide of cheap packaged crafts. The increasing interest in arts and crafts, together with increasing leisure time (voluntary or involuntary), seems to point to a need for dedicated craftspeople to encourage others in the soul-satisfying work of adding beauty to utility.

Margaret P. Spoor, c/o Noisy Crow Quilts, 99 Beechwood Hills, Newport News, Virginia 23602.

Wooden Boxes—A highly polished, beautiful block of black walnut. Only close inspection reveals that is is not simply a block, but a box. The inside is hollowed out, and the lid insert shaped correspondingly, so that the lid cannot be reversed and the grain always matches up. Size: 2½'' wide by 3¾'' long by 2'' deep. Minimum order: two boxes. $5.50 each, shipping not included.

Steven Foley—Woodworking is my profession and has been the sole source of my income for the last six years. The production of individually commissioned and designed furniture pieces is my specialty.

My work has been exhibited in the Craft Multiples show at the Renwick Gallery of the Smithsonian Institution, Washington, D.C., in the Portland Art Gallery, and in Portland's Contemporary Crafts Gallery, where I won first place among twenty Northwest entrants in furniture design.

Steven Foley, 908 Bickner Street, South West, Lake Oswego, Oregon 97034.

Ken Butterfield—I have been making my living as a professional glass artisan for five years. In that time I have never owned or operated a store-type business, preferring instead to seek a clientele through referrals and gallery exposure.

My wife and I have worked together from the beginning, each performing separate, specialized tasks to produce a finely crafted piece that will reflect our patience, pride and knowledge of materials and craft. Native and endangered wildlife have been our most enduring subjects.

We live in a dreary little coastal town which allows us to work with few distractions, free from the pressure to produce too much too fast. In this relaxed atmosphere we are free to reflect and create comfortable, usable and livable art glass.

Ken Butterfield, P.O. Box 1735, Cambria, California 93428.

Stained Glass Lamps—The cone-shaped lamp features calliope hummingbirds circling nasturtium blossoms. The delicate "fringe" along the bottom edge of this shade casts pleasant shadows in a dimly lit room. The background colors are green and brown. Orange is the dominant color of the flowers, while the birds are gaily-colored iridized glass. Lamp bases are made of the Brazilian hardwood imbuya. Each one is a little different. Lamps are fitted with two adjustable light-bulb sockets. All brass lamp parts are antique plated. Shade and base: 12" in diameter by 21" high. $1,095, shipping not included. The graceful bell shape of the Allen's hummingbird lampshade clearly shows the art of kiln-slumped glass. Nearly all the glass in this shade is bent in the kiln before assembly. The background color of this lamp is a warm caramel with green leaves, orange California poppies and multicolored birds. Shade and base: 12" in diameter by 23" high. $1,095 shipping not included.

Pewter—Pewter has long been renowned for its beauty, durability and usefulness. All of the items here are individually handmade of quality modern pewter, which contains no lead, and finished to a high polish. Dinner plate, 11'' in diameter, shipping weight 1¾ lbs., $24. Side plate, 6'' in diameter, shipping weight ¾ lb., $14. Soup/salad bowl, 6'' in diameter, shipping weight ¾ lb., $15. Serving/candy bowl, 8'' in diameter, shipping weight 1¼ lbs., $22. Mug holds 20 oz., shipping weight 1¼ lbs., $24. Bracelets are ½'' or 1'' wide in small, medium or large wrist size, shipping weight ⅓ lb., $13 each. All above items can be marked "Handmade for (your name)" or with special message. The pewter pipes are great for those "special mixtures." Shipping weight 1 lb each, $20. Specify lefthand, middle or righthand pipe. Prices do not include shipping.

Ken Roush—Ken has a background in mechanical engineering, but after several years of design work at the corporate level he felt a need to put his creativity into a more personal endeavor.

Pewter is a soft, warm, durable material which, over the years, attains a character and significance of its own. Ken feels that pewter items need to be presented in a modern style—one that incorporates a high-polish finish and smooth, uncluttered lines—however, retaining a hint of the classical shapes.

Ken works each piece individually and hopes that the personal attachment he develops for each piece will be shared by the person receiving it for years to come.

Ken Roush, 669 Twenty-fifth Street, Manhattan Beach, California 90266.

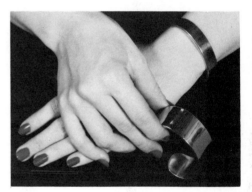

Colonial Nutcrackers—Each nutcracker is carefully and lovingly handmade of solid maple. The authentic costumes are painted in bright enamel colors; some natural wood is left showing to emphasize its luster and grain. To use as a nutcracker, lift the handle in the back and place the nut in the mouth. When the handle is pressed down, the nut cracks. The nutcracker may also be used as a bank. They are 15'' high and come as Ben Franklin, George Washington, Minute Man or Colonial Lady. Not shown are Captain Ahab, Union and Confederate Soldiers and many others. $25 postpaid.

Aspetuck Handcrafters—After graduating from the Philadelphia College of Art as a textile designer, I worked in New York for several years as a designer and colorist for several textile firms. Upon moving to Fairfield County, I free-lanced as a textile designer, until I became interested in crafts.

My family includes three teenage children and my husband Robert, an engineer, who collaborated with me on the design of our unusual nutcrackers, which I have been making for three years.

Dorothy Bernstein, c/o Aspetuck Handcrafters, 14 Eastwood Lane, Easton, Connecticut 06612.

Crocheted Neckpurse—The purse is made of cotton thread and should be worn as a necklace. It measures approximately 4½'' by 3¼'', and is available in green, blue, purple, yellow or red. $22, shipping not included.

Louise Weinberg—I have been making jewelry for six years and started crocheting jewelry last year. I am very involved with my crocheting right now. Since I have found a market for it and it is being accepted, I am very happy and busy. Ideally, I would like to continue as I am, living in the country and exploring my craft. I would like to be totally self-sufficient and this is a step on the way.

Louise Weinberg, Route 1, Box 87A, Blue Mounds, Wisconsin 53517.

Goblets—Individually hand-thrown goblets accented with four unique designs in soft blue and white. The stem is natural stoneware clay. These sturdy goblets are lead-free, dishwasher-proof and chip-resistant. Each goblet is 6'' high. A set of four weighs 5 lbs. packed. Set, $35.

Carolina Clay Pottery—I live in Raleigh, North Carolina, where I have worked as a potter since 1969. I graduated from the University of North Carolina in fine arts and then worked in a production folk pottery. I later established Carolina Clay Pottery, which makes a line of contemporary stoneware pottery and traditional children's clay toys.

My work ranges from functional ware to large lamps and hanging lights, garden lighting, decorative wall mirrors, contemporary hardwood furniture with ceramic insets, architectural planters, clay wall murals and fountains. I am also interested in liturgical murals.

Alice Proctor, c/o Carolina Clay Pottery, Route 1, Box 382A, Raleigh, North Carolina 27614.

Puppets—Mouth-action hand puppets delight young and old. Highest quality fake fur, sewn felt eyes, 9'' to 10'' high. Pictured here are Rooster (in blue, green, bright yellow, orange, black, white or olive); Hound Dog (in yellow, brown, rust, gray, white, beige or gold); Bird (in black crow, red, pink, canary yellow or blue). $5 postpaid.

The Mother Goose lap puppet is a life-size 27'' tall. It has yellow felt legs, yellow fur bill, white plush body and a print apron and hat. Gray and black bodies are also available. Color preference for hat and apron honored if possible (indicate first and second choice). $26.50 postpaid. Also available as a stuffed toy, $32 postpaid. List of other puppets $1 (refundable with order).

Merry Lyn Toys—Sewing hand puppets began as a hobby and an enjoyable pastime. However, it is now our only means of survival. For the past two years, my husband and I have lived completely from our craft. I sew and design; my husband sells. One room of our house is devoted only to sewing, but at times the stock overflows into other areas. So does the joy!

My approach to life is that of a humanist. What happens inside a child while he is doing something is what I care most about. I know feelings are the most important thing under the sun.

Puppets are a perfect medium for a child to use to express feelings. They have great do-it-yourself therapeutic value, as well as being a natural, participatory way to explore drama, creativity and spontaneity. In the experienced hand they are an unsurpassed teaching tool.

Marilyn McCurry, c/o Merry Lyn Toys, P.O. Box 191, Capitola, California 95010.

Leather Duffle Bag—The bag is made of prime, top-grain garment cowhide, double-stitched with durable nylon thread and reinforced at all seam ends with small brass rivets. The straps are made of vegetable-tanned harness leather; the button on the hand-stitched pocket is deer antler and all fittings are solid brass. Usually available in dark brown, light brown, rust or gold. Large: 18'' high by 13½'' wide, $42.40 postpaid. Small: 15½'' high by 11½'' wide, $31.80 postpaid.

Swadeshi Leather Shop— ''Swadeshi'' was the name of Ghandi's program to encourage cottage industries during the Free India Movement of the thirties and forties. Better known as the Spinning Wheel Program, Swadeshi came to symbolize self-reliance and integrity.

''Swadeshi'' is also the name of our leather shop. Here for almost ten years, Wes Stoft, designer and master craftsman, has guided numerous young apprentices and craftsmen in the creation of fine leather goods.

Apprentices learn self-reliance by completing each piece of work on their own. There is no sharing of work on any piece. That way each apprentice is completely responsible for the finished work. Integrity becomes an integral part of all work—both the process and the piece. Integrity is making each creation as durable as possible. There is an old English adage: ''The best is the cheapest in the end.'' We believe this is true.

Wes Stoft, c/o Swadeshi Leather Shop, 937A Sir Francis Drake Boulevard, Kentfield, California 94904.

123

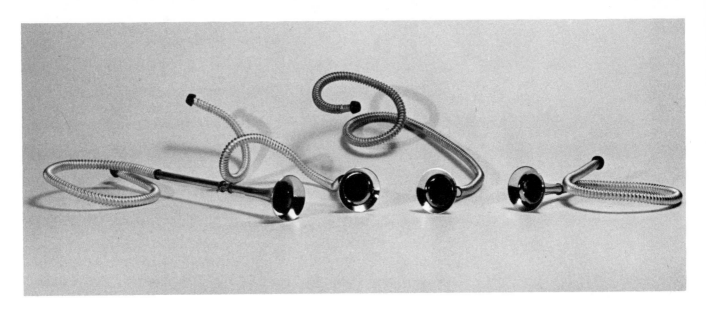

Corrugahorns—A whole new family of wind instruments was invented in 1973 by Frank Crawford. The Natural Corrugahorn consists of a corrugated brass tube with a flared bell at one end and a mouthpiece at the other. The Slide Corrugahorn has, in addition, a slide like a trombone. You play a Corrugahorn by simply breathing in or out through it. Greater air flow gives higher pitch. No lip control is needed; the sound is generated by the air bumping against the corrugations throughout the entire tube. The notes of the Natural Corrugahorn are in the same pattern as those of a bugle. The Slide Corrugahorn gets additional notes and can play a complete chromatic scale. The Corrugahorn tone quality is of great harmonic purity, somewhat like the upper register of a flute or like human whistling. Three models are available. A 14-page lesson book accompanies all models.

The 29'' Slide Corrugahorn in A: perfect for musicians and other perfectionists. Range without moving the slide is 3 through 12. Great for jazz or folk songs, since it gets a complete chromatic scale and has the range of an average human voice. $14.

The 24'' Bugle in C: a natural corrugahorn, its ''fundamental note'' is C, and its range is harmonics 3 through 10. Kids and beginners start out with easy bugle calls using harmonics 3, 4, 5 and 6. The lesson book then teaches how to ''finger flat'' each regular note, thus doubling the number of notes and allowing you to play in the lovely ''Balkan Minor'' scale. $6.

The 36'' Neckhorn in F: a natural corrugahorn, with range of harmonics 3 through 16. Worn around the neck with no hands needed. Many folk songs and jigs can be easily played. Perfect for playing blues in F while walking, bike riding, driving or accompanying yourself on guitar or drums. $8.

Add $1.50 per order for shipping.

Corrugahorn Manufacturers—Frank Crawford is a Berkeley astrophysicist who loves to play with sounds, to make music and to try and understand how it all works. These three elements, and happy accident, led him to stumble onto the Corrugahorn.

Frank Crawford, c/o Corrugahorn Manufacturers, 2826 Garber, Berkeley, California 94705.

Charms—Handmade original charms contain herbs to ward off evil and bad luck. They are designed for people with a rich fantasy life, who appreciate a special expression of spiritual needs, humor and day-to-day emotional survival. Wear on your person or hang on your wall to protect your home and those who enter it. Shaman (left), 6'' tall, $10. Lady's Home Companion (middle), 5½'' tall, $20. Shaman (right), 4'' tall, $10. Add $1 shipping charge per order.

Jean Ferris and Sheila Swiadon—Jean: I am an art instructor, designer and daydreamer. I feel a special affinity with children and design for the youthful curiosity, joy and pride in all of us. We have found working with spiritual charms and amulets offers great satisfaction in an area that transcends time, culture and geography. Sheila: Joining forces has been great fun. We have found a unique way to combine elements of jewelry, design and decoration in these charms. These are ornaments with a difference—they offer comfort and protection to people who need a personal power source in a hectic world. My studio is both a workplace and a retreat into an environment made for me by me. I love it.

Jean Ferris and Sheila Swiadon, 6533 Debs, Canoga Park, California 91307.

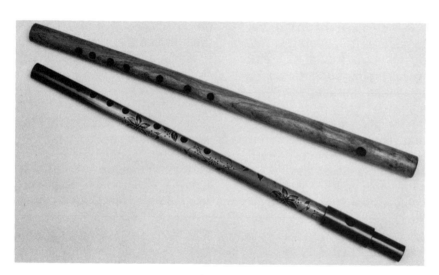

Copper and Wood Flutes—The copper flute has an elegant design etched into the metal, and is darkened and lacquered with a mouthpiece of contrasting color. The wood flute is made from the heartwood of the mesquite tree. Mesquite is hard and very stable; it will not warp, shrink or lose its tone. With time, the reddish-brown wood becomes burnished and the rich sound of the flute matures. Both are traditional transverse flutes, 18'' long, tuned in the key of G. They have a two-octave range. Corduroy case, instruction sheet and fingering chart included. $20 each.

Divine Flutes—When I play the flute, I am reminded by its few notes that there is a higher, more complete melody which is played within my being. The flute is a means by which I can relate my love for this complete melody, this divine harmony, to the world of men. I hope that by playing these flutes more, we can inspire each other to go deeper within until we touch that Divine Harmony which is our real home.

David Blackburn and Patrick Murphy, c/o Divine Flutes, P.O. Box 734, San Antonio, Texas 78293.

Pipes—All the pipes are hand-cut from 150-year-old Corsican Briar. They are individually carved and polished with an antique patina. Each has English rubber bits. I make seven basic shapes; each is original, unique and exclusive. $11 postpaid.

Wilson Bergerud—I studied for a year with Sven Jennsen, the master pipe maker of Denmark. Then, in Calabria, I learned the art of selecting briar. In Corsica I found the finest, lightest antique briar.

An erstwhile furniture designer, I express my creativity fluently in these burls of briar. I have been a professional pipe maker for twelve years. From time to time I have had an apprentice—an experience that has been mutually rewarding.

Wilson Bergerud, Box V, Norwood, New Jersey 07648.

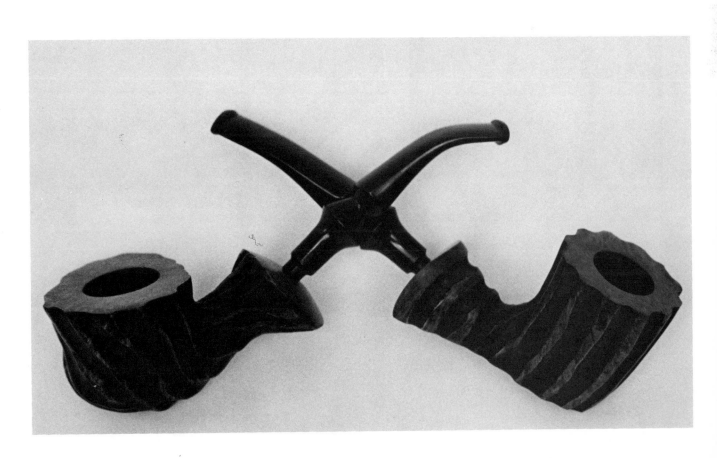

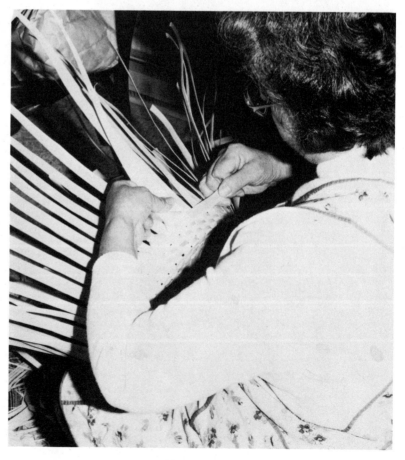

Mohawk Nation Sweetgrass Sewing Baskets—A hand-crafted basket is as unique as the person who makes it. Each basket is split, shaved, dyed and woven by one individual. The patterns are their own or are representative of their Nation's particular style. Mohawk baskets are made of black ash splints and are often decorated with fragrant sweetgrass. All the materials are gathered and prepared by hand. The black ash logs are hauled from the swamps and pounded with sledge-hammers to loosen the layers of wood. These layers are peeled off and further split and cut to the desired width and thickness. Some of these splints are dyed but most of them are left in their natural white to buff color. Sweetgrass is picked in the late summer and braiding the long strands continues into the winter. Only then can work on the baskets begin. Covered baskets, left to right: 8'' across, $10; 3'' across, $3; 6'' across, $6.50; 7'' across, $8; 10'' across, $15. Also available: extra-large or fancy, $17.50. Add 10% for packing and shipping.

Adirondack Pack Baskets—These ancestors of modern backpacks stand 6'' to 20'' high. They are made in the old style, without benefit of nails or modern tools. Left to right: 12'' high, $9; 6'' high, $3.50; 10'' high, $6. Add 10% for packing and shipping. Catalog 25 cents.

Mohawk Crafts Fund—Crafts are an important part of the life of the Mohawk Nation, many of whose people now reside on the St. Regis Reservation, which straddles the New York-Canadian border. The basket weavers on this reservation have established a special tradition of fine quality work, but a few years ago it seemed that the tradition was dying. Young people were not taking up the craft. The Mohawk Crafts Fund was organized to try to reawaken interest in traditional crafts by making their production economically rewarding. The idea was originally conceived in a business management class conducted on the Reservation by the Malone Extension of North Country Community College.

Mohawk Crafts Fund, 101 East Main, Malone, New York 12953.

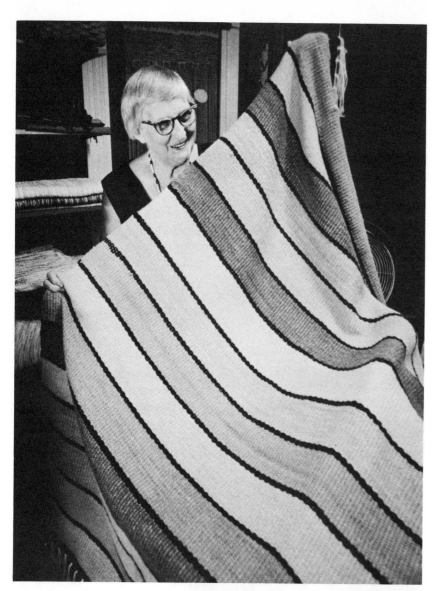

Weaving—The work shown, "Joseph's Coat," is a hand-dyed and hand-woven throw or wall hanging measuring 48" by 72". It is one of many designs. All wool. $62.50.

Wool-Art—I started weaving in 1957. I went to many fairs until 1964, when I opened my shop, Wool-Art. I buy hand-crafted items from other craftsmen who make good pioneer-style work and also sell my own weaving. My shop carries Indian baskets I buy from eighteen tribes.

Other than a small Social Security check, my shop is my living. It is in the front of my home, which is in a nice neighborhood near our beautiful Beaver Lake.

Elpha Kindred, c/o Wool-Art, 422 East Locust, Rogers, Arkansas 72756.

Stuart Golder, Route 1, Box 54A, Stout, Ohio 45684.

Silver Pendants—Each signed hollow sterling silver pendant is a one-of-a-kind work of art. Made by carefully fitting together and soldering two individually formed shapes which are cut from sheets of silver, they measure about 1½" by 1½". Shown with yard-long rattail cords with hand-made sterling silver tips; cords come in silver-gray, beige and black. Pendant $37 postpaid. Cord $12 postpaid.

Stuart Golder—I am a self-taught metalsmith living in the country and enjoying peace and quiet. I earn my living with my craft and fortunately live inexpensively. My special joy is making small containers of gold, silver and/or copper, with or without stones. These may be worn, carried in a purse or pocket, set on a table or tucked in a drawer.

130

The Crooked Stitch Shirt—Made of 100% natural cotton, completely hand-stitched in a running backstitch. Neck and arm tassles beaded with old ethnic beads from around the world, shell, stone, silver, wood and bone. Body and sleeve panels can contrast (as shown here), be all one color or be batiked. Available in natural white or hand-dyed sky blue, denim blue, brown, gold, coral, rose, lavender, pale yellow and turquoise. Batiks in earth or sea tones. All sizes. Dyed with body and sleeve contrast, $45 postpaid; natural white $40 postpaid; batiked $55 postpaid. For rare, higher quality beads add $7.50

Christopher Crooked Stitch—Presently there are about ten crooked stitchers here in the Ukiah area. We are people who are learning to live self-sufficiently on our land, in harmony with ourselves and nature. Our craft allows us this freedom.

I feel my clothing says the most about me. It is a very personal expression of how I feel about this culture which I am a part of, and what vision I hope to share with the people I live with. I am into a natural, meditation-guided lifestyle.

This year I hope to begin building my own house. I belive this environment has a great effect on my work. My craft sustains my environment, and my environment inspires my craft. I am happy being who I am and doing what I do, and would like to share this awareness with other people.

Christopher Hale, c/o Christopher Crooked Stitch, P.O. Box 604, Ukiah, California 95482.

Hobby Horse—Truly an old-fashioned toy, our horse is made for heavy-duty use and hardworking imaginations. It is made of heavy corduroy fabric with a hardwood pole and ball, and has a lightly oiled natural finish. Brown or blue, 42'' by 12'', shipping weight 4 lbs. $13.50, shipping not included.

Teddy Bear—Our teddy bear is of a traditional design, made from polyester with nose and paws of corduroy. Faces are hand-embroidered, giving each teddy his own personality. Dark brown, 17'' tall, shipping weight 3 lbs. $13, shipping not included.

Lucky Star Handicrafts—We have been making toys for about six years now, the last two professionally. Lucky Star was begun in response to a need we felt existed for thoughtfully designed, well-made soft toys. We feel that a growing number of people want to give the children in their lives a few made-to-last toys, rather than a number of mass-produced ones, the demand for which has been created by heavy advertising.

We live in a small town in Mendocino County, where we raise a number of different animals, have a large vegetable garden and lots of room to roam for our two children. Our workshop is a small old house on our property. Our business is a partnership in every sense of the word.

Bob and Karen Altaras, c/o Lucky Star Handicrafts, Star Route, Yorkville, California 95494.

Cloud Bottle—Brass and sterling silver (top) with brass tubing, blue glass beads at ends of tubing and feathers inserted through beads and tubing. Measures 2½'' high, 7/8'' in diameter. Other ''special'' bottles available. Weighs 1 oz., shipping weight up to 5 oz., $35.

Buffalo Pendant—Sterling silver with a bezel-set Indianhead nickel, silver-capped white dentalium shells (''money tusk'') and black glass beads. Buffalo head measures 2¾'' by 1¾''. Length from tip of horns to ends of shells is 5''. Length of glass bead chain with sterling silver clasp is 16'' from horn to horn.
Weighs 1 oz., shipping weight up to 5 oz., $40.

Lois Bertolino Handworks—Some of the most important things I own are tools. My tools are extensions of myself and are, to me, the beginning of the creative process. I'm good, but my tools make me better.

The best-quality raw materials are next—real cotton, wool and leather; copper, brass, silver and gold; gems for color and spirit. Then there are those ''gifts'' like finding an Indianhead nickel worn smooth in someone's pocket or an eyeglass lens found in an antique store (who looked through it?).

I bring the intangible idea to the tools and materials and try to make something tangible which embodies the idea and stands on its own. So these three things—tools, materials and the artist—come together and precipitate something separate, something capable of being perceived. Other important considerations are good color, form and composition hand-in-hand with fine craftsmanship.

I have been professionally selling and exhibiting my work across the country since 1969. Right now I'm concentrating on jewelry work and textile design with plangi (tie, fold or stick-dyed fabric).

Lois Bertolino, c/o Lois Bertolino Handworks, 3466 Cornell Place, Cincinnati, Ohio 45220.

133

Stoneware Slant Pot—These versatile hand-thrown planters are made of sand-colored clay, and then fired to beautiful shades of reddish-brown. We use special sumi brushes to hand-paint four different decorations: leaf, rosette, dot and Aztec (shown). The pots are left unglazed and come with drainage holes and matching banded saucers. Each planter measures 4½'' in height and 6½'' across the top. $7.50 postpaid. Being lifted *alive* from the spinning hump is a round white Sill pot, designed to sit on your window sills at home or the office. Black, white or sand, 4'' tall. Comes with a saucer. $4.50 postpaid. The little wall planter, shown with pencils, can be hung from a nail to hold a plant, brushes, peanuts, etc. In natural colors, 4½'' by 4½''. $4 postpaid.

Axner Pottery—Our family business began in January 1975. My businessman husband died suddenly that spring and my son Howard and I were caught up in the energy of a business that seemed to have an intense life of its own. I had to forget about my personal wish to become a potter and learn about running a business instead.

We are now in the process of happily mapping out our own paths to follow. I am back at the wheel, well on my way to becoming self-supporting. Howard is looking to carry on his own pottery venture.

I have had to learn pottery backwards. I can market the product, do the books and taxes, run the kilns, design the literature and pots. Now I am finally able to get to the beginning and my first love—the clay!

Howard Axner and Sophie Axner, c/o Axner Pottery, 100 Mingo Trail, Longwood, Florida 32750.

Silver Necklace and Bracelet—Disk, bead and ring chain is assembled from hand-formed and finished elements strung on a sterling silver chain with a sturdy hook and eye catch. The result is a rhythmic but not totally predictable flow of polished sterling silver surfaces. A 7'' bracelet weighs a full ounce and costs $83.50; a 17'' necklace weighs 3 ounces and is $188.50. Other lengths can be ordered at $10.50/inch plus $10 for assembly. All prices postpaid.

Moonface Paperweight—The moonface paperweight provides the advantage of being both a cheerful face on your desk and a cool, soothing object to hold when you are tense. Each face is part of a limited edition and is lost-wax-cast from approximately 2.5 ounces of sterling silver. I personally hand-file, smooth and polish each sculpture to retain the personality of the original. The face is 12.5mm (½'') thick and 35mm (1-3/8'') in diameter. $200 postpaid.

Gold Snowflake Pendant—This snowflake design is a mental distillation of several thousand snowflakes. I use a fine blade in a jeweler's saw to hand-pierce each flake from a heavy sheet of 14k yellow or white gold. Although I start with the same design each time, like real snowflakes, no two gold snowflakes turn out exactly the same. They measure 19mm (¾'') from tip to tip and 1.5mm (1/16'') thick, and work equally well as a pendant or a charm. Yellow gold, $60 postpaid. White gold, $65 postpaid. A 15''-long 14k yellow gold chain (as shown) is available with snowflake orders for $70.

Robert N. Hallett—Most of my designs are simple, strong expressions of a simple idea. I spend almost no time designing with pencil and paper because more and more my craft is my life and the design develops as part of the process.

Although it takes practiced eyes and hands along with a lot of technical knowledge to begin to do fine work with metal, it's the right tool that often does the magic. My favorites are some that were in use, helping to do fine work, long before I was born. Sometimes I learn as much from a tool as I would by talking with the man who used it. If nothing more, most old tools are beautifully handmade and are constant reminders of good craftsmanship and the reality of craft as much more than just a good design.

Robert N. Hallett, 428 Clifton Avenue, Glenshaw, Pennsylvania 15116.

137

Wall Hangings—Natural Swedish linen in plain weave with copper wires, 18'' by 40'', $75. Natural Swedish linen with iris pods, 6'' by 30'', $40. Natural Swedish linen with teasels, 9'' by 26'', $35.

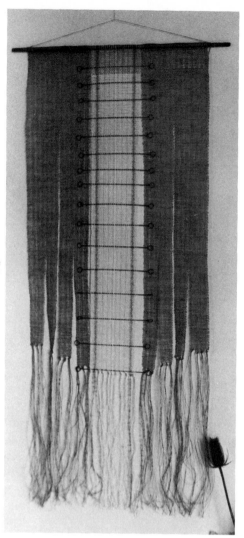

Margery Cosgrove—Crafts have been my hobby for thirty years. I've worked with fabric since I started making doll clothes at age ten. I was a painter for several years, but weaving and stitchery came very naturally and I enjoy them more all the time.

I love working with fabrics. Each fabric has its own personality, its own desire. Discovering them is an exciting adventure; you discipline them and they discipline you. When I dress my loom, usually in Swedish linen, I let the warp tell me what it wants to do, for each warp has its own message too.

Margery Cosgrove, 3218 Anniston Drive, Cincinnati, Ohio 45211.

Stoneware Sinks—These sinks are hand-thrown from a strong stoneware clay which is fired to about 2400°F. A totally functional overflow is hand-built to the bottom side of each sink, which fits into a standard 1¼" sink drainpipe. The finished sink is 14" to 15" in diameter, 7" to 8" overall height, has a volume of 5 to 6 quarts and weighs approximately 12 lbs. unpackaged and 16 lbs. packaged. The glaze design on each sink is unique. Each one is glazed with a combination of two colors: blue with brown accents, celadon green with black accents and earthy yellow with rust accents. $120 plus $10 packaging fee.

Susan Adame—I enjoy creating a ceramic design for an item and improving on it until it is aesthetically pleasing and completely functional. I believe that it is essential for a work to have both these qualities.

I have been throwing ceramics for five years. I work alone, out of my studio, and sell my hand-thrown sinks at the Tile Shop in Berkeley. I also make a variety of stoneware and porcelain functional ceramics which I sell at fairs.

Susan Adamé, c/o The Tile Shop, 1577 Solano Avenue, Berkeley, California 94707.

Stained Glass Panels—Our original designs are formed with antique and cathedral glass, copperfoil, solder and sunshine. Pictured here is one of Jay's windmill scenes. Each is different. Available in ambers and blues with coppery patina. Approximately 12'' by 15''. Shipping weight 5 lbs. $125. Also available, Mary Ann's wildflower panels, 8'' by 11''. State color preferences. Shipping weight 4 lbs. $55.

The Stained Glass Store—We need such a specific name out here, since the stained-glass revival is still taking place somewhere else. We envision a slowly growing business, as our rural location uses only so much glass. But we would rather live here than in the big city.

As far as we know, we are the only South Dakota members of the Stained Glass Association of America. Currently all income from our craftwork goes into expanding our glass stock and other supplies. This obviates the necessity of traveling to the nearest supplier, which is many days away by horse and wagon.

Jay: "A displaced New Englander—from Worcester, Massachusetts—and a South Dakotan by way of Cleveland and Chicago, I've come to feel the beauty of the prairie, where my family can live and breathe. The land of infinite variety has become the primary influence on our original designs."

Mary Ann: "Mothering, gardening, sewing and organization work kept me busy enough, but I got interested in stained glass. So Jay taught me what had taken him five years to learn by himself. We constantly consult each other to temper or refine our efforts, but our styles are distinct, and each of us executes every step of our own projects."

Jay and Mary Ann Paulukonis, c/o The Stained Glass Store, 814 Northeast Fifth Street, Madison, South Dakota 57042.

Wedding Rings—All individually designed. Contact me with thoughts of what you want expressed and the styles you like, and I will respond with a possible design. Other jewelry, such as pendants, bracelets, earrings and hair ornaments, available on custom order. Prices depend on complexity of design, weight and price of the gold used. Wedding rings in white or yellow gold, from $240 to $275.

Joan Giehl—My high is the give-and-take between someone needing something precious that speaks for them and the flow of intuition through my spirit and hands to give it back to them in a tangible form. We are both richer! The works grow from both of us, and growing leads me to new ideas. I want my work to be lived with daily, not locked away in museums. I want things I live with to have authorship—they speak to me and give meaning to my life, in contrast to our anonymous mass-produced, junk-oriented society. Understanding and experiencing my relation with nature is vital to creation—the beauty of my work becomes a reflection of the beauty of nature.

I feel that my fascination with gold and silver links me with craftspeople through thousands of years of tradition. That's important to me—important enough to pass on to my children and through our family.

Joan Giehl, 1248 North Eighty-sixth Street, Milwaukee, Wisconsin 53226.

Clown—Mesha T. Clown is a happy, energetic, feminine clown, who feels it is important for us to experience female clowns. Mesha emphasizes her femininity by wearing tights and a skirted costume. She delights children with balloon animals and pratfalls, and entertains adults with ball and club juggling, pocket magic and improvisational mime. She is assisted by Circus, her canine partner. Mesha offers a complete comedy and magic stage show, short fill-ins and supervision of children's activities. She is available for national craft-show tours or small one-show stands throughout the West. She is also happy to appear at private parties, grand openings and stage-show revues in the San Francisco Bay Area. Her rates are determined by performance time, length of show, travel and accommodations.

Mesha T. Clown—Mesha graduated from the University of Michigan after studying film and theater. She trained and performed with Mimetroupe, a professional mime company that tours Europe under the direction of Michael Filisky. Her circus skills were developed under the big top of the Pickle Family Circus. She also trained with Panov Olage from the Moscow Circus School.

Mesha Walczak, c/o Mesha T. Clown, 818A York, San Francisco, California 94110.

Wooden Chest—Pictured here in knotty pine. Available stained or unstained. Finished with Watco oil and wax. The chest is 13¼'' wide, 20'' high and 9¼'' deep. The upper drawers are 5'' wide by 5'' high by 9'' deep. The lower drawer is 10½'' wide by 3'' high by 9'' deep. The chest was originally designed for sewing and can include built-in spool rack for $5 extra. Shipping weight 22 lbs. $55, shipping not included.

Redwood Plate—Hand-turned. Each piece is individual unless matched sets are specifically requested. Finished with vegetable oil. Diameter is 11'', depth 1½''. Other woods available on request. Shipping weight 1 lb. 10 oz. $9, shipping not included.

Bodega Woodworking Company—I live on a sheep ranch in Northern California with several other families. I believe anything I can provide for myself directly is good—cutting firewood, growing a garden, building a house. Making my living as a woodworker is another facet of that philosophy. We are surrounded by so much poorly-made junk these days that it is a great satisfaction to turn out something useful, beautiful and solid. I feel as though I am making a small stand against the proliferation of trash.

I like the feel of the wood and the smell of it. Working with it occupies body and mind, senses and needs.

Becoming a woodworker was an important part of putting my life back together after I was injured in a car wreck. It provides me with a focus and a means of earning income on *my* terms. My shop is set up so I can do everything from my wheelchair. I've been doing this for six years now.

I particularly like building and designing things to fit people's special needs. I custom build cabinets, furniture—anything smaller than a house.

Nicholas Peck, c/o Bodega Woodworking Company, Box 123, Bodega, California 94922.

144

Silver Jewelry—We have a large selection of nature's artistry—leaves, fungi, seed pods, etc.—transformed into pendants. All have been cast in sterling silver and have sterling silver chains. The small alder cone is 5/8'' long, $9.50; the chain is a 16'' curb, $4. The large alder cone is ¾'' long, $9.50; the chain is 18'' rope, $5. The double alder cone arrangement is 1'' long, $11.25; the chain is an 18'' curb, $4.75. The large double alder is 1½'' long, $17; the chain is 22'' embossed cable, $7. The redwood cone is 5/8'', $16; the 20'' rope chain, $7. The sage calyx is 1½'' long on a 22'' cable chain, $26 altogether.

Weber Studios—While looking at the pictures of our sterling silver replications of nature's wondrous designs, imagine what has preceded them. See Alice and Martin, a couple in their sixties, at a Northern California ocean edge collecting the sand- and water-sculpted remainders of long-ago logging. Then see us in the dunes and washes of Southern California's desert discovering what's left of last year's blossoms and fruits. Now, see us at home by a creek in Central California gathering local cones, pods, leaves and fungi. Picture us in our studio where we select choice items from our searches and prepare them for casting, using the lost-wax process and finishing them to bring out textures and details. Then, see us joining other craftspeople at fairs and festivals to show these treasures.

During all the years that Martin was working as a research chemist and Alice was doing tax work, we both were developing as artists, too, through photography, evening classwork at art school and, later, teaching at the art school. We retired early from our professions to develop our talents. Art school enhanced our appreciation of nature's forms. The possibility of using these forms in jewelry led us to develop new methods which we combine with traditional ones to replicate natural objects.

The finished products have been so well received by people attending the shows that we have decided to continue to search for an ever wider range of natural objects that can be used in jewelry. We will even consider replicating your own wondrous find. The stimulation we get from finding things to preserve in silver or gold and the happy reception of the end product make up for the tedium, failures and disappointments that can occur in between.

Martin and Alice Weber, c/o Weber Studios, P.O. Box 423, Glen Ellen, California 95442.

Hardwood Table—Order in woods of your choice: birch, oak, maple, koa, teak, mahogany, rosewood, etc. Oval top 48'' by 72''. Leaves can be added to extend length almost indefinitely. Base sculpted from a laminated block. Shown: walnut and cherry table which opens to 10'. $2,200, shipping not included. Tables start at $1,500.

Hardwood Chairs—Swivel chairs with tilting backrests. Bases are turned on a lathe and the seats sculpted and shaped by hand. Chairs are 22'' square by 33'' high and weigh 25 lbs. Shown: walnut and cherry chairs. $600 each with arms; $500 without arms; cushions $30 extra. Shipping not included.

Peter Burt Company—I started my free-lance career in a warehouse studio in San Francisco. Fittingly, the very substance I work with seemed to beckon me to the ''wood'': the country, where I now live and work.

Even before the actual relocation, however, my work reflected the flowing organic forms of country life rather than the angularity of city life. The most important impression I wish to convey in my furniture is quality—in form, line, tactile sensitivity, mechanics, color and the kind of quiet monumental presence that will survive many generations.

Peter Burt Lauridsen, c/o Peter Burt Company, P.O. Box 1, Iowa Hill, California 95713.

Earthenware Plate—Herons on black ground. The plate is about 10'' in diameter and has two white herons with orange beaks and legs standing beneath an olive-green willow tree. High-gloss black background, lead-free glazes. A very elegant and delicate plate—it took about 35 hours to paint! $80 postpaid.

Earthenware Teacups—My favorite to make. They fit beautifully in your hand. A real pleasure to drink from, especially when filled with cognac. About 2¼'' across by 2½'' high. Pictured are gloriosa daisy teacups, with brilliant yellow flowers and bright green stems on a glossy black background. I do other flower, landscape, bamboo and face designs. $45 for 3 cups postpaid.

Gail Blank—I live in the forest in the Santa Cruz mountains with my two teenage sons, one dog and six cats. I put much of the forest into my pottery designs: the flowers which grow in my garden decorate my teacups. I spend about ten hours a day painting designs. The process is tedious and time-consuming, since I use three coats of each color. It can take ten to fifty hours to paint a pot, depending on the intricacy of the design.

In addition to making pottery, I teach ceramics every morning to high school students, and three afternoons a week I teach crafts to older people who have had strokes.

Soon I plan to make a series of porcelain dolls with leather bodies.
Gail Blank, 1017 Smith Grade Road, Santa Cruz, California 95060.

The Portmanteau—Made of oiled French back cowhide, in light or dark brown with molded horsehair handle and straps. The bag is suede inside; the buckles are solid brass. Sizes: 20'' by 6'' (shown), $250; 24'' by 10'' or other sizes by custom order.

Bladah Workshop—We have been working and growing in our leatherwork for five years. Our workshop/home is in the hills of Massachusetts, far from the bustling city life we were raised in.

All our work is done entirely by hand, and while this is very time-consuming, it allows us to create bags and cases of which we are very proud. We are happiest doing one-of-a-kind, custom-designed pieces.
Harvey Schaktman and Amy Reiser, c/o Bladah Workshop, Crittenden Hill, Shelburne Falls, Massachusetts 01370.

Leather Jackets—All jackets are hand-stitched and done totally by me. The man's jacket is a one-of-a-kind item and sells for $600. The woman's jacket is tan goat suede, with a dark green yoke and cuffs. There is a peyote bead design on the front and back yoke. $400.

Jan Faulkner—I've been working in leather clothing for seven years. I have taught classes and workshops, and have written a book, *Leathercraft by Hand*, which has just been released in England.

I love what I'm doing. I like selling through craft fairs, as I can have a direct relationship with the people who buy from me. This is the way I get feedback about what I do.

Jan Faulkner, Route 1, Box 2000, Grantville, Pennsylvania 17028.

Bracelet—This bracelet is completely fabricated from heavy gauge wire and sheet sterling silver. It comes with a fine mirror finish. The clean surfaces and smooth lines show the quality and natural beauty of the material. It is hand-crafted from a simple design and is sturdy and comfortable. Weight approximately 20 grams, 1'' wide. Wrist sizes 5¼'', 6¼'' and 7''. The bracelet is adjustable to accommodate all sizes, but feel free to specify your exact size. $31.50 postpaid.

Matt Maguire—Silversmithing has been my livelihood and lifestyle for over five years now. I learned the essence of the craft from a man living on the Russian River in California, and the nuances from experience. I live and work in Mill Valley, California, and I enjoy the responsibilities and freedoms of self-employment and self-sufficiency.
Matt Maguire, 23 Eugene Street, Mill Valley, California 94941.

Spinning Wheel—Saxony-type twin-belt tension-screw spinning wheel of early American design. It will spin, twist or ply any spinnable fiber in either S or Z twist. Hand-crafted from solid maple, metal parts are all brass (except ball bearings). Footman is made of leather. Hand-turned spindles are extra large for strength and appearance. Assembly and care instructions included. Danish oil finish. Spinning wheel $330 postpaid; with distaff $351 postpaid.

Four-harness Frame Loom—Continuous movable warp loom with tension adjustment, 1'' birch dowels cross-pegged into hand-crafted selected mahogany sides, 18'' by 36''. No extra accessories or threading necessary—warp goes directly on the loom—string heddles are attached last and may be changed with ease. Weaves 18'' wide on 4', 7' or 10' warps. Lightweight and very portable. Comes assembled with complete instructions, a 20'' tapered hardwood shuttle and rya stick. Danish oil finish. $40 postpaid.

Good Karma Looms—It is our goal to work within the spirit of karma yoga—to have each piece reflect our best efforts. Neal's relationship with tools and wood goes back over twenty years.

Neal Patterson, c/o Good Karma Looms, 440 West Fourth, Chadron, Nebraska 69337.

Emblems and Seals—Carvings made from selected sugar pine or mahogany. Finished naturally or painted. This plaque is 14'' in diameter, 1¼'' thick and about 4½ lbs. shipping weight. $65 and up, according to the complexity of the design. I will do any design. Wooden animals, name plates, desk plates, seals, dulcimers and antique firearms also done.

Mountain Dulcimers—An affinity for nature led to my vocation as a professional forester. Eventually my knowledge of trees led me to work with wood as a carver. I have been developing my own style of woodcarving since 1959. I have exhibited widely in the mid-Atlantic states and have been teaching carving since 1970.

S. Ronald Singer, c/o Mountain Dulcimers, 6144 New Leaf Court, Columbia, Maryland 21045.

Bone Earrings—Natural bone with sterling silver ear wires. A straight bone earring is about ¼'' wide and 1½'' long. A round hoop earring is about 1¾'' long. The bone is mostly white or cream-colored. $5.50 a pair, postpaid.

Richard Kemp—We are a family of eight. Some of the school-age children are also involved in crafts—stained glass, candles, silver jewelry and stuffed soft cloth toys and dolls.

We have used our trips to crafts shows as a teaching tool—the cost of selling, cost of materials, sales methods, making change and customer relations. And we get to see different parts of the country.

Richard Kemp, 131 Sunset Drive, Burlington, Vermont 05401.

Furniture Puzzles—The puzzles are an old American folk design. They are cut from one block of Oregon big leaf maple and are dipped twice in nontoxic Watco Danish oil. The small puzzle measures 1-5/8'' by 1¾'' by 4'' and has 9 pieces of doll furniture that nest together. The large puzzle has 13 pieces and measures 2¼'' by 2-5/8'' by 6''. Small $5, large $10.

Family Lonnquist Toys—We started making toys in the spring of 1974. Hardwood materials, original design and quality execution are our pride. We enjoy selling our products at the various markets and fairs in the Oregon area. Making wooden toys for children is fun. May you never get your salt mixed in with the sugar!

Family Lonnquist Toys, 500 Northwest Sixteenth Street, Corvallis, Oregon 97330.

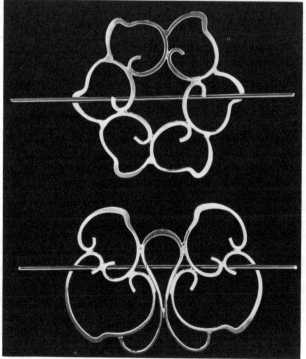

Barrettes—These delicately formed hair ornaments are made from sterling silver. They are approximately 4'' wide. $10. Also available in 14k gold.

Mike Knott—I've been making jewelry since 1970, after quitting as a philosophy major at Sonoma State College. First I taught myself and then I apprenticed under a silversmith in Sonoma County. I've sold on the streets in San Francisco and Berkeley and at numerous crafts fairs.

Arrays of metal
Bind up shining hair with ease
Joy to the wearer.
*Mike Knott, 1485 Timber Hill,
Santa Rosa, California 95401.*

Etched and Decorative Glass—We are presently engaged in custom work, and are planning to introduce a line of mirrors and general glass products. Prices vary, and are dependent on the complexity of design, execution and installation. Prices for custom work range from $15 to $50 per square foot. Prices of pieces shown: "Ted S. Smith," 20" by 30", $225. "San Anselmo Printing," 23" by 23", double etch, $200.

Out of the Blue—Although I am financially supported by my efforts in etched glass, I find great satisfaction in other means of expression. My background includes commercial art, cartooning, batik, candle making, carpentry, book design and illustration, and fine art.

Out of the Blue specializes in etched glass for doors, windows, cabinets, clocks, tabletops, arboretums, antique restorations and reproductions, vases, skylights and lamps. Our technology allows us to reproduce photographically any image onto stone, marble or wood. On occasion we have utilized stained and beveled glass in our designs, too.

Our services are available to other craftspersons who wish to combine their talents with ours. We also seek the opportunity to introduce alternative technologies to our craft, such as solar energy. Someday our etchings may even appear on automobile windows, skyscrapers and movie screens!

Gary Frutkoff, c/o Out of the Blue, 775 Anderson Drive, San Rafael, California 94902.

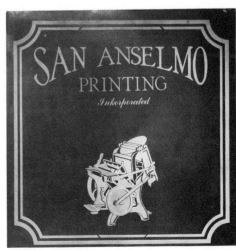

155

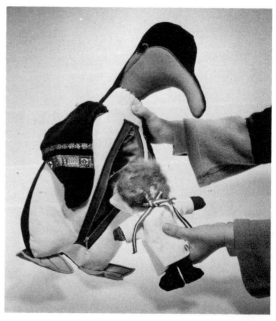

156

Knotty Babies—While the shape of the doll is repeated, the trims are endlessly varied. The cotton bodies are decorated with assorted braids, laces, ribbons and fabrics to form vests, suspenders, aprons and shirt fronts. Then hearts, flowers, buttons and bows are added to suit my fancy in making a happy doll. Long tubes of unstuffed fabric are knotted to form the arms and legs. This is a good doll for a baby or very young child, as small hands can easily grasp these arms and legs. From 18'' to 22'' long. Please specify boy or girl, $9.50 plus $1.50 shipping charge.

Admiral Bird and the Other Byrd—The penguin bird is made of black velveteen with heavy white cotton for his belly. The zipper pocket in his belly opens to a satin-lined pocket where the Other Byrd hides—a small doll dressed in a parka trimmed with bunny fur and adorned with medals for valor. The faces and trim on both dolls are appliqued with felt and machine embroidery, and contain polyester fiberfill. Measures 9'' wide by 24'' high, $38 plus $2 shipping charge.

Jonah and the Whale—Both Jonah and the whale are created from bright-colored cotton fabrics. The whale has velveteen fins, tail and belly. He has a zipper mouth lined with satin (so it feels good), which contains the small bearded figure of Jonah in appropriate dress for the occasion. All faces and trim are machine-embroidered, and the whale has jingle-bell eyes. All dolls are filled with polyester fiberfill. The whale is 12'' high and 20'' long. $28 plus $2 shipping charge.

Lisa Drumm—I have been making and selling dolls for approximately ten years. My husband Don and I own and operate a craft gallery in Akron representing fifty to seventy other craftsmen and our own work. Because we have very fine people working for us I am able to pursue my own craft while running the shop and doing some part-time teaching.

With Don and me both pursuing careers in crafts and sharing in the gallery operation, life is hectic but exciting. At times, we combine our efforts with me adding macrame to his metal forms. I started out in stitchery and still teach it summers at Penland School of Crafts. I moved into macrame and find pursuing intricate forms in fiber a challenge. When my oldest daughter (we have three) was very young, I started creating dolls for her and soon found myself with a market for them. The dolls have grown in complexity over the years and so has the market for them. Don and I often exhibit together in two-person shows as the coolness of the metal relates well to the warmth and color of the fibers.

Lisa Drumm, c/o Don Drumm Studios and Gallery, 437 Crouse Street, Akron, Ohio 44311.

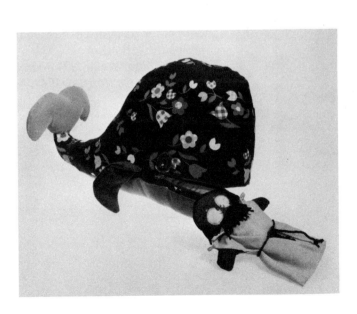

Batik Jackets—These reversible jackets are light, warm and wrinkle-proof. I batik and then paint one side of the jacket with permanent dyes. Then I quilt the fabric with gold thread outlining the figures in the paintings, resulting in a line drawing on the reverse side. I try to make the reverse-side drawings change the mood and expand the occasions for which the jacket can be worn. Jackets are backed in satin or denim, depending on the desired effect. The batiked side is made of cotton sateen or cotton twill. When ordering, tell me about your favorite colors, symbols, animals, artists, musicians, etc. I want to make you something you will not be afraid to wear. Also give your relevant measurements. $100 deposit with order. Total price $500 postpaid.

Genna Panzarella—I have always had a fascination with clothing and fashion, but I didn't connect it with my art until three years ago: I have been growing and learning the possibilities of clothing as a moving art form ever since. When I pushed my batik into quilting, I discovered that my fabric thickened and took on a sculptural dimension.

My feeling for wearing artwork has a rather primitive base. I feel there is a spirit in the coat—a power that carries from the artist and the coat itself to the wearer. I want my jackets to protect the wearer, cheer her, give her power and joy, warmth and comfort. I want the coat to present some inner core part of the wearer as well as the artist.

Genna Panzarella, 331 Jean Street, Mill Valley, California 94941.

Extension Lamp—Extension lamp for desk or wall (please specify clamp mount or wall mount). It is kept aloft by wooden nuts and bolts at the various joints and by a universal wooden joint at the acme of the lamp, permitting movement in a myriad of directions. The lamp stands 38'' to 40'' fully extended. It is constructed of white oak, big leaf maple, brass and glass. Woods are unstained and finished with natural-color wood oil. Shipping weight 4 lbs. Available with white frosted glass globe, $32, shipping not included; or bell-shaped amber glass shade, $35, shipping not included.

Jim Chapman—Four years ago, fate, karma, luck and the grace of ''le bon Dieu'' found me working in wood. After attending college, as a philosophy major, and years on the road, I was quite ready for roots. My woodworking, my wife's work as a graphic artist and my son's amalgam of both (he paints on wood) support all of us. We go on from here.

Jim Chapman, Checkered Mailbox, Vida, Oregon 97488.

Tabor—Double-headed, deep-booming frame drum with vellums wither-hooped and rope-tensioned or glued. Leather buffs for tuning, adjustable snare. Hang from the shoulder with a leather strap and play with a single stick or combination of hand and stick. Neck-laced 15'' tabor (shown above left), $150. Roped and hooped 15'' tabor (shown above right), $190. Shipping not included.

Tom Tom—Brightly painted with mandala-decorated drumheads.

Natraj, c/o Geetem Rajneesh Sannyas Ashram, P.O. Box 576, Lucerne Valley, California 92356.

Especially good for smaller children. Sturdy frame with hand-worked leather handle. Tom Tom 8'' in diameter (shown above center), $45. Tom Tom 10'' in diameter (not shown), $55. Shipping not included.

Tambourines—Middle Eastern proportions, rich tonal range, unlimited rhythmic possibilities. Hand-hammered or hand-stamped brass jingles shimmer lightly or jangle brightly. Each tambourine has its own unique sound color and use, solo or in concert. Tambourine, 15'', hammered jingles (shown on facing page, above left), $140. Tambourines, 8'', hammered jingles (shown facing page, above, on edge), $90. Tambourine, 10'' (shown on facing page, above right), $115. Jingle ring, brightly painted ring without head, 28 jingles, 8'' (shown on facing page, above, foreground center), with hand-stamped jingles, $48. With hammered jingles, 8'', $90 (not shown). With stamped jingles, 10'', $60 (not shown). With hammered jingles, 10'', $115 (not shown).

Hand-drums—A simple drum. The deep-rimmed drum sings in fuller ringing voice; the shallow rimmed drum sings in bell colors. Deep-rimmed hand-drums, 15'' (shown on facing page, it is the stack on the left, below), $90. The 15'' Bodhran, Spider Drum and Fire Drum shown in middle ground on page facing below may be special ordered. Prices on application. The 15'' shallow-rimmed Hand-drum (shown in foreground), $58. Shipping not included.

Natraj—Our drum making began with a dream and a magic drum that appeared out of the East one early spring in the hands of a wandering minstrel.

Swami Prem Avinash and Ma Prem Punita, with their littlest drum, Prem Lalit, live and work at Geetam (the Song) Rajneesh Sannyas Ashram, seventy acres of desert garden in the foothills of the San Bernardino mountains, a New Age community of the disciples of Bhagwan Shree Rajneesh.

Lamb Lamp—A lamp for hanging over table, chair or bookcase. Consists of a formed, welded natural steel top to which the shade ribs are welded. Wool, cotton or goat-hair yarn is then wrapped around the shade frame. Comes fully wired with three feet of chain. Height 22'', weight 15 lbs. $150.

Ice Cream Light—An indoor table lamp that's 24'' high. It has a welded steel pipe base and a six-sided shade covered with wool. Wired for 3-way bulb, weight 15 lbs. $160.

Eric Canon—I've been working at my craft for ten years. It is my full-time occupation; I have no other source of income. I operate as an individual, although my wife Carol wraps our lamp shade frames with yarn and occasionally I'll take on an apprentice.

We exhibit our work in Portland, Oregon; Honolulu, Hawaii; and Carmel, California. About eighty percent of my work is functional in some way, including such items as wood stoves, bird cages, beds, building hardware and a whole lot more. I specialize in lamps and lighting, but I'll try anything once. My idol is Harry Bertoia, and my goal is to work much as he did with functional architectural sculpture.

I was born and raised in Portland; I've traveled extensively. In 1967 the Bank of America made me an operations officer. It didn't take long for me to decide to change my occupation.

In 1969 Carol and I got together, our daughter Zafi was born and we all packed up and moved to Oregon. In 1972 my son Carter was born, we bought six acres and a run-down house in the mountains and started planning the house we finally built last year. We live a quiet life raising our kids, growing vegetables, collecting our chickens' eggs and maintaining our land.

Eric Canon, Route 1, Box 65, Gaston, Oregon 97119.

Laminated Wooden Containers—These elegant laminated boxes are excellent containers for jewelry, cigarettes or precious objects. Each box has a unique hardwood pattern resulting from the original process I have developed. The three flat-topped boxes in the upper row are $25, $17 and $44. Smaller and intermediate sizes are available. Pictured in the foreground are two intricately crafted curved-top boxes, $40 each.

William Jacquith Evans—For my own satisfaction I have crafted several unusual one-of-a-kind design pieces which have been exhibited in the California Design exhibit and at the Renwick Gallery of the Smithsonian Institution, as well as in the Museum of Contemporary Crafts.

William J. Evans, 6061 Merriewood Drive, Oakland, California 94611.

Porcelain Beds—No two beds are exactly alike; they come flat, rounded, four-poster, slab or with nudes sleeping in them. Single beds are 4'' by 6'', $30; bunk beds are 4'' by 6'' by 6'', $40. Box beds are 4'' by 6'' by 4'', $40 and have a top that comes off. Drawer beds have either one or two drawers, are 4'' by 6'' or 4'' by 6'' by 4'', and cost $60 or $90.

Egg Cartons—Like the beds, these are hand-built porcelain, fired to cone 017. They look real, but the insides are shiny mother-of-pearl luster. They come with or without a top and are the actual size. $40.

Adele Schonbrun—I have been in crafts for fifteen years, and have become more active now that my two children are growing up. Soon they'll be in school and I'll have even more time. I stopped teaching a year ago to devote more time to clay.

I'm concerned with the things a mother sees. Much to my surprise, I realized that the essential things of life are all containers, mentally or physically, just as a woman is.

Technically, working the clay when it is in its soft state is the most thrilling to me. I like the idea of showing its softness, preserving it in this state.

Adele Schonbrun, 33 Martins Lane, Berkeley Heights, New Jersey 07922.

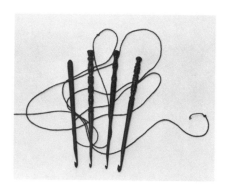

Crochet Hooks—We make hand-turned crochet hooks of rosewood. When available, we also work with lignum vitae, Osage orange, zebrawood and pau Brazil. These are some of the world's hardest and most beautiful woods. The hooks come in sizes F to Q (size H is the most common) and are approximately 7'' long. The width, of course, depends on the size of the hook. Prices vary according to the ornamentation and the rarity of the wood from $3 to $8 plus shipping charge (50 cents for up to four pieces, $1 for more). We also make rosewood chopsticks, pair $10; lace bobbins, $5; stilettos for drawn-work embroidery, $5.

Bill Dungan and Andi Dalton—We have been involved in this profession for four years, and are constantly making discoveries about wood. We are a partnership, working full-time at it, sometimes seven days a week and late into the night, and employing no other people—a true cottage industry.

We live in the Redwoods, along the Russian River. Few people live here, and it's very quiet. This gives us the time and space we need, both for ourselves and for our work. We are strongly committed to turning people on to the warmth and beauty of wood, and away from the plastic and metal that surrounds them. We believe we produce the most comfortable and beautiful hand tools possible.

Bill Dungan and Andi Dalton, P.O. Box 222, Rio Nido, California 95471.

Comforters—"Homestead comforts" are comforters made of downproof, off-white cotton filled with prime goose down. They are incredibly warm. Tube construction with seaming on the inside makes them very durable, too. Sheetcovers can be made from your sheets, or we can provide instructions for making them. Our featherbed comforters come in all sizes. Prices vary, depending on the amount of fill, but on the average, a full-sized comforter with 3 lbs. of fill is $150.

Fort Homestead Hermitage—We make a number of things as part of our "right livelihood" program at the Hermitage. These comforters are my contribution. Crafts are our major source of income and we have found it is the best way for us to make a living in a remote area and still pursue a spiritually-oriented life.

My personal background is of no account, although I might mention that I have had formal training in art, and take great pains to do my work well.

Peach Blossom, c/o Fort Homestead Hermitage, P.O. Box 6, Silver City, Nevada 89428.

Blanket of Earth Neckpiece—Bands of colored nylon, detail of bone rings, button closing. Available in four color combinations: Spring—tan background, various earth colors, rose, soft blue, light rust, white rings and button; Summer—rust background, bands of coral, royal blue, magenta, purple, orange, brown rings and button; Fall—brown background, bands of blue, beige, rust, red; brown rings and button; Winter—background of black, bands of beige, taupe, purple, white rings, brown button. Packaged weight 3 oz., 18'' by 4'' including fringe, $50.

Neckpiece with Bone Ring—Made with double cord, cowhorn ring, African lead bead, seed bead detail on ends. Button closing. Two colors: taupe with brown stripe, white button; brown with taupe stripe, brown button. Both have brown seed bead detail. Approximately 14'' by 3½'', $25.

Leather Bag—I've been making this bag for a long time now and have refined it considerably. It's made of a nice chap weight cowhide. It has mitred corners for shape and durability. There's a full-sized divider inside and a pocket on the back for your checkbook. Adjustable strap with buckle. Macrame detail on flap will vary, but will always be bold. Done with waxed nylon thread (Nyltex) and some natural ornament (bone, bead or ring). Inside divider's seams are sewn on my old treadle boot-patcher (it's got soul, folks), all other sewing is done by hand with waxed nylon. Needs saddle soaping every few weeks to keep looking great for a long time. Adjustable 36'' shoulder strap, 11'' by 13''. Warm brown leather, chocolate-colored macrame, black buckle. About 1¼ lb. packaged. $34, shipping not included.

Tina Johnson—My work is inspired by the things I love: the sea, the desert, African and Japanese textiles and design. I feel a great harmony with these things. I seek that harmony in my work. A quiet relationship between color and form, material and idea, that has the strength to stand on its own. I seek a union with the spirit of many cultures as well as the development of my own personal myth vocabulary.

I hope my pieces will inspire others to a heightened awareness of little things—details that can speak so clearly. Personal adornment can beautifully reflect the inner person—the one that wants to speak without words.

Tina Johnson, c/o General Delivery, Mendocino, California 95460.

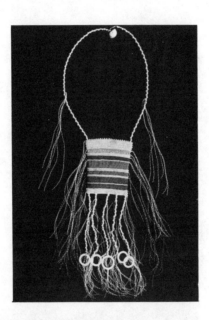

Frances Butler, c/o Goodstuffs, 6221 Hollis Street, Emeryville, California 94608.

Aprons—Hand-screened 100% cotton, completely washable. Bear design is chocolate brown, tan, orange and blue. Zebra design is gray, pink and black. Kits, $10 each postpaid. Finished aprons $14 postpaid.

Long Dress—Hand-screened 100% cotton, completely washable although dry cleaning is preferable. Fully lined, one size fits all (different hem lengths possible). Chocolate brown background, rust, gold and black figures of acrobats. Kit $53 postpaid. Finished dress $88 postpaid.

Goodstuffs—I had been printing fabric in my basement for several years when, five years ago, I opened a larger fabric-printing workshop in an old industrial section of town. The shop has sixty yards of table and now has several employees (three of whom are shown here). I also design yardage fabric, wall hangings, pillows, tablecloths and comforters and am very pleased to see others use my fabrics for their own projects. I began printing fabric as an outgrowth of appliqueing dresses and am still interested in sewing. I also make the aprons and dresses in kit form for those who would rather sew them up themselves.

White Porcelain Plates—One-of-a-kind sets of plates, handmade from porcelain with inlay coil decoration. Each plate is slightly different, but the set has an overall design continuity. Foot attached so the plates have a graceful curve and can be stacked. Diameter: 10½''. Set of 4, 7½ lbs., 20 lbs. packed, $64 postpaid. Set of 8, 15 lbs., 40 lbs. packed, $120 postpaid.

Carol Prier—I am a sculptor and a potter. I work primarily with clay. I find it a beautiful and amazing material in all its forms, fired and unfired. The rhythm of working between the functional and nonfunctional is like breathing: moving out to the uncharted grounds of sculpture, connecting again with a basic sense in making eating ware. Balance. The porcelain plates—slow, special work. Plates as individual pieces for beauty; plates to be eaten from each day. Porcelain for elegance and simplicity. I love this kind of making.

Carol Prier, 1711 Channing Way, Berkeley, California 94703.

Marimbas—Pictured is a "C" pentatonic marimba, which has a 2-octave range tuned to C-D-F-G-A. The mahogany tone bars are drilled and laced securely to a sturdy durable frame and produce a beautiful, glowing sound. Two 12'' mallets are included with each instrument. Weight: 7 lbs. $60. List of other instruments available.

Bird—I made my first drum out of a nail keg at fifteen, and I have been making instruments ever since. For the last six years, this has been my sole occupation—designing and making instruments of all shapes and sizes.

My shop is in a big old silver barn in an out-of-the-way alley in Sacramento. I work there with Jerry, my partner and friend, and Scott, a young neighbor lad who plays the tuba. There are no clocks on the wall—we just govern ourselves by the work at hand and flow with things as they happen.

I want people to make their own music. Music is play. I want to share the freedom I feel in music, so I make instruments that are simple and beautiful.

Charles Bardin, c/o Bird, 5116½ Fifteenth Avenue, Sacramento, California 95820.

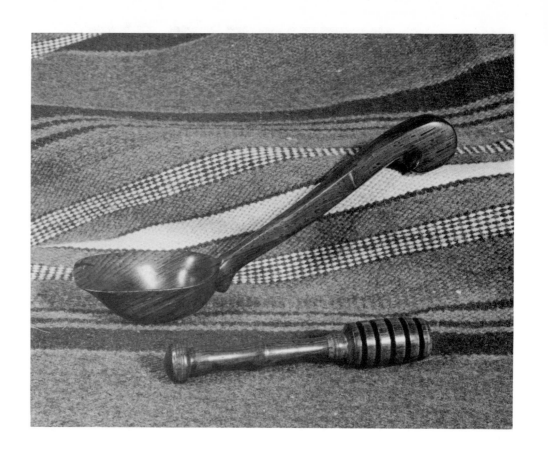

Carved Gemstone and Wood Wares—All pieces are individually designed and constructed, so prices will vary. Jade shuttle for inkle loom made from light, translucent Alaskan jade, about 6'' long, $25. Rosewood tasting spoon is 9'' long. The wood is moisture-proof and heat-resistant. $30. Rosewood honey dipper is moisture- and heat-resistant, $5. Serpentine mustard pot with blue jade lid and rosewood spoon, 4'' high, $95. (Pots range from $50 to $200.) Jade pipe carved from dark green British Columbian jade is 4'' long. There are two basic styles of pipe: one a single piece of stone, and one with a ring of some contrasting colored material and a rare hardwood stem-mouthpiece. They are also available in lapis lazuli, quartz, tiger's-eye and agate. These gemstone pipes are unique. Each is signed and dated with a diamond pencil. Jade pipe, $200. Special orders are our delight. Tell us what you want, how much you want to spend, and we will work something out. Our policy is ''satisfaction guaranteed'' for the lifetime of the item. All repairs are made free.

Light Touch Lapiderie—I have been carving stone for about nine years now and have never yet repeated myself. The material, with few exceptions, does not lend itself to repetition. A stone, like a snowflake, is unlike all others, both in chemical and physical composition and in actual form. The Eskimos have a saying: ''Look into the rock, see the form hiding in there, take away the extra rock.'' I tell my customers that the work they get is actually free; they pay for the stone I remove!

It we wanted to get rich, it would be easy to mass-produce some sleazy item. Instead we strive for quality, variety and joy in our work.

Robert Crawford and Frances Koliner, c/o Light Touch Lapiderie, P.O. Box 377, Sebastopol, California 95472.

Star Stove—Welded construction of 11 gauge steel with a cast and polished bronze door. Door and frame are precision-ground to provide an airtight seal. The stove stands 28'' high and has an average diameter of 20''. It will accommodate logs 6'' to 7'' thick. It features primary and secondary air adjusts, removable grates and an ample ash compartment. Shipping weight approximately 80 lbs. $295, shipping not included.

Box Stove—Airtight construction of heavy ¼'' plate steel, with 3/8'' plate used for the door and interior baffle. Adjustable draft design permits either up-draft or down-draft operation. Special preheating secondary air chambers assist combustion by providing additional oxygen in back of stove at grate level. Height 34'', width 18'', length 38'', weight approximately 250 lbs. Door opening 12'' by 14''. Oversized ash compartment needs emptying only every 2 to 4 weeks even with heavy or constant use. $495, shipping not included.

Randall Hunt—I am twenty-seven years old, working and living as a welder, librarian and resident craftsman at Arcosanti, Arizona. I have been welding since 1972 and have been producing and selling stoves since 1975. As a craftsman, I hold in highest regard the integrity of an object. Not only should an object be beautiful to the eye, it must be beautiful to use. Practicality must not be sacrificed for a well-turned line.

My designs are entirely original and constructed with care. I believe a hand-crafted object should be worth having and worth keeping. These stoves have been design-tested and I am proud to offer a full guarantee on workmanship.

To keep my work from becoming toil, I am naturally inclined toward producing custom and/or one-of-a-kind pieces. I would be delighted to discuss any special desires or specific applications you might have with regard to my stoves.

Randall Hunt, Arcosanti, Arizona 86333.

Oak Cradle—This solid oak cradle accommodates a standard 13'' by 27'' mattress pad. It is constructed from 1'' white oak stock, all pieces hand-selected and matched by our craftspeople. These pieces are then laminated, dowelled and assembled, without any metal reinforcement. A black walnut veneer is inlaid into the oak and the entire cradle is then rubbed with a Danish sealing oil. The cradle measures 25½'' wide by 31½'' long, and stands 23¾'' high. $175.

God'spun Honey, Unlimited—We are an unlimited partnership currently composed of Edward Lewis, Sidney Greenapple and Lowell Peters. Our objective is to offer products which cannot be improved upon. There are no sacrifices in design, materials or execution. Contrary to many of our previous experiences in which we were continually compromising and sacrificing, we are finding God'spun Honey, Unlimited, a unique experience in combining concepts, talents and, most of all, integrity with ideals.

God'spun Honey, Unlimited, 1166 Oak Hill Road, Lafayette, California 94549.

Star Dress—This is a child's dress done with textile paints and permanent dyes on cotton. The colors are bright reds and purples, with yellow and gold stars. Washable, colorfast, $60.

Sara Drower—When it comes to describing my work and my life (gad!), it comes out to balancing between work made to sell and work done for the sheer joy of creation. The rest is a balance too—we live in a suburb of Chicago, yet less than half a city block away from my house are woods and quiet beaches (if you get up early in the morning). To relax, I keep a wildflower garden and enjoy the galleries in Chicago. It's a good life.

Sara Drower, 127 Laurel, Wilmette, Illinois 60091.

Women's Waist-length Jacket—
Made of finest quality cowhide and
stitched with stretch-control nylon
thread that will not break as garment
fits to form of body. Shaped front and
back yokes and button cuffs.
Ponderosa pine wood buttons. Misses
sizes 8, 10, 12, 14. Dark brown (nearly
black), tan, chocolate brown, gold.
Shipping weight 3½ lbs. $92.50,
shipping not included.

**Women's or Men's Western-style
Shirt Jacket**—Contemporary shirt
jacket with Western-shaped front and
back yokes and cuffs. Hidden brass
snap closures in front and at cuffs.
Two front pockets. Made of finest
quality cowhide and stitched with
stretch-control nylon thread. Men's
sizes 38, 40, 42, 44. Misses sizes 8,
10, 12, 14. Dark brown (nearly black),
tan, chocolate brown, gold. Shipping
weight 4 lbs., $105, shipping not
included.

HideBound Leather Studios—Our
leatherwork experience began about
six years ago. Ginger has fifteen
years of experience in garment
construction, having worked in
several leather shops and studied
pattern drafting and tailoring at
vocational and technical schools. She
began to impart her knowledge of the
field to Mike and a new way of life
began.

HideBound had its origins as a
business on the back porch of a lake
cabin in Minnesota. Mike's first
commission was completed there—an
upholstery job on a classic sports car
that he accomplished with
upholstering instructions in one hand
and leather tools in the other.

Our work is done entirely in the soft
leather medium and, as such, is
generally quite different from the
work we have seen done in leather.
Our pieces range from fine hand-
laced garments utilizing age-old
Spanish lacing techniques to original-
design wall hangings and tapestries.

We are extremely interested in
promoting soft leather as a separate
artistic entity and are experimenting
continuously with new uses and
adaptations of the medium.

*Mike and Ginger Swartz, P.O. Box
1391, Pagosa Springs, Colorado
81147.*

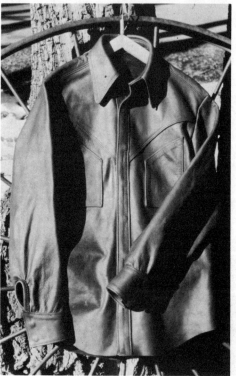

Hanging Chair—This soft, pliable chair hangs from a central pivot point in the ceiling and will swivel 360°. The top of the weaving is firmly attached to a solid red oak wood piece, which is suspended by braided leather. The chair comes in a single-person size (shown): 27'' wide, 20'' deep, 63'' high, weight 20 lbs. The two-person size chair is softly gathered at the top and attached to a linen-wrapped steel ring. It is 42'' wide, 24'' deep, 72'' high, weight 20 lbs. Prices: for commercially dyed and spun yarn $320 small, $400 large; for commercially spun, vegetable-dyed yarn $410 small, $480 large; for hand-spun vegetable-dyed yarn $620 small, $690 large.

Shoulder Bag/Backpack—In vibrant colors of the rainbow, with adjustable strap, measures 13'' wide by 16'' high. Custom-order in colors of your choice. Hand-woven of hand-spun, natural dyed yarn, $190; commercially spun and dyed yarn, $80.

Judith Suval—I am a wife, mother of two, gardener, worm grower, chicken rancher, angora rabbit raiser, builder, secretary and chief cook. I am also a spinner and weaver and I feel best when I am involved in some area of my craft.

My twenty-year involvement with textiles has been spontaneous and a work of love. When I discovered the joys of creating color from plants growing around me, my journey into spinning, dyeing and weaving began. As my family can attest, I will try anything that grows as a source of color!

Judith Suval, 455 Kourt Drive, Eugene, Oregon 97404.

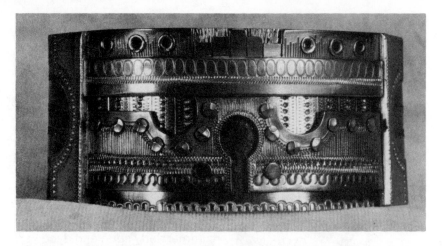

Bracelet—All pieces are constructed of copper, brass and sterling silver. Colors are moved and balanced through the use of layers, rivets, soldering and wire. Lastly, the metal is oxidized: the sterling becomes blue-gray; the copper, black; and the brass, golden. Decorative work includes stamping and engraving. This unique style of jewelry has been compared to medieval art and even to computers. Please give wrist measurement. $61 postpaid.

Belt Buckle—Buckles have a loop for the belt on the back and a hook on the other end for the belt holes. The hooks are made of thick round wire, and are soldered through the bottom layer of the buckle to insure durability. When ordering, indicate width of belt. $61 postpaid.

Nancy Moore and Tom Streb—Our life centers around a small house in the Finger Lakes region of New York. Our interests include fishing, needlework, wine making, wild turkeys, family and an English setter named "The Moose." We live in a secluded area, and "town" is an excursion, but we are more than content with staying home and making jewelry.

We choose to work only with metal, and rarely use stones in our jewelry. We feel that our jewelry is warm and personal, and quite distinctive.

Nancy Moore and Tom Streb, 5540 Dutch Street, R.D. #1, Dundee, New York 14937.

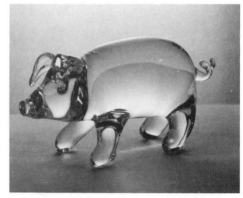

Glass Sculpture—The clear glass truck mounted on walnut base (above, left) has a special history. A local shipper started with two horse-drawn wagons around 1900. His third vehicle was this motorized one. A photograph of the original provided the design for this construction. Available with any name engraved on the side plaques. Size: 4'' wide by 4'' high by 10'' long. Shipping weight 10 lbs. $225, shipping not included. Whale (below) and Piglet (upper right) are both from the Small Friends Collection, all fabricated from solid clear glass. Whale, 2'' long, shipping weight ¾ lb., $3.25, shipping not included. Piglet, 1½'' long, shipping weight ¾ lb., $4, shipping not included.

The Glass Infinity—My work began with zoo animals because I grew up near the Washington Zoo. My work now includes food objects because of my passionate interest in cooking. I have also recently become concerned with the local traditions of Southern Illinois and reflect that in my designs.

Crafts have been my way of communicating with others since I was quite young. They are a tangible record of one's tastes, abilities, personality and environment. Consequently, whether I am cooking or blowing glass, my surroundings are always somewhat cluttered. My production is an attempt to control a medium of volatile beauty.

Lorenzo Cristaudo, c/o The Glass Infinity, R.R. #4, Carbondale, Illinois 62901.

Persimmon Tote Bag—The classical Chinese image of the persimmon symbolizes joy through its reddish color. This hand-screened bag is printed on tan chair duck canvas, which has a finish repellant to mildew and water. There's a velcro snap at the top and 26''-long black straps. It's 14½'' wide by 13'' deep. $14.

Bok Choy Tote Bag—Bok choy are delicious Chinese vegetables. This hand-screened bag is printed on neutral canvas. It has a velcro snap at the top and 26''-long neutral straps. It's 14½'' wide by 13'' deep. $10.

Pillowcases—Light-colored images are printed on khaki-colored polyester and cotton blends. They are machine-washable and need no ironing. The righthand pillowcase is an adaptation of Kuniyoshi's Miyamoto Musashi, the famous Japanese warrior who developed the double-sword technique in kendo. The lefthand pillowcase is my interpretation of a samurai of the Kabuki theater. Standard size $18 each, king size $19 each.

Luci Li—I graduated from the University of California in fine arts with an emphasis on painting and etching. Before my new adventure into screening, I worked as a medical photographer for an oral surgeon. My screening history is very short. I started out last winter with a book in one hand and a squeegee in the other.

I had a hard time thinking of a name for my company, so I named it after yours truly (not too arty, but basic!). I sign all my work in Chinese script, and use my chop (seal), which is my given name in ancient writing. I do everything myself, from beginning to end, including the labels. I hope to find a person to help me sew the bags, but until now, I have been the only labor I could afford.

Luci Li, 3031 Harper Street, Berkeley, California 94703.

Porcelain Birds—Tiny birds are sculpted from porcelain and salt-fired. Especially suitable as Christmas tree ornaments, these captivating iridescent birds can be hung anywhere. Each bird is equipped with a loop for hanging. Feather accents are hand-painted in your choice of blue, green or orange. Wingspread: 3'' to 4''. $5.50 each, 6 for $28.25 postpaid.

Bird Cups—Light porcelain cups are hand-thrown and salt-fired. A bird is etched into the surface of each cup and painted in rich colors. Choose among the following: bluebird, bluejay, finch, goose, hawk, eagle, heron, hummingbird, kingfisher, mallard, oriole, owl, peacock, quail, seagull or warbler. Iridescence adds brilliance to these 8-oz. cups. $8 each, 2 for $15 postpaid.

Marcia Skolnick Simonson and Don Simonson—Clay has been the focus of my life since I graduated from the University of California at Santa Cruz in 1966. Don's strong suits are etching, sculpture and his avocation—ornithology. His sculpture and etchings have been exhibited at the Smithsonian Institution and other galleries. We have built a studio and a salt-firing kiln named Smokestack Lightning on the banks of Seneca Creek.

The salt-firing process, first developed in the Middle Ages, yields a strong, durable glaze. First we coat the inside of the green (unfired) ware with a clear, lead-free glaze and decorate the outside with etched lines and colorants. The ware is stacked in the kiln, which is then fired to about 2300°F. When this extreme temperature has been reached, we throw dampened rock salt into the kiln through portholes, and quickly close them up again.

The salt melts in the white heat, and forms a gas which circulates among the pots. Soda in the gas combines with the alumina and silica in the clay to form sodium alumino-silicate, or glaze, on the exposed surfaces of the pots.

We throw salt into the kiln several times at maximum heat, completely covering the pots with successive coats of glaze. This process yields the prized "orange-peel" texture which can only be obtained by firing with salt. Later, as the kiln cools down from white heat to blackness, we may add tin chloride crystals. These volatilize like the rock salt, and kiss the pots here and there with iridescent pastel colors and rainbows. Real magic.

Marcia Skolnick Simonson and Don Simonson, Kirkhill Farm, 15811 Darnestown Road, Germantown, Maryland 20767.

Feather Jewelry—We use pheasant, peacock and guinea hen feathers as well as imported hackles. We use no dyes. Our feather bands are suitable as chokers, headbands or hatbands. They are available in an infinite array of designs, each one like a painting. Fine suede backing and ties are color-matched to each band. $8 postpaid. Earrings are available in all manner of feather design. Ear wires are sterling silver or 12k gold-filled. Shown here: super longs made of peacock and exotic imported hackles, $5 postpaid. Sizes range from 3½'' to 7'' long. Shown with earrings: large peacock-feather barrette, $6 postpaid; smaller barrette available, $4 postpaid.

Feathery Finery—Our base is in the championship town of Oakland, California. We love our work and each other.

Carolyn is the main creative force behind our work. She has an art background and has done teaching and writing in the art field.

Robert is our business manager as well as a craftsman in his own right.

Kevin, the youngest, has won art awards and usually handles our custom orders.

Carolyn Dismukes, Robert Bell and Kevin Hatfield, c/o Feathery Finery, 3254 Kempton Avenue, Oakland, California 94611.

Woven and Printed Textiles—
Colorful, soft, textured shawls of wool and mohair blends, 24'' wide by 80'' long, packed weight 2¼ lbs., $50. Tablet books, hand-bound with hand-printed fabrics, side hinging or top hinging, small (3'' by 5''), $3; medium (4'' by 6''), $4.50; large (5'' by 8''), $6. Shoulder bags (middle right), hand-woven with wool weft covering strong linen or cotton warp. Patterns: rainbow, cloud, sun, moon or geometrics. Sizes: small, 8'' wide, 9'' long with strap, 2'' deep, packed weight 1½ lbs., $33; large, 12'' wide, 12'' long with strap, 2'' deep, packed weight 2½ lbs., $48. Rag shag pillow (bottom left), polyester fiberfilled, 17'' by 17'', packed weight 5¼ lbs., $50. Honeysuckle pillow (bottom right), all wool with wavy geometric patterns in natural colors, 18'' by 20'', polyester fiberfilled, packed weight 3½ lbs., $32. Hand-woven wallets, made with wool weft and covering a strong cotton warp. Small, 4'' wide and 4'' long, $8. Large, 8'' long and 4¼'' wide, $11. Backpack: hand-woven with wool weft and strong linen warp. Designed in patterns: stripes, geometrics, landscapes, sun, moon and rainbow. Packs have leather straps and brass findings, are 12'' wide, 14'' long, 4'' deep and weigh 3 lbs. packed, $72. Specify color/combination choices. Shipping not included.

Mendocino Art Center Textile Apprenticeship Program—The Mendocino Art Center Textile Apprenticeship Program is an amalgam of the European-style apprenticeship and the American school system. We are twelve apprentices and two master instructors operating a producing studio five days a week, six hours a day for nine months of the year.

Mendocino Art Center Textile Apprenticeship Program, P.O. Box 36, Mendocino, California 95460.

Quilts—Three-dimensional quilts, wall hangings and stuffed sculpture of rare humor and delight are made of such materials as velour and corduroy, goose down and dacron, silk and old curtains. Qualities of color and texture are developed as a painter uses his palette. Give me your ideas and let me stuff them. Shown here: Washington quilt, 96" by 100", $600; flag quilt, 80" by 90", $400.

Shirl Salzman—Looking back, I suppose the newspaper-stuffed goldfish I produced as my first art project in grammar school probably turned me on to textile arts. My art history after that is blurred until just before high school, when I performed my first serious tantrum on behalf of my desire to take Art instead of Science. I arrived at UC Berkeley and admitted to never having heard of a major; I asked for examples. Those were the days of the revolution, and the world was lively and understandable for a romantic.

Eventually I majored in painting and received a sewing machine for my graduation. I made my living sewing for hippie shops.

My art education was not exactly practical, a fact brought home to me by a lady at an art jobs agency who, after a lengthy interview, politely told me, "Frankly, honey, you're unemployable." Somewhat relieved, I moved to Mendocino and did graphics, clothing and pottery. But one sunny afternoon a friend turned me on to making banners and quilts. Eureka!

To me techniques are only used in service of an idea. Only sculpting could bring certain conceptions to life. So I began making stuffed sculpture of scenery and jokes, and combining this technique with quilts when the ideas called for it.

Shirl Salzman, 1432 Bel Aire Road, San Mateo, California 94402.

Tipis—We make our tipis in the style of the Sioux, as described in *The Indian Tipi* by Reginald and Gladys Laubin. Our complete tipi includes a cover, liner, ozan (for additional warmth and dryness) and door flap. We use only the highest-quality materials in our tipis: marine vivatex, a pre-shrunk, double-fill canvas; and intrinsic cotton, a heavy cotton thread. Both are treated for water and mildew resistance and durability. Shown: our 15' tipi with 6' liner, $349. Brochure of our tipis, 25 cents. *Tipi Makers Booklet*, a detailed explanation of how we make our tipis, how to pitch and use one and other helpful hints, $3.

Tipi Makers—Back in 1970 I decided that I no longer wanted to be a chemist, stuck away in some laboratory. So I put my nose to the wind, my feet on the earth, made myself a tipi and headed into the mountains.

Along the way people told me how much they liked my tipi; finally one couple asked if I'd make them one. I did, and to this day the demand for tipis continues to grow.

Several friends now work with me making tipis. Together we feel that our work is meaningful. We sense that our tipis are opening new doors and channels for people who are searching for new ways of relating to the earth.

Jamie Jackson, c/o Tipi Makers, Box 9129, Mobile, Alabama 33609.

Stoneware Pottery—Our stoneware dining service comes in dark (Shaker) blue, light blue, tan, gold or antique gray. Included are 10'' dinner plate, $6; 8'' breakfast/luncheon plate, $5; 6'' bread-and-butter plate, $3; and 6'' soup bowl, $4. The service also comes with our Tobacco Tree design in brown or blue. Dinner plate $12, breakfast/luncheon plate $10, bread-and-butter plate $5 and bowl $6. Our son Jacques, shown with clean plate, enjoys a well-set table, including a single candleholder, $4; a 10-oz. mug, $4; plain goblet, $7; triple candleholder, $10; Tobacco Tree goblet, $8; and Tobacco Tree mug, $6.

The Elements Pottery—Linda Brousseau majored in pottery at East Carolina University with a minor in print making. After graduating in 1966, she and her husband moved to several locations in the Carolinas where Linda taught pottery. In 1970 the family moved to Danville, Kentucky, and began to produce pottery on a full-time basis.

Andre Brousseau was a mathematics and computer-science instructor until 1972, when he began helping out in the pottery. He has learned to throw on the wheel and has built some of the wheels they use. He has also built the jigger equipment which he uses to make all of the dinnerware.

In 1976 he resigned from teaching to work full-time with Linda and the children in their studio. The three oldest of their four children help in the pottery, trimming pots and pugging clay. The Elements Pottery is truly a family business.

Linda and Andre Brousseau, c/o The Elements Pottery, 629 North Third Street, Danville, Kentucky 40422.

189

Chairs—Cantilevered chair (opposite page), made of laminated ash with oil finish and leather seat. Also available in oak, beech, birch, maple and sometimes walnut. About 25 lbs., shipping weight 75 lbs., 47'' by 42'' by 24''. $936 (walnut $986), shipping not included. Spring Chair Design No. 3 (upper left) is made of laminated black walnut with oil finish, leather seat. Also available in oak, beech, birch, maple and ash. About 25 lbs., shipping weight 75 lbs., 30'' by 48'' by 66''. Walnut, $986. Other woods, $936, shipping not included. Sleigh chair (lower left) made of laminated red oak with oil finish, cotton macrame slings, leather head cushion. Also available in beech, birch, cherry, ash, maple and sometimes walnut. About 30 lbs., shipping weight 90 lbs., 28'' by 40'' by 72''. $1,560 (walnut, $1,610), shipping not included. Spring Chair Design No. 1 (lower right) is made of laminated ash with oil finish, leather sling. Also available in oak, beech, birch, maple and sometimes walnut. About 25 lbs., shipping weight 75 lbs., 54'' by 30'' by 36''. $832 (walnut $882), shipping not included.

William Leete—My work is done in an attempt to communicate a feeling of graceful movement and strength. Aside from visual and tactile stimuli, my work accomplishes this objective through actual movement of the piece and sitter while in use. Some of my support forms allow the user a springing movement of 6'' to 8''. Accomplishing this goal through the use of cantilevered linear elements, I have found it necessary to study engineering and mechanics.

William C. Leete, 201½ South Front Street, Marquette, Michigan 49855.

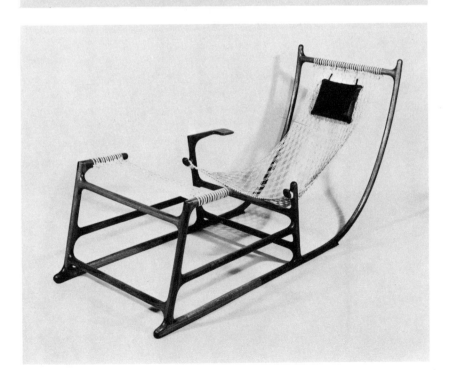

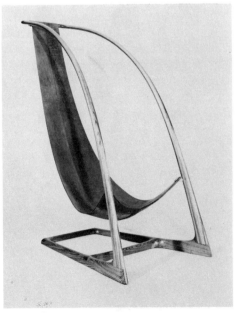

Leather Bags—Our bags are individually crafted of 3-oz. top-grain cowhide. Bags may be ordered smooth side out or suede side out, in dark brown, light brown, red rust or black. The Caterpillar (top left) has five separate compartments or ''cookie pockets.'' The bag is 18'' long, 23'' in circumference and 7'' high. Has adjustable shoulder strap plus handle across one end. $85. The Continental has 3 separate zippered compartments. Cookie pockets on either end are 2¾'' wide. Center compartment is 12'' long. Overall length 17½'', circumference 24'' and height 8''. $85. All postpaid.

Lloyd's of Leather—We started out in San Francisco in the late sixties, doing only hand leatherwork. We then bought a sewing machine and moved north to a very rural setting in Santa Rosa, selling leather garments to boutiques in San Francisco and, later, New York, Chicago and Seattle.

We now have a permanent home, a sound old house on a commercial lot in a mellow neighborhood. We do custom leather garments, moccasins and bags. Our business continues to grow in appreciation, and we have become members of the local Chamber of Commerce.

Kathy Sonheim and Lloyd Walton, c/o Lloyd's of Leather, 415 Goodman, Santa Rosa, California 95401.

Big Travel is designed for weekend jaunts. It has 2 small zippered pockets (5'' by 9'' by 2¼'') on one side and one large zippered pocket (8'' by 11¼'' by 2¼'') on the other, which has an extra flat pocket for maps. Un-attached cookie pocket accessory included. $125 postpaid.

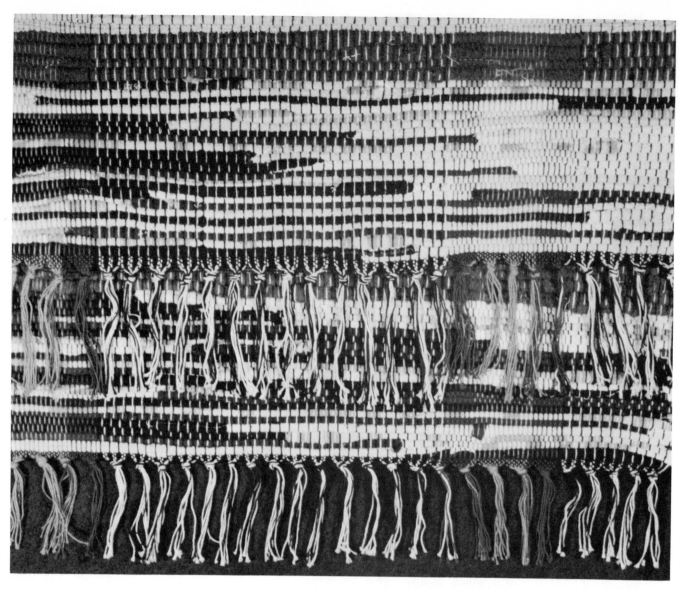

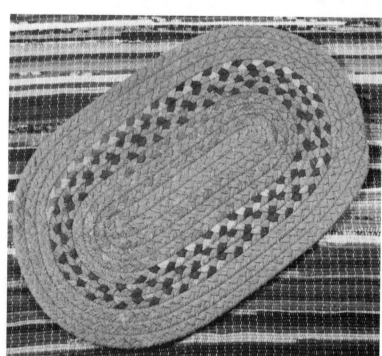

Rag Rugs—Our rugs are made of new wool rags or recycled miscellaneous rags, both machine-washable. Rag patterns are "hit-and-miss" (narrow strips) or broad strips of colors. Weaves are regular or San Francisco Everwearing Honeycomb ($4/yard extra). Sizes: 27'' by 54'', 32'' by 72'' and 36'' by 72''. Prices range from low of $5.50 (27'' by 54'' recycled rags, broad strips pattern) to high of $21.95 (32'' by 72'' new wool rags, hit-and-miss pattern).

Rag Carpeting—We make our rag carpeting in 27'', 32'' and 36'' lengths, sewn together ready to lay on floor. Materials, patterns and weaves same as rag rugs. Prices range from $4.95/yard (27'' recycled rags, broad strips) to $12.95/yard (32'' new wool rags, hit-and-miss, honeycomb). Only custom-made to your room measurements.

Rastetter Woolen Mill—The woolen mill we operate was started in 1840. It is now the oldest—and only—woolen mill in Ohio. My great-great-grandfather, who bought the mill in 1872, was a master weaver, weaving everything from 180''-long wool blankets to wool goods for suits. I am the fifth generation of male weavers to own and operate the mill.

My grandfather, who is now eighty years old and still weaving, started working for his grandfather at the woolen mill at age ten. When my great-great-grandfather died, my grandfather took over, concentrating on wool comforter making and weaving only rugs. After almost sixty-five years of weaving for a living, he was honored with a display of some of his rugs at the Smithsonian Institution in Washington, D.C. He still weaves the pattern displayed there, called "Brick and Block."

In 1973 my wife and I took over. Although we had no previous experience, we learned quickly and have prospered from my grandfather's wealth of knowledge. We have now doubled the number of looms going full-time. We've restored my great-great-grandfather's carding machine to its original working condition; it is now the oldest operating carding machine in the U.S.

Because we are a family-owned and family-operated business, we have very low overhead and all our prices reflect this savings. We specialize in custom work. We can make comforters from your wool or down, pillows from your feathers or rugs from your cut and sewn rags. Or we'll supply the materials.

Stop by if you're in the vicinity, and take a look at our carding, spinning and weaving operations.

Tim and Maureen Rastetter, c/o Rastetter Woolen Mill, Star Route, Millersburg, Ohio 44654.

195

Highchair—The highchair is made of Honduras mahogany and black walnut. It measures 46'' by 16'' by 16'' and weighs 45 lbs. $350, shipping not included.

Untitled Box—The box is made of beech and has two invisible Soss hinges. It measures 12'' by 8'' by 6'' and weighs 14 lbs. $125, shipping not included.

Richard String—As far back as I can remember I have worked with my father on the weekends in his workshop, learning how to work with wood. When I was sixteen, attending Cranbrook, the students and the environment inspired me to create. Now, after a few years of traveling, experiencing different environments and seeing people creating with their hands, I have found an environment and a medium that expresses my feelings and ideas.

At present, I am enrolled at Northern Michigan University in Marquette, Michigan. My major is furniture design. My goal is to work with and research wood and other materials, to support myself with my hands and my mind.

Each piece I create has an individual personality, reflecting the thought and time involved in producing a usable artifact. The challenge to communicate ideas with the hands is infinite.

Richard String, 229 Carey, Marquette, Michigan 49855.

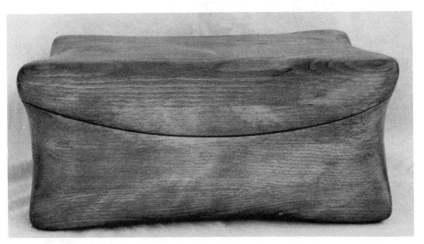

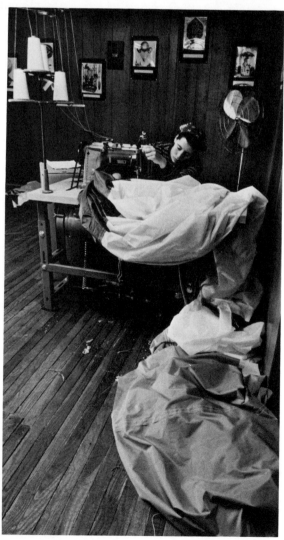

Balloons—We hand-craft wicker carriages for use with hot-air balloons. We also construct the envelopes, the balloon burner and the associated fuel system. The entire balloon system has been carefully designed as an integration of form with function, and is fully certified by the FAA. Our carriages provide a secure, logical, convenient location for flight controls, plumbing, fuel and burner. Carriages have a sculpted rattan structure that cushions even the worst landings. The triangular shape provides three useful long sides, and corner coves or pods into which fuel cylinders, instruments and controls are conveniently recessed. Sizes are 4.0, 4.5 and 5.5. Each size is designated in feet by its minimum floor dimension—from corner to corner to the midpoint of the opposite side. We have developed an envelope fabrication design that overcomes the deterioration problems that plague balloons made of nylon. Our coated polyester fabric outlasts nylon at least two to one. The T-Cote Polyester balloon fabric can operate continuously at 300°F. or 50° higher than any other balloon certified by the FAA. Our polyester envelopes can carry greater loads, go to higher altitudes and last several times longer than nylon ones. Prices range from $3,995 for the 4.0 DragonFly to $8,925 for the 5.5 FireFly.

The Balloon Works—Our only product is balloons. We hand-craft all parts here in the plant, using power woodworking, metalworking and textile sewing machines. None of these machines mass-produce but, rather, all are hand-guided and similar to home shop equipment. The Balloon Works is a closed corporation with three stockholders. We do not belong to any craft guilds, but many of our employees have an additional craft and individually belong to craft cooperatives here in North Carolina. We do a great deal of custom design work from customers' specifications or those of our own artists. The Balloon Works was chosen as one of the hundred finest producers of craft multiples in the U.S. as a Bicentennial project of the Renwick Gallery of the Smithsonian Institution, Washington, D.C.

Our plant is located in a rural area in the foothills of the Blue Ridge Mountains. We believe we successfully combine multiple production of a federally-specified product with the tradition of craftsmanship and create a viable company with a superior product.

The Balloon Works, Rhyne Aerodrome, R.F.D. 2, Statesville, North Carolina 28677.

199

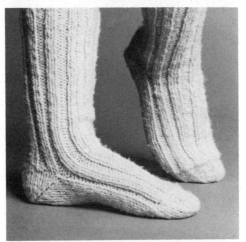

Hand-spun Yarn—Hand-spun 100% virgin wool yarn for knitting, weaving and stitchery. Wool of this warmth and durability cannot be found in any store. Naturally dyed with indigo, Queen Anne's lace, walnut shells and cochineal bugs in colors of the rainbow. One-ply weaving and two-ply knitting yarns, $4.75 per 3 to 4-oz. skein; stitchery yarn, $2.75 per 25 yards of 5 colors (reds, blues, yellows or mixed); naturally dyed yarn, $2.25 per oz.

Kits—Kit for knitting a Shropshire hat includes two skeins of natural off-white wool, instructions and personalized label, $14.25. Kit for Southdown socks includes instructions for knitting and care, special cloth label for your signature, and either 6 rainbow colors of naturally dyed yarn mixed with natural off-white, $29.50; 2 shades of naturally dyed yarn mixed with off-white, $29; or all natural off-white, sheep-colored yarn, $27.
Kit for Sok Kaleder, the sensible Icelandic shoe sock that can be worn inside boots, contains light leather soles, natural hand-spun wool and instructions, $7. All postpaid.

Shelburne Spinners—We are a nonprofit school set up to teach disadvantaged people how to hand-spin and market their own yarn. Our beginning came in trying to promote the agricultural land and heritage of Vermont, while producing something of value from start to finish with our hands.

After working together in the long task of preparing wool, we take carded rovings home to spin into yarn and finally return skeins to the shop, where we judge them for quality.

We have been purchasing three to five tons of wool annually in order to proceed through our nine involved steps of yarn preparation. We feel our yarn is unique for its rich natural colors and its soft yet durable design.

Martha Illick, c/o Shelburne Spinners, Box 651, Burlington, Vermont 05401.

Grandfather Clocks—These grandfather clocks are works of art, handcrafted from black walnut, the aristocrat of hardwoods chosen by generations of craftsmen. Each piece of wood has been carefully chosen for its particular place and matched one at a time. A clear lacquer finish makes the black walnut wood stand out beautifully. The movements are made in West Germany by famous clocksmiths and are fully guaranteed. Each has a moon-moving dial and 3 different chimes. Shipping weight is 175 lbs. The clock measures 18'' wide, 6'8'' high and 11½'' deep. $795 shipped freight collect.

Weather Stations—These weather stations are made of solid black walnut wood with an inlay of ebony and birch at the top, a recessed thermometer with brass trim, a precise barometer made in England and a hygrometer made in Germany at the bottom. Measures 10'' wide, 33'' high and 2'' deep, weighs about 5 lbs. $125 postpaid.

Donald Rapp—I have been involved in woodworking all of my life. From 1940 until 1970 I was a building contractor specializing in the best of workmanship. In 1970 I joined the Postal Service, and I hope to retire with a pension in another year or so. I have been making grandfather clocks (twenty so far) and doing other odd jobs of carpentry and cabinet-making in my spare time.

If the demand develops, I hope that I can work full-time making grandfather clocks.

Donald Rapp, 606 Lake Street, Chadron, Nebraska 69337.

1.

2.

3.

4.

5.

Knives—These knives are hand-fashioned from the finest quality carbon steel, which has been recycled from lumber-mill saw blades. The handles are made from the choicest exotic hardwoods. The sheaths are wet-formed to each individual knife and hand-sewn. The etchings are cut freehand into a wax resist and bitten directly into the steel with aqua riga acid. Thus, each etching is unique.

1. Chinese Chopping knife has a 4½'' blade, brass bolster, Lignumvitae handle and lion and girl etching. $160.

2. Carving knife has a 9½'' blade, brass bolster, Lignumvitae handle and leafy scroll etching. $230.

3. Filet knife has a 10'' blade, brass bolster, pau Brazil handle and birds of paradise etching. $165.

4. Light Kitchen Utility knife has a 6'' blade, pau Brazil handle and doves and roses etching. $80.

5. French Chef's knife—the most useful single kitchen knife—used for all chopping, dicing, and carving done on a board. The knife has a 7'' blade, pau Brazil handle, brass bolster, and fairy child etching. $160. Brochure available. Prices do not include shipping.

David Boye Knives—The knives are a product of a cottage industry in Davenport, California. The principle craftspersons responsible are David Boye and Dennis Bodewitz, who make the knives, and Francine Martin, who does etchings, and trains and supervises other etchers.

Philosophically, we feel that the knives offer us the opportunity to work creatively and under our own direction. The knives represent the loving synthesis of artistic expression and fine craftsmanship in a common useful object.

David Boye, c/o David Boye Knives, Box 187, Davenport, California 95017.

Silver Antler Tip Necklace—This necklace won a place in the Craft Multiples exhibition at the Renwick Gallery of the Smithsonian Institution. For the last six years I've made a limited number of these necklaces, no two exactly alike. Each bead is laboriously made in graduating sizes from flat sterling silver sheets. Each bead and cap is stamped with a radiating design. The antler is buffed to a deep amber color. Length 25¼'', $750, postpaid.

Belt Buckles—Designed for 2'' belts, these buckles measure approximately 3'' by 2½''. From left to right, Silver Skull, with copper horns on stippled brass landscape; Armadillo Rising, a silver armadillo rising from a copper earthscape on a brass background; Rising Sun, an age-old motif executed in three contrasting metals (sun and cactus in silver on a copper landscape with brass background). To construct such buckles is no easy task considering the three different melting temperatures of these metals. Each part is cut by hand, then silver-soldered flat together, after which the figures are stamped and engraved to a high degree of detail. Each buckle is buffed to a high shine which lasts indefinitely. $35.

Weldon Merchant—As a single individual craftsman, my sole support and life's blood is derived from the works my hands and mind concoct. There was no distinct beginning to my profession as an artist-craftsman. As a child growing up in rural Northeast Mississippi, I learned to work horn from my father, to pump the bellows in the blacksmith shop for the old smith while the horses were shoed, to make whips and whittle with the old men who sat by the fire passing wintry nights. Being raised in a rural environment where so many things must be made or repaired gave me a good basis for my life as a craftsman.

Presently I'm in the process of building my own dream studio/home, employing all of my metalworking, wood-butchering and sculptural skills. At the age of twenty-eight, I'm single and singly involved in my work and life, which flows as one with all around me.

Weldon Merchant, Route 2, Box 444, West Point, Mississippi 39773.

Picture Pillows—The "Palm Tree" and "Ocean Tides" pillows are 18" square. The applique of velvet, satin and corduroy in earth tones gives these pillows a rich textural variety. Pillows are kapok-filled, with zippered covers for easy dry-cleaning. The Palm Tree has shades of forest-green velvet, with a pale green satin sky. The sun is rust-orange and the tree trunk is brown. Ocean Tides has green land, a blue ocean with pale blue satin foam and a tan beach. The sky is blue with a gold satin sun. $30 each, shipping not included.

Quilts—Shown here at the Sausalito Art Festival, where my "California Coast" won the Best Seascape award. Appliqued velvets, satins and corduroys in earth tones. "Butterfly" available in blues and greens or browns and oranges. Filled with top-quality dacron polyester, they are warm, light and dry-cleanable. King or queen size. $395, shipping not included.

Jeri's California Quilts—I have always loved fabrics. The first quilt I tackled was a very special gift for a close friend. It took weeks to put together, but I found that I enjoyed every minute and the result was a success.

Before long someone asked to order one, and I was happy for the chance to create with fabrics again. Now it is a full-time occupation. My work has won prizes and is shown in galleries.

Although the many hours required and the high cost of fabric make financial survival difficult, I love my work and love the freedom of being my own boss.

Jeri Brittell, c/o Jeri's California Quilts, Industrial Center Building, Room 345, Sausalito, California 94965.

Hand-painted Eggshells—The birds that lay my eggs are all cared for naturally (as opposed to commercially), which makes for stronger eggshells from the start. Each egg is emptied, cleaned internally and externally, dried and painted in pen and ink and watercolors. Each is then coated with a glossy resin that protects the painting and strengthens the shell itself. Quail, chicken, duck, turkey, peacock and ostrich eggs are among those available. Colors include white, beige, brown, blue, green and spotted. The eggs are incredibly light and need to be packed carefully. Shipping costs, including insurance, are $2.50 per package. Ceramic stands are included with the price of each regular egg. Blackwood

Oriental-style stands for larger eggs are $2.50 each.
California Quail with California Poppies: painted on a brown chicken egg. About 1½'' wide and 2¼'' high. Painting continues around the egg. Predominant colors are dark and light brown, green, gold and blue. $17.
Unicorn: painted on a white duck egg. About 1¾'' wide and 2¼'' high. Painting continues around egg and contains violets, a tree and a crescent moon. Predominant colors: white, blue, purple-gray and green. $19.
Panda and Baby: painted on a light blue duck egg. About 1¾'' wide and 2¼'' high. Painting continues around the egg and contains bamboo plants and rocks. Predominant colors: black, white, green, gray and blue. $22.
Japanese Woman in Kimono: painted on a white duck egg. About 1¾'' wide and 2¼'' high. The painting covers two-thirds of the egg surface and contains a subtle design on the kimono. Predominant colors: black, beige and red. $21.

Anne Byrd Easley—Me?! Well . . . I don't really think of myself as an egg artist—or as an artist—or as a craftsperson. I have slipped into something I enjoy that I can make money at. I am lucky—I live in the mountains, in towers that my husband Dale is building on (and on and on . . .), with a huge pond, a lot of ancient apple trees, mud in winter, dust in summer and hundreds of bushes and wonderful plants all around. I work almost every single day in the main upstairs tower, sitting on a brass bed with pillows all around to minimize breakage while I work.

Weekends we drive far and wide to art and craft shows. Dale takes care of me and builds. Rita, our scruffy dog, takes care of both of us.
Anne Byrd Easley, P.O. Box 538, Boulder Creek, California 95006.

209

Personalized Stationery—Available in 130 styles, including families of Antiques, Emblems, Fish, Fowl, Menagerie, Bestiary, Victorians, Pursuits and Ornaments images. Custom orders welcome. Personalized note cards, 50/$26, 100/$34, 50 more/$12. Note cards with plain envelopes, 50/$33, 100/$44, 50 more/$16. Note card with personalized envelopes, 50/$52, 100/$64, 50 more/$22. Calling cards, 125/$22, 250/$28, 500/$40. Gummed bookplate and/or container label, 100/$15, 200/$22. Memo Pad, 5 pads of 100 sheets each, $20.

Subtle and Co.—It all started some years ago in a cottage in Normandy Village, a picturesque corner of Berkeley. Susan Subtle began producing calling cards for friends and acquaintances, using their own drawings, old woodcuts and what have you. She calls it "Your Name in Sights" and she's arrived at a distinctive look. The items range from party invitations to scratch pads.

Susan Subtle, c/o Subtle & Company, P.O. Box 9323, Berkeley, California 94709.

Lidded Bowl—Copper and/or nickel, electroplated onto the finished pot lids, highlights these shallow containers. During the controlled plating the metals develop rich textures with delicate networks resembling relief maps of the countryside. Inlays of brightly colored glazes introduce flashes of color into the metalwork on some of the lids. Metals are firmly bonded to the ceramic surfaces. Bowls are hand-thrown from fine translucent porcelain, available in 2 glazes: white or wood ash (caramel-brown, pebbly). Bowls are 1'' to 1½'' deep and 5½'' to 6'' in diameter. Weight: 2 lbs. packed. $40, shipping not included.

Dawn King—I like to think of my work as "jewelry for environments." I hope the pots will be selected to decorate homes just as people choose rings or necklaces to decorate themselves. My goal is to provide quality workmanship integrated into objects of beauty.

I am an ex-biologist and draw much inspiration from the forms and intricate structures of the living world. It would give me great joy to think that some of my work might remind people how closely entwined mankind is in the delicate network of life on the earth and in the universe.

Dawn King, 2950 Avocado Court, Newbury Park, California 91320.

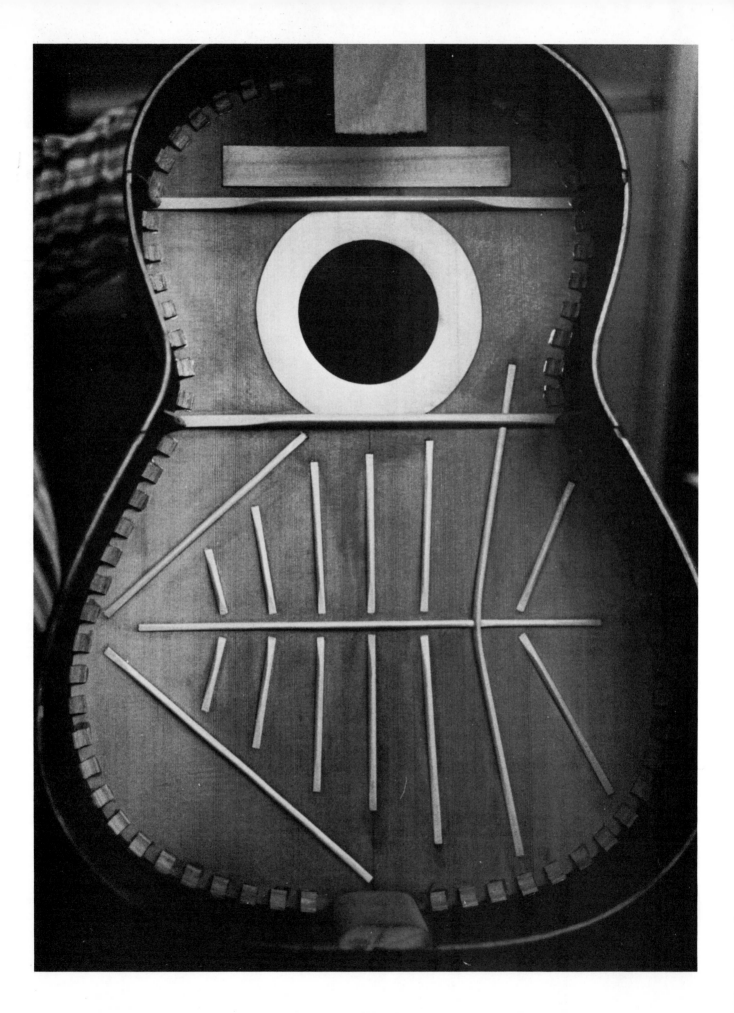

**Classical and Steel-stringed
Guitars**—Brazilian or East Indian
rosewood backs and sides, European
spruce or Western red cedar tops,
ebony fingerboards and ivory nuts
and bridge saddles. Instruments are
priced between $950 and $1,200,
depending upon materials and
aesthetic options. Custom order
inquiries invited. Guitar and case
packed for shipment weigh 15 lbs.
Shown: classical guitar, $1,000.

John Mello—I started to work on
instruments while completing a
degree in Communications at Oberlin
College. After saving enough money
to support myself during an
apprenticeship, I went to study under
Richard Schneider, a luthier whose
work I admired. Upon completion of
the apprenticeship I opened an
instrument repair and restoration
shop in Detroit. After two years I
moved to Berkeley; I now have a shop
in the basement of a local music store.
 It is hard for a young guitar maker
to build a reputation, particularly with
the prices hand-crafted instruments
dictate. At present repairs and
restorations make up a large part of
my income. As my reputation grows,
however, I hope to devote most of my
time to the construction of
instruments of my own conception.
 *John Mello, 2277 Shattuck Avenue,
Berkeley, California 94704.*

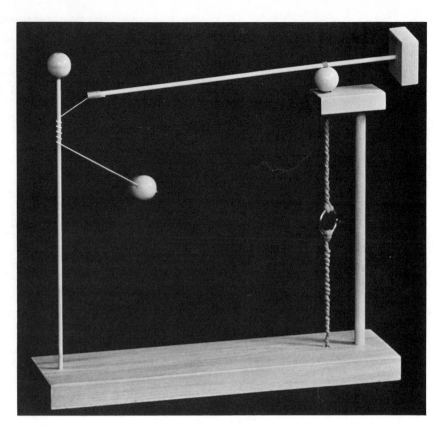

Wooden Toy—Swing Thing is an entertaining amusement device that also has educational value. Its action demonstrates several important concepts dealing with energy and motion. This modern American folk contraption is an instructive toy for inquisitive children, and intrigues people of all ages. Hand-crafted from wood and oil-finished, it comes in a boxed kit and is friction-fit for easy assembly in home, office, car or plane. It stands 10'' high assembled. $5 postpaid.

Solar West—Solar West is a partnership of a university professor and his son who operate out of their home workshop. They have been in business two years. Swing Thing was invented and patented by the father-son team as a result of their interest in gadgeteering.

Solar West, P.O. Box 1843, Fort Collins, Colorado 80522.

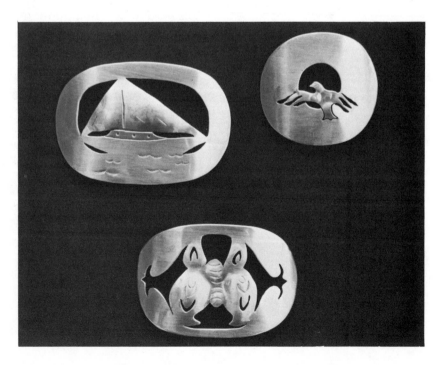

Belt Buckles—My buckles are made from brass or silver for 1¾'' belts. They measure 2-1/8'' by 2½'' or 2-1/8'' by 3''. Shown here are ship, bird-and-moon, and butterfly designs. Also available in sunburst and bird-and-mountain designs. Brass, $15, silver $115.

Brian Wizard—I have been an independent artist-craftsman for five years. I am a graduate of the School of Expressive Arts at California State College at Sonoma. I make my living off my own creative energy, providing my customers with many items of art and craft, including earrings, buttons, roach clips, coke tooters and hardwood walking sticks.

Brian Wizard, P.O. Box 755, Sebastopol, California 95472.

Kite Winder—This 4½'' by 4'' by 10'' clear acrylic kite winder is not only a marvelously manageable and easy-to-control reel for small kites, but quite elegant as a showpiece to set out on the shelf. Included with the reel is 50' of black 10 lb. test strength nylon cord and a brass kite clip. $14.95.

Hollis Dayton—I am—as many of my friends have labeled me—an industrial designer and a pack rat. I feel my perhaps overdone collecting of objects helps stimulate new ideas, but I'm not so sure my theory always works.

When I'm not working on my industrial design projects or collecting things, I enjoy the outdoors. We live in a wooded area outside Cincinnati and our creek is one of the most pleasurable places I know. Snow skiing and backpacking are my main escape outlets when I've had too much of school. The skiing tends to be difficult, as Ohio has to be one of the flattest states. But I usually manage a few trips during the season.

Hollis Dayton, 577 West Galbraith Road, Cincinnati, Ohio 45215.

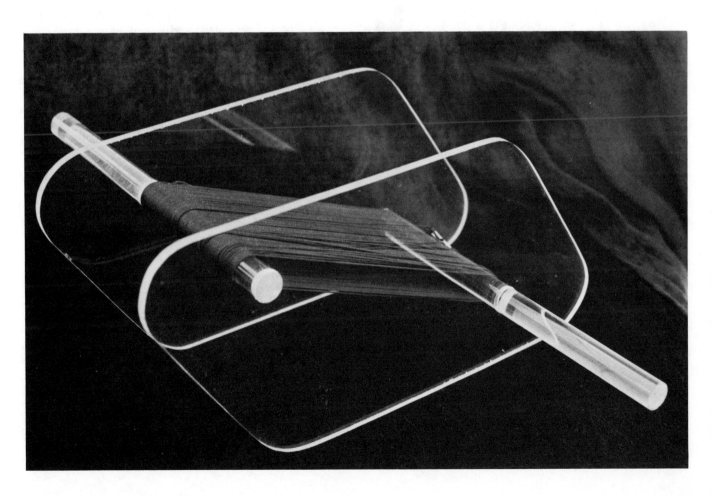

215

Metal Bells—Since 1958 Paolo Soleri has designed a series of original bells sculpted using the typical foundry sand-casting technique. These bells are distinctive insomuch as the well-known earth-forming method is augmented with patterns applied to the walls of the bell mold. The poured molten bronze then captures the sand patterns making each a Cosanti Foundation Original. Bells shown are: #376, $34; #176, $25; #276, $32, #476, $120. Shipping not included.

Paolo Soleri—"Cosanti" is from two Italian words meaning "before things." Arcology, Soleri's fusion of architecture and ecology, is the methodology that recognizes the necessity of the radical reorganization of the sprawling urban landscape into dense, integrated, three-dimensional cities.

The metal bell project is part of the growing economic base of the town of Arcosanti, which is being built as a full-scale demonstration of Paolo Soleri's theories. Thus these bells are not only beautiful to look at and a wonderful wind instrument, they are also products of a visionary attempt to transform the world.

Cosanti Foundation, 6433 Doubletree Road, Scottsdale, Arizona 85253.

Pillows—Designed by Sara Kramer in a variety of colors. Pillows come in sizes: 9'' by 12'', $25; 13'' by 14'', $30; 15'' by 16'', $35.

Wall Hangings—Large woven wall hangings reflect depth of visual insight with quality craftsmanship. Weavings are designed by the project artist and produced by the combined skills of the workers in the Studio. ''Counterpoint from Bolinas,'' created by Louaine Elke, $1,450. ''Introduction,'' created by Danielle Hochman, is an all-wool tapestry in brown and rust with wrapped weft, tapered fringe, $400.

Tenaya Weavers—We enjoy the stimulating combination of each person having his own work plus the sharing and interchange of ideas which brings energy and talents together in the creation of a new piece. This is of central importance to the operation of our studio.

We are a profit-sharing cooperative with an apprenticeship program for new members.

Tenaya Weavers, c/o Louaine Elke, P.O. Box 501, Kentfield, California 94904.

Buffalo Bird—Custom-designed dulcimer with two separate fingerboards to be played by two music lovers, facing each other, legs, interlocked, instrument on their combined lap. Each fingerboard embraces 2½ octaves of tones selected from the diatonic scale. There are two separate sound chambers designed to produce sympathetic tone qualities. The three-stringed fingerboard has a soft, ethereal quality. The six-stringed fingerboard has a very clear, strong, resonant sound and is designed to be played with complicated chord structures. Fingerboards, sides and back are British walnut. Top is Northern Red Cedar and was chosen for its straight grain and highly-valued acoustical properties. The supporting structural members are of Honduras mahogany, chosen to accentuate the bold lines of the walnut and cedar. Buffalo Bird is 12½'' wide by 40½'' long by 2½'' deep. $2,100.

Kuba—This dulcimer was created as an acoustical experiment. The two ''arms'' are hollowed and act as shock absorbers for the resounding air. The base side is abbreviated. The resulting sound is a clear, deep-throated mid-range tone with a very short sustain, highly reminiscent of the mandolin. Made of cherry, spruce, Honduras mahogany, Indian rosewood and American walnut.

Kuba is 14½'' wide by 39'' long by 2¾'' deep. $1,900.

If you are interested in having one of these musical oddities created for you, share your time and thoughts with me. I will sit in my Northern Vermont studio and design five or six alternates and through correspondence with you come up with a musical sculpture which is unique and created especially for you. (No traditional Appalachian mountain dulcimer orders taken.)

Ken Riportella—The dulcimer is a vehicle through which one can transcend inner fear and frustration. It brings us in touch with a pure, uncluttered inner self, filling us with a good sense of who we might become.

Out on the frontier, frolicking naked in a climate of innovation and change, the form of the sculpture is inseparable from the sound. It is interdependent with its function. No doubt there is tremendous joy and fulfillment in creating out of mere sticks of wood an art form that is so alive, so robust that it literally sings with you. I mold this wood, as if it were clay, into amorphic freeform beings. As a craftsperson my mission is to create by illusion. As a human being my mission is to put total love and devotion into all I create.

Ken Riportella, East Calais, Vermont 05650.

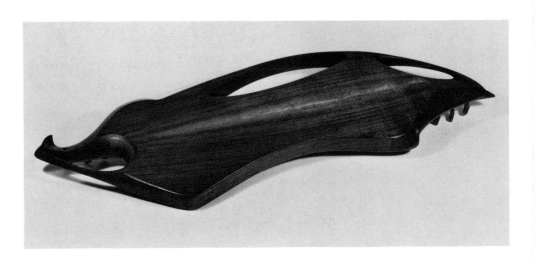

Hooded Cape—The cape is woven with mohair, brushed wool and a nubby wool blend imported from Ireland. It has been brushed with a natural teasel to increase its luxuriousness. Leather or natural wood buttons accent the front closing, and one size fits all. Petite sizes can be made by special order. The available colors are: Sand Mist (a soft gray-beige), Almond Mist (a darker gray-brown, Gray Mist (a silver-gray-white) and White. Yarn swatches of colors available upon request. Terms: ⅓ deposit with order, balance C.O.D. Style #35, $260.

Tweed Tunic—This pullover tweed tunic is a combination of imported Donegal Tweeds and hand-spun wools in several color combinations. Yarn samples are available for $1 in the following colors: brown/beige (shown), gray/beige, white/white, rust brown/brown, soft silver green/cream. Small (8 to 10), medium (12-14) and large (16 to 18). Special men's sizes may also be requested. Terms: ⅓ deposit with order, balance C.O.D. Style #30, women's sizes, $160; men's sizes, $175.

Mandarin Jacket—This mandarin-collared, fully lined short jacket is woven with white mohair and a textured gray/tan wool blend imported from Ireland. Elegant enough to be worn as an evening jacket, it is also sporty enough to be worn during the day. Hand-crocheted loops and double glass or mother-of-pearl buttons accent the front. Small (8 to 10), medium (12 to 14) and large (16 to 18). Terms: ⅓ deposit with order, balance C.O.D. Style #34, $230.

Woodland Weavery—I am the major textile designer for Woodland Weavery in Pittsburgh, Pennsylvania. Woodland Weavery is primarily known for its production of interior furnishings including pillows, carpets, draperies and large tapestries for industries and private firms.

My designs are inspired by the earth: the textures of rocky hillsides, the regular patterns of plowed fields, the softness of drifted snow. Weaving these elegant pieces in such a rustic setting is so correct. I do a lot of walking in the woods near my home and I do a lot of contemplating before I see a new design on the surface of a tree or in the bottom of a pond. When I need a color I go to the earth: soft golds, rusts and greens are hand-dyed using vegetable matter as the coloring agent.

Woodland Weavery has a new brochure which is available for $2.

Rebecca Jane Noble, c/o Woodland Weavery, 623 Center Avenue, Pittsburgh, Pennsylvania 15215.

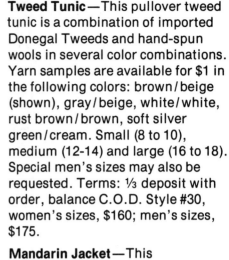

Porcelain Necklaces—The pendants are individually made from raw porcelain. They are a combination of freehand drawings and impressions of organic matter such as sea shells and sea urchins. Glazing is done with my own special formula. The beads begin as powdered porcelain, to which high-fire stains and water are added to form colored clay. Each bead is then hand-rolled, fired and polished to a smooth finish. Specify 18'' or 24'' necklace length. The Earth (bird and tree), amber and brown, $10. The Sea (hills, water and sun), blue and tan, $10. The Sky (star) blue and brown or amber and brown, $10.

Lena Orlando—My home is on the Mendocino coast; all of my work reflects the environment around me. Intricacy and perfection in the designs drawn by nature astound me: the ruggedness of the sea, the clarity of the night sky, the ease with which birds soar.

My medium is porcelain and along with the jewelry displayed in this catalog, I do clocks, wall-mounted oil lamps and candleholders, all of which attempt to present a glimpse of our natural environment.

I guess if an artist's work comments on the times in which we live, my comment is ''Stop, listen, look around and please, stay still long enough to really hear and see.'' We need this earth.

Lena Orlando, P.O. Box 403, Point Arena, California 95468.

Steel and Glass Furnishings—All pieces are hand-forged and welded in limited editions. Stained-glass inlays are placed in carefully selected areas of most pieces. Steel chair: 58'' high by 22½'' wide by 19½'' deep. $275. Music stand: the design of the upper portion comes in 10 variations, determined by where the music is held. Dimensions: 20'' wide by 56'' high by 15'' deep. $80. Music stand with wooden tripod: peacock motif in cobalt blue and emerald green glass. $1,000. Shipping not included.

Lawless Studios—I first began working with steel in 1971 under Konstantine Milonadis, artist-in-residence at the University of Notre Dame. In 1976 I organized my studio in Buffalo and began to explore the possibilities of combining stained glass with other materials such as steel, wood and concrete—those materials which best reflect the spirit of this age.

Billie Lawless, c/o Lawless Studios, 324 Highgate Avenue, Buffalo, New York 14215.

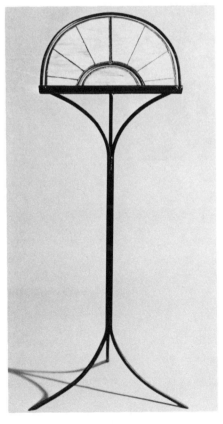

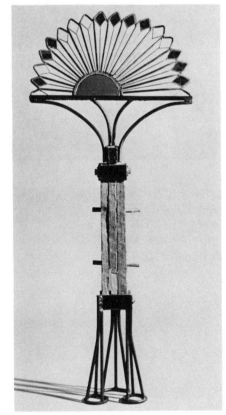

223

Bob and Bill Ayre, c/o Ayre & Ayre, 1825 Kentucky North East, Albuquerque, New Mexico 87110.

Jewelry—All of our jewelry is available with selected lace agates. Most pieces are available with picture jaspers, petrified dinosaur bone, palm wood and other agates. Indicate your color preferences. Picture jaspers are usually about 20% higher than agate. Rings (left to right): stone size 1½'' by 1¾'', $35; stone size ¾'' by 1-1/16'', $30; stone size ¾'' by 1½, $35; agate with 6 garnets, $75. Bracelets (left to right): domed heavy metal (brass) with stone, $35; 3-wire, 1½'' by 1¾'' agate, $55; 2-wire, 1½'' by 1¾'' agate, $50; 3-wire, 1½'' by 1¾'' jasper, $65 up. All prices postpaid. Catalog, $1, refundable with order.

Ayre & Ayre—A father-and-son team of contemporary metalsmiths. Bob gave up a career in electronics five years ago and has been making jewelry ever since. Bill picked up on his father's work but branched out and worked for several jewelry shops in Albuquerque for two years. In early 1976 they joined to form Ayre & Ayre Silversmiths. Bob is now forty-one and Bill is twenty.

Peasant Dress—We hand-brush hot wax through our own stencils, hand-dye the material and sew it in our own designs. Our cotton batiste peasant dress is available in violet with Grecian geese (as shown), or in terra cotta with African gazelles. The dress comes in sizes small (6 to 8), medium (10 to 12) and large (14 to 16). $110 postpaid. Hand-crafted scarves, sarongs, blouses and skirts also available in various colors and designs.

Ariadne's Thread Works—The Works is evolving into a true cottage industry. My apprentices and I are learning more and more about batik, weaving, pattern making and clothing construction, textile history, dyeing and world culture. We are very serious about our work and hope that our company grows strong and inspires other people to start their own small businesses as an alternative to the textile mills and sewing sweatshops prevalent in our society.

My batik designs grow out of very ancient or traditional motifs in the arts and crafts of a variety of cultures. I hope that those who wear my clothes will be enchanted by both the product and the system of work and cooperation that produces the threads of Ariadne.
Deborah Henry, c/o Ariadne's Thread Works, 2611 Fulton Street, Berkeley, California 94704.

M Square—A participatory manipulative sculpture and mechanism for placing planes in space. A nondestructible toy for aesthetic play, the M square is alluring to adults and children. This unique and original sculpture concept is featured in the collection of the Museum of Modern Art in New York. The double square configuration is just one of a family of forms that I have developed over the last seven years to explore the hinge. Shown here are a few of the configurations possible, but what makes the piece remarkable is the interaction that takes place in the process of reforming the shape. Made of .040'' brass plate formed with integral hinges and steel pins. Overall size is 5'' by 7''. Comes in brown flannel pouch. Edition limited to 500. $50, shipping not included.

Merle Steir—My preoccupation is with large sculptures and the occasional publishing of maquettes as related to my sculptural concerns. I make both limited and unlimited editions of my sculptures depending upon the nature of the piece.

My recent professional experience includes being an instructor at several New York art schools, as well as art consultant to the District of Columbia Redevelopment Land Agency in Washington, D.C.

Merle L. Steir, 237 Centre Street, New York, New York 10013.

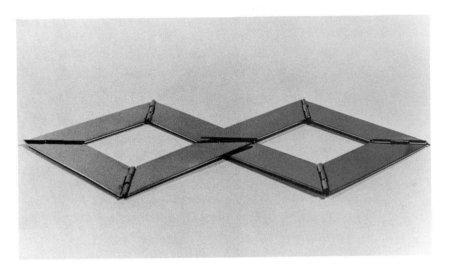

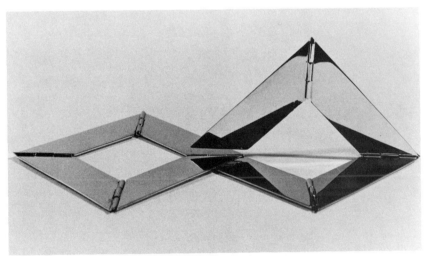

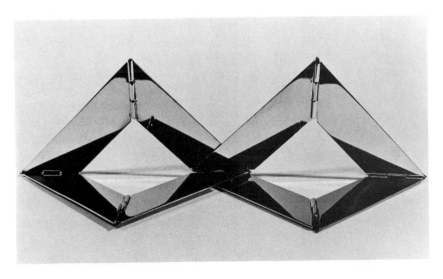

Dolls—Lewis Carroll doll was originally done as a joke, as Alice is almost a cliche with doll artists and no one had ever done Lewis before. I found his picture in a book of his own photography and he appealed to me. He represents a sample of my portrait work, which I do on commission. The Lewis doll is 28'' tall. He has a porcelain head and human hair eyelashes and brows. The hairs are applied one at a time directly to the head. He wears a three-piece Victorian suit. $252 postpaid. Baby doll is about 8'' tall. It has a porcelain head and hands and a soft stuffed fabric body, constructed to assume many of the positions and attitudes of a real infant. This doll has human hair eyelashes and comes dressed in either a modern stretch suit or a traditional christening gown. $42 postpaid. The Muses (opposite page, top and right) are female figures 21'' high. They have porcelain heads, necks, hands and feet, muslin bodies stuffed with sawdust, turning heads and arms wired for positioning. Their wigs are human hair, and their human hair eyelashes are singly applied. Available dressed or nude, $102 or $82 postpaid. Dolls are made in limited editions. Each is signed, numbered and copyrighted. Orders will take about 4 months. Deposit of ⅓ required with order.

Panna Hess Dolls—Dolls move something in people, touch a part of them that's deep and personal. Everywhere I turn I find incredible interest. Doll making is a highly personal art form. Dolls are soft, they move, sit in your lap, hang out in your living room, listen, wait for you to come home. It's really an intimate relationship.

For me, as an artist, doll making is the best of all possible worlds. I sculpt, I paint, I design, I make wigs, clothing, shoes, accessories, jewelry and furniture. Small has always been enchanting to me. I never outgrew a devout belief in the "little people," and as no one had every quite "caught" them the way I saw them, I decided it was for me to do.

There are many aspects of the process which are difficult, tedious and exacting, and yet every time a doll is completed and is sitting there grinning at me, my joy is so complete that I pity all the people in the world who are not doll makers.

Panna Hess, c/o Panna Hess Dolls, 480 Sixth Avenue, Salt Lake City, Utah 84103.

Velveteen Pouches—These pouches are 100% cotton velveteen, hand-embroidered with DMC thread and glass beads. Available with drawstring or ribbon. The pouches are fully lined and come in almost any color. They are 6'' wide and 9'' high. $18 postpaid.

Compton O'Shaughnessy—My husband and I are trying to fix up a two-hundred-year-old log house in a lovely hollow, with pure water very close by. I am most interested in the healing herbs that proliferate all around us.

My embroidered mandalas are an outgrowth of my own centering and the joyous celebration of the rainbow patterns of all life everywhere. It's wonderful! Wonderful!

Compton O'Shaughnessy, Route 1, Box 159, Vesuvius, Virginia 24483.

Patchwork-edged Butcher Apron—Made from natural or blue denim, this apron fits both men and women, and is completely washable. There are no exposed edges or seams for strength and longevity. About 25'' by 22'', $12.50 postpaid.

The Patch Works—I began to understand the unique craft heritage I was endowed with when I came to the Midwest in the late sixties. Here were women making beautiful, traditional hand-sewn crafts I had seen only in pioneer museums in my mother's home state of Utah.

In 1974 I began to organize a cooperative sales effort and coordinate the designs for a line of handmade items. Women from all walks of life came to me—coal miners' wives, woodcarvers' wives, students, senior citizens and even professors' wives. They are the living fabric of the tradition.

Judith Tomlinson Trager, c/o The Patch Works, 801 South Johnson Street, Carbondale, Illinois 62901.

Ceramic Pins—Finely hand-painted pins made individually. Both underglazes and overglazes are applied for bright colors and detail. From 2 to 5 kiln firings are needed to produce a finished pin. Pins range from ½'' to 1¾'' in length. A safety clasp is epoxied to the back of each pin. Top row: fried egg, flying heart and red heart, $1 each. Middle row: golden eye duck and sundae, $1.50 each; Eskimo pie, ice-cream cone and popsicle, $1 each. Bottom row: auto, palm scene star and truck, $2 each. $5 minimum order, shipping not included.

Bob's Dog-Gone Ceramics—From a basement workshop in hilly Oakland come Bob's Dog-Gone Ceramic Pins. Button Bob has been making ceramic jewelry for five years and has developed more than thirty designs.

Robert Sumner, c/o Bob's Dog-Gone Ceramics, 5416 Lawton Avenue, Oakland, California 94618.

Jewelry—Sterling silver and stones. Gold prices on request. From left to right: lotus ring is lost-wax cast from an original wax carving, $35. Split-wire bracelet comes with either rectangular or oval stone. Shown with Biggs jasper, $175. Band ring comes with oval, round, teardrop or rectangular (with rounded corners) stone shapes. Shown with malachite, $40. Wing ring, $35. Gypsy ring pattern wraps around the stone. Its effect is created by pierced overlay and oxidation of the bottom layer of silver, $35. Tuley sunrise is a cut-out overlaid pattern of a stylized sunrise (sunset?). Stone shape is always a long oval, as shown, $35. Fleetwood is the Cadillac of ring designs, $30. Band ring with Biggs jasper, $40. Silver box with lace agate stone. Size and shape of each box is determined by the stone set in the top. Made with silver 1mm. thick, collector's quality, $60.

John Bagley and Carol Hotchkiss—We were both in publishing before starting business together. Two years ago we pulled into Guerneville and found a shop space with two redwood trees growing up through the back porch. We also found Leo and Terry and Rick and Jack and all the gang. We're now a working "family." Our common goal is to own a ranch where we and our children can live and grow together.

Our life and work are integrated—no one can see where one stops and the other begins. If we aren't digging rock, making jewelry or cutting stones, we'll be working on our machinery. Our whole trip revolves around love and love of rock. People say, "They must have rocks in their heads!" We do! By the time we're through we'd like to give Tiffany and Cartier a run for their money.

John Bagley and Carol Hotchkiss, 17140 River Road, Guerneville, California 95446.

Fans—We weave and construct natural fibers, fronds, dried flowers and feathers into fans of many sizes, shapes and styles. These fans run the gamut from exotic to whimsical. They are often functional and certainly beautiful. Our fans are originals or reproductions of ancient shapes and styles. Guinea hen feather fans, above and below, $36 each. Peacock feather fan, $27. Shipping not included.

Fanne's—Our day-to-day involvement with fan making grew out of an interest in the historical information, the countless stories and samples we've seen. The usefulness of the fan, as well as its beauty and playfulness has come alive for us.

We work as a family. I have been involved with weaving and other arts since childhood, professionally since 1966. Our lives really revolve around our garden, where we now grow almost all of our own materials for use in making fans (as well as most of our own food), and our studio-workshop where we sort, prepare and clean materials and make our woven flower fans and dream over new creations.

Pamela Yates, c/o Fanne's, P.O.Box 323, Graton, California 95444.

Woven Pillows—Patterned pillows made from Scandinavian and Mexican wool with polyester stuffing. Four colors in each pillow—two complementary colors with related hues, or four bright contrasting colors. Each pillow is individually designed. Size: 16'' by 16'', $36 postpaid. Also available in 30'' by 30'' size, same materials plus a fluffy, thick wool roving in one of the four colors. $83 postpaid.

Wendy Niles—The textiles field is one of diverse experiences, and I enjoy all of them.

Most important of all, I enjoy my association with the vital crafts movement that is now consistently offering the public well-made, individually designed, hand-crafted products. The integrity of handmade objects is unquestionable and the joy of creating them is unequalled.

Wendy Niles, Box 473, Richmond, California 94807.

Batiks—My batiks are often representational, with subjects not usually depicted in batik. The work shown here is done on Irish linen with Procion dyes unless otherwise indicated. The finished batiks have been dry-cleaned to remove all wax, and then mounted on ¾'' by ¾'' stretcher frames.

Noah's Ark: white, yellow, gold, browns, reds, gray and black; 23'' by 33'', $50, shipping not included.

Three Japanese Beauties: pale yellow, coral, periwinkle, turquoise, dark blue, black, white background, 22'' by 28'', $40, shipping not included.

Stitched Figure with Peacock: black stitching on white cotton-polyester fabric; peacock's tail is batiked fabric (blues, greens and purple) appliqued to padded background, 13'' by 20'', $40, shipping not included.

Beer Drinkers: yellow, gold, orange, greens, available with either a dark red or a dark green background, 10'' by 10'', $15, shipping not included.

Fourth Dimension Batik—I have been working with batik since graduating from college with a degree in political philosophy four years ago. I was amazed to discover there was actually more of a demand for batik than there was for political theory, and batik has subsequently become my only source of income. I work alone, since I am the only one brave enough to enter the fume-filled pit—my studio.

My batiks have been predominantly decorative; however, I have been experimenting with functional pieces recently: placemats, backgammon boards, purses and scarves. I try to keep my prices reasonably low, because I feel that well-designed and executed crafts should be within the reach of the average person's means.

Phyllis Charles, c/o Fourth Dimension Batik, 42 Maple Avenue, Hamilton, New York 13346.

Silver Pin—Fabricated hollow rectangular box is 20-gauge silver. Dimensions: 1½'' wide, 1½'' high, including drop, and 3/8'' deep. The box has a satin finish. The drop is carved epoxy which is highly polished and then riveted into a hold encircled by round wire in the center of the rectangle. The drops, which are carved individually, may vary. $58.

Daryl Toth—I majored in photography and then sculpture at the Rhode Island School of Design. My senior year I became very interested in metalwork and since then have devoted all my energies to learning more about metalsmithing.

My first year out of school I waitressed, worked in a factory and designed costume jewelry. I now share a shop, Trillium, in downtown Providence, Rhode Island.

Daryl Toth, 385 Westminster Street, Room 57, Providence, Rhode Island 02903.

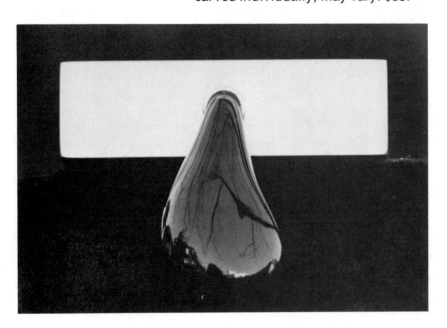

Wool Blankets—All blankets are 100% wool. Many patterns, colors and styles available. The blankets are about 6' long and 3½' wide. Indigo, red and white blanket 39'' by 58'' plus fringe shown on lap of artist, $200 postpaid. Blanket in shades of gray and brown with some purple and red shown in background, $200 postpaid.

Kay Marshall—I was born in 1943 in Anchorage, Alaska. My present goal is to become self-supporting through the production of beautiful handmade items. My blankets are for color and warmth. If I have time I dye the yarns with vegetable dyes. I like to keep as close as possible to the essence of the material—unspun unbleached wool. I use wool for warmth, pattern for structure and try to allow the material as much freedom as possible.

Kay Marshall, 820½ ''I'' Street, Anchorage, Alaska 99501.

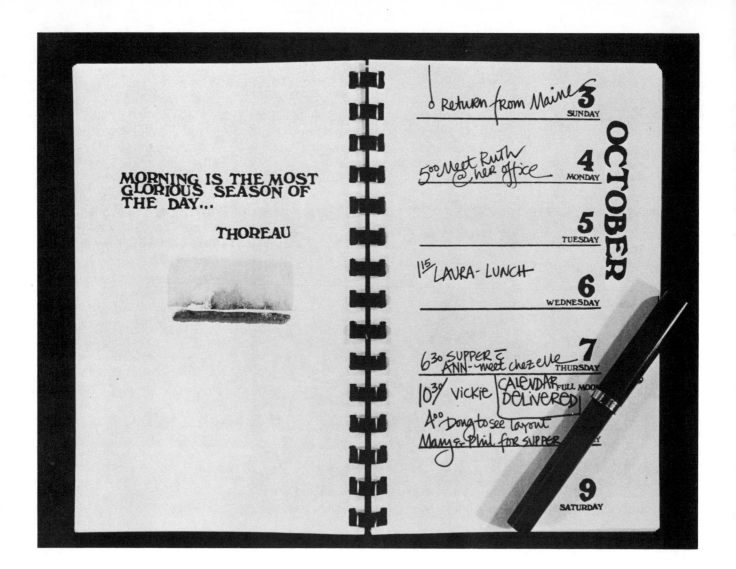

MORNING IS THE MOST
GLORIOUS SEASON OF
THE DAY...

THOREAU

Return from Maine **3** SUNDAY

5⁰⁰ Meet Ruth @ her office **4** MONDAY

5 TUESDAY

1¹⁵ LAURA- LUNCH

6 WEDNESDAY

6³⁰ SUPPER & **7** THURSDAY
ANN- meet chez elle

10³⁰ Vickie CALENDAR FULL MOON
DELIVERED

4⁰⁰ Doug to see layout
Mary & Phil for supper

9 SATURDAY

OCTOBER

A
BOOK
FOR
1978

AN
ENGAGEMENT
CALENDAR

SUSAN RIECKEN

Calendar—An engagement calendar for 1978 with weekly format and space to write notes and appointments for each day. The calendar contains quotes from the writings of Emily Dickinson, Thoreau, Whitman, Shakespeare and others. Full moons, new moons and the first day of each season are marked. The calendar is produced by combining mechanical offset and hand-printing with hand-carved stamps. Letters and numerals are printed in brown ink on off-white stock; the illustrations are brightly colored. Heavy covers, handy pocket for schedules or receipts, sturdy comb-style binding, 5½'' by 8''. Limited edition. $6.50 postpaid.

Notes—The notes are hand-printed using hand-carved stamps and brightly-colored designers' inks. The paper is heavy, off-white card stock with a slightly textured finish. Heart or heart-in-hand design in red, purple or turquoise, with envelopes in a complementary color. Cards measure 4½'' by 6¼'', packages of 10, $3.75 postpaid.

Susan Riecken—I am a free-lance graphic artist and have been making the calendar since 1971, when I made an edition of twenty-five copies. The size of the edition has grown each year. I've done teaching and consulting in the Boston area as well as in Worcester, Massachusetts and Baltimore, Maryland.

Susan Riecken, 9 Vincent Street, Cambridge, Massachusetts 02140.

Raw musk ox wool as worn by model.

Hand-spun Alaskan yarns—Yarns from Aleutian sheep, musk ox, wild mountain goat, wild red and white fox, beaver and martin. All yarns are skeined on a niddy-noddy and banded in the middle. Prices are per 2 ounces, shipping not included. Alaskan sheep, $4; wild mountain goat, $5; wild red fox, $5; wild white fox, $10; beaver, $5; martin, $5.

Natural Alaskan Dyes—Packaged in plastic bags with instructions for dyeing. Arctic willow catkins (greens with alum and copper); Arctic willow leaves (brilliant yellow with alum); Arctic larkspur (light blue); Arctic pink poppy (rose); dogwood (red); Northern bedstraw (yellow, red); Alaskan goldenrod (yellow, red); Siberian aster (yellow); Alaskan chrysanthemum (yellow); mastodon flower (green); senec (beige); white tundra daisies (yellow); green tundra moss (beige); wild onion (yellow). $1 for 2 ounces, shipping not included.

Anne Howard—I was born in El Paso, Texas and spent most of my childhood in Mexico and South America. I taught in Washington, D.C., South Dakota and Idaho before coming to Alaska. I now teach among the Eskimo people of Nunivak Island.

I am very interested in spinning, dyeing and ethnic garments.

Anne Howard, P.O. Box 12, Mekoryuk, Alaska 99630.

Kerosene Oil Lamps—Hand-thrown stoneware bases. Safe and efficient lighting. Uses plain kerosene or scented lamp oil. Instructions included. Pedestal lamp, 19'' high, 16-oz. capacity. Heat-resistant glass chimney included, $18.95 postpaid. Large lamp, 16'' high, 32-oz. capacity, chimney, $17.95 postpaid. Small lamp, 14'' high, 16-oz. capacity, chimney, $11.70 postpaid.

Egg Separator—These little guys are great! What you do is break the egg into the top, tilt the bowl and pour the white out of the mouth. Lead-free and dishwasher-safe, 4'' wide by 3'' high. $5.45 postpaid.

Cheese Grater—Does the job and looks great on the wall, 5'' wide by 6'' high. $5.45 postpaid.

Heartstone Pottery—A family business in the truest sense. I am the chief designer and potter. My wife Rhona is responsible for the bookkeeping, shipping and criticism. Our children Eric and Shannon are in charge of screaming, yelling and general jumping around.

We live in the rural coastal hills of Northern California. Being close to the earth, to the air and water, is an essential part of what and who a potter is. We feel a close contact with the elements that is conducive to ceramic creations of the highest caliber.

It takes a lifelong dedication to become a master craftsman, and along the way there are some very nice pots possible. We do lots, including vegetable steamers, birdfeeders, honey jars, wine goblets and decanters, among others.

M. P. Martin, c/o Heartstone Pottery, Star Route, Whitethorn, California 95489.

241

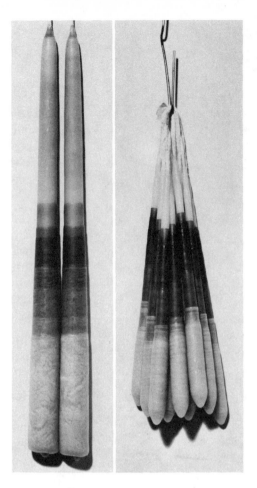

Candles—These wax candles are formed by repeated dippings in especially blended and dyed waxes. There are six color groups to choose from: warm, cool, earth, pastel, assorted and neutral. Each design is individual. They burn with a steady, smokeless flame and are dripless, except in strong drafts. Box of 6 different sets, 3 pairs each of 11½'' candles, $18. Box of 8 different bunches, each bunch made up of twelve 4'' birthday candles, $6. Shipping not included.

Waxen Candles—I studied painting at Pennsylvania Academy of Fine Arts and was awarded two traveling scholarships for travel-study in Europe

I have been making candles since 1967. I am experimenting with new dyes, building new equipment and planning a craft gallery called ''Craftplane,'' which is scheduled to open this fall in Philadelphia.

James Evans, c/o Waxen Candles, R.D. 3, Bloomsburg, Pennsylvania 17815.

Batik Paintings—These batik paintings are ordinarily done on 100% cotton fabric, but occasionally I work on silk. The average size is 28'' by 20''. They are mounted on corrugated board and matted on cardboard of a suitable color, ready for framing. Each batik is one of a kind. All are still-life compositions. Shipping weight 1 lb. $25.

Prabhakar Poola—I was born in India in 1947. After finishing high school in my hometown, Gudiyattam, I went to art school in Madras for six years. I come from a family of professional weavers and dyers, but for some dubious reason, I never showed any interest in weaving.

I was attracted to the dyeing process at an early age, and eventually to the resist-dyeing process called batik. For the past six years or so craft work has been my main source of income.

Prabhakar Poola, 488 Spruce Street, Berkeley, California 94708.

Denim Jackets—Appliqued, embroidered, fully lined jackets made from old and new denim and washable fabrics. Specify colors you'd like used. All sizes. $45.

Susan Swab—Making the realistic fanciful is a challenge I find irresistible. The fantasy world I enter while working designs is influenced by my many travels. I re-create these different locales on my jackets, using yarns, appliques, beads, ribbons, rhinestones and embroidery.

I opened my own clothing store early in 1975 in Stillwater, Oklahoma, a small college town. It was primarily a jeans store, since I bought old and new jeans by the bale. As a service to my customers and a hobby for me, I also decorated the jackets and jeans. In addition, I made bedspreads, wall hangings, ski vests and many other things. They were well received, and after one and a half years, I sold my store. I have since been working from my house.

Susan Swab, 4214 South Wheeling, Tulsa, Oklahoma 74105.

Wooden Toys—Shaped from solid blocks of carefully selected red birch, these toys are so sturdy I am willing to make free repairs to any one a child can break. I use hardwood wheels and axles, and parts are secured with a nontoxic two-ton test glue plus a pressure fit that I can't undo. Then I sand the hell out of them and apply a natural vegetable oil finish. Shown: Big Tractor, $20; Baby Tractor, $6 (both opposite page); Tractor-trailer, $18; Aeroplane (bottom), $12; Fat Bug (right), $6.50. Not shown: square-wheeled Wobble Bug, $7, which I sell as a back massager for adults. All prices postpaid.

Whimsical Woodcrafts—I have been interested in woodworking since I was a child. I had some experience building custom furniture in New York. I fell into toy making over five years ago while out of a job.

My first year in business I approached a local toy shop that had expressed interest in my line. After some discussion, however, the owner decided not to handle my toys— because they were too well-built. He actually told me that there would be no profit in it for him because my toys would last and the parents wouldn't be back in his shop buying replacements for a long time.

I vowed then and there to make a perfectly unbreakable toy that would be thoroughly enjoyable. And I believe I have done just that.

Hugh Gundry, c/o Whimsical Woodcrafts, 203 South Fair Oaks Avenue, Pasadena, California 91105.

Aluminum Kitchenware—Cast in our own foundry with a hand-buffed finish. May be used on top of the stove or in the oven, as one would use any metal kitchenware. Top row: soup tureen holds 4 quarts, measures 9'' in diameter by 9'' high, weighs 8½ lbs., $45; skillet holds 2¾ quarts, measures 7'' in diameter by 4'' high, weighs 5½ lbs., $38; loaf pan measures 5½'' wide by 8½'' long by 3'' deep, weighs 2 lbs., $28. Bottom row: 6-cup muffin pan measures 7'' wide by 16'' long, weighs 3 lbs., $32; casserole holds 2¾ quarts, measures 8'' wide by 11'' long by 3'' deep, weighs 5½ lbs., $38; casserole holds 2½ quarts, measures 5'' wide by 8'' long by 3'' deep, weighs 5 lbs., $38. Catalog available. $2 shipping charge.

Don Drumm, 437 Crouse Street, Akron, Ohio 44311.

Don Drumm Studio—Don Drumm has been a pioneer in the use of aluminum as a sculpture and craft medium. He has operated his own studio and foundry in Akron, Ohio for eighteen years. He creates a wide variety of sculpture and craft items ranging from large architectural wall murals to small functional items for the home. As a full-time practicing craftsman, Don has found it a real challenge to come down from creating a ten-story concrete wall mural or a 20'-high Cor-ten steel sculpture piece and go back into the studio to work on new designs for casseroles.

All of our aluminum pieces are created through the sand-casting process, which goes back to biblical times. The forms are carved in sand and molten metal is poured into those molds. As the casting is taken from the mold, the mold is destroyed, requiring preparation of a new mold each time. The casting piece then demands considerable finishing, filing, buffing and polishing to bring it up to our standards of quality.

Cast and Welded Metalwork—The colors I use vary from the silver-gray to the pigeon blue of steel; from the yellows of brass to the subtle greens, blues, yellows and red-browns of copper and bronze patinas. My fireplace tools are made of iron and brass and weigh 16 lbs. The tools are 25'' long; the stand is 42'' high on a 16'' diameter base. Shipping weight 36 lbs. $200. The music stand is made of iron, brass and copper. It is 50'' high on a 14'' diameter base and weighs 20 lbs. Shipping weight 40 lbs. $160. The parrot cage is 36'' wide by 24'' high by 18'' deep. It comes on a stand which is 36'' high and has a 20'' diameter base. The cage and stand are both made of iron and weigh 100 lbs. $600. Prices do not include shipping.

Steve Hersch—I like contrast. I like tight, well-controlled forms kicked in the ass by rough, nappy textures. I like materials that still have the scream of the earth left in them. I like the play between the tragic and comic that keeps things human—a blend of the past and present, a mix of classical and modern forms. I like things that keep a balance between the outrageous and sublime, forms that dance between symmetry and asymmetry, the subtle that has its origins in the obvious. Paradox.

Steve Hersch, 15305 Seventy-eighth Avenue North East, Bothell, Washington 98011.

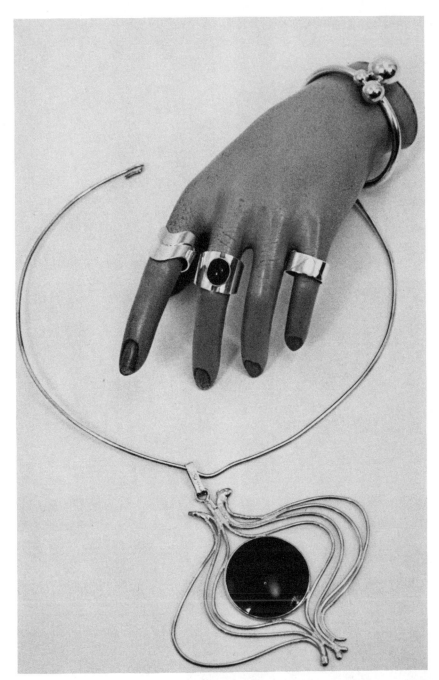

Hand-fabricated Gold and Silver Jewelry
—Cut from pieces of metal, formed, joined and soldered. All of the jewelry is made of sterling silver and/or solid 18k gold with the techniques of European goldsmiths. Each piece is signed. If you lose weight, I'll gladly re-size your ring free. Ring boxes available if requested. Shown on mannequin's hand: sterling silver bracelet, $40. Rings, left to right: sterling and 18k gold ring, $48; sterling ring with jade, tiger's eye or onyx center stone, $40; sterling and 18k gold ring, $38. Sterling necklace with onyx or carnelian center stone, $65. Shown on human's hand: sterling bracelet with onyx or Wyoming jade, $60. Rings, top to bottom: sterling ring, $35; sterling ring, $35; sterling and 18k gold ring, $38.

Hannelore Gabriel—A German goldsmith who received her training at the Goldsmiths' School in Essen, West Germany, Ms. Gabriel served a four-year apprenticeship with a master goldsmith. She has worked as a professional goldsmith for jewelry firms in Germany, Holland and South Africa.

In 1974 she set up her own design studio in Madison, Ohio, with her husband Ray. Her work has been shown in leading galleries and shows in major cities including New York, Chicago and Miami. She has taught jewelry making in her studio and at Oberlin College.

Hannelore Gabriel,
1469 Rosena Avenue,
North Madison, Ohio
44057.

Top, Egyptian shirt; middle, Turkish coat; bottom, French cheesemaker's smock.

Top, Syrian dress; middle, Gaza dress; bottom, Rumanian blouse.

Folkwear Patterns—Based on traditional clothing from all parts of the globe, designs perfected by centuries of daily use have been reproduced for modern home sewing in full-scale paper patterns which adjust to fit all sizes. Each pattern is printed on heavy paper and can be used repeatedly. Guide sheets and pattern layouts are included, as are designs and instructions for authentic handwork techniques wherever appropriate. These basic ethnic garments can be sewn quickly and easily because they evolve from a system of triangles and rectangles. The simple lines enhance your choice of fabric. French cheesemaker's smock, Egyptian shirt, $2.50; Rumanian blouse, Black Forest smock, $3; Gaza dress, Syrian dress, Turkish coat, Afgani Nomad dress, $4; and Little Folks, a collection of eight patterns for children in one package, $4.50.

Folkwear—Folkwear Ethnic Patterns are the creation of three California women of diverse but complementary backgrounds: Barbara Garvey, Alexandra Jacopetti and Ann Wainwright. Ann translates authentic examples of ethnic clothing into designs for the contemporary figure. She has designed for major dress manufacturers, collects ethnic clothing, and feels that it is exciting to work on "lifetime dresses" that will never go out of style or be prohibitively expensive. Barbara writes Folkwear's sewing instructions. Three years as a computer instructor, programmer and systems analyst for IBM produced some of the techniques that Barbara now applies to Folkwear's "much more exciting" endeavor. The researching, diagramming and explanation of the needlework and handcraft techniques accompanying the patterns are done by Alexandra, a well-known weaver and fiber artist. She is shown in the picture working on handwork instructions with Penelope Kramer.

Barbara Garvey, Ann Wainwright, Alexandra Jacopetti, c/o Folkwear, Box 98, Forestville, California 95436.

Quilted Jackets—Made to order in cotton. A combination of hand and machine quilting is used, in your choice of pattern, either "Log Cabin" (shown) or "Wild Goose Chase" (a triangular pattern). Colors as you desire—vibrant to subtle, or predominantly blues, greens, reds or browns. These jackets, after a few wearings, begin to conform to your body. Quilted material has an inherent elasticity which makes a flexible and very comfortable garment. The batting is Dacron polyester fiberfill. Machine-wash gently, tumble dry gently or line-dry. Jackets weigh approximately 12 oz. $75 postpaid.

B. B. Doriss—I live in the backwaters of Mendocino County. When I go to the city, I go to fabric stores and bookstores. My reading and research about quilting is as absorbing as the doing! I'm currently putting together a study of contemporary applications of traditional nineteenth-century motifs. The Amish and Mennonite quilters of the mid- to late-nineteenth century particularly fascinate me.

Other than quilting, I'm pretty well-balanced. My husband, Steve Doriss, is a woodworker whose tool chests are also in the catalog. Really fine work, I think. It's helpful to have a different outlook on design in the house. Our nineteen-month-old daughter has the best of it all—parents who are *doing*, and doing what they love.

B. B. Doriss, P.O. Box 1635, Fort Bragg, California 95437.

Stoneware Coffee Pot—Hand-thrown coffee pot includes 3 pieces: pot, lid and funnel for paper filter. Comes in two color combinations: semi-matte white glaze with cobalt blue banding and semi-matte gold-brown glaze with glossy black-mocha (shown). Pot with filter inserted is about 12'' high, with a capacity of 1 to 1½ quarts.

Perforated spout is suitable for the brewing of loose tea. Pot should be preheated with warm water before use and should not be placed on stove element or open flame without a trivet. Weighs 4 lbs. $30. Set of 4 mugs, $20. Shipping not included.

Jim Stanley—My wife and I live and work on a forty-acre homestead we share with another family, just east of Oregon's Cascades. Since we have no electricity, I have had to re-learn throwing on a kick-wheel—but I have found the slower pace more in keeping with my surroundings.

I am primarily involved in functional stoneware, but I like to play with nonfunctional sculptured forms as well. Other interests include a bit of small-scale farming, experiments with solar heat and wind generation, part-time school-bus driving and V.W. mechanicking.

Jim Stanley, P.O. Box 274, Dufur, Oregon 97021.

Ojo de Dios—The Ojo is a colorful and authentic talisman believed to bring good health, good fortune and long life to those displaying it. They are derived from the Huichol Indians of northwestern Mexico, who base much of their everyday living on the power of the god's eye. "Falling Star" is a traditional style ojo in shades of rust, tan, brown, orange and yellow. This ojo and others may be furnished in any color shades to match your decor; other styles have from 4 to 36 arms. Highest quality yarns are used; 3 lbs. packaged weight. $30.

Evelyn Davis—What started as a simple hobby has become a very important part of my life.

A photographic and written record is kept of every ojo I make, and I have hundreds of yarn sample plus a large inventory of yarns and frames.

Evelyn Davis, Star Route #1, Box 305, Wild Horse Mesa, Sedona, Arizona 86336.

Raffia Dolls—My raffia dolls can be used in a number of ways during the long autumn decorating season or as a welcome addition to any doll collection. They are not intended to be a young child's toy. When ordering please state your preference of calico or denim clothing and the predominant color desired. Custom orders will be filled if customers send about ⅓ yard of each of two or three desired fabrics. $11 per pair postpaid.

Phyllis Jones—I have not seen your first catalog, but it sounds like the answer to my prayer for a way to sell my craft items. The craft store I sold through last fall has had to go out of business. We rural Kentuckians enjoy making crafts for ourselves but we have a poor market for ready-made items such as these.

After teaching home economics for a few years I decided to stay home with our children and practice what I had been preaching! My husband and I recently purchased a farm near the small community of Summer Shade because we enjoy country living. It is not a "farmers's farm," however, so we are attempting to develop other means of income in order to become independent. By using my sewing skill to make wreaths, dolls, sleeping bags and anything else you might suggest, I hope to contribute to our family farm venture. I promise to fill all orders as long as they come and the Lord God grants me health and life on this earth.

Phyllis Jones, Route 2, Box 92, Summer Shade, Kentucky 42166.

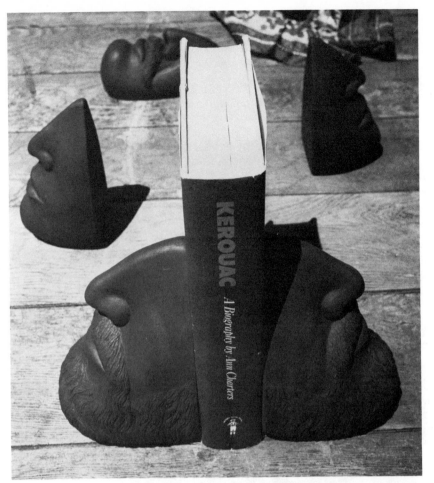

Cast Book Ends—These book ends come in chocolate, bone or bronze colors. They are made of gypsum materials which are as strong or stronger than nonferrous materials. They have holes in bottom for mounting on wall as shelf brackets. $18 per pair, shipping not included. Also shown: clothes hooks, chocolate color only. $7 each, shipping not included.

Darius Strickler—I have been making faces out of any available materials since I was very young. The pattern grew and carried over into and through my art education until it developed into a full-time endeavor. For the last two years I've been expanding and promoting my works through shows and shops in the Northeast. I have plans to increase the "nose" line to include toothbrush holders, salt and pepper sets and other functional oddities.

Darius Strickler, Route #3, Box 512F, Boone, North Carolina 28607.

Paddles—Unfinished pine butter paddles are sanded smooth, tapered and ready for use. The paddles are reproductions of Early American apple butter paddles. Small: 4'' wide by 22'' long. In unfinished pine, $4; with a nontoxic sealer, $4.50; with stain and lacquer, $5. Large: 4½'' wide by 35'' long. Plain paddle, $6; with nontoxic sealer, $6.50; with stain and lacquer, $7. All prices postpaid.

The Acorn Workshop—Lynn and I operate the Acorn Workshop to supplement the income from our daytime jobs. We've been involved in craftwork several years. We greatly enjoy working on our crafts and appreciate hearing from other craftspeople on just about any old thing. We are hopeful, Mother Earth-type folk, and want to remind you to plant a tree.

Randall and Lynn Caldwell, c/o The Acorn Workshop, Box 2172, Falls Church, Virginia 22042.

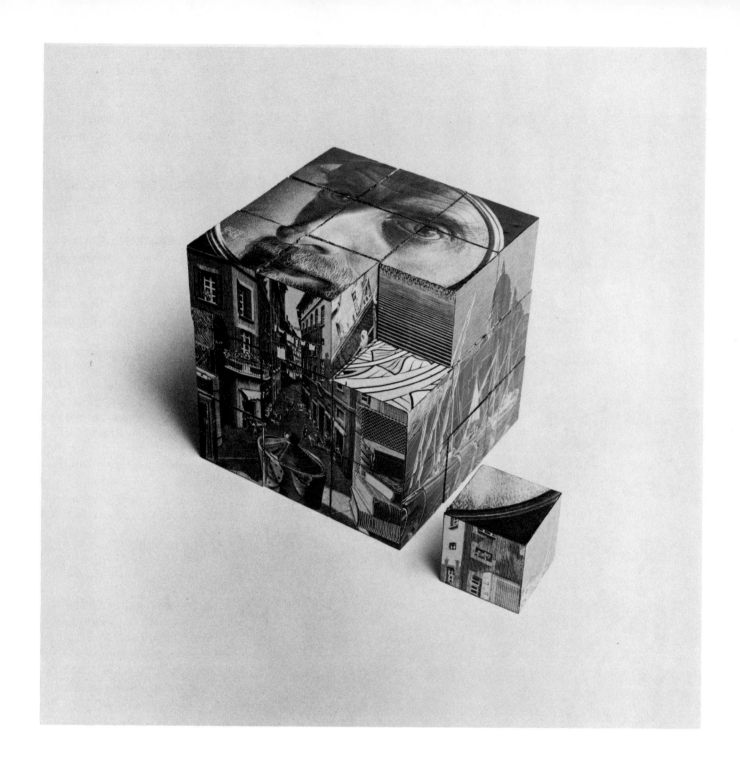

256

Cube Puzzle—This is a 27-block cube puzzle featuring art by M. C. Escher and measures 4½'' by 4¼'' by 4½''. When accurately assembled, the cube makes six 3-block by 3-block pictures on its outside facets, plus six more 3-block by 6-block pictures when opened on its interior axes. $75, shipping not included.

Pooh, Etc.—Block puzzles made for children of all ages ranging in theme from Winnie the Pooh to Michelangelo to Steam Tractors. Each set of puzzles makes six different pictures, one at a time, with the same artist or theme on all six sides. Yellow pine blocks are covered with art reproductions (we also work with original art), and finished with four to twelve coats of hand-brushed polyurethane. Puzzles range in size from four to three hundred blocks. Four-piece puzzles are $7.50, six-block sets $10 and nine-piece puzzles $12.50. Puzzles from ten to fifty pieces are $1.35 per block, and over fifty pieces, $1.50 per block. Since each set of puzzles is completely handmade, and no two are ever alike, you may specify any artist or theme when ordering. Please specify number of blocks desired and artist or theme. Our block size is always 1½''.

Homestead Puzzle Company—The handmaking of Six Way Puzzle Blocks has become much more than a business for us; it has become a lifestyle. In our seven-year journey from a small army-surplus tent (where we first began making puzzles) to our present home/shop near Fredericksburg, our family has grown to include two sons—Ezra, five, and Beany, six—a Weimaraner named Hilda, an awful lot of cats and a wide assortment of friends. But Shadow, our black Belgian sheepdog, who has been with us since the beginning, still takes care of us all.

After several years of perfecting our technique as puzzle makers, we realized that there was more to being a craftsman than doing fine work. We feel that it is the obligation of each craftsperson to educate the public not only to appreciate his work but to recognize fine workmanship in all mediums.

In the course of attending art shows and after long talks with fellow craftspeople, we have come to the conclusion that craftsmen must take more responsibility in the creation of their marketplace. Having the courage of our convictions, we have for the past five years run one show each year, usually for a charity or nonprofit organization. Our primary thrust in these shows has been to bring together top craftsmen from throughout the United States with an emphasis on demonstrations of seldom-seen traditional crafts.

After all the ups and downs of seven years as full-time professional craftspeople, we still wouldn't trade our life for any other—it's very rewarding to hear your son say, "When I grow up I want to be a puzzle maker like Mommy and Daddy."

Roland and Nancy Denny, c/o Homestead Puzzle Company, Box 64, Mason Route, Fredericksburg, Texas 78624.

Functional Stoneware—My pottery is fired to about 2300°F. in an electric kiln. It is ornamented with brushed oxide of iron, cobalt and copper, then coated with an impervious lead-free glaze. All my pieces are dishwasher-safe. The teapot is 6'' wide by 8'' high, weighs 2¼ lbs., holds 1½ quarts and costs $20. The sugar bowl and creamer are each 4½'' wide by 4'' high, weigh 1½ lbs. each, hold 1 pint each and cost $15 per set. Mug is 3¼'' wide by 4½'' high, weighs 10 oz., holds 10 oz. and costs $5. The wine set consists of a ring decanter and six cups. The decanter is 7'' wide by 8½'' high, weighs 2¼ lbs. and has a capacity of 1 quart. The cups are 2½'' wide by 3'' high, weigh 4 oz. each and hold 5 oz. Set costs $35, decanter alone, $20. Please add 10% for shipping.

Andrew Quient—I am an independent production potter and teacher, operating my own studio in Glen Cove, Long Island. I have been working in pottery since 1965. I hold a B.A. in humanities and a Bachelor of Architecture degree. My background has given me a strong foundation in design process. I have designed and built potters' wheels, and have extensive experience as a kiln fireman in the production of stoneware, porcelain, raku and salt-glazed ware.

Andrew Quient, 5 Highland Road, Glen Cove, New York 11542.

Leather Hats—Igor's fine hand-stitched hats are made from buffed top-grain cowhide for comfortable, durable, distinctive wear. They come in a versatile tan color with a dark brown braided leather band, and are available in sizes Small, Medium, Large, Extra Large and Extra-Extra Large. Send us your head measurement in inches. All hats are carefully cut, stitched and shaped entirely by hand. $38 postpaid.

Igor's—I have been professionally involved in crafts since I graduated from high school ten years ago. I originally worked with batik, selling mainly through art shows. Later I moved into leather, making deerskin and sheepskin jackets and other garments for a craft shop in Tahoe City, California.

I met my wife and we moved to Walnut Creek, where we worked for Foothold Sandalmakers for almost a year, learning the leather goods retailing business and producing various leather items on a limited production-line basis.

From this background, we formed our company—Igor's—to produce fine leather hats. The business is our sole income and much to our delight is providing us with a comfortable living. The many steps from hide to finished product we carry out mainly in our well-equipped workshop; the only exception is the time-consuming work of stitching by hand which, weather allowing, we do sitting under the surrounding pines. We have found a community where we will probably stay and raise our first child.

Tom and Monika Banwell, c/o Igor's, P.O. Box 409, Grass Valley, California 95945.

Triangle Pocket Pipe—This pipe has a fairly large bowl, yet is small enough to be carried in your pocket. Each pipe is made of fine hardwood in the shape of a perfect triangle. The mouthpiece section is cut off and reconnected by a high-tension unbreakable spring on either side, which provides a strong seal for excellent draw. This mouthpiece can be flipped over onto any of its three sides and moved into position either as a cover for the bowl, as one mouthpiece, or as two mouthpieces. Satisfaction guaranteed. Measures 2½'' by 2½'' by 1''. $5.95.

Wooden It Be Nice—We have both been in the arts since our early years and have a solid background in graphic arts. In early 1975 Gary sold his life insurance policy and bought a wood lathe; from there we turned to woodworking. Our appreciation for the natural beauty and utility of fine hardwoods provides us with inspiration to create functional items that flow with their natural wood grain. We have made natural wood products that range from turned salad bowls and cannisters to our pipes.

Gary and Janet Stephens, c/o Wooden It Be Nice, P.O. Box 634, Glen Ellen, California 95442.

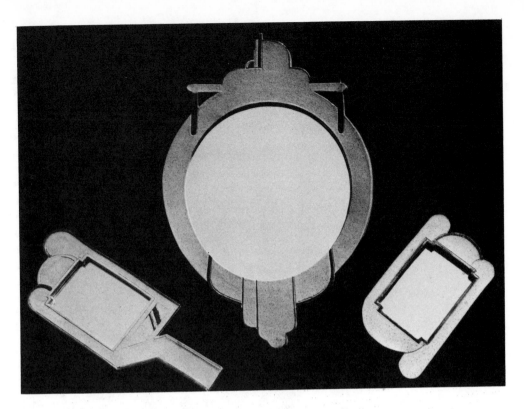

Ceramic Mirrors—Executed in Art Deco Style. Available in a variety of earth tones: brown, cream, blue, green, ochre. The round mirrors are made to be hung and measure 20'' at the furthest point. $50 postpaid. The rectangular handmirrors can also be hung. They measure about 4'' by 6''. $10 postpaid.

Sheila Speller—I am a working craftsperson in the Cincinnati area. Presently I am with the Cincinnati Recreation Commission as an art resource specialist. We are attempting to stimulate interest in the visual arts among a variety of age groups, from tots to senior citizens.

These mirrors represent the culmination of my interest in the decorative motifs of Art Deco. My involvement with this style began in Cincinnati with the furor that was generated when several complete Art Deco buildings were slated for demolition. I chose clay as a medium for these mirrors because its manipulative properties allow me to execute the intricacies of Art Deco within these forms.

Sheila Speller, 3130 Bishop #3, Cincinnati, Ohio 45220.

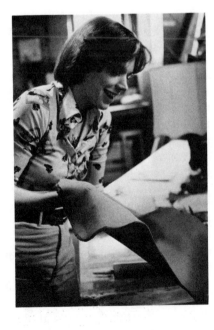 

Drawstring Pants—Made from 100% cotton and dyed with Procion dye, a high-quality fiber-reactive dye. Dye yields brilliant colors and will not fade or run. The pockets are batiked in a variety of colors and themes: mythical (dragons, unicorns), rainbow scenes, shooting stars, desert scenes, sun and moon, and peacocks. Because they have a drawstring, two sizes fit almost everyone. White with batik pockets, $18.50. Dyed blue, green or brown with batik pockets, $21. Sizes: small to medium and large to extra-large. I also make batik mobiles and stuffed animals.

Monica Dunnington—I was born and educated in London. I left England six years ago to travel in the States and have since made this country my home. My two-year-old daughter Jessica and I live under the redwood trees on the Russian River. I have set up a studio next to my house where I paint, work on my batik designs and teach beginners the basics of the art of batik. I also travel the crafts-fair circuit for fun and enlightenment and to stay in touch with the world.

Monica Dunnington, P.O. Box 806, Guerneville, California 95446.

Ruana—A versatile garment which can be worn as a poncho, shawl or tunic. Pure 100% virgin wool, rugged in texture like the terrain of the Colorado sheep who grew the wool. Hand-washable, 36'' by 54''. Natural white, wine, desert sunset, magenta/orange. $65, shipping not included.

L. J. Carlin Company—After steeping myself in my craft, I left the academic world to earn a living with my hands. Because hand-weaving with hand-spun yarns is a pleasurable but labor-intensive processs, I have evolved an intermediate technology in which twentieth-century textile techniques are scaled to the individual artisan.

I want my work to be worn and enjoyed by people; I want the tactile qualities of my work to be felt, not just seen. From raw wool all the way to the wearable piece, my garments are made by hand and meant to convey a single message: if we revive our renewable resources such as wool, and return to the human scale, we will rediscover a world that is personal, harmonius and satisfying to the human spirit.

Lee Carlin, c/o L. J. Carlin Company, 2209 Fourth Street, Boulder, Colorado 80302.

Spinning Wheel—This castle-style spinning wheel was designed with the production spinner in mind. It has a spindle-to-drive ratio of about 15. There is a 7/16'' orifice and each bobbin can hold ½ lb. of wool. The wood is coastal tan oak and ball bearings are used throughout. The wheel is 18'' wide, 36'' high and 22'' deep and weighs about 35 lbs. $175.

Crispin Hollinshead—I have a degree in mechanical design and have been designing ''things'' for fifteen years. I have been working wood for a living for almost four years and have recently focused my energy on spinning wheels. Anyone thinking of buying one of these should realize that I am constantly improving the design as I grow and learn. Therefore, what is shown is not what will be built. Life is growth and change. I have chosen to be alive.

Crispin B. Hollinshead, Box 541, Mendocino, California 95460.

Refrigerator Magnets—All are precolored with permanent, nonfade lifelike pigments. Bread dough magnets are hand-shaped from bread dough mix. After baking, they are coated several times with polyurethane and decorated with poppy, caraway or sesame seeds. Shapes: braid, twist, knot, spiral, and various loaf shapes. $1 each, 3/$2.75, 6/$5. Clay magnets are completely handmade from a low-fire decorative clay compound. The clay is nonporous and waterproof. Tomato, pumpkin, asparagus, watermelon slice, crookneck squash, mushroom, eggplant and peanut (not shown), $1 each, 3/$2.75, 6/$5. Fast food series are made from low-fire clay compound. Cheeseburger, french fries and hot dog are colored appropriately. Burger, $2.75; fries, $2; dog $1.50; set $5.

Crafty Things Boutique—I was born in the Bay Area and have lived here all my life. I majored in anthropology at San Francisco State University. What does a young married woman do with an anthropology background and a fascination for the Mayan civilization? She works as a legal secretary.

For the past five years I've been working as a wife, homemaker, mother of two small boys and avid vegetable gardener. When I became interested in clay, my husband and I converted one room of our home into a workshop/studio for me.

My work has become a great part of our family life. I work on my craft every day, usually at our kitchen table, which is constantly covered with stacks of clay, tubes of epoxy, rolls of magnetic tape, tools and half-full cups of cold coffee. It is all quite hectic, but very satisfying.

Sandra Patterson, c/o Crafty Things Boutique, 669 Kirk Glen Drive, San Jose, California 95133.

Doll Kits—My doll-house dolls are of pink bisque and pink or black luster, fired to 2,000°F. I start with an idea, model the doll, make the mold, pour, paint, glaze and fire the doll myself. I sell the dolls as kits, including head, arms, legs, body pattern and instructions for assembly. Write for a catalog describing all the dolls available. "Granny" and "Jed Clampett" doll kits $15 apiece, postpaid.

Ann Decker—Eureka Springs is an unbelievable little town full of craftspeople and their shops, writers, poets and artists. It's called the "Little Switzerland of the Ozarks": seven months of tourists, five months of beautiful quiet.

From 1941 to 1954 I had a modest little doll mail-order business. I had to give the business up when my husband died and get back to earning my living. I moved to Eureka Springs in 1968 and began to make dolls again in 1973. All of my business is mail order, but I love to have people look me up in my studio—an unusual pie-shaped room in a turn-of-the century, turn-the-corner building right downtown.

Ann Decker, 79½ North Spring Street, Eureka Springs, Arkansas 72632.

Hand-drawn Notecards—Reproduced from pen and ink drawings on a stiff cream paper. Printed in green ink, 5'' by 6½'' folded. Each package contains 6 notes of one design and 6 seals. Package $1. Four designs available: Laurel Creek (shown), Sugar Tree, Log Cabin and Farmhouse. Fine-quality black-and-white prints of Laurel Creek and Sugar Tree, 16'' by 20''. $10 each.

Cindy Pacileo—I grew up in a large and creative family where I was encouraged to draw before I could write. Long woodsy walks and full days of creekin' crowded my childhood. These early earthy experiences later became the natural subjects of my professional artwork. And so they have remained.

Recently I moved from my Ohio home to a farm in the Blue Ridge Mountains of North Carolina to be closer to the sources of my art. In the drawing of Laurel Creek you see detailed one of my favorite friends: the quiet pool above the dashing little waterfall I love to visit.

Cindy Pacileo, Route 2, Box 136A, Vilas, North Carolina 28692.

Soft Sculpture Mobile—Each mobile is a signed work of art, consisting of 16 pillows of vibrant colors including hand-painted rainbows, blue stars and white clouds. All revolve around an orange sun and yellow moon. They are suspended by transparent nylon cord from smoothly sanded natural hardwood supports. The pillows range in size from 5½'' to 7½'' in width and are made of 100% cotton chintz. They are stuffed with polyester fiberfill. The mobile weighs 1 lb. 6 oz. $66.50 postpaid.

Cindy Grantham—Involved with crafts most of her life, Cindy Grantham's only form of employment now is her craft work. She has won several awards for her unique and colorful designs.

Cindy Grantham, 6900 Roswell Road, North West, Apartment Q-20, Atlanta, Georgia 30328.

Natural Containers—Completely hand-crafted, each container is a one-of-a-kind item. All our materials are gathered by the three of us from the Southern California coastal and inland regions. The wood is avocado and the stone, alabaster, which we prospect ourselves in the Anza-Borrego and Mojave deserts. The colors range from rich reds to striped blacks and whites to golden yellows, pinks, purples and tans. Pictured are alabaster and avocado hand boxes, ranging in size from 4" by 4" by 6" to 5" by 5" by 8", and in weights from 1 to 3 lbs. The flat box is $40, the other two are $35 each. The laminated alabaster box is 6" by 6" by 14", weighs 10 lbs. and costs $125.

Susan, Paul and Tom—We live between the cracks in the sidewalk as do most artists and craftspeople in this country, trying to make an honest living doing what we choose to do, what we feel most productive and significant doing. We share materials and selling, but each of us creates our own pieces, has developed our own style and solved our own aesthetic and technical problems.

After years of being a religious printer and photographic production engineer, Paul says of art, "It sure beats working for a living." After seven years as a rehabilitation-counseling coordinator in the mental health field, Susan says, "I have no choice. Working with my hands, bringing form to my intuitive ideas is all I can do and remain sane." Tom says, "Don't invest your life in something someone can take away from you—my art is my own."

Susan Zalkind, Tom Driscoll, Paul Hawkins, 145 Edgeburt Drive, Leucadia, California 92024.

Rocking Horses—Solidly built, hand-carved wooden rocking horses. Built of Douglas fir, glued and dowelled at the joints (no nails, screws or staples are used), hard-carved and sanded to a smooth finish. Each is finished with either walnut stain and oil, or paint. Each horse comes with a suede-covered saddle with adjustable wooden stirrups, a hand-woven saddle blanket, a splayed rope mane and tail, and a rope halter. Available in three sizes (size is measured from the saddle to the floor and from chest to rear end). Small: 20'' rocker with 6''-wide body (suitable for children up to three years of age). Medium: 24'' rocker with 8''-wide body (suitable for children up to ten years of age). Large: 30'' rocker with 8''-wide body (suitable for children of three to grown adults). The small horse comes with an English saddle; the medium and large horses come with Western saddles. No two horses are exactly alike. Shipped by private carrier. Small, stained $175, painted $200. Medium, stained $250, painted $275. Large, stained $300, painted $325. Shipping not included.

William Hale—I was born and raised in New Jersey, educated in business at the University of Pennsylvania Wharton School, reluctantly joined the business world for six months, then joyfully withdrew and began searching for alternatives. Fortunately, at the age of twenty-eight, I happened upon wooden rocking horses. Now, three years later, my life is dedicated to wood. I live in Maine and am enamored of its provincial, almost calculated backwardness. I will probably stay here. I will always be making rocking horses. It is my love. It is my life.
William Hale, 60 Brackett Street, Portland, Maine 04102.

269

Storybook Doll Patterns—Characters include Stanley and Sally Possum and their family, the Wizard of Oz gang, the Little Red Hen and many others. The patterns are full-size with complete instructions provided. The Little Red Hen and Possum family patterns include storybooks. Possum family patterns, $3.50; Wizard of Oz patterns, $4; Little Red Hen pattern, $2.50. Lots more dolls—catalog $1.

Mother Goose's Place—Thelma Jennewein designs the Storybook doll patterns. She has been married for twenty-six years and is the proud mother of seven children, aged six to twenty-three. All of her children help her in her work, stuffing dolls and packaging patterns.

Thelma is a third-generation doll maker. In an average week the family produces about fourteen dolls. In addition to the full-time demands of doll making and the mail-order pattern business—and the seven children—Thelma also demonstrates the art of doll making at craft shows and is writing a book. There is never a dull moment in the Jennewein household!

The family dream is to go back to the simple life—to the farm where they lived years ago. They hope to realize this dream in a few years, for the farm life is always beckoning.

Thelma Jennewein, c/o Mother Goose's Place, P.O. Box 98, St. James, Missouri 65559.

Silk Yarns—I buy white and beige silk yarns from around the world. I dye them with dyes extracted from nature—from leaves, flowers, barks and heartwoods. The colors are made permanent by the use of mordants such as iron and aluminum, which act as fixatives through a natural chemical interaction. Before 1856, all textiles were colored this way. The cost of the yarns varies with the dyestuff used and the time it takes to do them. They average $16 per ½ lb. Sample cards of natural silks and silk colors available for $1 each.

Cheryl Kolander—I am a self-taught dyer and weaver. I was born in Oakland and grew up in Berkeley. Now I live on a small mountain farm in Southwest Oregon with a growing family of children and animals. We love visitors!

I have a dream about going around the world searching out other natural dyers, especially those who are the last survivors of a vanishing tradition, to record their work. I am currently working on a book about silk for hand textilers.

Cheryl Kolander, 276 North Myrtle, Myrtle Creek, Oregon 97457.

Leather Travel Bags—Made from latigo and moccasin leathers in 6-oz. to 10-oz. weights in combination. Colors: earthy reds, browns and yellows. Every bag has an adjustable strap, latched lid, side and bottom tie straps, specially designed porcelain beads and a minimum of 12 individual pockets. All stitch drawings, appliques, and extras such as silver conchos, back-carry straps or snakeskin inlays are original work unique to each bag. Design and overall dimensions vary according to customer's specifications. Bag shown is 14'' wide, 12'' high and 9'' deep. Repair or reconditioning free. $200, shipping not included.

Guitar Gig Bags—Made of 10-oz. latigo leather lined with ¼'' shearling, double-zipper closure, hand-carry strap and adjustable shoulder strap. Double thickness leathers on sides and bottom to insure instrument safety. The buckled front pocket has several interior compartments which allow space for sheet music, strings, tools and picks. Seams are machine-sewn with dacron-polyester thread and double-line stitched. Monograms are available. Approximate weight is 10 lbs. The bags come in beige, tan, golds, browns and reds. Specify manufacturer, size and kind of instrument. $300, shipping not included.

Scorpion Springs Leatherworks—Established in 1972 as a cottage industry, we now have two partners and two apprentices.

Lynn began leatherwork in 1968, then fled the city for the Nevada hills, to her present state of happy involvement. Barbara is a student of the arts, searching out that ''something else'' which may give real value and make a person really happy, instead of the illusory ''goods'' with which we are surrounded in ordinary life.

Lynn Nardella and Barbara Raymond, c/o Scorpion Springs Leatherworks, P.O. Box 34, Steamboat, Nevada 89436.

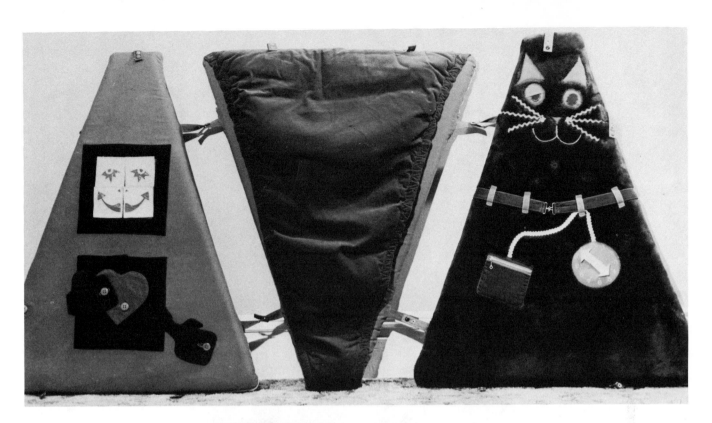

© 1976 by Dog-Gone Toys

Pup Tent—A developmental toy for children. Tent consists of three triangular modules designed to be safe, durable, cleanable and educational. Modules are foam rubber encased in muslin, 38'' wide by 46'' high by 3'' thick. Over this goes the designed surface coverings with five background sides of corduroy and one of fake fur. Designs used include puzzles, clocks, buttons, alphabet, etc. Zippers allow easy removal for cleaning. Weight: 14 lbs., 20 lbs. packaged. $225, shipping not included.

Dog-Gone Toys—I have been involved in designing and making educational toys since 1972. I have developed and tested three versions of the Pup Tent before being satisfied enough to offer it to the public.

I do the designing, pattern making, purchasing, cutting, manufacturing, testing and selling. When I am swamped I have another craftsperson help with the sewing.

Toy making allows me to explore and combine areas such as sewing, silk screening, soft sculpture, creative environments, modular furniture, etc.

Gaytrell Jane Lapp, c/o Dog-Gone Toys, P.O. Box 857, Woodland, California 95695.

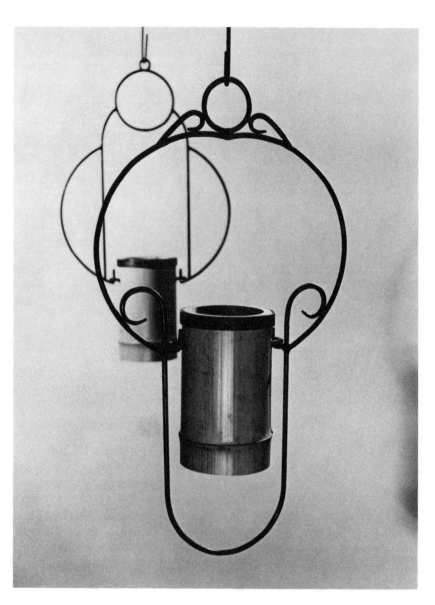

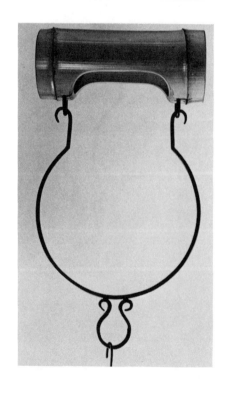

Iron and Bamboo Hanging Planters—
The bamboo is fumigated and sealed
with a varathane finish. The metal
can be either primed, painted or
treated with animal fat for a more
natural finish. Bamboo holder size
varies: around 6'' in diameter by 14''
long for horizontal type; 6'' in
diameter by 9'' long for vertical.
Overall lengths vary from 12'' to 20''.
Prices, including an S-hook to adapt
to chain, vary from $15 to $18
depending on design.

Lantern—The glass chimney is 12''
long and 4½'' in diameter. The
ironwork is quenched in animal fat,
then hand-rubbed to give a dark
protective coating. Lantern is 12½''
wide, 26'' long. All work is done with
forge, anvil and hammer. Accessories
in the form of hooks, chains,
wall-hangers and stands can also be
provided. Packaged weight 15 lbs.
$50.

Hammer and Wool Design—I was
born in Honolulu, but spent most of
my adolescence in the San Francisco
Bay Area. In 1967 I was drafted; upon
my discharge in 1969 I returned to
Hawaii to live and to finish my
education.

I was always interested in arts and
crafts, but never really pursued my
interest until 1970. My motivations
are really diverse and subjective. I
have always marveled at handmade
objects, especially those objects that
reflect a lifestyle or depict a means of
survival. For example, the early
Japanese farmhouses were built
according to tradition. The
woodworkers' skill is demonstrated
by the fact that some of the old houses
still stand. There is not a nail to be
found in those structures. I marvel at
their simplicity of design, efficiently
solved engineering problems and
aesthetically pleasing composition.
From them I learned quality and
tradition.

In 1973 I was hired to help extract
pipes and machinery from an old mill
where sugar cane was converted to
raw sugar. These sugar mills helped
to settle the Islands and formed the
nucleus of our economy for many
years. There were mill wrights and
blacksmiths, who fixed machinery,
fabricated new parts and created tools
for specialized jobs. I spent much
time looking at the old tools and
talking with the men who had worked
the mills. I learned from their
ingenuity and developed my skills
through trial and error.

Everything a person meets with
creates an impression. In recent years
my awareness has increased
immensely because I have learned
new things and clarified past
experiences. I feel that this is my
forte as an artist/craftsman: my
abilities of perception, ultimately
creation, encompass all aspects of
human behavior. The act of creation
is not singular, but a continuing spiral
that grows with awareness and
honesty.

*Ernest S. DeCoito, c/o Hammer
and Wool Design, 87-739 A Meaulu
Road, Waianae, Hawaii 96792.*

Mittens—Made of 100% water-repellant wool, in natural tones with colors for accent and design. Please send an outline of each hand and your color preference. $16 postpaid. Trigger-finger mittens (with thumb and index finger separated), $18 postpaid.

Socks—Hand-spun 100% wool with lanolin and oils intact. I use vegetable-dyed yarns and Canadian yarns for pattern accents. The sole, toe and heel are 2-ply yarn with 15% nylon for extra strength. The socks are 10'' high from the ankle and have replaceable heels. Please send an outline of your foot and your color preferences. $25 postpaid.

One-of-a-Kind Hats—Hats of 100% wool, mainly crocheted. In earthy colors and naturals. Strong, simple designs that are intricate in combination. Please specify head size, style of rim and colors preferred. $18 postpaid.

Annie Landon—I work at home, twenty-five miles from a small town in the mountains of Northern Idaho. I have lots of time, lots of space and not much money. So the control of my creations from source to finished product is both economical and necessary.

I am driven by the urge to use everything available around me, from the moss on decaying trees to the feathers the chickens molt each fall. The plants of the field and forest are useful for food and also for coloring wool. I am dedicated to wool and love the raw colors with their built-in oils and weather protection. Black, grey, brown, cream, white—a flash of golden onion skin thrown in—each fleece is different.

The enjoyment I have in making each article should come through in the finished product. There is something new happening every time I pick up a needle or hook and start to make an item. I'm willing to try anything.

Annie Landon, Route #5, Box 103, Priest River, Idaho 83856.

China and Porcelain Dolls—Opera heroines are porcelain with wigs. They are signed, dated and numbered. Each kit is $49.15; assembled and dressed as shown, $250 each, postpaid. China Rag (center of page) is 14'' tall. Each is painted differently, dated, numbered and signed. Kit with head, arms, legs and pattern for body, $15.25. Complete as shown, $25.65 postpaid. Send for catalog describing many more dolls.

Mark Farmer Co. Inc.—We are starting our fourth decade of making china and porcelain dolls. Our first dolls were reproductions of the more popular nineteenth-century china dolls. The years have enabled us to realize many more of the old designs and to add a few new ones of our own. We have been a family business since 1946.

Mark Farmer Co. Inc., 38 Washington Ave, Box 428, Point Richmond, California 94807.

Mackintosh Furniture—My primary concern is to design things that work for people and to do it in such a way that my products can both stand alone and harmonize with my clients' existing furnishings.

I work in wood not so much out of a love for the material as such, but more because wood seems to be the most suitable substance from which to make the kind of furniture I want to make.

As for design influences, I guess I have to admit to a half-dozen or so, mostly from the twentieth century, but the overriding factor in my designs is grace, in both line and proportion.

Steven Mackintosh, c/o Mackintosh Furniture, Route 315, Deansboro, New York 13328.

Quilt Stand—The stand is 33'' wide by 33'' high by 12' deep. Shown here in walnut, $250; also available in cherry, butternut and ash, $240 postpaid.

Wall Clock—The clock is 14'' wide by 23½'' tall by 3'' deep. Comes with mounting system. Shown here in cherry, $320; also available in walnut, $340 postpaid.

Bathroom Baubles—Our bathtub soap dish is slab-constructed, high-fired stoneware with a removable soap rest. Earth-tone matte glaze, 4'' wide by 6'' long by 3'' tall, $16.50 postpaid. Our Oral Hygiene Center is slab-constructed stoneware and porcelain. It accommodates four toothbrushes and toothpaste, and measures 13'' wide by 7'' high by 2'' deep, weighs 3 lbs. $25 postpaid.

Brophy Clay—Humor plays a central role in our lives and in our clay work—which is a major part of our lives. Whenever we are especially tickled by an idea, we run out to our studio to put it in clay.

Prior to our involvement with clay, we both received B.A. degrees in psychology from Stetson University in Florida. We went to Nashville, Tennessee, where Jay obtained a Ph.D. in psychology. Our return to Florida in 1969 began our adventure in clay.

Sandy works full-time at running the pottery, while I work at it on a half-time basis. We have a well-organized and spacious studio with power wheels, slab roller and an eighty-cubic-foot car kiln.

Jay and Sandy Brophy, c/o Brophy Clay, 415 Mead Drive, Oviedo, Florida 32765.

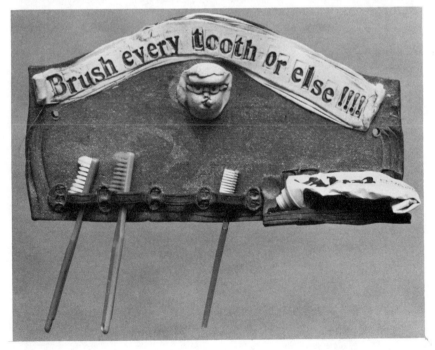

Marbled Paper and Marbled Cloth—
Boxes and containers of cardboard,
wood and metal covered with marbled
paper or marbled cloth in sizes from 1
to 50 cubic inches. Prices range from
50 cents to $1 per cubic inch.
Individual sheets of paper (12'' by
18''), $3 each. Cloth for sewing (same
size), $4. Purses, drawstrings,
scarves, placemats and napkins also
available.

K. Franklin Spoor—I have been
fascinated with the pattern, color,
texture and history of marbled paper
for nearly four decades.

I was introduced to printing and
advertising early, as an apprentice in
a large commercial art studio in the
forties. Since then I have been
primarily involved in the study and
teaching of history and English. I am
hoping to found a press after I retire
from teaching.

This is my personal attempt to
revive and extend the decorative, and
often highly guarded, seventeenth-
century craft of marbling. I am
interested in learning more about the
history of marbling and establishing
contact with present practitioners of
the craft.

*K. Franklin Spoor, Beechwood
Hills, Newport News, Virginia 23602.*

Baskets—These baskets are made of gold, green or brown pine needles found in the Santa Barbara area. This craft is Indian in origin, so many of my designs have a distinct Indian feeling. The stitching has been done with raffia. Many of the baskets are decorated with pheasant and owl feathers, bells and wooden or heishi beads. There are three basic shapes, although each basket made will vary: the rounded bowl, the U-shape (not shown) and the vase. Large bowl, 8'' in diameter, $20.50; large vase, 10'' high, $20.50. Other shapes and sizes: small $12.50, medium $15.50. All postpaid.

Margie Caldwell—I have been making pine-needle baskets for three years, after having explored various areas in textile and fiber. Basketry supplements my full-time teaching job.

As people become increasingly aware of their natural environment, they also become more aware of processes utilizing natural materials. I enjoy sharing the skill I have acquired through the creation of beautiful and lasting objects which use totally natural fibers. The tradition of the craft is also important: to use an idea which has been around for centuries, and to use it in a new way is part of the evolution of our thinking and creativity. My basketry students become convinced of the skill and craftsmanship involved in each piece.

Margie Caldwell, 1750 Hillcrest Road, Santa Barbara, California 93103.

Spinning Wheel—This contemporary spinning wheel is made entirely of hardwood. It has a ball-bearing drive wheel and 1'' diameter orifice. The bobbin holds 24 oz. of yarn up to 1'' thick. Unique features include the hookless flyer with sliding yarn guides for a smoothly filled bobbin and effortless unwinding, with no hooks to cause snags. The Pirtle Spinner can be delivered with the orifice on the left or right for the ''long draw'' spinner. The spinner is 24'' wide by 32'' high by 11½'' deep. It weighs between 35 and 45 lbs., depending on wood selected. Spinning head and stress parts made of hard maple; frame and treadle from shedua, oak, maple or mahogany. Demountable for storage. Mahogany $150, oak $165, maple $175, shedua $185, postpaid.

Pirtle Spinner—Our lives changed six years ago when Bev went into a weaving shop to buy yarns for a macrame project. Until that time she had taught elementary school, preschool and children's crafts. Seeing the yarns in the shop aroused her interest in weaving and subsequently in spinning.

After experimenting with several different spinning wheels, Bev decided she needed a spinner that could spin very bulky as well as fine yarns. Paul, who had already made most of the furniture in their house, used his woodworking talents to craft a wheel which would be a piece of fine furniture as well as a smoothly operating spinner. Now he too enjoys weaving and spinning—which, along with his woodworking, provides a welcome release from the pressures of his engineering and management profession.

Bev and Paul Pirtle, c/o Pirtle Spinner, 21501 St. John Lane, Huntington Beach, California 92646.

Rings—Each ring is a unique conversation piece that can be taken apart and easily reassembled into the original pattern. The pattern is based on the ancient design used for the Turkish ''Harem rings'' which were given by the Sultan to each wife to insure her fidelity. Each ring is individually hand-woven into an intricate pattern of interlocking bands of silver or gold. Our easy-to-follow instructions make it simple to fathom the working of the ring. Rings are available in styles of 4, 6, 8 or 10 bands in either sterling silver or 14k gold. Include exact ring size to ¼'', number of bands, and material preferred when ordering. Top left, $38 silver, $232 gold; middle left, $28 silver, $180 gold; bottom left, $24 silver, $120 gold; top right, $12 silver, $87 gold; middle right (snake), $80 silver, $240 gold; bottom right (twist), $16 silver, $102 gold. Add $1.50 shipping charge.

Norman Greene—As a young man, Norman became involved with the timeless beauty and cosmic intricacies of these rings. He fled the East Coast to sample the wonders of California, settling in Berkeley in 1971, where he started producing fine hand-crafted items. Norman and his colleagues have been doing business for six years. They hope that you will enjoy the complexities and fun of the rings as much as they enjoy making them.

Norman Greene, P.O. Box 8451, Emeryville, California 94662.

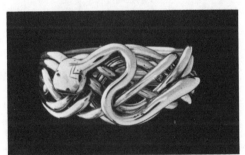

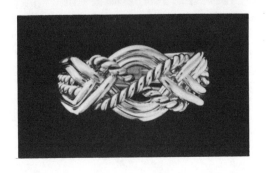

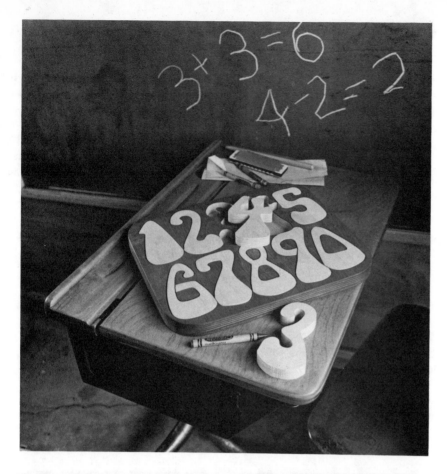

Name Puzzle—Puzzle is approximately 4'' by 8½'' by ¾''. Longer names require a larger piece of wood. This is our favorite puzzle. Since each name is a unique design, we feel a certain familiarity with our puzzle recipients. After all, we know their names! Names up to 6 letters, $9. Each extra letter, 75 cents. Shipping not included.

Alphabet Puzzle—Puzzle is 13¾'' by 9½'' by ¾''. The individual letters average 2½'' high and are easy for kids two years and older to handle. If you aren't much at putting puzzles together or spelling out words, then stacking the letters can produce interesting towers. $18, shipping not included.

Numeral Puzzle—This puzzle measures 11¾'' by 9½'' by ¾''. Each numeral is 4'' high. The pieces are heavy on the bottom to help them stand up. How are you at math games? Arrange the numerals 1 through 9 on a three-by-three grid so that any three numbers added vertically, horizontally or diagonally all add up to 15! $12, shipping not included.

Jim and Judy Williamson—We have tried to make a sturdy toy with lots of play value. The wood (a twelve-ply birch lamination), the glue and the stain are durable and child-safe. Whether the letters or numbers are used independently or as a puzzle, they should provide years of enjoyment.

We started the puzzle business three years ago as a hobby. It has now grown to where we are both working full-time on it. We have found the life of the craftsman austere at times, but uniquely gratifying. We feel that it is important and rewarding to simplify the relationship between ourselves and our work. At the end of each day we know exactly what we have done for a living. This certainty makes us both proud and grateful.

Jim and Judy Williamson, 108 Lorraine Court, Berea, Kentucky 40403.

Lady Pillows—These Art Nouveau pillows are made of printed cottons and satin embroidery on linen. They have a velvet backing and polyester-filled inner pillows. Measuring 14'' by 14'', the pillows display a variety of colors. $52 postpaid.

Children Collage—I use upholstery material almost exclusively in these collages, especially brocades, velvets, damask, matelasse, antique laces and trims—I like unusual material of any kind. The collages are machine-embroidered and lightly stuffed to give form and dimension. They come stretched and ready to hang, and are 18'' by 25''. $205 postpaid.

Eleanor Loecher—I've been doing fabric collage on my own for about four years now. I started years ago doing designs for women's magazines. When the editors themselves started buying my things, I started putting my pieces in art and craft galleries.

   The house we live in was built in 1820, and I share my attic studio with a bell-ringing ghost. I use everything around me as subject matter—the woods, my daughters, the wildlife and as much fantasy as I can conjure.

   Eleanor Loecher, R.D. #1, Box A35, Sandy Hook, Connecticut 06482.

Wind Chimes—These chimes have an especially delicate but full sound. They are made of white earthenware clay with impressed flower designs, stained to bring out detail. Specify color for stain when ordering (darker colors show up better). Chimes have from 5 to 7 pieces and average 6'' in diameter, 24'' in length; lengths can be suited to your specifications. $22 postpaid.

Alba Studio—I am a member of the Highwater Crafts Center, a crafts cooperative, and the Western Carolina Arts Coalition. My studio is located in an old warehouse in Asheville rented by the cooperative. Members include five potters, four woodworkers, one printer and one blacksmith; we are the only group in this area working together in this way.

Sarah Struby, c/o Alba Studio, P.O. Box 705, Asheville, North Carolina 28802.

Zafu—Traditional round meditation cushion with carrying handle. Stuffed with kapok, an organic fiber imported from the Far East, each zafu comes with an opening tucked inside one of the pleats for addition or removal of kapok. Mats and cushions are double-sewn and hand-tufted, and come in black, royal blue, kelly green, chestnut brown, marigold yellow, plum purple and blue denim (add 10% for denim). Zafus measure 7'' high, are 12'' in diameter and weigh 2½ lbs. $14.50, shipping not included.

Zabuton—A mat used under the zafu or alone for meditation or any other living activity. Filled with cotton batting, the Zabuton is available in two sizes: 27'' by 34'' or 30'' by 34''. $17, shipping not included.

Samadhi Cushions—We operate within the framework of Karmê-Chöling, a residential contemplative community devoted to the Buddhist discipline of meditation, study and work.

Although not all of us here are directly involved with the Samadhi project, we all benefit by it—not necessarily financially, but as one of the three expressions of our way of life—practice, work and study.

The project is rather a unique and exciting attempt at incorporating a certain lifestyle with the energies needed to flourish in the business world. Our success is proof that one does not have to sacrifice either.

Samadhi Cushions of Karmê-Chöling, Barnet, Vermont 05821.

Cloisonne Enamel Pendant—The "Pair of Birds" pendant pictured is cloisonne enamel in a specially designed hand-wrought setting, $350 postpaid. It is shown with a completely hand-fabricated silver chain, $125 postpaid. For each order I design from the idea expressed by the customer, and then decide the method and the materials to use.

Nicholson Designs—My first involvement with jewelry and design began while I studied creative art in college. It seemed to me a wonderful way to merge the creative force with a medium that people could become directly involved with. Since that time I have worked intently towards developing a style that reflects my personal/spiritual perceptions. My work is my sole occupation, as well as a sort of personal yoga.

Barbara Nicholson-McFadyen, c/o Nicholson Designs, P.O. Box 64, Wilmington, North Carolina 28401.

Raku Lamps—I make these lamps in Oriental styles and shapes. A soft wash of pastel color runs through the cracked, semi-matte white glaze. A full palette of colors is available, and custom color schemes can be mixed for an additional charge of $5 per color. Hardware is made of heavy brass with a matte black finish. Lamps are prewired, but do not include shades. Sizes are 12'', 16'', 20'' and 24'' (ceramic section); the lamps weight 10, 20, 30 and 40 lbs., and cost $35, $45, $55 and $65.

Russell Gamble—I began working in the ancient Japanese raku technique of low-fired, porous earthenware seven years ago. Raku is a rustic, primitive method of firing involving basic materials and equipment. It is fully developed and controlled by the potter in a spontaneous and personal experience. The completed piece carries unique markings resulting from the process it has endured, giving it a feeling of great age and ruggedness.

Russell Gamble, P.O. Box 1915, San Jose, California 95109.

Pipes—Our pipes are made from the same materials used by natives and settlers. The bowl is soapstone; the stem, maple. Soapstone is a multicolored, easily worked rock with a heat-tolerant quality. Our rock comes from the Sierra Foothills near the town of Railroad Flats, California. Maple is used for the stems because of its strength. We prune the trees, then burn out the pithy center of the wood, which gives the pipes a sweet taste. Each pipe comes with a leather bag for bowl protection. Wire stem cleaner and screen filter included. Large stems 12'' to 15'', $13.50 postpaid. Small stem 5'', $9 postpaid.

Mountain Pipes—We're both Aries. Our heads, hearts and souls rest in the mountains. At the moment our bodies reside in Fat City, California. Pipes have been our trade for six years, and we put much care, concern and energy into our work.

We dig up our own rock, cut our hardwoods and search for magic. We would never kill anything for use in our pipes. Smoke with peace in your heart.

Vince and Jodi Castanon, c/o Mountain Pipes, P.O. Box 2245, Stockton, California 95201.

Harpsichords—Pictured is a French double manual harpsichord, a reproduction of an extant 1769 instrument designed by Pascal Taskin. The harpsichord measures 91'' by 36¾'' by 11¼'' and has a range of 61 notes—FF to fff. The entire case is made of solid poplar. The maple or oak wrest-plank and other cross members are let into mortises in cheek and spine and secured with trenails as in the original. The harpsichord is strung with low tensile wire, which best simulates early iron wire and produces a tone rich in harmonics at early pitch. Other models available. Delivery time 18 to 20 months. $6,200.

Early Music Stand—This is a wooden stand designed especially for early music performance. Hand-crafted from solid cherry, it is then oiled and hand-rubbed to a satin finish. The desk tilts and adjusts in height from 26'' to 48'' so you can play comfortably sitting or standing. $98.

Richard Lee—Mr. Lee has been researching and making harpsichords for the past six years. While satisfying the demand for elegantly styled, well-built musical instruments and stands, the sales of these creations also allows him to sustain his research of early harpsichords. He uses authentic construction methods and woods to make precise copies of important extant instruments.

Richard J. Lee, 75 Homer Avenue, P.O. Box 277, Palo Alto, California 94302.

Whitesmith's Wares—All my products are forged of low-carbon steel, the closest thing to iron still available commercially. To prevent rust, simply keep the piece lightly oiled with vegetable oil. Hardware can be painted, oiled, sealed with a varnish or polyurethane, or left to acquire a patina through rusting. Skimming ladle, 18'' to 20'', $36; keyhole spatula, 14'', $21; spatula,

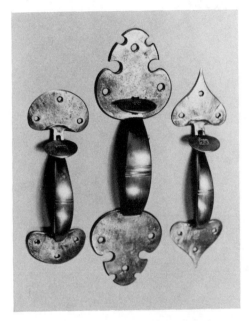

15'', $9; ladle, 20'', $45. Interior kidney bean latch, 7½'', $18; exterior latch, 14'', $60; interior onion latch, 9'', $21. Before ordering latches, please determine whether house construction is suitable. The door must be mortised, staple points must go through the door and the doorjamb will have the keeper driven into it. Hearth toaster, 18'' by 13½'' by 6'', $125; candle stand, 60'' tall, $1,500.

Peter Ross—For the last five years I have been concerned primarily with the iron and steel objects one might find in an eighteenth- or nineteenth-century house here in New England. This includes hardware, lighting devices for candles and oil, cooking utensils and fireplace equipment.

Many of these items were made not by the blacksmith, but by the whitesmith, who was responsible for pieces of greater refinement and finer finish. Generally those pieces were filed and/or ground to remove all marks of forging.

I forge all my work freehand from bars and sheets. Forge-welding produces the smoothest transitions and flow of lines, and is the type of welding used during this period. Finishing is done with files, not in retaliation to industry, but as a means of achieving the character and quality often found in ironwork of this period.

Although I work with period iron, I am rarely called on to copy a piece exactly. Often the designs are my own and involve combinations of motifs to fit specific areas and periods. Some pieces are entirely spontaneous and have no conscious connection with any other existing work.

Ironwork constitutes my sole means of earning income. I work alone and have been here on the coast of Maine for over a year. However, for the last four years I have actively pursued a career in ironwork through various apprenticeships and study experiences. All of my work is done on order. I can work from sketches, rubbings, books, photos and original artifacts.

Peter Ross, Old Ferry Road, Deer Isle, Maine 04627.

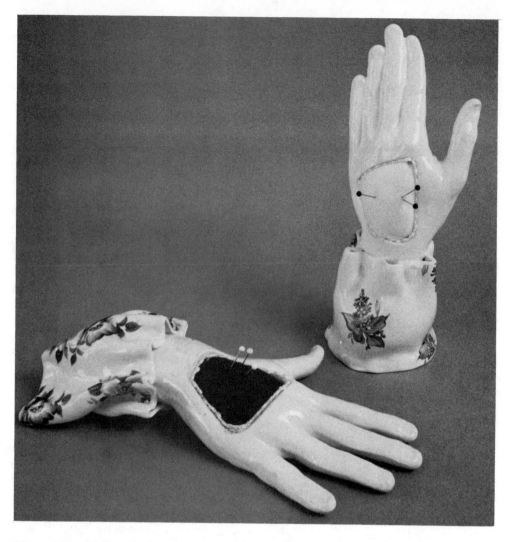

Pincushion—Life-size hand-shaped pincushions are made with earthenware and velvet. White only with brown, white, burgundy or purple velvet cushion and coordinated color decals. Shown here are flat open palm and upright palm. Upright fist and flat palm (fingers together) are also available. Shipping weight 1 lb. $40.75 postpaid.

Susan Potts—I live on a small farm in Wisconsin with Leo and Morgan, my calico cat and cairn terrier. I grow vegetables and work full-time and overtime as a potter.

I consider the expression of humor one of the most important aspects of my work. Most of my work is a direct reflection of the influences around me. Because I work with body parts in combination with articles of everyday life, I consider most of my ceramic constructions to be self-portraits.

Susan Potts, Route 1, Box 138, Cedar Grove, Wisconsin 53013.

Stoneware Rice Bowls—These bowls are 7'' in diameter and weigh 14 oz. They are glazed with temmoku, a glossy black glaze. The temmoku is made with the wood ash from my workshop stove and with Albany slip, a clay mined near Albany, New York, that was used for generations as a liner glaze in New England salt-glazed stoneware. Lead-free and easy to live with on a daily basis. $6 each, shipping not included.

Dancing Man Pottery—I have taught school in Chicago, edited a trade magazine, fought fire and rounded up wild horses in Eastern Oregon, and turned wood in Maine.

I've been potting full-time back here in Massachusetts now for five years, the last two in a chicken barn that served as both home and studio. Recently we bought a home of our own—more than a hundred and twenty years old, with twelve rooms, a barn with one thousand square feet of workspace and an attached garage-cum-kiln shed. Ah, luxury—making it back to the middle class.

Where is Roland White?
Jim Salem, c/o Dancing Man Pottery, #4 Severance, Shelburne Falls, Massachusetts 01370.

293

Placemats—Linen and special rug wool are combined to make an easy-to-care-for placemat. A wide choice of colors are available; a variety of herringbone patterns are used. Mats measure 11'' by 18'' plus fringe. $3.50 each.

David Haywood—I am a professional craftsman and have earned my living for the past seven years from my craft. After serving an apprenticeship to a traditional weaver, I set up my shop and began production. All my looms are antiques, and I have many other pieces of antique spinning and weaving equipment which I use in daily production.

David Haywood, 804 Cockletown Road, Yorktown, Virginia 23690.

Wooden Toys—My hardwood toys are rubbed with nontoxic linseed oil. Tractor of hard maple, $14, and its oak and maple disk, $10. Maple whale that bounces along on eccentric oak wheels, $11.50. Maple mastodon, $11.50, all postpaid. Cherry or walnut slightly more.

The Maple Horse—I began making toys four years ago. Gradually it has become my living. Last year I became a full partner with Paula Jacobssen, the lady of my life. Our business, The Maple Horse, is in downtown Bloomington, Illinois. We sell toys, quilts, hand-spun wool, blown glass, pottery, leather goods and graphics.

We thoroughly enjoy making toys, but we enjoy seeing children derive pleasure from them more. We see our toys as alternatives to cheaply made, crass, mass-produced items.

Things that make us happy are horseback riding, camping, bluegrass music and spending time with three-year-old Katie. We love the Midwest and hope to have land here someday with three cats, two dogs, a cow and a pig.

Darrell Schapmire, P.O. Box 11, Towanda, Illinois 61766.

Moccasins and Boots—Our moccasins and boots are built inside and out, using the best, soft, sturdy glove-tanned cowhide we can buy. Standard colors are sand, rust, brown and black. Long-lasting soles are made of oak leather or rubber and neoprene material. Pictured from left to right are the Apache boot, 7'' high, $50; the deluxe child's moccasin, $35; and the moccasin boot, 7'' high, $95.

Freespirit Leatherworks—My name is Cristy, and my dad is Don. As we traveled about the country doing fairs and selling our wares, Don taught me leatherwork. Besides moccasins, I make soft leather caps, handbags, vests, shirts and jackets.

Don started making footwear about ten years ago, after he dropped out of his lofty position in an electronics firm. He says, ''I had time to think about footwear and decided to make the best, most substantial mocs and boots I could make. It seems that just about the time a pair of commercial shoes become really comfortable, the damn things fall apart. I hope to correct this by making the shoes comfortable to begin with, by using the best leather available and by using a sole that can be replaced by almost anyone. I think we have corrected that problem.''

Cristy and Don Collins, c/o Freespirit Leatherworks, P.O. Box 128, Vineburg, California 95487.

Japanese Flutes—The Shakuhachi is an end-blown flute tuned to a pentatonic scale. By various fingerings and by controlling the angle of the mouthpiece against the lip, all twelve tones of the Western chromatic scale can be produced. The quality of a Shakuhachi is determined largely by the quality of bamboo that is used. Heavy, thick-walled bamboo make more mellow and sensitive flutes. Thinner-walled flutes have a harder sound, a slightly more resonant tone which is by no means unmellow. More expensive flutes are those cut closest to the root. $15, $20, $30, $45 and $60 flutes are available. Pictured: Shakuhachi in the style of the Kinko sect. Two-piece construction with hardwood plug and sterling silver bands. Bamboo was cut cured and seasoned for 4 years before being fashioned into a Shakuhachi. $175. One-piece construction, $135.

Monty Levinson—Ralph, Mike and Peter showed me the first Shakuhachi; crude but magical. And Tom, who will be a master himself someday, and Steve in Japan introduced me to the ways that are now vanishing. A passing interest became a life's work and, more importantly, a way of life. The spirit took up residence and we settled into a routine, day to day. Any craft, in the true sense of the word, must develop from the most mundane aspects of one's existence. Like air or water or fire, the most astounding is also the most common.

Monty Levinson, P.O. Box 294, Willits, California 95490.

Belt Buckles—Our solid brass belt buckles are individually hand-constructed to fit belts 1'', 1¼'', 1½'', 1¾'' wide or any custom size. Whales: we donate $10 from each whale buckle to Greenpeace, an organization working to save the whales. Specify species if you like. Plain, $15; inscribed ''Save Our Oceans,'' $20. Superboat: any boat that requires 10 or more piercings to saw. This boat is a square-rigged tops'l schooner, $20. Sunset, $15; also oval, $16. Oval boat, $15; also rectangle, $14. Each boat is different. We make all modern rigs with marconi or gaff-rigged sails. For custom work, send a photo or accurate drawing of boat from abeam (side view), $15, or $20 with the boat's name. Oval tree, $13; also rectangle, $12. All postpaid.

David and Barbara Bowman—We left our last ''job'' in 1972 when our son Reid was six months old. After four years, now that we're no longer living at the bare survival level, we find that working for ourselves allows us a lot of freedom to grow creatively, socially and personally. We are able to invest some of our time and energy in save-the-earth projects, such as opposing nuclear power development and supporting the whale movement.

David and Barbara Bowman, Box 738, Berkeley, California 94701.

© 1976 by Helen Morris

Sweaters—These hand-knits may help to prevent chilblains from taking over the earth. The design's yoke is a head and chest protector. There are pockets and a drawstring at the neck. Available in oiled worsteds, boucles, tweeds, recycled denims, silks and flaxed linens. Acrylic and orlon, in all colors: small $41, medium $43, large $47. Bulky, 4-ply wool: small $49, medium $53, large $57. Hand-spun wool, in all natural colors and tweeds: small $70, medium $80, large $90. Shipping not included.

Helen Morris—I began knitting as a lark. I wound up designing after finding most of the patterns uninspiring.

Eventually I hope to raise sheep and goats and sell my own hand-spun yarn. I am also writing two books: one on healthy cheesecake recipes and one on antique spinning wheels.

Helen Morris, 535 North Bath Street, Santa Barbara, California 93101.

Woven Pillows—Hand-spun and woven of wool, angora (from our own rabbits), cotton, mohair, synthetics and/or dog hair. Each one is unique in its color combinations, fibers and texture. They are mostly natural shades of off-white, browns and grays. Some have touches of color, beads or shells added. Please request shades, colors, fibers, beads. Pillows are 12'' by 12'' and have fabric backing. $25 postpaid.

Joan Siegel—I am a self-taught spinner and weaver, and a retired speech and hearing therapist. (I retired seven years ago at the age of twenty-three.) I live in the country where we raise our own sheep and angora rabbits for their wool. I make all kinds of things with the yarns I spin: socks, hats, sweaters, mittens, etc. The list is constantly growing.

I find working with fibers very relaxing and enjoy watching the designs and textures take shape as I weave. It's very satisfying living in the country, growing food to eat and raising animals for fibers to make yarns for clothes.

Joan Siegel, Route 1, Box 54A, Stout, Ohio 45684.

Salad Bowl Set—Made of 210 pieces of exotic wood veneer laminated in molds. Only two molds are used since the entire set is made of two basic 90° curves. Each bowl is about 6'' square by 2½'' deep. Set weighs 4 lbs. $375.

Purse Mirrors—These small clam-shaped purse mirrors have a pivoting top which, when open, exposes a 2¼'' mirror. They are made from various exotic woods and cost $10 each.

Exotic Wood Designs—Gary Stam and Lynn Allinger work together in a partnership, producing wooden accessories. Gary is a graduate of the School for American Craftsmen at Rochester Institute of Technology and has a B.F.A. in woodworking and furniture design. He teaches woodworking evenings at R.I.T.'s College for Continuing Education, where Lynn first became involved with wood as one of Gary's students.

Gary Stam and Lynn Allinger, c/o Exotic Wood Designs, 50 Mulberry Street, Rochester, New York 14620.

Landscape Pillows—This is a three-part pillow set of an idyllic scene. The sky is dyed so that it has a dark-to-light shaded effect. The pillows are 16'' square and 4'' deep, and are done in blue-greens or shades of brown. The materials used are satins, velvets and brocades. Each pillow weighs 1½ lbs. packed. There is a cityscape set available at the same price: $120 for three pillows, $80 for two pillows, $40 for one pillow.

Rainbow Pillow—This is a happy pillow, a celebration pillow. Color combinations: either blue, red, orange, yellow and white, or brown, tan and beige. Made of satins, cotton pique and textured polyesters. Large, 12'' square, 1½ lbs. packed, $18. Small, 7'' square, 1 lb. packed, $10.

Bob and Carol Nude Pillow Sets—Bob and Carol are sensuous and whimsical at the same time. And definitely provocative. Each pillow is 14'' wide, 17'' high and 4'' deep. They are made of satins, prints, brocades or whatever you like, in your color combinations. A custom portrait nude set can be made from a photo for an extra $30. Packaged weight for each pillow is 2 lbs. Three-pillow set $180, two pillows $120, one pillow $60.

Margaret Cusack—Born in Chicago in 1945, Margaret has lived in New York since 1959 and in Brooklyn since 1971. She received a B.F.A. *cum laude* from Pratt Institute, majoring in graphic design. Margaret has since worked as a graphic designer, set designer and advertising art director. In 1971, she won an Emmy award for set design for station WETA-TV in Washington, D.C. Since 1972, Margaret has worked as a free-lance illustrator and craftsperson in appliqued collage—fabric artwork. The NYC Bicentennial Corporation chose her as a contributor to the Crafts Revisited Program, and she was an exhibitor in the U.N. International Women's Year Art Festival.

Margaret Cusack, c/o Margaret & Frank & Friends, 124 Hoyt Street, Brooklyn, New York 11217.

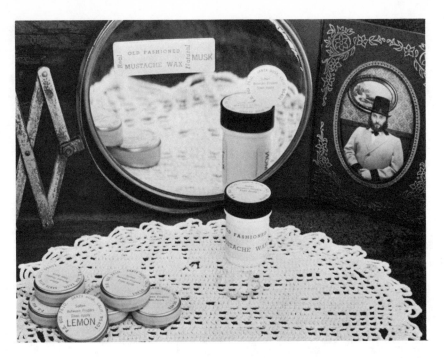

Lloyd Walton—I was born in Kansas and raised in a children's home and a reform school. I have been on my own since I was fourteen. I joined the service in 1961, then worked in gas stations and factories until 1967, when I dropped out. I spent the next few years in the Bay Area teaching myself leatherwork. I am also a sewing-machine repairman, horse trader, graphic artist, gardener and carpenter, and I raise bees, rabbits and a few other things.

Right now my partner Kathy and I have a home next to our leather shop. All our business with people is conducted on a personal basis. I do a lot of barter. I help people find homes and jobs. Giving information that helps people turns me on.

The mustache wax thing has been in me for over a year. Now the dream is a reality in the shape of a product designed to hold a mustache and please one's nose. No loans, no family —only faith, hope, determination, will power, tears, sweat and sacrifice brought it all together. And love.

Lloyd Walton, Real Natural Old-fashioned Mustache Wax Co., P.O. Box 7610, Santa Rosa, California 95401.

Mustache Wax—Dr. Walton's Real Natural Old-fashioned Mustache Wax is created, blended, packaged and sold by man with a mustache. We use a blend of natural ingredients and honest-to-goodness beeswax. Available in spearmint, lemon, musk, orange, almond, strawberry, vanilla, and pineapple scents, or unscented. Half-ounce, wide-mouth, milk-glass jar, $3. Six-pack of ¼-oz. tins, $6.

Pyramid Pillow—Made-to-order for you in your color choices of all-wool yarns with coordinated cotton velvet facing and backing. Size: 14'' by 14'' by 3''. $135. *Jerry's Two-Needle Pyramid* booklet describes this new technique for creating pyramid forms on mono canvas, $3 postpaid.

Aardvark Adventures in Handcrafts —The interrelationship of threads, fabrics and designs has been a lifelong interest for me. My desire is to share my enthusiasm and knowledge with others.

Jerry Zarbaugh, c/o Aardvark Adventures in Handcrafts, 1191 Bannock Street, Livermore, California 94550.

Pendants—Made totally by hand, using sterling silver and natural stones. The chains are also sterling silver and are available in 18'' or 15'' lengths. Please specify which length you desire. Various stones are also available: lace agate, banded agate, golden tiger's eye, tree agate, goldstone, carnelian, mother-of-pearl, jade (black or green) and moss agate. Please remember to specify stone and chain length. Small pendants, $12. Large pendants, $13.

Stephen Freeman—Although I have been interested in jewelry design and fabrication for most of my life, I have only been doing it in a professional capacity for two years. Prior to that I led a fairly varied life, working in occupations ranging from auto mechanic to professional psychologist and university instructor. Although I receive a great deal of satisfaction from working directly in the metal, I still feel a very strong desire to work with younger craftsmen who are just getting started. To achieve this end I am in the process of trying to go back to school to get an M.F.A. so I can teach jewelry and metalsmithery.

Stephen Freeman, 5411B Chesterfield, Austin, Texas 78751.

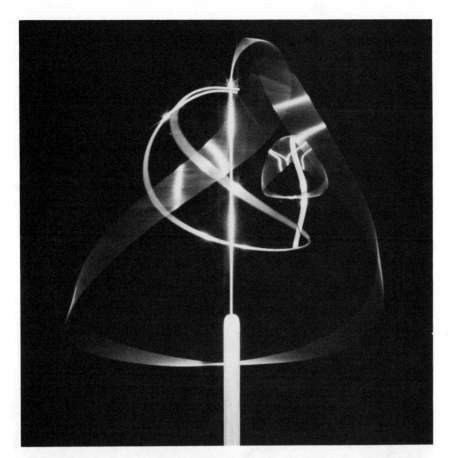

Kinetic Sculpture—My sculptures are made of chromed steel, acrylic and/or walnut. The sculptures are manually started and move gracefully or playfully. A photo brochure is available for $1.25. Quadruple mobile is a stationary mobile, 30'' wide by 30'' high, $200. Tear drop mobile is a moving mobile, 48'' wide by 6' high, $450. Shipping not included.

Randy Georgi—My sculpture has evolved as my principal source of income after several years of selling various media. My work ranges from wood sculpture and photography to found objects, plastics, pen and ink and chrome. I've developed pieces designed for wind and motors, as well as those that simply sit still.

I began seven years ago by opening a crafts store in Berkeley prior to the street artists' appearance. I now have a workshop in a rural area just north of San Francisco.

Randy Georgi, 1212 15th Avenue, San Francisco, California 94122.

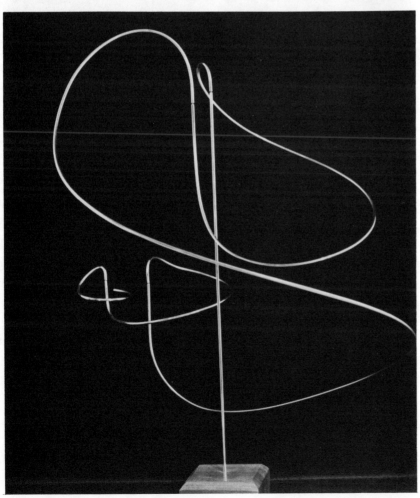

Tiffany-style Lampshades—Take a step back in time with our elegant stained-glass lampshades. Our original designs are crafted with the old copper foil method, a time-consuming process which involves designing the mold, cutting the glass, grinding the edges, copper-foiling and burnishing each piece and then flowing solder onto the copper foil both inside and out. There are no solder joints to disturb the gentle, flowing lines. Our tulip lamp is composed of 3 sections: the neck, a soft light green; the body, which can be yellow, peach, orange or red; and the petal, colored to contrast with the body. Shade is 9'' high, base is 11½'' high; assembled height 22½''. Solid brass cap is 4½'' wide. Tulip lampshade $75, with flowered panel $85. Grecian lady base, $28. All prices postpaid.

Little City Stained Glass—My wife and I live in San Francisco. We love our work and love working together to create something that will endure past our lifetimes. Polly and I try to bring beauty into being, so we can be proud to say that we have enhanced your lives with our workmanship.

Peter and Polly Zajda, c/o Little City Stained Glass, 1234 Eighth Avenue, San Francisco, California 94122.

Western Stock Seat Saddles— Custom-designed for work or show. Bowman tree foundation or special-order trees—Arab, child's, trick riding. Made of cowhide with rough or smooth side out exteriors. Sheepskin underlying skirts and optional suede fancy-stitched seats. Adult-size seats 15'' to 18''. Popstitching, rawhide-rolled horns and cantles, all silver ornaments and inlaid work done by special request. Specify colors: hides are natural buff but can be stained or dyed to your liking. All exposed surfaces are coated with a leather wax for protection. Original stamped floral designs. Stirrups and cinches included in price. Approximate weight 40 lbs. unpackaged. $400 and up. Shipping not included.

Mervin Ringlero—Born in 1917 and raised on the Lehi and Soboba Indian Reservations, Mr. Ringlero has been a saddle maker for nearly thirty years. He began as an apprentice to his father in Arizona. For twenty years he worked with the San Fernando Valley Saddlery Company and Ellis Saddle Company in Southern California as an anonymous craftsman.

His work has been recognized as perhaps the finest example of leather floral tooling and stamping in the world of saddle construction. His individually designed floral pattern stamping is marked by its delicacy and control. He helped to create a legend of saddle making. Now the man and his work can be identified in the forefront of the ranks of Native American master craftsmen.

Mervin Ringlero, c/o Horsemen's Haven, 33527 Rosedale Highway, Bakersfield, California 93307.

Chair—The chair is made of Eastern oak with oak veneer inserts for the seat and the back. It is finished with Danish oil, which gives it a golden honey color and brings out the natural richness in the wood. It measures 30'' high by 17'' wide by 18½'' deep and weighs 13 lbs. For structural strength, the chair pieces are secured with machine bolts (shown) or countersunk woodscrews capped with plugs. $75.

Table—The tabletop is solid 1'' Eastern oak. The table measures 33'' wide by 72'' long by 29'' high, and is finished with Danish oil. $275.

Frank Bletsch Designs—I have been designing and building custom wood furniture for four years, and it is now my principal source of income. I work mainly by myself, but hire people occasionally. My background is in the arts and industrial design. My furniture has been featured in the California Design 76 exhibit and in Sunset Books.

Frank Bletsch, c/o Frank Bletsch Designs, Upstairs at 2366 Valley Street, Oakland, California 94612.

Cradles—Early American design, made of ¾'' clear pine and held together by ¼'' hardwood dowels and glue. The rockers are 1¼'' clear pine. The outside of the cradle is stained. The inside is left the natural wood color. The headboard has two birds carved on it, as my trademark. Width: 16'' at bottom, 20'' at top; 34'' long, 32'' high. Shipping weight: 35 lbs. $180, shipping not included. Also available in maple, shipping weight 50 lbs., $215, shipping not included.

Cradle Bassinet—My own design, made out of ½'' clear pine. The rockers are 1½'' clear pine and are easily detachable to allow use as a bassinet. Sanded smooth and finished with polyurethane. Measures 16'' wide at bottom, 17'' wide at top. It is 34'' long and 23'' high, shipping weight 23 lbs. $90, shipping not included.

The Woodcarver—I have been involved in woodcarving for six years. I am one of many artists and craftspersons who have shops or studios in our remodeled warehouse. I have a combination gallery space and work area in my shop so that customers may see how the work is done. I also do special-order woodcarving and find it necessary to share ideas with the customer while the work is in progress.

Joseph Thompson, c/o The Woodcarver, 725 West Alder, Missoula, Montana 59801.

Pillows—Batiked and machine-quilted 14'' by 14'' pillows, firmly stuffed with polyester batting. They are available in several patterns (Sunrise, Geometric, Mixed Flowers, Tulips, Daisies, Fern) and about ten color combinations (yellow/green, pink/purple, blue/navy, etc.). The backing is white with the characteristic batik ''crackle'' in all three of the dye colors (first and second dyes plus the resulting third color mixture). $20 postpaid.

Ginevra Bayles — My batik and sewing work are a part-time business and source of income for me. I have been doing this for four and a half years, mostly on an individual basis. I participate in almost all the local craft events and sell through various stores around the country. My two children, husband and I have lived in Eugene for five years and have settled into the proverbial happy home in the country! He is a photographer and we are lucky enough to have sufficient room for us both to work in our house.

Ginevra Bayles, 85060 Spencer Hollow Road, Eugene, Oregon 97405.

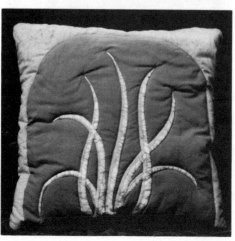

Church Vestments—Special vestments for ministers of all religions. Each design is individually made after a personal consultation and reflects the inner person who wears the vestment as well as the religion he or she moves within. Items are hand-stitched and executed in mixed media—embroidery, applique, quilting, off-loom weaving and batik. Colors and styles are chosen individually. Robes are available in caftan style or Russian style (shown here). They are fashioned of 100% cotton calcutta and are fully lined. Shipping weight 6 lbs. Basic robe (undecorated) $85. Fully decorated robe (neck, sleeves, front, back) $350. Stoles are available in any style or fabric. Shipping weight 1 lb. $40. Set of four stoles, $150. Shipping not included.

Vestments and Paraments by Mary Becker—I live in the hills by the Santa Monica Mountains with my two children. My life has been in a state of flux—growth and change these last few years. I feel very deeply that my talent and creativity are in my hands, and my work is a joy to me. My lifestyle is such that I make enough to be comfortable with my children, and to pursue the classes and workshops that broaden my craftsmanship.

Mary Becker, c/o Vestments and Paraments by Mary Becker, 20935 Marmora, Woodland Hills, California 91364.

Hammocks—Our hammocks are made of soft, textured, weather-resistant polysynthetic rope. This greatly reduces the problems of rot, mildew and shrinkage. Rope ends are knotted and fused with a hot iron. The multistrand interlocking weave makes for strength, comfort and beauty. Large hammock 60'' by 84'' body size, overall length 14', weight 10 lbs., $49. Medium hammock 54'' by 82'' body size, overall length 13', weight 9 lbs., $42. Small hammock 48'' by 82'', overall length 12', weight 8 lbs., $37. All prices postpaid.

Twin Oaks Community—When Twin Oaks began in 1967 there were eight people living on a 123-acre farm outside of Louisa, Virginia. They took their inspiration from B. F. Skinner's *Walden Two*. We are now seventy-eight people and though we have learned a great deal about the shortcomings of Skinner's techniques, we still strive for similar goals. We share everything, from income and expenses to the common cold. Though we call ourselves a nonracist, nonsexist, noncompetitive community, we spend a lot of time wondering if we can live up to it. It's hard work.

We started making hammocks nine years ago, and we've learned a lot about that too. We now make them better, faster and with more pleasure than we did then. The jig we use to weave the body of the hammock is specially designed so that two people can weave together. Hammock weaving suits us as it is work that can be done at any time that the worker chooses.

Twin Oaks Hammocks, Twin Oaks Community, Route 4, Box 169, Louisa, Virginia 23093.

Educational Puzzle—Creative Cubes comprise 30 wood cubes 2'' square. Each set makes six different puzzles, each containing basic valuable information for the young learner. Children develop perceptual, motor and problem-solving skills while assembling the puzzles. The six puzzles show: a map of the United States; various animal shapes; the color wheel; the alphabet; numerals 1 through 20 in figures and in dots, and various math symbols; and four seasons, twelve months and seven days of the week. $53 postpaid.

Bicentennial Bell—Shaped from an actual 1976 quarter into a small bell with a sterling silver clapper, $9.

Creative Cubes—Lorenzo Baca is an artist of Native American descent. His mother is Isleta Pueblo and his father is Mescalero. Mr. Baca is a creative silversmith with an innovative line of jewelry; he also holds a credential for teaching kindergarten through ninth grade.

His work has been exhibited at the California Museum of Science and Industry in Los Angeles and the Morris Museum of Arts and Sciences in New York City. He is a published poet and writer.

Creative Cubes are the result of his desire to fill the need for a toy that can entertain, educate and aesthetically please the player all at the same time. His philosophy is that the most beautiful object is simple in shape and natural in material.

Lorenzo Baca, c/o Creative Cubes, P.O. Box 1353, Sonora, California 95370.

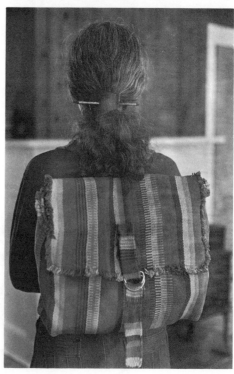

Rug—This 3' by 5' rug is woven with a traditional Swedish Krokbragd threading; changes in color and treadling create the design. The warp is cotton and the weft is all wool, sheared and processed in Maine. High-quality materials and the nature of the weave make this rug very thick and heavy, yet soft and luxurious to the touch. Each rug is woven with five colors in the design. Three color ranges are available: red to orange warm tones, blue to green cool tones and brown to cream neutral tones. Designed by Janet Ressler. Shipping weight 8 lbs., $175.

Knapsack—This hand-woven knapsack is functional and beautiful. It is a roomy 12'' wide by 16'' high by 6'' deep, with extra-long adjustable straps. The all-cotton weave is strong and warp-faced. The colors are a bright and cheerful rainbow in stripes and patterns. Machine-washable. Designed by Sheila Denny-Brown. Shipping weight 2 lbs., $34.

Tote Bag—The tote is woven of rainbow-colored cotton. It is 13'' wide, 15'' high and 5'' deep, with strong handles of the same weave and a small fringe around the top. Machine-washable. Designed by Sheila Denny-Brown. Shipping weight 2 lbs., $22.

North Country Textiles—We are a cooperative of six Maine weavers: Sheila Denny-Brown, Bobby Dickerson, Ron King, Carole Ann Larson, Janet Ressler and Joan Shapiro. We work in our own studios and meet twice a month to conduct business, discuss designs, share news and hold open workshops.

Our work is both individually and cooperatively designed and produced, allowing us to carry a wide range of articles and fill orders promptly.

Several of us teach weaving, one at the university level. We have studied weaving and design at such varied institutions as Cranbrook, Haystack, the University of Maine and the Radcliffe Institute, but many of our skills have been self-taught through years of weaving. We have a year-long apprentice program which provides training and jobs in our under-employed section of the country.

We enjoy living very simply, wasting little. Our looms require no other power than from our own bodies. Several of us are part-time farmers, and we all live in rural areas. We feel that making a living as a weaver is a rare opportunity to live in an independent and satisfying way, responsive to our unique Maine countryside. We are all committed to maintaining the highest levels of quality and design, and to help spread the growing public awareness of fine craftsmanship.

North Country Textiles, Box 176, Route 175, South Penobscot, Maine 04476.

Animal Puzzles—Our puzzles are made from 2'' hardwood which is sanded and rubbed to a polished natural wood finish. This hardwood block is then cut into a number of interlocking pieces. The puzzles which we are presently making vary in number of pieces from six to fourteen. However, this is subject to customer requests. Left to our own devices, we determine the number and shape of pieces attempting to show the mood of the particular puzzle character. We are presently making the following puzzle characters: duck, elephant, hippopotamus, train, house, whale, turtle, apple, butterfly, car, chicken, dachshund, cactus, mouse and kangaroo. The physical dimensions as well as the design vary slightly with each puzzle. However, the dimensions approximate 2'' thick, 10'' to 14'' wide and 6'' to 8'' high. Each puzzle is $7 postpaid.

Dana Kay's Crafts—Our craft business presently represents about half of our income, but is rapidly developing into a full-time operation. We have dabbled in the craft business off and on for about ten years with the hope of one day developing a pleasurable business. Two years ago we made the commitment and hope we will realize the goal of ''full-time'' within the next year. The ''we'' I refer to is my family—three children, my wife and myself. It's a family business. Each one shares in the work, the responsibility and the rewards. But most of all we just enjoy the opportunity of sharing with each other and the fun involved in doing something which we all enjoy together.

Albert Dudek, c/o Dana Kay's Crafts, 824 North Lafayette Avenue, Morrisville, Pennsylvania 19067.

Drawstring Pants—Simplicity of pattern and fabric make these 100% cotton drawstring pants versatile as well as extremely comfortable. The drawstring design enables these pants to be roomy and adjustable. Customer should specify desired color and design. White pants with any choice of color for the pattern along the bottom is preferable, but pants can be made in other solid colors. Send usual pants size for correct fit. Shipping weight 1 lb. $50. (Children's and extra large pants priced accordingly.) Matching cotton shirt, $60. Specify size. Shipping not included.

Hooded Sweaters—This is the closest you can get to wearing the sheep's clothing. These sweaters are woven with unwashed wool, making them water-repellant and somewhat warmer than washed wool sweaters. The fiber still contains lanolin, which causes this water-repellancy as well as a slight odor. Sweaters can be made with either ¾-length sleeves or full-length sleeves. Send normal shirt size for correct fit. Shipping weight approximately 4 lbs. $100, shipping not included.

Harriet Behar—I am striving for self-sufficiency and it is teaching me frugality and self-confidence. I feel my work is of high quality as I project good feelings towards everything I do. Every creation is a learning experience and a one-of-a-kind item. Recently I have been expanding out into the community, seeking to demonstrate and share my skills with others.

Harriet Behar, Route 2, Box 63A, Blue River, Wisconsin 53518.

Appetizer Tray—Use this stoneware appetizer tray for serving vegetables, chips and crackers with guacamole and other dips. It is made in two pieces—plate and dish—for easy cleaning and storage, and is dishwasher-safe. Please specify small or large, and choose which glaze number you prefer: #1, white and shiny black, as shown. #2, white and turquoise. #3, white and light yellow. #4, glossy yellow and dark brown. Small, 11'' wide by 2½'' high, 3½ lbs., 6 lbs. shipping weight, $20. Large, 15'' wide by 3'' high, 5 lbs., 8 lbs. shipping weight, $30.

Crocheted Bags—These unusual bags are whimsically and uniquely crocheted using soft colorful wool yarns and lined with cotton fabric for lasting strength. Each bag is one of a kind, crocheted with any variety of colors. Tell me if you prefer your bag large (about 15'' by 16'') or medium (about 13'' by 14''), symmetrical or asymmetrical, and what sorts of colors you like. Shipping weight 2 lbs. Large, $46. Medium, $38.

Linda Dowdell and Ed Hoe—We have been professionally involved with crafts for four years now. Before moving to Vermont we had a partnership—Fiberwheel Pottery and Weavery in Saranac Lake, New York—and we are now forming another partnership in Vermont as Sarsaparilla Studios.

Pottery is Ed's sole source of income and textiles is half of Linda's. The rest of her income comes from her work as a musical accompanist for modern dance at neighboring colleges and various dance companies.

A commitment to rural living is a strong part of our lives, and combining it with the production of fine crafts has been our main goal for a long time. Our work reflects a desire to produce crafts that are beautiful and interesting, and that serve a function, things that people can use. We hope people can become more accustomed to buying and using people-made products, instead of the machine-made objects that currently clutter our lives and culture.

Linda Dowdell and Ed Hoe, c/o Sarsaparilla Studios, R.D. #1, Hollow Road, Shaftsbury, Vermont 05262.

Fruit and Vegetable Tiles—Each vegetable or fruit consists of four 4¼'' by 4¼'' by ¼'' white body commercial tiles that are handpainted. Turnips: light brown and earthtones with green stems and tops. Carrots: orange with green tops. Lettuce: green with yellow and white highlights. Lemons: yellow with green leaves. Other fruits and vegetables are available. Packaged weight for each fruit or vegetable is 3 lbs. $20 per fruit or vegetable, shipping not included.

Swimming Fish Mural Tiles—Six 6'' by 6'' by ¼'' white body commercial tiles that are hand-painted. The fish are various types: bass, tuna, etc., with varying colors of salmon, blue, gray and black. They are surrounded by a watery blue color glaze. Packaged weight 5 to 6 lbs. $55, shipping not included.

Fish with Border Tiles—Six 4¼'' by 4¼'' by ¼'' white body commercial tiles that are hand-painted. The fish is of grey/blue tones with a sprinkling of black spots, surrounded by a black and white checkered border. The fish is available in other colors. Weighs 4 lbs. packaged. $25, shipping not included.

Susan Tait—Hand-painted tile has been a folk art in many countries and cultures throughout the world. It is an art that has been handed down through the ages. The growing demand for hand-painted tile has resulted in importation of tiles from Mexico, Portugal and Holland. In 1973, while teaching art at the School of Arts and Sciences in San Anselmo, I became interested in the hand-painted tiles of Europe.

Much of my imagery in tile has been in the ''trompe de l'oeil'' style. This means, literally, ''deception of the eye.'' I like to use this approach to give a three-dimensional quality to ordinarily flat tile.

Susan Tait, c/o The Tile Shop, 1577 Solano Avenue, Berkeley, California 94707.

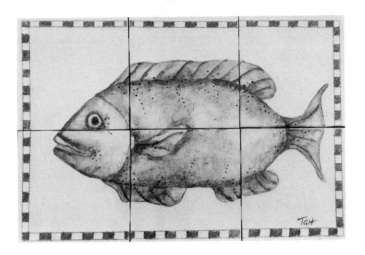

Marbled Bookmarks—Marbled printing is an ancient craft of Turkish origin. The process is done by boiling a special moss in water to make it into a thick sizing. Drops of oil-base inks are floated on the surface of the sizing, and pins and nails drawn through the inks to create patterns. The patterns are then picked up with paper that is laid on top of the sizing. These bookmarks come in assorted colors with a paper backing in a coordinated color and a wool tassel. They are 5¾'' long. $1 each. Shipping charge of $1 for orders under $15.

Marbled Crafts—I am from Georgia, and worked in New York as an artist before turning to marbled printing as a crafts profession. I find it a challenge and a joy. It has flexibility and tremendous potential. I enjoy working with a medium which is relatively underdeveloped, because its boundaries haven't been set yet; there is a sense of innovation about working in the craft.

Kay Radcliffe, c/o Marbled Crafts, P.O. Box 1138, Stuyvesant Station, New York, New York 10009.

Wool Shawls—Can be worn as luxurious wraps, lap robes or couch covers. All wool and woven in traditional twill patterns. This is a sturdy blanket-weight piece that is supple and durable enough to be used actively yet still retain its original beauty. Over 36'' wide, 72'' long. $85, shipping not included.

The Jade Shuttle—My partner Paul Besco and I are weavers. We earn most of our livelihood from the sale of our wares at crafts fairs and through our own studio gallery.

We weave wool, cotton, linen and silk into beautiful durable fabric in traditional patterns and contemporary colors. Our pieces feel homey and are practical as well as beautiful.

Owen Orser, c/o The Jade Shuttle, 8875 Water Road, Cotati, California 94928.

Witch, 10'' tall, $45
Witch, 12'' tall, $55
Clown, $50
Emmet Kelly Clown, $60
Clown, $50

Tiny Tim, $25
Schoolteacher, $40
Student, $20
Newsboy, $40
Toy Maker, $40

Character Dolls—My handmade character dolls are fully clothed and hand-stitched, made of sculpey, bread dough, wax and wood. They are arranged on a wire frame, then cased and stuffed. Dolls are bendable. I also make apple-head dolls, hand-painted stuffed dolls and miniatures for doll houses. Prices range from $10 for doll house occupants to $150 for portrait and special-order dolls. Shipping not included.

Hope France—I am the mother of seven children, now all grown, who have given me twelve beautiful grandchildren. My husband has made me a workshop and display area for me in our basement, so everything is compact and handy.

I spend every possible moment making these exciting little people. They are all completely different, as I work for character in every little face and try for expression in the hands.

I have been working with crafts for eight years, and so far it is a hobby with me, although I have sold my dolls to collectors.

Hope France, 2426 Wismer, St. Louis, Missouri 63114.

Carved Ducks and Geese—My ducks and geese carvings are strictly decorative (not suitable for use as decoys). They are carved from barn beams 75 to 100 years old, that were hewn with an axe or adz at the time the barns were built. We have a supply of cherry, black walnut, oak and wormy chestnut that will last for many, many years. I use only hand tools to do the carving. I make seven species of ducks and geese, and each carving is about 7/8 life-size. Since each carving is done by hand, there is usually a waiting period of about four months per bird. They weigh 5 lbs. packaged. $100.

The Carbon Copy—I gave up a busy, lucrative life in the rich Midwest to move to this tiny mountain town about two years ago, and I plan to stay here carving for many more years. I plan to keep on making each carving by hand, one at a time.

Wood carving is our main source of livelihood, although my wife Shirley and I also operate a photography studio at our place of business. We belong to our local Art Guild and we each teach classes in both photography and wood carving.

David Ritter, c/o The Carbon Copy, 16 North Broadway, Red Lodge, Montana 59068.

Stoneware Oil Lamps—These wheel-thrown, hand-painted stoneware lamps are available in a variety of colors and motifs: spiral, in black, brown or blue on white; primitive goat, in black and blue on white; Egyptian ibis, in brown and black on white; striped flower, in black and blue or black and brown on white; and bull's-eye, in black and blue on white. They are approximately 4'' wide and 3'' high, including covers. $10 postpaid.

Sandra Dalton—All my income comes from sales and teaching of my craft. I work independently, and from time to time in conjunction with other local potters.

I have been involved at this level for about five years. Making pots from clays I've dug from local hills, teaching, a simple life in the country . I've found it possible to make my living this way.

Sandra Dalton, 971 Alleghany Star Route, Nevada City, California 95959.

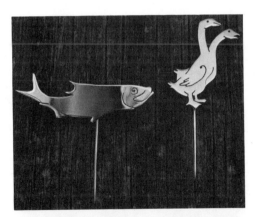

Jewelry—Stickpins are highly polished red brass, hand-pierced and sawed. Flashing trout (2½'' wide by ½'' high), $10. Honking geese (1¼'' wide by 1¾'' high), $10. Sterling silver pelican's foot (2'' wide by 1¼'' high) is hand-sawed, dapped and soldered, and comes with an 18'' hand-constructed chain. $52.

Paula Jo Everett—I'm a metalsmith. My studio is in my home in Ojo Caliente, a gathering of adobes along a ten-mile stretch of river.

We heat our house with wood. On cold nights we like to make the stoves dance. We usually go up into the mountains once a week to get wood and catnap in the sun. I bake every day and seem to appreciate in size as a result. We love our life—the hardest art form to master—in this adobe.

Paula Jo Everett, P.O. Box 498, Ojo Caliente, New Mexico 87549.

Clutch Ball—A popular toy in mountain homes for over a century, these balls were originally made from quilt scraps. These are made with calico prints and matching solids, stuffed with washable foam. Diameter: 6''. $2.75, shipping not included.

Mountain Handicrafts—My business is operated as a partnership with my two sisters, although there are many craftspeople who join us in producing our crafts.

I was born in the isolated mountains of Kentucky and have been involved in crafts since childhood. I served with VISTA for three years. During this time I organized and taught many craft groups.

Mossie Wilson Goodin, c/o Mountain Handicrafts, Silver Route, Box 149-B, Williamsburg, Kentucky 40769.

© 1976 by Indian Images, Inc.

American Indian Needlework Kit—The Chippewa (Ojibway) Head Band Kit includes bound 10-point interlock canvas, design graph, needle, leather thongs, 3 tin cones, 32 tile beads in 2 colors, 12 marabou fluffies, heavy felt backing, history of the tribe and complete, easy-to-follow instructions. Available in red/white/blue, navy/rust or brown/gold Persian wool yarn. $11 postpaid.

Indian Images—Crafts have always been a part of my life. The love and empathy for Native Americans and their culture and art is more current. Indian Images, Inc. provides a business of my own which expresses these two loves. For the first time in my life I am doing something where all aspects of the work are enjoyable. I think it shows—in my work and in my life. And I hope that friends who purchase my pieces and invest in producing them share with me some of this pleasure.

Carolyn Klein, c/o Indian Images, Inc., P.O. Box AA-271, Evanston, Illinois 60204.

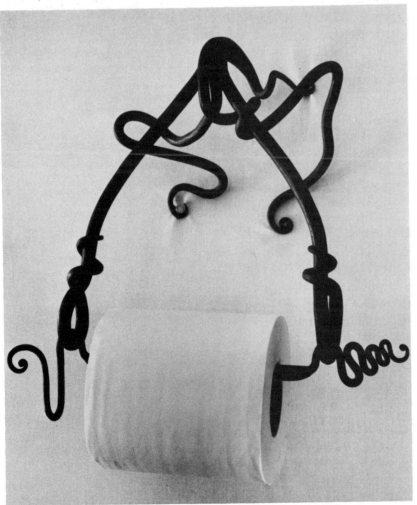

Toilet Paper Holder—Made of mild steel that has been hot-forged on an anvil. The natural protective finish is a mixture of beeswax and linseed oil. Holder attaches to the wall with three screws and bar lifts out for easy paper change. Size: 11'' wide by 10'' tall by 5'' deep, 2 lbs. $50 postpaid.

Peter O'Shaughnessy—I am a self-taught blacksmith, and have been earning my entire income through the sale of my craft for five years. My work—forge welding, riveting, upsetting, heating and bending—is done on an open coal forge.

I live in a small rural community, but I am by no means isolated from others who are also pursuing a life with clean air, clean water and natural foods. I am very happy to be earning a living through the use of my hands.

Peter O'Shaughnessy, Route 1, Box 159, Vesuvius, Virginia 24483.

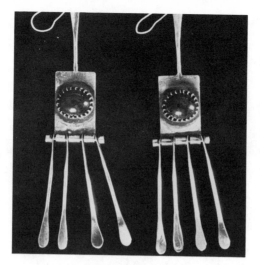

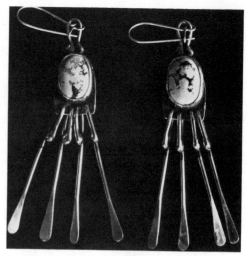

Silver Jewelry—Sterling silver rings with bright metal rims and medial panel surrounded by textured dark antique areas. Maximum width of man's ring 10mm., $50; woman's 9mm., $45. Sterling silver earrings with hinged pendants and choice of stones: carnelian, jade, malachite, amethyst, red jasper, Elat chrysocolla. Maximum length 3''. $40. Sterling silver earrings with pendant elements. Choice of stones in long oval bezel setting: turquoise, carnelian, jade, malachite, red jasper, Elat chrysocolla. Maximum length 2'' $35.

Ophir Jewelry—A partnership of artisans Yvonne Giambrone and Fred Scales. We are engaged in the design and production of gold and silver jewelry, often set with precious and semiprecious gemstones. Pieces are fabricated by forging, piercing, soldering, applique, and the lost-wax method.

Fred Scales, c/o Ophir Jewelry, 420 Riley Street, Santa Rosa, California 95404.

Leather Address Books—The 4'' by 3¼'' address book features a hand-embossed border encircling an inset of pressed flowers. The flowers are sealed on a velvet or satin background. The book is fashioned in soft pigskin or calfskin and contains replaceable alphabetized pages. Brown or gray pigskin suede; natural tan leather. $5.50 each.

Sylvia Nissley—I have designed framed arrangements of dried flowers in the Victorian tradition for several years. My partner was engaged in the design and production of handbags and footwear for many years, and now makes custom books.

The flowers we use are grown by friends and in our own garden. Wildflowers are selectively picked on hikes and camping trips.

Playing classical piano and chamber music are my other delights.

Sylvia Nissley, 338 Fourth Avenue, San Francisco, California 94118.

Medallion Quilt—Our quilts are made with cotton and polyester fabrics, stuffed with glazed dacron polyester batting and either tied or hand-quilted. We will use complementary fabrics based on the color of your choice so that each quilt will be one of a kind. Color choice: light blue, dark blue, red, green, brown, yellow. Each quilt weighs about 5 lbs. Machine-washable. Available in four sizes: 70'' by 90'' tied $110, hand-quilted $200; 80'' by 90'' tied $120, hand-quilted $210; 85'' by 95'' tied $130, hand-quilted $220; 100'' by 100'' tied $150, hand-quilted $240.

Jean Pekarek and Sally Tingley—We love to make quilts and work to improve the quality every time we make another one. We have been making quilts for a relatively short time, but have been sewing all our lives. We are now increasing our knowledge of sewing through patchwork. It's satisfying to make something that is both creative and useful.

Jean Pekarek and Sally Tingley, 1918 Grant Street #2, Berkeley, California 94703.

Stained Glass—All the items are made of hand-cut and assembled glass using the copperfoil technique. The six-compartment box measures 18'' by 6'' by 2''. It is made of antique glass in an assortment of pastels. The compartments all have top openings. $120 postpaid. The Gypsy panel is constructed of antique and semi-antique glass and has a wood frame. It measures 19'' by 17''. The main colors are green and blue. $120 postpaid. The Bow Box measures 8'' by 6'' by 3''. It is made of antique glass with light blue and light green ribbon. $120 postpaid.

Carol Sitarsky—She has been experimenting with stained glass for four years at the Brooklyn Museum Art School, the New School and the Metropolitan Museum at the Cloisters. Her innovative technique, combining stained glass with tinted mirror, will be featured in the upcoming *Mirror Book.*
  Carol Sitarsky, 323 East Ninetieth Street, New York, New York 10028.

Dolls—Despite their name, ''Friends of the Child'' are not only for children, but also appeal to fantasy-loving grownups. They work well as book ends or doorstops, and are just as happy to sit around unemployed. All of the friends are made with 100% cotton velveteen, which I dye in very bright colors. Some have satin features. The main body is filled with birdseed and the remainder with polyester fill. Sun and moon dolls are 25'' long and weigh 5½ lbs., $35 each.

Pat Landskron—I'm happy to share my work with you. I've studied many aspects of art, looking for a medium that suits what I hope to express.

For most of us, the true fulfillment of our ambition lies in the response of people to our craft. For the last several years I've worked in various textile forms, and ''Friends of the Child'' has been my most rewarding venture.

Pat Landskron, P.O. Box 16, Forestville, California 95436.

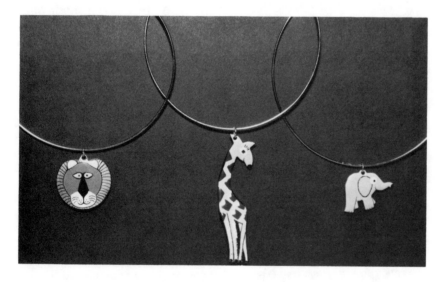

Enamel Zoo Animal Jewelry—All animals are shaped to curve outward or inward. They are counter-enameled, and designed so that there are no sharp points. Giraffe pin or pendant, 3½'' tall, $6.75. Elephant pin, pendant or tie tack, 1½'' long, $4.50. Lion pendant, 1½'' in diameter, $5.50. Specify chain or choker for pendants.

Susan Whitfield—After graduation from college, I held several secretarial jobs and worked with enamel for recreation. I had no art classes in school, so am primarily self-taught. However, I grew up in an artistic environment. My father is a sculptor and I now work in his studio. I have gained a great deal from my parents' talents and abilities.

I have one ongoing guide in my work: to create fine-quality pieces rather than large quantities.

Susan Whitfield, c/o Tintagel Studio, Route 8, Topeka, Kansas 66604.

Victory Box—The box is made of copper-foiled stained glass, with a brass-plated victory buckle. It has a blue background, with red and white stripes. It measures 7'' by 7'' by 3'', weighs 2¼ lbs. packed. $40, shipping not included.

Cradle of the Sun—I became involved with stained glass in 1970, struggled through a period of trial and error, and then was fortunate enough to apprentice with a Latvian stained-glass master, who helped me immensely.

Daniel C. Gamaldi, c/o Cradle of the Sun, 4374 Twenty-fourth Street, San Francisco, California 94114.

Stuffed Animals—Dimensions, weight and color vary with each animal, depending on fabric and personality. I use velvets and velours and stuffing is polyester fiberfill. General color requests are invited, and I like custom orders for new animals. Bodies are machine-stitched; the stuffing, assembly and embroidered eyes are done by hand. Shown: Unicorn, $48. Also available: Stegosaurus, $65; Basic Flying Dragon, $125. All prices postpaid.

Vlada Rousseff—My earning my living as a craftsperson has evolved one day at a time. I have a fine-arts background and was taught to make things I wanted or needed. Somehow it all keeps flopping around and falling together in new ways.

Painting and papier-mache and making clothes to suit myself led to designing for others. In 1970 I started a summertime shop in Stockbridge, Massachusetts, specializing in handmade clothes and crafts.

The transition from dresses to soft-sculpture animals seems very logical and pleasing to me. Besides the summer shop I do craft shows and have a line of handbags. I am getting into wall hangings.

Vlada Rousseff, 113 Mercer Street, New York, New York, 10012.

Teaset—High-fired stoneware glazed in warm ochre with reddish brown highlights. Teapot has reed handle and is 5'' wide by 7'' high. It comes with or without four teacups. Teaset with cups, $24; teapot only, $21.

Pier 9 Pottery—I hand-throw each piece individually on a kick wheel, so there is an interesting variation to each. I also mix my own leadless glazes. My studio is on Pier 9, which is part of the original San Francisco Waterfront. It is a peaceful place to work, by the water with the tugs docked nearby.

Carolyn Means, c/o Pier 9 Pottery, Pier 9, Embarcadero, San Francisco, California 94111.

Reversible Tree Pendant—Made of sterling silver and a natural stone (in this picture, the stone is light green serpentine). Lace agate, carnelian and jade are also sometimes available. The other side of the pendant shows the stone and a bezel setting. The sterling chain may be requested in any length. The pendant is 1½'' by 1-1/8''. $38 postpaid.

Barbara Edwards—I am an individual craftswoman who has been doing business in Berkeley for four years. Making jewelry provided my full income until a year ago when my daughter was born. Until she learns to hold a torch, jewelry will be a half-time profession for me.

I listen to loud music when I work and watch the hummingbirds slurp nectar from the lemon tree outside my many-paned window. My garden is full of flowers and I am easily distracted. I worked for a year in a windowless garage workshop and made a lot of jewelry, but I didn't enjoy it nearly as much as I do with my sun-porch workshop.

Barbara Edwards, 1321 Milvia Street, Berkeley, California 94709.

Name Train—Lay it down or stand it up. This puzzle goes together only one way and when completed, it spells your favorite little person's name. Made of ½'' 7-ply hardwood, with finished sides. Each letter is hand-painted in a bright color. $7 per letter (engine included free) plus $1.50 shipping charge.

Chunky Lion—Big, bold and brightly hand-painted ½'' 5-ply hardwood cut into big chunks that are easy for small hands to grasp. Fun silhouettes help form the completed puzzle. Over 20'' high. We will cut the child's initials into this one, if you wish. Lion (shown), owl and frog, $65 each postpaid.

Wooden Jigsaw Puzzles—Hand-cut to order. Shapes and cuts that delight children of all ages make these puzzles extra special. They are made from ¼'' 5-ply hardwood and backed with walnut. You may have your name or whatever cut into it. An excellent puzzle for a family gift. Dated and signed by the craftsman. A puzzle of 25-30 pieces, designed for ages 3 to 5, $45; a more complex, 110-120 pieces puzzle for ages 5 to 7, $95; and the most intricate, 140-160 piece family puzzle, $130.

Centre Chimney Crafts—Our craft shop and studio are on a dirt road that winds through the hills of Canaan, New Hampshire. We are small by choice, and do consistently high-quality work. We go directly to the mills to select the finest wood and have it custom-made to our exacting specifications. The result of this is a several-ply hardwood board of unparalleled beauty and quality.

My background is in graphic design. I had my own advertising design business outside of Boston for twelve years. Eight years ago I escaped with my wife and three children to the country where the air is clean, the fishing is good and I can practice my craft without too many hassles.

Dave Tibbets, c/o Centre Chimney Crafts, Canaan, New Hampshire 03741.

Robin Freeman, c/o Robin Freeman Design Studios, 2526 Shattuck Avenue, Berkeley, California 94704.

Studio Stool—Knock-down stool is 24'' high. Unfinished fir, $9. Clear-lacquered fir plywood, $12. Birch or mahogany, $20. Rosewood or walnut plywood with hand-rubbed oil finish, $40.

Studio Easel—Tilts, rigid construction, 90'' by 24'' by 36'', will accommodate 7' canvas. Assembled, unsanded basic model, $45. Hemlock fir, with Renaissance-type peg arrangement (as shown), $50. Utility finish, $60. Furniture finish and wood knobs rather than wing nuts, $80. Easel in oak or mahogany, $190. Options: floor rollers, $7.50; extra-wide tray, $2.50; pastel forward-tilting device, $2.50. Free catalog.

Robin Freeman Design Studios—For the past eight years I have made half my living from design and building. In addition, I am a teacher, writer, and community organizer in aesthetics, the environment and peace. I am the sole proprietor of my studio and occasionally hire co-workers and apprentices.

Japanese-style Crab Rubbings—These rubbings are made by putting a special paint directly on a real crab, placing a piece of textured rice paper over it and rubbing until an impression is made. Backed and wrapped in acetate, 14'' wide by 12'' high. Please specify color: red, blue or green. $17 postpaid.
Fish rubbings (Gyotaku) are also available and are made in a similar manner. I can't guarantee what type of fish I'll have on hand, but I usually have some needlefish, among others. Inquiries invited. Price depends on size of fish.

Michael Phillips—Since I am an avid fisherman, I naturally was drawn to the Japanese art of making rubbings from fish and crabs. I lived for many years on the East Coast, where I printed about forty different types of fish. I am now doing California's fish and crabs.
Michael Phillips, P.O. Box 356, Stinson Beach, California 94970.

Jewelry—These pieces are cast from models carved in wax. They are 14k solid gold. Small seahorse, $59 postpaid. Large seahorse, $79 postpaid. Egyptian queen pendant, $145 postpaid. Solid gold 15'' chain optional—add $7.50.

Auric Jewelers—Designing and making jewelry has been my life's work for the past ten years. Being a jeweler feeds me both spiritually and financially, and has become a lifestyle. My wife, Caroline, also makes jewelry, and we support ourselves doing art shows and craft fairs, and by displaying at several fine galleries. It makes us feel good to realize there are pieces of our jewelry all over the world.

Irwin Licker, c/o Auric Jewelers, Star Route #550, Ramona, California 92065.

Weaving—This variation of the South American ruana is more versatile than a poncho or a shawl. It's as elegant as a cape, as warm as a blanket. Made of 100% wool in commercial or natural dyes. One size fits nearly everyone, but extra-large ones can be ordered. Specify color ranges or preferences, such as blues, blue/green, rust/gold or send yarn or fabric swatch or picture as a guideline. Shawls and blankets also available. Ruana (48'' by 54'' plus fringe), $50. Extra large (54'' by 60''), $60. Add $15 for natural dyes.

Mariana Mace—I like to weave beauty for people to use on a daily basis. When you wrap yourself in warmth and color, in something that has been crafted with time and care, it can't help but make everything else a little more special.

Mariana Mace, 40 Harper Street, San Francisco, California 94131.

Hand-painted Silk Kimonos—Hand-made of fine-quality China silk, painted with colorfast silk dyes in brilliant and quiet colors: blues, browns, golds, violets, greens, sunrise tones. Specify background color: silver-gray, sand, chocolate brown, white or blue. Designs are natural images, each different: phoenix, lotus, knots, moonbows, etc. Wrap-front kimono with pockets and waist tie in one size, jacket-length, $100, full-length, $150.

Silk Scarves—Hand-painted in colors and design of your preference. Large, in kimono-weight silk, 18'' by 52'', $35. Small, lightweight silk, 14'' by 40'', $25. Square, lightweight, 30'' by 30'', $25.

Janet Orth—Using clothing as a vehicle, I have found a way to bring the visual harmony of color and two-dimensional design into a sensory experience in the daily world: soft as an imagined cloud against the skin, fluid and changing as a tree whose leaves stir in the breeze.

In Indonesia, batik masterpieces are commonly worn as wrapped sarongs with the better side to the inside, against the skin, for the inner self to absorb the magic that the artist has transferred into the garment through the symbolism of the design.

My works, as do all creations made with care by hand, also embody the magic of spirit. The work is complete when the new owner puts it on.

Janet Orth, 468 Pleasant Hill Road, Sebastopol, California 95472.

Leatherwork—Men's and women's wallets: dyed, antiqued, with neatlac finish; a number of designs to choose from, 9¼'' by 3-3/8'', $12. Skeet shooting bags (top left and top right) with two pockets, 7'' high by 8'' wide, to attach to your belt, $30 each. Pistol caddy (top center), 11'' long, comes in several designs, $30. Not shown: handbag with tooled deer family has adjustable strap. Fully lined, 7½'' by 9½'' by 3½'', $55. Handbag with tooled horse has adjustable strap, measures 7½'' by 9½'' by 3½'', $50. Clutch purse, 4'' by 7¼'', $20. Shipping not included.

Richard Labrecque—My craftwork is my principal form of employment and income. My wife and I work as a team. She handles the bookkeeping and the business side. I do the leatherwork, and she is learning the trade. I have been working with leather for two years. I have been doing very well with my business, but I would like it to be better, so that we can open a shop of our own.

At present I'm incarcerated at the Hampshire County House of Correction in Massachusetts. I would like to have a steady business going when I am released.

I will take special orders, but I must have a picture of the desired artwork and dimensions for the item.

Richard Labrecque, 66 Division Street, Easthampton, Massachusetts 01027.

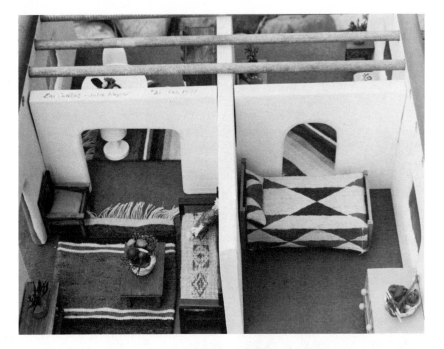

Las Casitas—I was born in the Midwest, grew up on the East Coast and have lived in Northern New Mexico for five years. I have an M.F.A. in sculpture from the Rhode Island School of Design. I now live in an adobe house in a small rural town with my husband, our little girl, a dog, a cat and some chickens.

I have been making doll houses for a year. The first house was designed and made for my three-year-old daughter, Molly. Since then I have made and sold them through friends, friends of friends and wholesale. I designed these houses to be beautiful in themselves, but at the same time sturdy enough for children to play with.

In addition to the doll house shown, I make furniture and custom doll houses, with a lot of help from my husband and parents when things get frantic.

Julie Wagner, c/o Las Casitas, Box 758, El Rito, New Mexico 87530.

Adobe-style Doll House—Made of 1'' pine, painted with quality latex paint. Doll house has four rooms, a painted particle-board roof and stained floor and vigas. The sections are slotted and come apart for shipping and storage. Measures 24'' by 24'' by 9-5/8''. Shipping weight 26 lbs. $54, shipping not included.

Ceramic Planter—Three holes in the pot bottom allow water to flow and settle in the trough of this one-piece planter. The inside is unglazed and the clay is wedged with grog to allow the plant to breathe. Outside decoration is painted with oxides or incised through an oxide to the clay color. The planter is then dipped in a matte of shiny glaze and fired to cone 8 in an oxidation atmosphere. Can be made with any design or motif. Planters are about 6'' in diameter by 6'' high. Prices range from $12 up. Planter shown, $25 postpaid.

Mary Seyfarth—I never dreamed that I would become a potter. I graduated from a college that had an outstanding ceramics department, but I spent my time in the library or cross-country skiing. The lure, fun and excitement of clay began for me in a night class at a local college.

I have traveled and lived in the Northwest and Southwest, and find the American Indian designs of those areas both handsome and inspiring. For me, the life, the excitement and even the bewilderment of clay is summed up in a quote from Conrad Aiken: ''I plunged into the center and found it vast.''

Mary K. Seyfarth, 1442 Forest Avenue, Highland Park, Illinois 60035.

Reversible Denim Jumper—The jumper is created from quality navy brushed denim with machine embroidery. It features an appliqued doll pocket on the denim side and a patchwork print or gingham on the reverse side. Washable. Sizes 1 through 6X. $17.50 postpaid.

Patty's Hang Ups—In 1974, after twenty years as an accountant, I decided to embark on a long-awaited dream: to earn my living through a textile craft. My work had to be different and good enough to support my family. I began with weaving, and now I work with juvenile clothing and soft toys. These things never fail to bring a smile to the faces of passers-by at craft shows. It leaves me with a feeling of pride and pleasure.

Patricia Farrington, c/o Patty's Hang Ups, 339 Fourth Avenue #2, San Francisco, California 94118.

Brass and Silver Jewelry—Top row: (left and right) 2'' hammered cuffs: brass $10, silver $40; (center) 2½'' cuff: brass $11, silver $45. Bottom row: (left) wire bracelet: brass $12, silver $25 (please state wrist size); (center) cuff with lock: brass $15, silver $45 (please state wrist size); (right) hammered bracelet, 2½'' wide at points: brass $12, silver $45. Shown on model: necklace comprised of three rectangles with soldered jump rings. The center piece is 1'' by 2''. Total length of necklace 16'': brass $10, silver $30.

Barbara Sucherman—I have been doing art in some form ever since I can remember. I began making jewelry two years ago. I'm not sure why I began—but the sheen of the metal, the play of light on its surfaces, the many textures, the mystery of fire and strange chemicals, new forms . . . they all seduced me.

I have experimented with many different ideas. The concepts expressed here are just a few of the multitude that interest me.

Barbara Kruglick-Sucherman, 1260 Ridgewood Drive, Highland Park, Illinois 60035.

Tipi—The standard 18' tipi is ready-made of white duck with door and liner. It also comes without the liner and in kit form. Tipis come in 16', 18' and 20' sizes and can be made of heavier material. Water-resistant and mildew-resistant; seams are lapped and double-sewn with heavy polyester thread. Tipi shown, 18' with door and liner, $148, shipping not included.

Pam Connett—No dwelling excites the soul like the tipis of the Plains Indians. They are beautiful, efficient in space and heat distribution and spiritually satisfying.

I made my first tipi in Colorado in 1971, and later began to live in one. I now live in upstate New York and make tipis for others who, like me, seek a lifestyle in harmony with nature.

Pam Connett, 1006 Spring Street Extension, Groton, New York 13073.

Windvane—The windvane shown is available complete or in ready-to-assemble kit (no brazing needed). Width 34'' from pointer to wake, 58'' high, 18'' across the compass spokes. Made of bronze, with aluminum sails, the constantly active schooner rides on an oil-impregnated bronze and sealed ball bearing atop a spring steel tapered vertical shaft. Complete, $150; kit, $90, shipping not included.

Bruce Haig—Bruce makes whimsical and functional metalwork in El Granada, California. ''People around here go in more for wind than windvanes, bottles more than fountains, but every once in a while I get a job to do a gate, a planter or a whirligig.'' His sheet copper sculpture has been shown and acquired locally by people who have a particular nook and an unusual notion about enhancing a garden, a wall, a roof, an existence. He welcomes correspondence and visits from those who wish to discuss windvanes, fountains, gates, sculpture, life and politics.

Bruce Haig, R.R. 1, Box 400-C, Half Moon Bay, California 94019.

Cindy Sägen, c/o Little Wide Awake, 6311 Thornhill Drive, Oakland, California, 94611.

Early American Schoolbook Quilt and Block Kit—Alphabet and matching pictures, circa 1840, are hand-silk-screened in 8'' squares, on washable 100% cotton twill. Easy sewing instructions guide you in making one 44'' by 66'' quilt top or a set of 9 big alphabet blocks (stuffing and backing not included). Color choices on white fabric are black, brown, blue, red and red-white-and-blue. Kit, $25.

Little Wide Awake—I love fabric and the endless design possibilities and functional properties within its scope. Combining enlarged graphics from old children's books with photo-silk-screen on fabric enables me to give these enchanting illustrations to kids in a dynamic, durable, colorful and washable form. Learning is playing. My children love to play with interchangeable forms and create their own space. Learning is a by-product of that play.

343

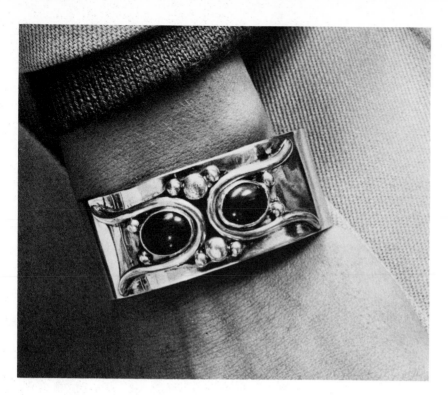

Sterling Cuff Bracelet—My work is contemporary jewelry, wearable and unique. It subtly incorporates the classic motifs of Art Nouveau, Art Deco and Egyptian art with my own intuitive strokes. This bracelet is made from sheet silver with silver applique and matching jade cabochons, or other stones as requested. Women's size, 1'' by 5½'', $60. Men's size 1'' by 6½'', $65.

Vitrice McMurry—After my beginnings in art academia at Louisiana State University, I worked on jewelry in an idyllic country setting filled with aspiring and inspiring artisans. I now live in the city and am becoming a little more worldly and professional in my approach, but I still keep those years of meditative work as my inspiration. To persevere in this life, one has to keep one's dedication to that world of the beauty of simplicity and function teamed with intuitive imagination.

Vitrice McMurry, 8232 Hickory Street, New Orleans, Louisiana 70118.

White Stoneware Vase—Also available in porcelain. Hand-thrown with applied decoration in turquoise, blue, green, yellow and any combination of these colors. About 9'' high. $25 postpaid.

Sally Weaver—I love the speed with which the original thrown form is completed. The white clay body lends itself to subtle or dramatic color changes. I am currently working with applied colored-clay decorations in intricate designs and textures.

My pieces are delicate, but just as durable as any other stoneware. I hope people will feel free to enjoy them both decoratively and functionally.

Sally Weaver, 5530 Ecoff Avenue, Chester, Virginia 23831.

Jasper Buttons and Boxes—Made from jasper and jasper agate found in Sonoma and Mendocino counties in Northern California. Buttons are cut from slabs into 5-, 6- and 7-sided shapes with diamond saws, ground smooth on wet grinding wheels, drilled and polished. Rich earth tones of yellow, red and brown. Dime size, 80 cents each. Nickel size, 90 cents each. Quarter size, $1 each. Half-dollar size, $1.10 each. Boxes are made in the copper foil technique. Polishing the stone takes most of the time in making the boxes. Box 2½'' by 4½'' by 1½'', $30; box 4'' by 6'' by 1½'', $40. All prices postpaid.

Harry Hostetter—I am a welder by trade, and build all of my own machinery. I started rock hunting fifteen years ago as a hobby, and spent all my spare time on excursions up and down the creek.

What was once a part-time hobby has evolved into a full-time occupation. Packing out rocks—sometimes for many miles—is hard work. But it is exciting and rewarding too. My lapidary is above money. It is a big part of my life.

Harry Hostetter, c/o Translucent Lapidary Art, 2825 Lynn Road, Sebastopol, California 95472.

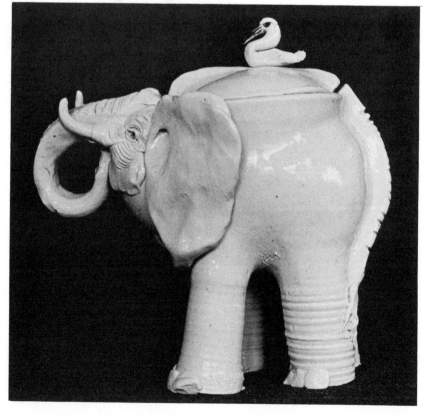

Endangered Species
Pottery—Functional, high-fired true porcelain animal sculpture about endangered species. The Lion Mug comes in white or tan. There's another version with his mouth open. Both 3½'' wide, 3'' high, 6½'' long, $26.50 postpaid. The Elephant Sugar Bowl comes in pure porcelain, white or soft blue-gray, with a white egret on the cover, 3'' wide, 6½'' high, 6½'' long, $36.50 postpaid. The Owl Planter has a braided hanger, branch and brass-covered ring. He's available with a brown, white or pale blue-gray glaze, 9'' wide, 9'' high and 7'' deep, $73 postpaid.

Natalie Surving—Clay is my life. There are never enough hours to work with it. I love the long hard hours of digging clay, processing it in a pug mill, hauling it home and wedging it for use. I treasure Staten Island's fine deposits of white clay.

I spend most of my days and often far into my nights creating new pieces in my basement studio. My son, daughter and husband come down frequently to meet my new creatures, pay a visit and lend a hand.

In eight years of potting, I haven't quite mastered the final step in the process—saying goodbye. It's hard to let go of something I have created and loved, and accept in its place the communion it carries between myself and its new owner.

Natalie Surving, 44 Pommer Avenue, Staten Island, New York 10304.

347

The Goodfellow Review of Crafts—Berkeley's own Huck Finn, soccer-player extraordinaire Christopher Scheer, is seen here holding a copy of the Goodfellow Review of Crafts. The Review is a monthly journal that promotes high-quality craftsmanship. Produced by the editors of this Catalog, the Review features columns written by craftspeople about their work, book reviews, gallery and guild information, lists of regional and national crafts fairs, marketing tips and survival instructions on everything from copyright protection to health-hazard warnings.

Most important, the Review hopes to encourage craftspeople in their lifestyle and work, and help focus attention on issues that affect them. It is also intended to serve as an information resource alerting the general public to developments in the world of crafts. $8 per year, Canada $10.

The Goodfellow Review of Crafts, P.O. Box 4520, Berkeley, California 94704.

The Goodfellow Catalog of Wonderful Things, 1974 Edition—The first edition of this book, published in January 1974, introduced a new dimension in marketing hand-crafted items. It was conceived and personally produced—from fact gathering through typesetting to distribution—by Christopher Weills. It was a remarkable conceptual achievement—and a beautiful piece of work in itself.

Although it enjoyed spotty distribution and limited availability at the time of its publishing, the original Catalog was, happily, a critical success. If you would like a copy of this rare First Edition, write to us. Although it may no longer be useful as the mail-order catalog it once was, the original catalog can be enjoyed simply for its historical interest. $3.50 plus 30 cents for shipping.

Goodfellow Catalog, P.O. Box 4520, Berkeley, California 94704.

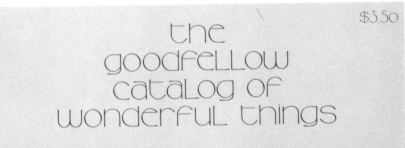

$3.50

the goodfellow catalog of wonderful things

Major Crafts Fairs

Crafts fairs are an excellent way for crafts producers and consumers to get together. For many crafts-people, these fairs are necessary to their economic survival. For visitors, they are good places to find well-made merchandise and to see demonstrations of various crafts. On the following pages we have provided information on fifteen of the most important crafts fairs in the country.

Baltimore Winter Market—The Winter Market is a recent outgrowth of the Rhinebeck Summer Market. Like its New York counterpart it aims to make American crafts accessible to major retailers, designers and galleries.

The first Winter Market, held in February 1977 in Baltimore's Civic Center, presented work by 400 top crafts-people from states east of the Mississippi. Booth space was divided between traditional and contemporary crafts. Many well-known craft guilds were present, among them the Southern Highlands Guild, the Kentucky Guild of Artists and Craftsmen and the West Virginia Artists and Craftsmen's Guild.

The Winter Market is sponsored by Northeast Craft Fair, Ltd., a subsidiary of the American Crafts Council. It runs for four days; the first two are restricted to wholesale trade. Admission is $2.

Baltimore Winter Market, Constance Stapleton, Route 1, Box 109 A, Middletown, Maryland 21769.

Craftsman's Fairs of the Southern Highlands—These fairs have been held for the past thirty years. The summer fair takes place in July in Asheville, North Carolina; the fall fair, in October in Knoxville, Tennessee. Each runs for five days. Both are sponsored by the Southern Highland Handicraft Guild.

Over 100 craftsmen—all of whom must be Guild members—exhibit at each fair. Traditional crafts featured include coopering, patchwork clothing and quilts, ceramics, vegetable dyeing, wood carving and basketry. Contemporary crafts include jewelry making, macrame, screen painting, batik and stenciling. Daily demonstrations of basketry, shuck-doll making, vegetable dyeing and spinning are given. Entertainment includes folk music and dancing. Admission for adults is $2.50; for children $1.

Craftsman's Fairs of the Southern Highlands, c/o the Southern Highland Handicraft Guild, P.O. Box 9145, Asheville, North Carolina 28805.

Farmington Crafts Expo—This festival, now in its sixth year, is sponsored by

American Crafts Expositions. Over 200 craft exhibitors participate; visitors number over one hundred times that figure.

The Crafts Expo is held annually, on the first weekend in June, at the Farmington Polo Grounds in Farmington, Connecticut. All exhibits are juried. Admission is $1.50.

Farmington Crafts Expo, c/o American Crafts Expositions, P.O. Box 370, Farmington, Connecticut 06032.

Frederick Craft Fair—This fair, sponsored by National Crafts, Ltd., is now in its third year. It is held annually in early June at the Frederick Fairground in Frederick, Maryland, forty miles from Baltimore and Washington, D.C.

The Frederick Craft Fair runs for five days; the first two are limited to wholesale buyers. Over 1,500 applicants from around the country compete for entry; only one-third that number are chosen.

The atmosphere is festive. The fairground buildings themselves are funky late-Victorian—and a real part of the occasion. Bluegrass music and the aromas of home-cooked food further delight the more than 40,000 visitors to the fair.

Frederick Craft Fair, c/o National Crafts, Ltd., Noel Clark, Director, Gapland, Maryland 21736.

The Great River Roads Crafts Fair—This three-day fair was established to encourage the production and support of crafts especially among people in this area of the South. It aims to honor our pioneer heritage and emphasizes crafts basic to survival in the early days of this country.

The fair, now in its fifth season, is held annually in early October at the Natchez Convention Center in Natchez, Mississippi. It is sponsored by Trinity Episcopal School and features the work of 75 juried craftspeople.

Craft demonstrations are encouraged for their educational value. Entertainment includes folk music, dulcimer playing and traditional singing. Weekend passes cost $3 for adults, $1 for students; children admitted free.

The Great River Roads Craft Fair, Box Elder Lane, Natchez, Mississippi 39120.

Greater Milwaukee Craft Fair—This fair is held annually on a weekend in late November, in Milwaukee's Wisconsin State Fiar Park. It is now in its fifth season.

All entrants are juried; 165 are chosen from across the nation. Visitors number about 15,000.

Crafts exhibited include leaded glass, macrame, enameling, lapidary, cornhusk crafts, painted eggs and stitchery. Live entertainment and demonstrations are featured.

Greater Milwaukee Craft Fair, 1655 South Sixty-eighth Street, West Allis, Wisconsin 53214.

Indian Summer Arts and Crafts Festival—This fair has been in existence for over twenty years. It is sponsored by the Marietta Area Arts and Crafts League and the Marietta College Art Department. $500 in prize money is awarded.

The Indian Summer Arts and Crafts Festival is held annually in Marietta, Ohio, for three days in September. Over 100 artists and craftspeople exhibit and sell their work.

The festival celebrates the rich American heritage of arts and crafts. Demonstrations are encouraged as a way of educating the public to quality craftsmanship. Wandering minstrels play and sing among the over 15,000 visitors. Admission is 50 cents for adults.

Indian Summer Arts and Crafts Festival, c/o Arthur Howard Winer, Director, Marietta College, Marietta, Ohio 45750.

Kentucky Guild of Artists and Craftsmen's Fair—Two four-day fairs are held at Indian Fort Theater in Berea, Kentucky. The spring fair, now in its eleventh season, is held in late May and draws crowds of close to 20,000. The fall fair, now in its third season, is held in late September, with attendance around 13,000.

Over 100 juried Kentucky artists and craftsmen participate in each of these fairs, both of which feature contemporary and traditional crafts. The heritage of the self-sufficient Kentucky pioneers comes alive in the work of traditional basket makers, quilters, blacksmiths and knife makers. The pots, bonnets, woven coverlets and vegetable-dyed, hand-spun yarns displayed are much the same as those made over 200 years ago in the Kentucky mountains.

Appalachian music, puppetry, folk tales and dancing add to the festivities. Admission for adults $2, for children 50 cents.

Kentucky Guild of Artists and Craftsmen, Box 291, Berea, Kentucky 40403.

KPFA Christmas Crafts Fair—KPFA is a listener-sponsored FM radio station serving Northern California with community-oriented programming. The fair it sponsors provides a major source of support for the station.

The fair is held on the two weekends before Christmas, at Pauley Ballroom in the Student Union Building on the University of California campus in Berkeley. More than 12,000 people attend; there is a 50 cent donation in lieu of admission charge.

The fair is juried; over 300 fine craftspeople in all fields are selected. Displayed items represent the wide range of crafts produced in Northern California.

KPFA Christmas Crafts Fair, c/o KPFA, 2207 Shattuck Avenue, Berkeley, California 94704.

Minnesota Renaissance Festival—This annual fair runs for five consecutive weekends in late August and early September. It is held on grounds just outside Chaska, Minnesota, about twenty-five miles southwest of Minneapolis. Over 140,000 people attend.

The festival is a re-creation of the color, atmosphere and pageantry of an Elizabethan royal fair. Participants clad in period garb display their arts and crafts in the more than 200 thatched, stone shops and studios on the fairground. Demonstrations of various crafts are given.

Entertainment includes Elizabethan games, jousting, traveling theater, clowns, horse races and food. Admission for adults is $3.75, for children $1.

Minnesota Renaissance Festival, Route 1, Box 125, Chaska, Minnesota 55318.

Pacific Northwest Arts and Crafts Fair—This fair, now in its thirty-second year, is the largest outdoor arts and crafts fair in the country. The three-day event is held annually in late July at Bellevue Square in Bellevue, Washington. It is sponsored by the Pacific Northwest Arts and Crafts Association and draws crowds of over 10,000.

More than $10,000 is awarded to 900 artists, craftsmen and filmmakers participating in the fair. Fifty-five craftsmen are further selected to demonstrate their talents and compete for over $600 in prizes on the Craft Mall. A special juried "super show" for professional-quality crafts, with $1000 in prizes, is another special feature. In addition, a number of Northwest music and drama groups provide free daily performances.

Pacific Northwest Arts and Crafts Fair, Pacific Northwest Arts and Crafts Association, 10310 NE Fourth, Bellevue, Washington 98004.

The Prater's Mill Country Fair—The Country Fair is held semiannually, on Mother's Day weekend in May and on Columbus Day weekend in October. It takes place at historic Prater's Mill just outside Dalton, Georgia, and draws crowds of 15,000 to 20,000 people.

Over 125 artists and craftspeople participate. All work is juried, and must be handmade of natural materials. Special emphasis is placed on traditional crafts—blacksmithing, spinning, weaving and Dalton's own hand-tufted bedspread making. There are demonstrations of many crafts.

Homemade food, mountain music, fiddlers, gospel singers and square dancers help to re-create the atmosphere of an old-fashioned country fair. In addition, the old 1859 grist mill is in operation during the fair. Admission is $1.

The Prater's Mill Country Fair, 101 Timberland Drive, Dalton, Georgia 30720.

Renaissance Pleasure Faire—The Pleasure Faire is held twice a year. It is a springtime Maying festival in Southern California and a fall harvest festival in Northern California. The spring festival, now in its fifteenth season, runs for six consecutive weekends in April and May at the old Paramount Ranch in Agoura, California, forty miles from Los Angeles. Over 350,000 people attend.

The fall festival, now in its tenth year, runs for six consecutive weekends in late August and September at Black Point Forest in Marin County near San Francisco. It draws crowds of 250,000.

California's meadows come alive as authentically costumed participants re-create the splendor of Elizabethan England. Over 200 craftspeople display, demonstrate and hawk their wares along the lanes and byways of the Elizabethan-like marketplace.

Craft competitions in the spirit of the Renaissance craft guilds are held daily. Special workshops open to the public offer expert instruction in the language, dress and drama of the period. Entertainment includes traditional games, juggling, tumbling, pageants and parades.

Visitors are encouraged to come in costume. Admission is $4.95 for adults, and $1.95 for children.

The Renaissance Pleasure Faire, c/o Art Blum Agency, 627 Commercial Street, San Francisco, California 94111.

Rhinebeck Summer Market—This major crafts festival, now in its twelfth season, is sponsored by the Northeast Craft Fair, Ltd., a subsidiary of the American Crafts Council. It features the work of 500 outstanding individual craftspeople from twelve Northeastern states. Over 1500 craftspeople compete for these 500 places, and the preselection process guarantees the high quality of the show.

The fair runs for five days in late June at the Dutchess County Fairgrounds in Rhinebeck, New York. The first two days are reserved exclusively for wholesale trade. At this time major retailers, home-furnishings buyers, interior designers and gallery and shop owners purchase crafts for resale.

Over the years, the fair has grown from a small group of craftspeople seeking new and enlarged marketplaces into a major annual event drawing over 40,000 visitors. In addition to the regular craft displays, there are daily craft demonstrations and workshops, plus craft supply, material and equipment shows. Admission for adults is $2; children are let in free.

Rhinebeck Summer Market, c/o Northeast Craft Fair, Ltd., 153 Main Street, P.O. Box 10, New Paltz, New York 12561.

West Virginia's Mountain Heritage Arts and Crafts Festival—This is a three-day fair sponsored by the Jefferson County Chamber of Commerce. The summer festival, now in its sixth year, is held the second weekend in June. There is also a new fall festival, but its date is yet to be determined.

The fair is held in a spacious country setting near Harper's Ferry, West Virginia. Over 125 juried craftspeople exhibit and sell their work. Demonstrations are encouraged.

The festival prides itself on its low-key, noncommercial, restful atmosphere. Folk dancing, singing, apple-butter making and Appalachian folk music are some of the activities available to the 35,000 to 40,000 visitors each year. Admission is $2 for adults, $1 for children.

West Virginia's Mountain Heritage Arts and Crafts Festival, c/o Jefferson County Chamber of Commerce, Box 430, Charlestown, West Virginia 25414.

On The Road Selling Crafts—A Few Insights

by R. Duane Ferre

Duane is the Goodfellow Review's oldest regular correspondent. His stories and insights from the roads of America have become a favorite feature. As a peripatetic craftsman-philosopher, Duane has encountered almost every pitfall of itinerent salesmanship. He has also reaped the rewards of this freedom.

Since before recorded time vendors have plied dusty trade routes, seeking their fortunes in the teeming markets of strange and distant lands. Squatting beside crowded pathways, they spread their ragged mats and hawk their wares to those who would stop and bargain.

In 1971 I left my office job and joined that primitive fraternity of vagabonds, wandering the asphalt alleys of America selling a modest but clever sort of wire jewelry. I've traveled enough miles to go to the moon. But instead I went to Bar Harbor and Long Branch, to Gatlinburg and Gainesville, to Taos and Eugene, to San Luis Potosi and Oaxaca. Never have I taken a trip which didn't realize a profit. It has been my good fortune to travel at will and still put money in the bank. For those readers contemplating a similar nomadic existence, the following is a quick harvest from my experiences.

Getting Started

Poverty is society's way of saying you're doing something wrong. It takes a long time—sometimes *years*—to find the right combination of skill, product, location and presentation to be successful in craft sales. It would be easiest if during this experimental period one had an additional source of income with which to pay the bills.

A constant battle rages within me between the forces of pure craftsmanship and business acumen. It's a personal decision as to how much each of us is willing to compromise creativity to pander to the commercial desires of a generally tasteless buying public. I picked wire jewelry as my commodity after considering the following criteria:

1. Am I proud to put my name on it? Am I committed to *quality*?

2. Is the product *handmade*? This is a requirement for all craft shows. If I'm just a vendor, I need to go to flea markets. (I've never found flea markets a very good place for selling crafts.)
3. Is the *price* acceptable to the customer yet sufficient to give a fair return for my labor?
4. Can I *supply* enough items to meet a reasonable demand?
5. Is my product easily *transportable*? (It would be difficult to go on tour specializing in 20-ton concrete statues of King Kong.)

Finding Craft Shows

The best source for finding craft shows is from craftspeople themselves. By going to a local craft show and talking to the participants I can usually learn of regional publications which list shows in that area. Many craft magazines, such as the *Goodfellow Review of Crafts*, include lists of such publications as well as individual craft shows. I have planned several nationwide tours just by using the *National Calendar of Indoor/Outdoor Art Fairs*, compiled by Henry Niles, 5423 New Haven Avenue, Fort Wayne, Indiana 46803.

Another possibility is through official government sources. I just make up titles such as "State Bureau of Tourism" and send letters to capital cities asking about craft shows. The letters are forwarded to the proper offices and the responses are quite helpful. If I want to visit a specific area, a letter to the Chamber of Commerce may produce a list of annual events.

Once I started attending craft shows, my name began to get on various mailing lists. Now I get more unsolicited invitations than I can handle.

Getting In

I have a rule of thumb: the easier the show is to enter, the less I want to participate. Benefits, church bazaars and shows sponsored by new or incompetent promoters are often so poorly organized and badly publicized that they aren't worth attending. Entrance into most successful

355

shows is juried. Each applicant must send slides or pictures of recent works. A panel of judges then select the best. I have found that it helps to apply early, in case there are quotas for each type of craft. Another trick is to be from far away—organizers are flattered that I would drive 800 miles to be in *their* show. (Living in Texas, I'm used to driving long distances to shows. It sure is a luxury to be in areas like the Northeast where every few *miles* there's another city!)

Getting accepted is only half the battle. It is then necessary to read the rules and proceed accordingly. Some events require specific costumes or display decorations. Consider the following behests, just a few from the eighteen-item diatribe of one fair organizer:

• NO LIGHTS, except battery-operated permitted. Only exception: equipment used by craftsmen and lights for sketch artists, but batteries must be in a plastic or wooden box.
• No picnicking on the mall at any time.
• No toddlers, children or pets at any show. Please make arrangements to leave them AT HOME.
• All tables must be covered on all four sides to the floor—not with white sheets. All supplies must be out of sight at all times.
• NO CONFIRMATIONS are sent—your check is your receipt. Applications and checks will be returned to you if the show is filled. If you reserve a space in a show—you are responsible for paying for that space. NO REFUNDS for any reason after closing date!
• All problems should be taken up with the Director of the show—NO EXHIBITOR may go to the mall manager, security, janitors, electricians or merchants.
• Unprofessional conduct, inappropriate dress and not manning your exhibit are due cause by Directors for removal from mailing list or show.
• No placing of chairs or anything else, in front of stores—at any time!
• Leather craftsmen—Absolutely not more than ten (10) buckles to be exhibited without belts. You are leather craftsmen NOT BUCKLE SALESMEN—NO BUCKLES SOLD SEPARATELY.

An increasing number of cities are providing street markets for the selling of crafts. Usually a city license is required, which may or may not be easy to get. In Boston one may get a vendor's license, but a myriad of restrictions and police harassment make selling virtually impossible. One of the nicest events I have attended was the Saturday Market in Eugene, Oregon. In Austin, Texas, I sold on the streets every weekend for a year until the city council restricted the market area to a few blocks and allowed them to be overrun with importers. Street selling is a whole different ball game than the refined atmosphere of a well-organized craft show.

Selling

I love the excitement of traveling and meeting new friends. In the final analysis, however, the purpose of my trip is monetary. In my case it takes about $300 per week to "break even." Through necessity I've developed a few practical principles of salesmanship:

1. *Visual impact* is essential. Frequently two exhibits sell almost identical products, yet one person is far more successful than the other. Presentation is the secret. Color, arrangement, and accessibility are paramount. At the same time one's display must be easy to assemble, windproof, and protected from the elements.

2. *Attitude* is the second ingredient of good salesmanship. I have found that my newly designed pieces of jewelry almost always sell faster than the more established ones, even though the customer has no way of telling which is which. The difference, I contend, is my own response to each of the styles: excitement over one, lackadaisical about the other. It is sometimes difficult when the coffers are empty and the show is a bust not to express one's boredom and frustration. Yet I have been the most successful when I have put making money out of mind and concentrated on communicating with each visitor in a joyful and sincere way.

3. *Bargains* are the pot of gold at the end of a shopper's rainbow. Offering sales and discounts are time-tested methods of increasing business. I apply this principle in several ways, starting with prices that are high enough to allow for a bit of flexibility.

My favorite is the inclement weather discount. After all, if people bother to come in foul weather, they should be rewarded. I have a sign that says RAINY DAY DISCOUNT—10% OFF. As soon as the sun appears, the sign disappears.

Another application is the multiple purchase discount: "I can't discount one pair of earrings, ma'am, but I can give you a good deal on three pair," or "Tell you what, if your friend also buys a necklace, I'll knock a dollar off for both of you." Selling wholesale also falls under this category. For anyone willing to spend over $100 I give 40% to 50% discount.

Sometimes people don't have very much money and just plain can't afford the full price. Soft touch that I am, I usually reduce the price so that the jewelry can have a happy home.

4. *Attention grabbers* will sometimes stop an otherwise uninterested passerby and result in a sale. I frequently make one or two items which are totally ridiculous, either because of their size or materials, such as giant rabbit fur ear hoops. After people stop to laugh at them, they often see something else which they do like and make a purchase. The funny thing is, even the ridiculous ones eventually sell!

Signs work the same way. As corny as they are, I get the most response from these two: "CHECKS ACCEPTED—IF THEY'RE GOOD" and "JEWELRY CUSTOM MADE WHILE YOU WAIT (AND WAIT . . . AND WAIT . . . AND . . .). A little humor relaxes people and reduces their inhibition about buying.

5. *Price* is relative. I always make one or two very special (and thus expensive) items, which are the center of attention. Most visitors can't afford them. However, relative to those items everything else seems very reasonable.

6. The foundation of a good *reputation* is built on quality merchandise, reasonable prices, and friendly, efficient service. No-thing makes me happier than to return to an area where I have sold before and have a former satisfied customer rush up to my display with her friends, exclaiming, "This is the jewelry I was telling you about . . . ."

Keep On Truckin'

I have a friend who lives on Long Island who never has to drive more than 15 or 20 miles to go to a craft show. For him that's an ideal situation. For me, however, attending craft shows is primarily a means of financing my principal interest: traveling.

Ingrid, my first van, was converted into a very comfortable camper. Many craft shows provide campsites or parking areas for campers. My second van, Ingrid Too, while being much more economical, is much smaller and contains only a bed. I usually stop at campgrounds where, for a few dollars, I can use the facilities, pool, showers and recreational equipment.

The past half-decade has been the most exciting and creative time of my life, a dream come to fruition partly through the freedom made possible by selling wire jewelry. It's my hope that if you're on the brink of involvement in crafts, these basic comments will encourage you and help you get started. I never said it was easy, nor will you get rich, but with the proper frame of mind, making and selling crafts can be challenging and rewarding.

Vendor dressed to sell—note vulnerable look cast by his gaze. Hat for sun stroke. Beard fights dust. This is not Duane, but it could be.

Pottery booth—ready for action.

Writing a Crafts Book

by Dona Z. Meilach

Dona Z. Meilach has written more than thirty books, on almost every kind of craft. Her most recent include: A Modern Approach to Basketry *and* Creating Modern Furniture. *Her work has inspired others to make and appreciate quality craftwork. Here she shares some of her experiences.*

How often have you read through a new craft book and muttered, "Why didn't I write that?" or "I could write a book on the craft I know best." The idea begins to grow. You visualize what your book would look like and what you would say. Your fantasy builds, you imagine yourself at autograph parties and appearing on television. Offers pour in for lectures and workshops. Your artwork sells as fast as you can produce it. Visions of royalty checks winging their way to your mailbox bring a sweet smile to your lips.

Fact or fiction? What is the truth about writing a book? How do you go about it? What is involved in effort, time and money?

Writing is a craft of its own that requires motivation, analysis, study and practice. If you are not familiar with such terms as point of view, transition, pacing sentences, anecdotes, or the use of interviews and quotations, enroll in a class on writing for publication. Subscribe to magazines such as *The Writer* and *Writer's Digest*. There are as many publications devoted to the literary arts as there are to the visual arts.

Since the majority of craft books today rely heavily on black-and-white photography you may want to master the use of a camera and lighting and discover what can be done in the darkroom. Learn about custom photo processing rather than relying on drugstore film processing.

If you can hire a professional photographer you won't have to be adept at camera technology; but if you do the photography, you can express your artistry and emphasize the details you want underscored.

When a book requires many photos (some of mine have between 500 and 700), hiring a professional book photographer would make the cost prohibitive. A book with 500 photos may require shooting about 2,000. If you prefer your own drawings your photography problems and costs are lessened.

Now You Are Ready to Sell Your Idea

Would-be writers who ignore learning the ins and outs of publishing usually think they must have a completed manuscript before they approach a publisher. They may spend years gathering material, writing, typing fingers to the bone—and then end up with an unsaleable manuscript. To avoid such trauma first concentrate on selling an editor your *idea*. You must convince him of your ability to produce a book that offers something better or different than any other book on the market. You do this *before* you have written the book. How?

Thorough research is the first requirement. Analyze every current book on your subject by consulting *Books In Print* and *Forthcoming Books* (ask your librarian). Do not rely on local libraries and bookstores for your research; many stores order only a few of the thousands of books on the market.

After evaluating the books, determine how they differ from one another and from your idea. Then make a list of all potential publishers by consulting current volumes of *The Literary Marketplace* and *The Writer's Market*. These provide names and addresses of publishers, special projects editors, the types of books they want, numbers of books published in the previous year and other pertinent information. Write to publishers for catalogs so you can compare back-listed titles, too.

Now you are ready to write an enticing "query," the initial step to catapulting your idea onto an editor's desk. Essentially, a query is a one- or two-page letter asking the editor if he would be interested in the subject. The letter should demonstrate that you know how to write and should explain what you are going to write about, your qualifications for writing it, why the book will serve a need and who will want to buy it. Your query letter must spark his interest, whet his appetite to hear more. Almost every how-to-write book has sample query letters to help you compose your own.

You can send several of these letters to different publishers simultaneously (not copies, but originals), then wait for answers. If you prefer, you may ask a literary agent to market the material for you. However, the probability of an unpublished author attracting an agent is unlikely—and frequently the author can learn more by doing it himself.

Let's assume you have done everything right. You will receive several reject letters, then one day the anxiously awaited positive response arrives. The editor will ask to see your proposal. You're ready . . . almost.

Your proposal should be professionally and meticulously prepared. It must be typed on one side of 8½ by 11 bond paper and consist of:
• A cover letter summarizing the book and describing the market in greater detail than your query letter.
• A brief analysis of competitive books and why yours differs from those already available. If it's a new subject, stress that point.
• A detailed outline of the proposed contents, chapter by chapter, including subheads and possible ideas for demonstrations and/or specific projects and patterns.
• One sample chapter (sometimes three—but not necessarily in consecutive order).
• Samples of your photography and/or drawings.

Think of the proposal packet as "you"—your ability as an artist, writer, photographer, researcher, teacher. On the strength of that material rests the decision of whether or not you will be given a contract to write the book.

Now It Begins

Your proposal is promising and convincing. Your editor calls or writes, and terms are discussed. A contract indicating the terms of the advances, royalty, deadline and so forth is sent through. If you are unfamiliar with contract procedures, see "The Recommended Trade Book Contract: The Contract Guide," available from the Author's Guild, 234 West Forty-fourth Street, New York, New York 10036. Talk to other writers about their contracts—we all learn the hard way what should and should not be in contracts. Generally, you are given an advance against future earned royalties, the percentage of the sale price of each book.

You will probably receive half on acceptance of the final manuscript.

Are you guaranteed publication yet? No way. Now the work begins. You realize you must produce an acceptable book within the time stated in the contract, which could be three months to three years. Usually, an advance will not cover your living expenses, so you won't be able to desert your job, family and daily responsibilities. The book will be an added load to your already busy schedule.

You gather your material. If the ideas and experiences you wish to write about are your own, you can establish working times at odd hours during the months to come. If it is a project that requires correspondence with artists, museums and galleries, or travel to photograph and interview other craftspeople at work, the book then becomes a full-time job in itself. It requires careful organization and record keeping of every letter, every photo sent to you, every original piece of artwork that you may have to photograph and return, every release and permission form. You may have to telephone artists to request more or better photos, information about techniques used and perhaps a personal statement.

Once photographs and artwork are under control, the amorphous mass of material and research must be organized into a cohesive, logical entity. It's time to write. And rewrite. And revise. And rewrite. You must correlate photos into the manuscript. If you have a knowledge of layout and graphic design you might be able to "dummy" the book yourself—but actually this is a function of the publisher.

Now the final manuscript must be typed in duplicate. It should be proofread by someone who knows the vocabulary of the craft form as well as proper grammar and punctuation.

Finally, the book is finished. You pack it, phone your editor that it is on its way via United Parcel or the postal service, and pray that planes, trucks and trains do not crash, succumb to floods, lightning or other natural disasters.

Acceptance!

The manuscript—with your sweat and blood invisibly but indelibly mingled with the type—is read by the editor. The happiest ending would be that he would phone you and shout joyfully, "It's the greatest thing to hit world literature! We'll rush it to the presses!" Unlikely. He will read it carefully and with the editorial blue pencil, make corrections, ask questions in the margins, request clarifications. He may send it to another editor for a similar reaction. And a final decision. Is it publishable?

How could it *not* be publishable? Remember, your second advance is paid only *on acceptance*, not on submission. Would your editor dare reject it? He would . . . and often does. For any number of reasons. For one, the editor's job is to edit, not to write or rewrite. One frustrated author I know rewrote a manuscript three times under editorial direction but still could not get it to jell. The manuscript was finally rejected. Luckily for the author, an important clause was in the contract: "In the event of rejection, the initial advance does not have to be refunded." At least she had some of her costs covered.

But let us continue with our positive thinking. Your book is accepted with minimal editorial queries. You willingly make the requested changes to the editor's satisfaction. You wait impatiently for the 12 to 24 months it can take for a finished book to be in your hands.

Is It Worth It?

What about those costs? What can you hope to make for your time and effort? Let's establish a hypothetical ledger— strictly a guess-timate!

All costs incurred to produce the book may be deducted from taxes as business expenses. You must establish a bookkeeping system and record every penny you spend for postage, envelopes, paper, staples, typewriter ribbons, photography, shipping and depreciation on typewriter and cameras. You can also record mileage at the allowed rate for trips essential for interviews and photography. Whether or not you can deduct an office at home is subject to current IRS rulings.

For ease of figuring, let's establish a book with 200 pages, with two to three photos per page, which breaks down to a cost of $20 per page or $4,000. The income that book will produce depends on the market's potential, advertising budget, publicity, timeliness and other factors. A hard-cover craft book may sell for $10 per copy. Your ten percent royalty on each copy sold is $1. If the book sells 10,000 copies (a respectable number for a hard-cover book), you estimate a return of $10,000 spread out over the length of time that book is in print, which could be from four years to about twelve years. You've already received part of it as your advance; you will not receive additional money until enough books are sold to cover that advance.

The ledger tips out as an estimated $10,000 income: $4,000 expenses or $6,000 profit. But don't bank on that. Foreign sales do not earn the full ten percent royalty. Some books do not sell 10,000; they may sell only 3,000 or 5,000. Too many end up on the "remainder" tables of bookstores. Paperbacks can realize greater sales, but before you sharpen your pencil be forewarned that paperback royalty rates are less and the books sell for less than hard-covers.

Is writing a book worth the time, effort, energy and costs? It's as big a gamble as playing the tables at Las Vegas. With luck, royalties can be like annuities for several years. But there are fallout aspects that cannot be measured in money. The day you hold in your hands a completed book that you wrote is a day you won't soon forget. There is a satisfaction, a sense of accomplishment and a belief in the viability of your idea. You forget the long nights, rewrites, checking galleys— you forget the labor pains. You wait for the world to rock, to take notice of your creation.

Sorry. That doesn't happen with a craft book. With the thousands of books published each year, every publicity agent and author is fighting for time and space in the media. Somehow craft books do not have the general appeal of novels and political exposes. You will be grateful for good reviews in craft publications and happy when you find your book in the card file of a library.

You will gain prestige in the eyes of your peers and may be asked to lecture occasionally or present a workshop. Generally, you have your moment of glory and go about your business of creating.

Will it be another book? Only if you have become addicted to a type of masochism that is peculiar to authorship.

Crafts Book Publication and Promotion

by Elyse Sommer

Elyse Sommer is an agent, author and promotional consultant. She has published sixteen crafts books, among them, Career Opportunities in Crafts *and* Rock and Stone Craft. *Here she outlines the relationships involved in getting a crafts book published. It should be of interest to any potential author.*

As I write this my three hats are constantly in use. This kind of juggling of interests is not uncommon to craft writers. Your own "extra" hats may be those worn by the teacher, selling artist or supplier. The reason for this diversification is partly due to the wonderful versatility inherent in a crafts career and also because diversification insures a measure of economic security. Since being an author's agent is the role I have played the longest, let me start with some guidelines for author-agency relationships.

Agent

As I stated in *Career Opportunities In Crafts*, you don't *have* to have an agent to sell your crafts book. Make your decision as to whether you need or want an agent *before* you contact one. To beginners who ask me, "Is it worth it to have an agent?", my answer has always been, "If you're not sure, then you shouldn't have one." An agent cannot sell a poor manuscript or negotiate spectacular terms for a beginner.

The last point, of course, brings up the matter of actual agency costs. The base percentage for author's agents is 10% on domestic sales, though this may rise to 15% for first-time books in specialty or small earnings areas. Whatever the commission, it applies to all your earnings. An author-agency contract contains a special clause stating that all monies earned are paid to the agent who in turn sends a new check, minus commissions, to the author. This arrangement continues even if you and the agent should terminate your relationship.

Choose an agent as carefully as you would a doctor. To help in the selection process check the *Literary Market Place* and *Writer's Market*, both of which carry listings detailing how long an agent has been in business and his area of specialization. Even better, check people you know who can make personal recommendations. However, if your friend is a novelist and his agent specializes in novels, this may not be the right person for your book.

Give your agent the opportunity to really work for you. First, provide a solid sales package. Just because the agent knows the editors does not mean they will buy an idea without some written and visual backup for the agent's "pitch." Secondly, keep the agent informed about what's happening with you. A good agent will encourage direct author-editor contact, but don't agree to do things like special cover designs without checking out possible remuneration through the agent. Also, if you write articles or give lectures, send on information which might suggest possible future book assignments.

Collaborator

In her discussion of how one progresses from book idea to acceptable manuscript, Dona Meilach makes it clear that the responsibilities are manifold. One way to cope with the many tasks involved is to work with a collaborator. There are three basic types of crafts-book collaborations: author-illustrator, author-photographer and author-crafts artist.

Author-Illustrator Collaborations

If your book requires a large number of sketches it may be necessary to work with an illustrator. Illustrators work on a flat fee or an advance-royalty basis, usually sharing a 75%-25% split in favor of the author. Do not, however, hire or commit yourself to an illustrator before you have sold your manuscript. As a rule, publishers deal with free-lance technical artists familiar with the requirements of their particular publishing houses. But if you know an illustrator with whom you work well, by all means suggest him.

What about responsibilities—you to the illustrator and vice versa? The sketch-illustrated book begins with the author.

In addition to the manuscript you will be expected to provide rough sketches, diagrams, snapshots or actual samples of the items to be illustrated. A xerox of the manuscript (made by the publisher) and of your box of samples then go to the artist. In preparing the sketches, the illustrator, if he is experienced and alert, may see flaws in the written how-to descriptions—or he may ask that you alter some descriptions. Xeroxes of the artist's sketches and suggestions are then sent to the author for okay and correction.

Author-Photographer Collaborations

In the adult-book field, photographic illustrations are becoming the preferred type. Unlike the illustrator who works directly with the publisher's art director, the photographer for a crafts book has no contact with the publisher. Since the validity of your book will hinge on numerous and good-quality photographs it is important that you at least know how to obtain the necessary photos and have an idea of your costs in order to judge the fairness of any proffered advance and/or photo expense payments.

Photographers rarely share in book royalties. Payment is negotiated either on a flat fee or per diem basis. To arrive at a manageable fee, estimate the number of photographs you plan to use and multiply this by $1 to $3 per finished print.

The following rules should be carefully observed for the sake of a good book and a continued good relationship with your photographer.

• Plan your photo sessions efficiently. If you photograph a series of demonstrations, have all your photo setups lined up in an orderly fashion so that pictures can be snapped without unnecessary delay.

• When making samples, choose your colors and materials with the photographer's problems in mind. Avoid colors which wash out or which require special filters.

• When arranging on-location shots, make sure the artist whose work you are photographing is aware of your needs for space, backgrounds and so forth.

Author-Crafts Artist Collaborations

When a crafts artist and/or teacher does not have the time or inclination to shoulder the organization, research and writing of a book, it is best to leave such tasks to an experienced crafts writer. This way, the artist is free to provide all the samples for the book (her own and contributing artists'), while the writer determines the organization, researches the introduction and writes the captions and

text. Sometimes both authors are also artists and they divide the work, with each responsible for writing up his or her own contributions, but collaborating on the introduction or bibliography, for instance. But be flexible. If one does more work than the other, so be it. The division of money is almost always an even 50-50 split. The publisher should be asked to draw up contract copies for each party, and monies are sent to each as it becomes due.

Promotional Consultant

Most reputable publishers have promotion departments. Does this mean that once your script is complete and approved you can sit back and wait to be invited to autograph parties and national television promotional tours?

Unlikely. Even big publishers with departments to handle media publicity, promotions and special sales have to face the reality of competition from a staggering list of new titles published each year—a growing number of these in crafts.

One of the most valuable promotional consultants for any publisher is the author. Here are some ways in which you as an author can and should insure maximum sales and exposure for your books:

• Arm the publisher with all possible information. Provide the publicity department with the names of specialized publications which may not be familiar to them. Mention any special slants you feel would make your book noteworthy (for example, local people featured in your book).

Give the special sales department lists of atypical book outlets such as suppliers and cataloguers. Let the promotion department know about events where your book might be promoted.

• Secondary sales of portions of books to magazines (first or second serial rights) are not easy to make; quite often magazines expect to reprint material as "free publicity." However, if you do an article or design things especially for a certain magazine, your book will be mentioned as part of your by-line so that you are being paid even as you publicize your book.

• If you are featuring the work of other artists in your book, make sure they receive a copy. This is not only a necessary courtesy, but it also makes good business sense, for these people usually in turn promote the book, by selling it at shows, fairs or in their shops.

• If you teach, lecture or sell, arrange with your publisher to become your own bookseller. If you don't teach or lecture but would like to, use the book to open your own doors. The kind of lecture most frequently arranged by publishers is the store tie-in where the author (unlike other lecturers) is not paid. Do this if you want the experience—but don't be surprised if only a modest number of books are sold. I have made it a principle never to lecture or demonstrate without at least receiving an honorarium, unless I have carefully ascertained long-range publicity. Book authors, like artists, are too generous (or is it insecure?) about giving away their time and energies.

The business of arranging one's own promotional activities brings me to one final point which may be of particular interest to readers of this Catalog. It is the matter of doing the whole publishing thing yourself—not vanity publishing but self-publication. For craftspeople this can be a valid and satisfying enterprise. I refer those interested to some of the stories of self-publishers featured in *Career Opportunities in Crafts*.

Book Reviews

Compiled by Bette London

The following reviews were written by practicing craftspeople. Each was asked to review the books he has found to be the most valuable in his particular field. We hope these reviews will be of interest to the beginner and the hobbyist as well as to other active craftspeople.

BATIK

Contemporary Batik and Tie-Dye: Methods, Inspiration, Dyes. By Dona Z. Meilach. Crown Publishers, 1973. $4.95.

Dona Meilach's batik book is the only one that you need to own. It has 450 photographs, 19 of which are color plates. The information regarding resist techniques is definitive.

I've used it since I began batiking, at which time I appreciated the simply stated explanations of wax application, dye progression and wax removal methods. I still turn to the book for reference and for inspiration for subject matter and display alternatives. The section on dye classification, conversion tables, wax melting points and supply sources is particularly useful.

This book successfully conveys the magic and mystery of the batik process. That magic is the reason I do batik; it is exciting to read a book by someone who shares that feeling.

Maureen Rosenblum

Batik with Noel Dyrenforth. By John Houston. Bobbs-Merrill Company, 1976. $9.95.

Batik with Noel Dyrenforth is a visual delight. It is filled with color reproductions—the only way batik can be truly experienced in print.

Mr. Dyrenforth's background in graphics has enabled him to expand the batik process significantly. Some of his distinctive designs are portrayed here in easy-to-follow working projects.

This book presents a strong personal statement about one man and his batiks. It covers all aspects of the medium and teaches a very personal style which can be copied or incorporated by experienced craftsmen into their existing modes of

work. It is a worthy addition to a batiker's reference library.

Stephen Blumrich

Recommended Books—Beginners

Designing in Batik and Tie Dye. By Nancy Belfer. Davis Publications, 1972. $3.98.

Robin Grey's Batiker's Guide. By Robin Grey. DTC Publications, 1976. $4.95.

Batik Reviewers

Stephen Blumrich studied fabric design in Linz, Austria. He has taught several workshops on the subject and his work has been featured in numerous exhibits across the country, including Craft Multiples at the Renwick Gallery of the Smithsonian Institution in Washington, D.C. His work has earned many awards.

Maureen Rosenblum is a full-time designer/craftswoman in batik, currently living in Milwaukee, Wisconsin. Her work, primarily batik dolls, is displayed at selective design stores and craft shows.

CERAMICS

Clay and Glazes for the Potter. By Daniel Rhodes. Chilton Book Company, 1957, 1973. $12.50.

Stoneware and Porcelain: The Art of High-Fired Pottery. By Daniel Rhodes. Chilton Book Company, 1959. $7.50 cloth, $3.95 paper.

Daniel Rhodes's *Clay and Glazes for the Potter* became a standard reference book soon after publication in 1957. It contains valuable information for students and professional potters on glaze ingredients and calculations, clay types and the formation of ceramic bodies. The new edition includes a section of color plates to complement over 100 black-and-white photos of past and present ceramic art and updated text.

A companion book, *Stoneware and Porcelain*, covers materials, techniques and traditions of high-fired pottery. Rhodes begins with historical and contemporary attitudes toward porcelain and stoneware and continues through the formulation of high-fired clay bodies. Photos illustrate concepts of good form and design.

James Meyer

Finding One's Way with Clay. By Paulus Berensohn. Simon and Schuster, 1972.

Paulus Berensohn's book really defies

categorization. It would be useful to a beginning as well as advanced potter. He gives life to the often overlooked and maligned pinch pot, with specific directions, photographs and simple exercises to develop this skill. Interspersed among these exercises are meditative techniques for approaching clay. Berensohn uses the process for quieting the mind and centering the self in order to let the imagination flow. It is this blending of the definitive and the meditative that makes this book so appealing.

Marcia Crapo

Glazes for Special Effects. By Herbert Sanders. Watson-Guptill, 1974.

Glazes for Special Effects describes exotic and seldom-used glazes and glaze techniques. It is probably the most important work on crystalline glazes to date. Equally valuable are the sections on copper reduction glazes and wood and plant ash glazes.

For ceramicists who work with low fire clays there is a section on luster techniques, underglaze decoration and decals. A chapter on raku glazing and firing techniques, which has enough formulas to keep most potters experimenting for a long time, ends the book.

James Meyer

New Ceramics. By Eileen Lewenstein and Emmanuel Cooper. Van Nostrand Reinhold Company, 1974.

In the introduction, the authors state that their book is "an illustrated survey of what is happening in studio pottery today." Excellent black-and-white as well as color photographs, present a clear, concise, up-to-date panoramic view of outstanding ceramics by potters around the world.

This book is an excellent reference source, valuable for the student and professional potter or teacher and for the amateur who loves objects made of clay.

Angelo Garzio

The Potter's Challenge. By Bernard Leach. Dutton-Sunrise Inc., 1975.

Bernard Leach has contributed significantly to the world of ceramics through publications over the last fifty years. Now we have *The Potter's Challenge*, a wonderful book for the contemporary potter or anyone interested in beautiful pottery.

Leach's book describes issues faced by every potter: technique versus creativity and the problem of what makes a "good pot." He offers a section entitled "First

Steps" on making and decorating pots. There is also a diagrammed analysis of a pot followed by photographs of "exemplary pots."

Marcia Crapo

Pottery Decoration. By Thomas Shafer. Watson-Guptill, 1976. $15.95.

This very beautiful book illustrates virtually every known decorative technique. Hundreds of photos, many in color, that portray historical and contemporary techniques will inspire beginners and professional potters.

The first part of the book covers sculptural decoration, including carved, impressed and added designs. Part two treats color decoration.

Ceramicists and potters who are not master throwers will find valuable information on how to decorate and enhance their pottery in unusual and beautiful ways.

James Meyer

Raku. By Christopher Tyler and Richard Hirsch. Watson-Guptill, 1975. $15.75.

The authors of this book explain raku's history, beginning with its origins in Japan, through its adoption and adaptation by American potters. Raku forms and firing techniques are discussed in detail and beautifully illustrated. Valuable information on raku clay and glazes is provided plus easy-to-read diagrams on building a raku kiln.

James Meyer

Recommended Books—Beginners

Ceramics: A Potter's Handbook. By Glenn C. Nelson. Holt, Rinehart & Winston, 1972.

Ceramics: Techniques and Projects. By Sunset Books. Land Books, 1973.

Making Pottery Without the Wheel. By Carlton Ball and Janice Lovoos. Van Nostrand Reinhold Company, 1974.

Pottery Workshop. By Charles Counts. Macmillan/Collier, 1976. $4.95.

Advanced

Ceramic Glazes. By Cullen Parmelee and Cameron G. Harmon. Cahners Publishing Company, 1973.

Ceramic Formulas: The Complete Compendium. By John Conrad. Macmillan Publishing Company, 1973.

Ceramics for the Artist Potter. By F. H. Norton. Addison-Wesley Publishing Company, 1952.

The Kiln Book. By Frederick Olsen. Keramos Books, 1973.

Kilns: Design, Construction and Operation. By Daniel Rhodes. Chilton Book Company, 1968.

Pioneer Pottery. By Michael Cardew. St. Martin's Press, 1969.

A Potter's Book. By Bernard Leach. Transatlantic Arts, 1940.

General Reference

Illustrated Dictionary of Practical Pottery. By Robert Fournier. Van Nostrand Reinhold, 1973.

Pottery: Form and Expression. By Marguerite Wildenhain. Pacific Books, 1962, 1973.

Pottery Form. By Daniel Rhodes. Chilton Book Company, 1976.

Raku: Art and Technique. By Hal Riegger. Van Nostrand Reinhold Company, 1970.

The World of Japanese Ceramics. By Herbert Sanders. Kodansha International USA, 1967.

Ceramics Reviewers

Marcia Crapo has studied ceramics for the last eight years at Arizona State and in Berkeley. She is currently teaching at the Mug Shop in Berkeley and pursuing her own development as a potter in a small studio group composed of good friends.

Angelo Garzio is a professor of Ceramic Art at Kansas State University. He has received several grants and numerous awards and exhibited in over thirty one-man shows in the United States and abroad. Mr. Garzio is a periodic contributor to Craft Horizons and Ceramics Monthly.

James Meyer has taught pottery for several years and has been a regular contributor to the Goodfellow Review of Crafts. He is currently living and working in Oakland, California.

ENAMELS

Experimental Techniques in Enameling. By Fred Ball. Van Nostrand Reinhold, 1972, $10.95.

This is the first and only book to attempt an in-depth exploration of nontraditional enameling techniques.

It begins with a thorough explanation of basic procedures, then delves into an exploration of liquid enamel, metal inlay, foil and mesh structures, overlays of unexpected materials, firing variations, chemical surface treatment and the correction of technical problems.

Liberal illustrations include line drawings of procedures, black-and-white photographs of work in various stages of progress and an eight-page color group of enamels. The works illustrated are remarkable for their manipulation of material, but are generally weak in design and expressive content. Still, this book goes a long way toward encouraging an intuitive approach and extending classical limitations.

Suzanne Muchnic

Step-By-Step Enameling. By William Harper. Golden Press, 1973. $2.95.

This book is the most qualitatively illustrated enameling book available and the best buy on the market today. *Step-By-Step* provides basic instruction in traditional and modern techniques, methods of finishing and use of materials.

It includes step-by-step instructions for projects using the techniques of cloisonne, basse-taille, champleve, grisaille and plique-a-jour. Illustrations include clear line drawings and an excellent assortment of photographs of work by the finest and most creative contemporary enamelists.

Suzanne Muchnic

Recommended Books—Beginners

Enameling for Beginners. By Edward Winter. Watson-Guptill, 1962.

The Art of Enameling. By Margaret Seeler. Van Nostrand Reinhold, 1969.

General Reference

Enamel Art on Metals. By Edward Winter. Watson-Guptill, 1958.

Enameling on Metal. By Oppi Untracht. Chilton Book Company, 1962.

The Enamelist. By Kenneth Bates. Funk & Wagnalls Company, 1975.

Enamel Reviewers

Suzanne Muchnic is a practicing artist, teacher, technical consultant and free-lance writer in the arts. Her work in enamel has been exhibited throughout the United States and England. She is currently the Los Angeles editor of Artweek.

GLASS

Creative Glass Blowing. By James E. Hammesfahr and Claire L. Stong. W. H. Freeman and Company, 1968. $9.

Probably the best book outside of the many technical handbooks dealing with torch-working, *Creative Glass Blowing* offers the novice information on procedures and the manipulation skills required by both the scientific and novelty fields.

Marvin Lipofsky and Andy Magoanz

The Encyclopedia of Working with Glass. By Milton K. Berlye. Oceana Publications, 1968. $15.

Although published in 1968, this book continues to serve as a resource and reference aid, covering such topics as drilling, cutting, laminating, blowing and lampworking. It offers a diverse, although somewhat dated, synopsis on glass. This compilation of technical information deserves a place in every glass artist's library.

Marvin Lipofsky and Andy Magoanz

New Glass. By Otto Rigan. San Francisco Book Company, 1976.

New Glass, which looks at twenty-four West Coast stained glass artists and their work, is the first book about younger artists who treat stained glass in unconventional ways. Rigan calls this new direction an "omni-movement"—"without a declared manifesto, statement of purpose or any restrictions whatever." Some might call it a mishmash of divergent styles.

The excellent photographs by Charles Frizzell are the main content of the book. An introductory chapter by Otto Rigan provides a historical summary of the evolution of stained glass.

The body of the book consists of individual sections for each artist. In each section, Rigan's introduction is followed by the artist's statement. There are black-and-white photos of each artist in his/her studio and photos of some of the artist's work. The center section of the book contains sixty-four pages of color photos of windows by the twenty-four artists.

Peter Mollica

Studio Glassmaking. By Ray Flavell and Claude Smale. Van Nostrand Reinhold Company, 1974. $8.95.

Studio Glassmaking deals primarily with the technical aspects of glass-working and studio operation. Although not intended as dogma, the information here will be valuable to any glass artist. Flavell and Smale, themselves glass workers, wrote this book to fill the gaps in technical knowledge that continually present themselves to the studio glass artist. The book contains numerous black and white photographs and drawings to illustrate several procedures and techniques involved in the creation of glass objects. It is by far one of the most objective and concise texts on the studio glass movement and the existing technology in England and Sweden.

Marvin Lipofsky and Andy Magoanz

Recommended Books—Beginners

Stained Glass Primer. By Peter Mollica. Mollica Stained Glass Press, 1971. $2.95.
Techniques of Stained Glass. By Patrick Reyntiens. Watson-Guptill, 1967. $15.

General Reference

The Complete Book of Creative Glass Art. By Polly Rothenberg. Crown Publishers, 1974.
Glassblowing. By Frank Kulasiewicz. Watson-Guptill.
Glassblowing: A Search for Form. By Harvey K. Littleton. Von Nostrand Reinhold Company, 1972. $14.95.
Stained Glass: Music for the Eye. By Hill, Hill and Halberstadt. Scrimshaw Press, 1976. $9.50.

Glass Reviewers

Marvin Lipofsky is the chairperson of the Glass Department of California College of Arts and Crafts. These reviews were done under his supervision by students in the department with special assistance from Andy Magoanz.

Peter Mollica apprenticed to Chris Rufo in Boston, studied design with Ludwig Schaffrath, and currently lives and works in California, designing stained-glass windows.

JEWELRY

Contemporary Jewelry: A Studio Handbook. By Philip Morton. Holt, Rinehart and Winston, 1970, 1976. $15.95.

This excellent book is used by many craftspeople as a college text. It covers all of the basic techniques plus many advanced ones useful in jewelry making and metalsmithing.

Information is well organized and well illustrated with diagrams and photographs of contemporary American and European metal jewelry.

Techniques covered include soldering, forming, riveting, fastenings, hinging, casting methods, stone setting, enameling and tool making. Electroforming and photo etching are introduced.

Revised in 1976, much new material has been added including over 400 additional photos of the work of many fine European and American jewelry designers. Unfortunately, Morton's own work is the weakest represented.

Florence Resnikoff

Design and Creation of Jewelry. By Robert Von Neumann. Revised edition, Chilton Book Company, 1972. $12.50 cloth, $5.95 paper.

This book, by an instructor of jewelry making, offers a fresh approach to the subject. It contains illustrations for various projects with simple, easy-to-follow instructions. Many pieces presented are works by students using modern techniques. The chapters on traditional Japanese work, modern electroforming and photo etching are particularly interesting.

Mike Knott

Handwrought Jewelry. By Lois Franke and William L. Udell. McKnight and McKnight, 1962. $11.32.

This book deals with the fabrication of metal objects through forging, bending, soldering and forming procedures. It is an excellent introductory text for high school and college students. Photos of work processes and illustrations of finished work are excellent. The section on designing for jewelry is outstanding.

Harold O'Connor

Metal Techniques for Craftsmen: A Basic Manual for Craftsmen on the Methods of Forming and Decorating Metals. By Oppi Untracht. Doubleday, 1968.

Perhaps no other single publication available is being used by so many jewelers today. This book can easily be termed the "Bible" of the trade. Liberally illustrated with photographs and drawings, it covers a wide range of activities including Tibetan bronze casting, Indian and Japanese repousse, Mexican ornamental ironwork, Spanish sword etching, English engraving and contemporary Scandinavian hollowware. Complete with charts, tables, sources of supplies and an extensive glossary and bibliography, this book is a must for both beginners and old hands.

Mike Knott

Metalwork and Enameling. By Herbert Maryon. Revised edition, Dover, 1971. $3.50.

This book covers many facets of the jeweler's and silversmith's processes including various raising techniques, production spinning methods, and Japanese alloys and coloring processes. One of the most interesting sections, illustrated with photos, presents seventy-two different designs which can be made from various shaped wires. Other chapters offer an extensive coverage of enameling techniques, inlaying of metals, etching and layout methods.

Harold O'Connor

New Directions in Goldsmithing. By Harold O'Connor. Dunconor Books, 1975. $7.50.

The Jeweler's Bench Reference. By Harold O'Connor. Dunoonor Books, 1977. $12.50.

Harold O'Connor has written and published two workshop handbooks which I have found invaluable. These books are written by a man who is a producing, exhibiting jewelry designer passing along information and knowledge which he has garnered through the years.

Directions gives helpful information on creating thin hollow form, saving precious metal, texture transfer, lathe uses, plastics in jewelry and sling casting, and the making of your own equipment.

Bench Reference, a small, sturdy, wire-bound book, suitable for use on the workbench, is filled with information cover to cover. It contains many tables and formulas—determining materials needed for special shapes, coloration and alloying of metals. Also included is information on reclaiming scrap and mercury gilding, ideas for original fastenings and discussions of the esoteric techniques of mokume and reticulation.

Florence Resnikfoff

Recommended Books—Beginners

Creative Gold and Silversmithing. By Sharr Choate and Bonnie C. De May. Crown Publishers, 1970. $9.95 cloth, $5.95 paper.

Step-by-Step Jewelry Making. By Thomas Gentille. Western Publishing Company, 1974. $4.95 cloth, $2.95 paper.

Advanced
Engraving on Precious Metals. By Wolpert and Morton. N. A. G. Press. $7.95.

The Goldsmith's and Silversmith's Handbook. By Staton Abbey. W. S. Heinemann, 1968.

Jewelry Making by the Lost Wax Process. By Greta Peck. Revised edition, Van Nostrand Reinhold, 1975. $8.95.

General Reference
Metal Jewelry Techniques. By Marcia Chamberlain. Watson-Guptill, 1976. $16.95.

Jewelry Reviewers

Mike Knott is a professional jeweler living and working in Santa Rosa, California. For over seven years he's been doing custom work, attending crafts fairs, and selling his wares to shops throughout the Northwest.

Harold O'Connor has studied, worked, taught and lectured in many countries and has exhibited widely around the world. He is author of New Directions in Goldsmithing (Dunconor Books, 1975), Procedures and Formulas for Metal Craftsmen (1976) and The Jeweler's Bench Reference (1977) and the director of Dunconor Workshops in Crested Butte, Colorado.

Florence Resnikoff has been working in the field of jewelry and metalsmithing for over twenty years. She has had many one-person exhibitions, including ones at the de Young Museum in San Francisco and at Stanford University. She is currently exhibiting at invitational shows and is on the faculty of California College of Arts and Crafts.

LEATHER

Brendan's Leather Book. By Brendan Smith. Outer Straubville Press, 1972.

This is a good beginner's book for those interested in "funkier" styles of leatherwork. Many different projects are described, with diagrams and easy-to-follow line drawings. The book deals with simple projects such as belts and sandals, as well as hard-leather purses. The concentration is certainly on harder leather, which is easier for the novice to handle. The excellent foreword details what to look for when buying leather and tools.
Fredda Cassidy

Encyclopedia of Rawhide and Leather Braiding. By Bruce Grant. Cornell Maritime Press, 1972. $10.

Bruce Grant's *Encyclopedia* can solve every conceivable problem the leatherworker will have in trying to combine two or more pieces of leather. Grant assumes that you will be making a professional-looking finished product, and that you will want to embellish your piece with some fancy lace or braid work. The text, divided into several chapters, provides written explanations and diagrams. Grant seems to be familiar with every known type of braid.

Other chapters deal with button-making, hobbles and Turk's-head knots. Although it assumes considerable knowledge of leatherworking, as well as an idea of knotwork, the book can be used by anyone working in either hard or soft leather, clothing or bag work. It can also be an excellent guide for those interested in expanding their ideas about macrame and embroidery. No fine leather shop or leather craftsman should be without this invaluable source of information and ideas.
Fredda Cassidy

Everything About Sewing Leather and Leather-like Fabrics. Vogue Patterns, Butterick Fashion Marketing Co., 1971.

This is the most advanced source I have come across on sewing soft leather with a sewing machine. The book discusses mostly clothing, but the techniques are also pertinent to sewing soft leather.

The book assumes that you already know how to sew, and that you want a high quality product when you are finished. While discussing how to finish your goods professionally, it also looks at designing and laying out patterns, choosing leather, and stitching and finishing your piece. I highly recommend this volume to anyone interested in stitching soft leather on a machine. The clearly presented drawings are a delight.
Fredda Cassidy

Introducing Bookbinding. By Ivor Robinson. Watson-Guptill, 1968.

This book, a step-by-step guide to bookbinding, offers just about all the information a beginning binder would need. It begins with basic definitions and terminology. Then it describes and illustrates the materials and tools to any reader's satisfaction.

Because the procedure is so well illustrated, one could follow this guide and, with minimal trial and error, end up with a bound book.

The book's only drawback is the author's continual reference to professional equipment which most beginners in the field would lack. We need to rely on our ingenuity to improvise tools, and Mr. Robinson never acknowledges this.

Amy Reiser

Leather as Art and Craft. By Thelma Newman. Crown Publishers, 1973. $8.95 cloth, $5.95 paper.

This is one of the best general sources on new and traditional techniques and processes of leatherworking. Ms. Newman states her belief that leather has no limitations. More striking is her approach; she treats the medium with a reverence which it seldom receives elsewhere.

While her history of leather is too brief to be really useful, her main thrust —exploring the ways in which contemporary craftspeople are utilizing their material—is very informative.

She uses numerous photographs to illustrate the procedures used in such processes as molding, stitching and batiking. While not a how-to book, it does provide the interested reader with all sorts of ideas and approaches to handling leather.

Amy Reiser

Working with Leather. By Xenia Ley Parker. Charles Scribner's Sons, 1972.

Parker's delightfully comprehensive book succeeds on two counts: it conveys large amounts of pertinent information to the new craftsperson, and simultaneously nourishes the imagination with provocative ideas.

The introduction and first chapter are complete and informative. They supply the reader with historical background about leather and provide basic criteria for distinguishing hide types and weights—skills necessary to anyone truly interested in the art.

Theoretically and factually sound, Parker's book displays a talent for to-the-point instructions. I highly recommend it for anyone ready to plunge into leatherworking. It would also be a useful and welcome addition to the libraries of experienced leathercrafters.

Ginger Swartz

Recommended Books

Leather Craftsmanship. By John Waterer. Praeger Publishers, 1968.

New Directions in Bookbinding. By Philip Smith. Van Nostrand Reinhold, 1974.

Leather Reviewers

Fredda Cassidy is a practicing leather artist and owner of the Golden Calf, a leather shop in Berkeley, California.

Amy Reiser is a practicing craftswoman living and working in the hills of western Massachusetts, doing all her work entirely by hand.

Ginger Swartz has been working in leather for over fifteen years. She studied pattern drafting and tailoring at vocational-technical schools and now works almost entirely in soft leather.

METAL

Art of Blacksmithing. By Alex W. Bealer. Funk and Wagnalls, 1969. $10.

Modern Blacksmith. By Alexander G. Weygers. Van Nostrand Reinhold Company, 1974. $8.95 cloth, $4.95 paper.

Art of Blacksmithing is a comprehensive source for anyone interested in the craft. Bealer covers its history, illustrating and describing basic techniques such as drawing, forming, upsetting and forge welding. Part of the book shows how to make tools, hardware, home utensils, weapons and decorative work.

Modern Blacksmith is another valuable resource. Weygers clearly explains the basics of forging, presents a good section on tempering and hardening, and includes color charts showing the heat glow and oxidation spectrums for steel. Weygers, a stone and wood carver, uses the rest of his book to describe the essentials of tool making.

Both books encourage improvisation and advise the keeping and use of a good scrap pile (something I'm especially fond of). Both are illustrated; Weygers' includes a glossary, Bealer's has an index and bibliography.

A working knowledge of iron is essential to both industry and art. Wood, stone, plastic, paper, fiber, and indeed, metal itself, could not be cut, carved, formed, pushed or pulled without it.

Steve Hersch

Recommended Books—Beginners

Metalworking. By Oscar Almeida. Drake Publishers, 1971.

Advanced

Machine Tool Operation. By Burghardt, Axelrod and Anderson. McGraw-Hill.
Welding Engineering. By Boniface Rossi. McGraw-Hill.

General Reference

The Complete Illustrated Tool Book. Edited by Clark and Lyman. Galahad Books.

Metal Reviewer

Steve Hersch has worked as a mechanic, welder, fitter and sculptor. He has also taught blacksmithing to community college students. His sculpture is exhibited at select galleries.

WOOD

Antique Country Furniture of North America. By John Shea. Van Nostrand Reinhold Company.

One of the best books on the subject, *Antique Country Furniture of North America* contains a comprehensive picture collection representing a dozen different regional influences on American country furniture. The French Canadian, Southern Plantation and Texas German pieces are particularly striking.

In Section Two of the book, the photos are arranged to allow the reader to compare various regional influences on particular pieces. Tables, chairs, chests of drawers, cradles, desks and other pieces are included in this section.

A rudimentary discussion of some of the joints and techniques used in woodworking shows what to do, but not how to do it. The final section, a large collection of measured drawings, can easily be followed by someone with woodworking experience and equipment.

Tom McFadden

A Cabinetmaker's Notebook. By James Krenov. Van Nostrand Reinhold Company, 1976. $13.50.

Krenov's unpretentious book, with beautiful photographs and lucid prose, distills the thought of a master woodworker. It describes how he got there, where he's still going, and offers ideas for beginners on the path, as well as his reflections on wood—from its beauty to its demands. I return to the book frequently for inspiration from a man who

has not knuckled under to commercial demands.

The application of his fundamental methods leaves little chance of distorting final shapes. Hand carving and planing with handmade planes produces most of his final shaping. He stresses the importance of the feel of the wood between the fingertips. His simple lines, along with his expressive joinery, make this work truly inspiring.

Steve Doriss

Cabinetmaking and Millwork. By John L. Feirer. Charles Scribner's Sons, 1973. $24.95.

This work—which is *the* textbook on this subject—is the most comprehensive description of modern machine woodworking methods and equipment I have seen. There are separate chapters on nearly every available piece of machinery, and on nearly all of the techniques a modern woodworker needs.

Slanted to machine woodworking, the book devotes minimal space to hand methods. The section on construction covers the basics very well. This is a reference book that anyone interested in woodworking will benefit from.

Tom McFadden

Country Furniture. By Aldren A. Watson. Thomas Y. Crowell, 1974. $9.95.

Aldren A. Watson's *Country Furniture* is an engaging description of the life and techniques of the furniture maker in the late 1700s. Outstanding illustrations by Watson on nearly every page cover everything from selecting, cutting and air drying fine hardwoods to applying hardware to the finished piece of furniture.

The section on woodworking methods has step-by-step illustrated instructions for numerous operations, including hand-cut dovetails, carvings, turnings and bentwork. Woodworkers and others interested in ''Americana'' will find this interesting.

Tom McFadden

Encyclopedia of Furniture Making. By Ernest Joyce. Drake Publishers, 1971. $14.95.

A classic, this covers everything from tools and materials to techniques and actual examples. A thorough coverage of the whole range of furniture making—from trees to table tops—makes this book extremely useful. Its main value for me is that it acts like a springboard: when I have a vague notion, or when I'm totally uninformed about a topic, I can consult this book and it will point me in the right direction.

Sections on characteristics of wood, joints, carcase construction, specific furniture types, plus an emphasis on handwork, help make this a necessary reference work.

Steve Doriss

Planecraft. By C. W. Hampton and E. Clifford. Woodcraft Supply Corporation.

The book on planes. It deals with plane basics (use, adjusting, sharpening, techniques), types of planes (a thorough chapter on each) an interesting history of the plane, plus a small section in the back on the workbench and some workshop hints.

I find this small book valuable on two levels. First, the use of the plane, a basic hand tool, is covered well. Second, as machines take over a larger and larger share of the duties of the woodworker, it is helpful to keep handwork in mind—for there are some tasks for which handwork is superior to machine work.

Steve Doriss

Recommended Books—Beginners

Cabinet-Making for Beginners. By Charles Hayward. Drake Publishers, 1971.

De Cristoforo's Complete Book of Power Tools. By R. J. De Cristoforo. Harper & Row, 1973. $12.95.

Fine Furniture for the Amateur Cabinet-Maker. By Andrew Marlow. Macmillan Publishing Company, 1955.

Good Furniture You Can Make Yourself. By F. E. Hoard and A. W. Marlow. Macmillan Publishing Company, 1972. $3.95.

How to Build Your Own Furniture. By R. J. De Cristoforo. Barnes & Noble. $2.95.

Woodworking and Furniture Making for the Home. By G. W. Endacott. Drake Publishers, 1971.

Advanced

Know Your Woods. By Albert Constantine. Charles Scribner's Sons, 1972.

Windsor Chairmaking. By Michael Dunbar. Hastings, 1976. $9.95.

Woodwork Joints. By Charles H. Hayward. Drake Publishers, 1970.

General Reference

Creating Modern Furniture: Trends, Techniques, Appreciation. Crown Publishers, 1975. $12.95.

Furniture Treasury. By Wallace Nutting. Macmillan Publishing Company.

Wood Reviewers

Steve Doriss came to woodworking with a background in architectural design. He is presently involved in a small cabinet shop concentrating on tool and instrument chests and basic cabinet work.

Tom McFadden is a professional woodworker earning his living making custom furniture in Mendocino County, California. He exhibits at select fairs and art centers.

TEXTILES

Handspindles. By Bette Hochberg. $3.95 paper.

The familiar drop spindle has been only one of many handspindles used to produce yarn or thread for fabrics. *Handspindles* is the first book to survey the whole field.

This historical overview, entwined with spindle folklore, is illustrated with photographs and woodcuts of spindles and spindle whorls past and present (including today's aboriginal cultures). The author has categorized these numerous styles into ten distinctly different types. Illustrated directions show how to use the spindles and each one is discussed in relation to various fibers and the types of yarn.

Directions on how to spin are easy to follow; notes for teachers make it useful for class. A chapter on selecting spindles explains how design affects performance.

With this book we have a readable discussion of hand and wrist distaffs and how they can be used to produce smoother yarn.

Susan C. Druding

Handspinner's Handbook. By Bette Hochberg. 69 pages, 36 illustrations. $3.95, paper.

Whether a beginner or advanced, you'll want this handy manual by your spinning wheel. The first section gives step-by-step instructions on spinning; the drawing out of fibers; speed spinning; producing thick, thin and textured yarns;

washing; carding; setting the twist and allowing for shrinkage.

The second section, which abounds with information about more than twenty natural fibers, makes this the first book to provide a worldwide guide to animal and vegetable fibers for handspinners. Each fiber is fully dealt with: how its chemical and physical properties influence the way in which the fiber spins, plus tips on selecting, storing and spinning each fiber.

With this book alone it is possible to become a fast, competent spinner.

Susan C. Druding

Your Handspinning. By Elsie Davenport. Select Books, 1964. $4.50.

For a long time this was *the* book on handspinning (with both a drop spindle and spinning wheel). This is a very thorough, somewhat opinionated book taking the reader step-by-step from whole fleece to finished yarns ready to weave, knit or crochet. There may be an occasional British term which confuses the American reader, but don't be put off. This book is packed with useful information for the spinner and would-be spinner. Ms. Davenport both tells you how to spin and deals with the care, maintenance and choosing of a spinning wheel. She deals at length with preparing and spinning flax (starting with the seeds) and other fibers. There are also good chapters on yarn design and finishing. A very solid, valuable book.

Eleanor Adams

Spinning Wheel Primer. By Alden Amos.

This is not another "how to spin" book; it's a look at the spinning wheel as a machine. If you want to build, buy or just understand it, this is the book for you.

Good diagrams and simple explanations of the pros and cons of the various mechanisms aid the non-mechanically minded. Alden even gives his formula for the "ideal wheel"; while you might not agree with him, you will better understand your own prejudices.

Gail Grogan

Nature's Colors: Dyes from Plants. By Ida Grae. Macmillan Publishing Company, 1974. $14.95.

Nature's Colors is an attractive, well laid-out book on natural dyeing with an emphasis on West Coast plants. It's exciting to realize that so many potential sources of "natural colors" surround us all the time—even in the city. There are a great many very specific formulas covering a wide color range; however, I have found it difficult to duplicate the colors which Ms. Grae obtains—possibly due to differing mineral content in the water used. Also, I find Ms. Grae overly optimistic in estimating the light-fastness of many of the colors she obtains. Otherwise, the book is very clear and easy to follow—a good presentation of the possibilities.

Eleanor Adams

A Handweaver's Pattern Book. By Marguerite P. Davison. John Spencer, Inc., 1975. $12.

If the intrigue and delight of a pattern built into heddles and treadled out captures your fancy, look what's available! This classic handbook, written in 1944 and now in its sixteenth printing, documents a thousand possible weaves on the four-harness loom, and challenges you to create even more. Black-and-white photos of fabric samples all made of the same kind of thread provide a basis for comparison. Clear, consistent diagrams for threading and treadling make the complicated comprehensible. A source book, it should be used in combination with a basic weaving text.

Carolyn Dyer

The Technique of Woven Tapestry. By Tadek Beutlich. Watson-Guptill, 1974. $11.95.

By leading the patient craftsperson through the process with remarkable diagrams and photos, British artist Beutlich deflates the idea that flat woven tapestry is difficult. Dressing both high and low warp looms, he discusses heddles, tensions, tools, the building of the web, fibers and finishing. Rya rugs as wall hangings are examined. Glossary, bibliography and list of suppliers in the U.S. and England are included. Design is crucial, he says, it determines whether a tapestry turns out to be art or just some dangling fibers. Beutlich, known for his strong composition, advises simplicity.

Carolyn Dyer

New Key to Weaving—A Textbook of Handweaving for the Beginning Weaver. By Mary E. Black. Collier-Macmillan, 1975. $13.95.

This book is one of the oldest, most complete textbooks for beginners. First published in 1945, it still maintains the flavor of weaving as a home craft. The seventeen chapters cover basic information such as loom workings, loom-controlled weaves, finger-manipulated weaves, special weaves and the theory of drafting. For each weave or technique, full, detailed information is given.

There is only one problem—the drab, uninspiring illustrations. On the whole, however, it is an excellent in-depth how-to book, very useful for beginners.

Ida Grae

The Techniques of Rug Weaving. By Peter Collingwood. Watson-Guptill, 1972. $17.50.

In *The Techniques of Rug Weaving*, Peter Collingwood—one of weaving's foremost names—may well have written the most authoritative guide available to handweavers. Since it is written "from the point of view of a professional, not a hobby weaver," it approaches the full scope of rug weaving techniques with exacting detail, careful instructions and working diagrams. A master of his craft, he leads into each technique, from warping the loom to infinite finishing methods, with clear explanations that can be of value to even the most experienced. An invaluable resource and reference, his book is a must for every serious handweaver.

Judi Keen

Textiles of Ancient Peru and Their Techniques. By Raoul D'Harcourt. University of Washington Press, 1962, 1974. $8.95.

This scholarly work, first published in Paris in 1934, is a superb source of techniques and ideas for the textile artist. D'Harcourt painstakingly researched numerous loom and non-loom techniques of the pre-Spanish Peruvians (including double cloth, gauze, passementerie, plaiting, braiding and felt).

The techniques are described in detail and analyzed in terms of design, motif and use in early Peruvian society.

One cannot help but marvel at the flowering of textile arts in ancient Peru, while lamenting that many of the techniques which produced the exquisite pieces pictured in D'Harcourt's book have fallen into oblivion.

Joan Reid Saltzman

Beyond Craft—The Art Fabric. By Mildred Constantine and Jack Lenor Larsen. Van Nostrand Reinhold, 1973. 295 pages. $35.

A coffeetable look-book of considerable beauty, *Beyond Craft* is a solid source for understanding contemporary fiber art. Reviewing design and weaving movements of the early twentieth century (especially the Bauhaus), the authors explore the artists' studios, galleries and commercial interiors. Definitely not a how-to volume, it offers no magic formulas—only challenges! And the authors concentrate on the superstars.

Carolyn Dyer

The Textile Arts. By Verla Birrell. Schocken Books, 1973. $7.95.

A friend describes certain quiet, unassuming people as "deep, deep wells," which is how I've come to regard the Birrell book. She has a cohesive overview of the textile picture that integrates weaving, embroidery, single-element processes like macrame and lace with surface decoration like dyeing and printing. Birrell's interest in archeology adds richness to the techniques and makes us develop an appreciation for what's gone before. I find myself playing games with her as my own research progresses—"Hey, Verla, bet you skipped machine embroidery! Well I'll be. . . . There it is, Fig. 174, work of the Mayan Indians of Yucatan!"

Robbie Fanning

The New Basketry. By Ed Rossbach. Van Nostrand Reinhold, 1976.

The book, a well-illustrated discussion of many new trends, techniques and materials in textile arts today, goes far beyond the realm of basketry or raffia weaving. It focuses on the basket as an art form, which is technically not a weaving, but more like a "fiberwork," or fiber construction. The photographs explore work being done by artists—not basketmakers—using basketry as a form of expression in fiber. Rossbach explores "fibrousness" and demonstrates how the "new basketry arose out of handweaving." He emphasizes the union of basketry and other textile arts in relation to techniques and materials used in three-dimensional works. The volume is an excellent study in the use of many types of fiber, a worthy companion and follow-up to his *Baskets as Textile Art*.

Arlene Noble

The Quilt Design Workbook. By Beth and Jeffrey Gutcheon. Rawson Associates Publishers, Inc., 1976.

The book explains how to chart and implement the design of a quilt. It describes cutting, piecing, sewing, quilting, binding and finishing techniques. The last half of the volume contains actual patterns and directions. This book differs from those that have come before it in focus, design and format. Although it does not replace those volumes which primarily survey quilts and quiltmakers, it is an excellent supplement to any quiltmaker's library.

Arlene Noble

Recommended Books—Beginners

The Art of Weaving. By Else Regensteiner. Van Nostrand Reinhold, 1970. $15.95.

Elements of Weaving. By Azalea Stuart Thorpe and Jack Lenor Larsen. Doubleday. $10.95.

Stitches of Creative Embroidery. By Jacqueline Enthoven. Van Nostrand Reinhold, 1964. $9.95.

Advanced

Design on Fabric. By Johnson and Kaufman. Van Nostrand Reinhold, 1976. $6.95.

Designing on the Loom. By Mary Kirby. Select Books, 1973. $6.

Inspiration for Embroidery. By Constance Howard. Charles T. Branford Company, 1969.

The Needleworker's Dictionary. By Pamela Claburn. William Morrow and Company, 1976. $19.95.

Vegetable Dyeing. By Alma Lesch. Watson-Guptill, 1971. $7.95.

General Reference

American Quilts and How to Make Them. By Carter Houk and Myron Mille. Charles Scribner's Sons, 1975.

Baskets as Textile Art. By Ed Rossbach. Van Nostrand Reinhold Company. $14.95.

Dyer's Art: Ikat, Batik, Plangi. By Jack Lenor Larsen et al. American Crafts Council, 1976. $35.

Fabric Printing: Screen Method. By Richard Valentino and Phyllis Mufson. Bay Books, 1975. $3.95.

Molas: What They Are, How to Make Them and Ideas They Suggest for Creative Applique. By Rhoda Auld. Van Nostrand Reinhold Company, 1977.

Primary Structure of Fabrics. By Irene Emery. Textile Museum, 1966. $25.

Quilts in America. By Myron and Patsy Orlofsky. McGraw-Hill, 1974.

Sheila Hicks. By Monique Levi-Strauss. Van Nostrand Reinhold Company, 1974. $15.

Textile Collections of the World. Edited by Cecil Lubell. Van Nostrand Reinhold Company.

Trapunto and Other Forms of Raised Quilting. By Mary Morgan and Dee Mosteller. Charles Scribner's Sons, 1977.

Textile Reviewers

Eleanor Adams is an apprentice in the Mendocino Art Center Textile Apprenticeship Program.

Susan Druding is a practicing fiber artist and proprieter of Straw Into Gold, a large retail and mail-order fibercraft outlet.

Carolyn Dyer received her B.A. and M.A. from Mills College. She is a teacher, gallery owner and producing and exhibiting artist specializing in traditional tapestry. She writes for Artweek and Fiberarts.

Robbie Fanning is editor/publisher of Open Chain, the Newsletter of Threadbenders, author of Decorative Machine Stitchery (Butterick Publishing Company) and a new book on ethnic embroidery which will be published by Butterick.

Ida Grae has been a producing craftswoman since 1951. She is the author of Nature's Colors—Dyes from Plants (Macmillan Publishing Company, 1974), Dressing the Loom (1954, 1975) and a new book, The Book of Handwoven Garments (1978). Ms. Grae is the winner of major textile awards and is currently teaching in her own studio.

Gail Grogan is an apprentice in the Mendocino Art Center Textile Apprenticeship Program.

Judi Keen is an apprentice in the Mendocino Art Center Textile Apprenticeship Program.

Arlene Noble is a librarian at Stanford University, a handweaver, book reviewer for The Goodfellow Review of Crafts and an indexer for Artweek.

Joan Reid Saltzman is a textile artist living in Berkeley. She currently teaches loom and non-loom weaving at Fiberworks Center for the Textile Arts.

Crafts Reference Books

Research compiled by Arlene Noble.

Business

Career Opportunities in Crafts. By Elyse Sommer. Crown Publishers, 1977. $10.95 cloth, $5.95 paper.

Crafts Are Your Business. By Gerald Tooke. Canadian Crafts Council, 1976. $3.50.

Crafts as Business—1975. American Crafts Council, 1975, 10 pages. $2 members, $3 nonmembers. Marketing and other business topics—annotated bibliography.

The Crafts Business Encyclopedia: How to Make Money, Market Your Products, and Manage Your Home Craft Business. By Michael Scott. Harcourt Brace Jovanovich, 1977. $10.

Crafts for Fun and Profit. By Eleanor Van Zandt. Doubleday & Company.

The Craftsman's Survival Manual: Making a Full- or Part-Time Living from Your Crafts. By George and Nancy Wettlaufer. Prentice Hall, 1974. $5.95 cloth, $2.95 paper.

Craftsmen in Business: A Guide to Financial Management and Taxes. By Howard W. Connaughton, C.P.A. American Crafts Council, 1975. $4.95 members, $6.50 nonmembers.

Creative Exploration in Crafts. By Gretchen M. Anderson. Prentice-Hall.

Creative Selling Through Trade Shows. By Al Hanlon. Hawthorne Books, 1977.

Design and Sell Toys, Games and Crafts. By Filis Frederick. Chilton Book Company, 1977.

Encouraging American Craftsmen. By Charles Counts. Available through the Superintendent of Documents, U.S. Government Printing Office, Washington, D.C. 20402. 1972, 36 pages. 45 cents.

Exhibiting Spaces 1975-76: Artists' Bay Area Marketing Handbook. By Felicity Pruden. Mother's Hen, 1975. $5.95.

The Handicraft Business. Small Business Reporter Series. Bank of America, Department 3120, P.O. Box 37000, San Francisco, California 94137. 1972, 16 pages. $1.

How to Earn Money from Your Crafts. By Merle E. Dowd. Doubleday Company, 1976. $7.95.

How to Make and Sell Your Arts and Crafts. By Lois S. Becker. Frederick Fell.

How to Make Money with Your Crafts. By Leta W. Clark. William Morrow & Company, 1973. $6.95.

How to Sell Your Arts and Crafts: A Marketing Guide for Creative People. By Loretta Holz. Charles Scribner's Sons, 1977. $12.50.

How to Sell Your Crafts. By Ruth Wucherer. Drake Publishers, 1976. $4.95.

How to Start and Operate a Mail-Order Business. By Julian L. Simon and Mae G. Simon. Second edition, McGraw-Hill Book Company, 1976.

How to Start Your Own Craft Business. By Herb Genfan and Lyn Tatezsch. Watson-Guptill Publications, 1974. $7.95.

Planning Your Craft Show. United Maine Craftsmen, R.F.D. 2, Litchfield, Maine 04350, 22 pages. 60 cents. Helps groups who plan to sponsor a craft show.

The Potential of Handicrafts as a Viable Economic Force; An Overview. U.S. Department of Commerce. 1974, 52 pages. 65 cents. Available from U.S. Government Printing Office, Washington, D.C. 20402.

Sales Success at Crafts Fairs. By Arthur E. Koski. Finn Craft. $1.

Selling as a Professional. By Michael Higgins. The Working Craftsman, Box 42, Northbrook, Illinois 60062. Reprints from columns. 65 cents each; four reprints $2.60.

Selling Your Crafts. By Norbert N. Nelson. Van Nostrand Reinhold Company, 1967. $3.95.

Selling Your Crafts and Art in Los Angeles: The Complete Source Book for Amateurs and Professionals. By Lila Weingarten and Kendall Taylor. Wollstonecraft, 1974. $3.95.

Selling Your Handcrafts. By William E. Garrison. Chilton Book Company, 1974. $4.95.

Successful Craftsman: Making Your Craft Your Business. By Alex Bealer. Barre Publishing Company, 1975. $9.95.

Legal

Legal Forms for the Designer. By Lee Epstein. Contract Books, 1969.

Legal Guide for the Visual Artist. By Tad Crawford. Hawthorne Books, 1977.

Tax and the Individual Artist. By Bay Area Lawyers for the Arts, 25 Taylor Street, San Francisco, California 94102, $2.50. New pamphlet explains the effect of the new Tax Reform Act on artists.

Tax Guide for Small Business. Publication 334, Internal Revenue Service, U.S. Government Printing Office, Washington, D.C. 20402. Issued annually to help small businessmen with tax preparation.

What Every Artist and Collector Should Know About the Law. By Scott Hodes. E. P. Dutton, 1974. $9.95.

The Visual Artist and the Law. By the Associated Councils of the Arts, the Association of the Bar of New York City and the Volunteer Lawyers for the Arts. Revised edition, Prager Publishers. $10.

Source Books

Alternative Shopping: A Guide to Handcrafted Wares in California, Santa Cruz to San Diego. By Deborah Eddy. J. P. Tarcher, 1972, 1973. $3.95.

American Artist Product Directory. Billboard Publications, 44 pages. $1. Lists manufacturers and national distributors of art and crafts supplies, brand names, and books, new product news.

American Crafts Guide: A Comprehensive Directory to Craft Shops, Galleries, Crafts Schools, Museums and Studios of Individual Craftsmen Across the United States. Edited by Marion May. H. M. Gousha Company, 1973. $3.95.

Artisan Crafts Guide to the Craft World. Edited by Barbara Brabec. O & E Enterprises, P.O. Box 398, Libertyville, Illinois 60048. $5.50. Lists artists and craftsmen, shops, galleries, studios, instruction, publications and services.

The Best Things in Life Are Free: A Directory of Free Craft and Hobby Materials. Edited by Mark Weiss. Drake Publishers, 1972.

Contemporary Crafts Market Place. By the American Crafts Council. R. R. Bowker Company, 1975. $13.95.

Craft Shops/Galleries U.S.A. American Crafts Council, 1973. $3 members, $3.95 nonmembers. A nationwide directory of outlets selling American crafts.

Crafts Sources: The Ultimate Catalog for Craftspeople. By Paul Colin and Deborah Lippman. M. Evans and Company, 1975. $12.50 cloth, $5.95 paper.

Craft Suppliers. American Crafts Council, 1974. $2 members, $3 nonmembers. Two-part directories of supplies and their sources.

Crafts Supplies Supermarket: A Directory of Supplies, Tools, Materials and Equipment. By Sarah Rosenbloom. Oliver Press, 1400 Ryan Creek Road, Willits, California 95490, 1974. $3.95.

Create Your Place. P.O. Box 196, Reynoldsburg, Ohio 43068. Titles available: *Miscellaneous Craft Supplies & Distributors*, $3.95; *Beads of All Types*, $4.50; *Ceramics and Earthenware Supplies*, $3.95; *Jewelry Supplies*, $4.95; *Jute and Macrame Cords*, $4.95; *Needlepoint & Weaving Supplies*, $4.95; *Sewing Notions & Material*, $2.95; *Leather & Woodworking Supplies*, $2.95; *Decorating Accessories*, $2.95.

Handmade in Ontario—A Guide to Crafts and Craftsmen. By Susan Himel and Elaine Lambert. Van Nostrand Reinhold Company, 1976. $5.95.

Health Hazards Manual for Artists. By Michael McCann, Ph.D. Foundation for the Community of Artists, 1975. $2.

Lapidary Journal Buyers Guide. The Lapidary Journal, P.O. Box 80937, San Diego, California 92138. $2. Issued annually. Lists retail and wholesale dealers.

Leather Manufacturers Directory. Shoe Trades Publishing Company, 15 East Street, Boston, Massachusetts 02111. $8. Lists all U.S. and other tanners, sources for everything used in tanning.

The Mail-Order Catalogue: Suppliers, Kits, Finished Items, Publications, Home Study Courses, Organizations, Services. By Margaret Boyd. Chilton Book Company, 1975. $7.95.

Mail Order U.S.A. By Dorothy O'Callaghan. P.O. Box 19083, Washington, D.C. 20036. $3. Evaluates over 2,000 mail-order catalogs in U.S. and Canada. Hard-to-find clothes, foods, books, toys, sports, equipment, handicrafts, supplies and tools.

Mail Order U.S.A. By Margaret Rose. 4820-D 41st Street, NW, Washington, D.C. 20016. Lists approximately 1,000 catalogs on everything, including hundreds on crafts supplies. $3.

National Guide to Craft Supplies: The Craft Yellow Pages. By Judith Glassman. Van Nostrand Reinhold, 1976. $6.95.

New York Guide to Craft Supplies. By Judith Glassman. Second edition, Workman Publishing Company, 1974. $2.95.

1976 Handweavers Guild of America Suppliers Directory: A Listing of Firms Specializing in Supplies and Equipment for Weavers, Spinners and Dyers. By Handweavers Guild of America. 998 Farmington Avenue, West Hartford, Connecticut 06107, 1976. $4.

Profitable Craft Merchandising. P. J. S. Publications, News Plaza, Peoria, Illinois 61601. June 1976 issue contains indexed directory of suppliers and manufacturers of crafts supplies. Monthly, $5/year.

The Sensuous Gadgeteer. By Bill Abler. Running Press, 38 South 19th Street, Philadelphia, Pennsylvania 19103. $3.95. Common shop practices are shown, explained and illustrated.

Spinning Sources List. The Weaving Craftsman, Box 42, Northbrook, Illinois 60062. $2.50. Sources of supplies, equipment, books, dyes.

Where to Get What. By Margaret Rose. 4820-D 41st Street, NW, Washington, D.C. 20016. $2.25. Lists hundreds of craft supply catalogs.

Wholesale Arts & Crafts Directory. G & J Distributors, 4523 West Labath, Santa Rosa, California 95401.

Photography

Photographing Crafts. By John C. Barsness. American Crafts Council, 1974. $3.95 members, $4.95 nonmembers.

Photographing Your Product for Advertising: A Handbook for Designers and Craftsmen. By Norbert Nelson. Van Nostrand Reinhold Company, 1971.

Photography for Artists and Craftsmen. By Claus-Peter Schmid. Van Nostrand Reinhold Company, 1975. $9.95.

Photography Market Place. Edited by Fred W. McDarrah. R. R. Bowker Company, 1975. $14.95.

Bibliographies

American Crafts Council, Reference Bibliographies. Compiled by the Research & Education Department. On the history and processes of craft media, including periodicals and *Craft Horizons* articles. Fiber, 1976, $5 members, $6 nonmembers; Clay, 1977, $3 members, $4 nonmembers; Metal, 1975, $3 members, $4 nonmembers; Wood, 1975, $3 members, $4 nonmembers; Glass, 1975, $2 members, $3 nonmembers; Enamel, 1975, $1 members, $2 nonmembers.

Applied and Decorative Arts: A Bibliographic Guide to Basic Reference Works, Histories and Handbooks. By D. L. Ehresmann. P.O. Box 263, Littleton, Colorado 80120, 1977. $15.

The Butterick Fabric Handbook: A Consumer's Guide to Fabric for Clothing and Home Furnishings. Edited by Irene Cumming Kleeberg. Butterick Publishing, 1975. $2.95.

Crafts Today. By R. M. Harwell and A. J. Harwell. Libraries Unlimited, P.O. Box 263, Littleton, Colorado, 1974. $9.50. Spare time guide: information for hobbies and recreation. Bibliography.

Female Artists Past and Present. Second edition, The Women's History Research Center, 2325 Oak Street, Berkeley, California 94708, 1976. $6.

Packaging/Shipping of Crafts. American Crafts Council, 1976, 12 pages. $2 members, $3 nonmembers. General and specific recommendations for various media, list of supplies, shipping agents, export information, bibliography.

Production Logbook for Spinning. Straw Into Gold Editions, Straw Into Gold, 5533 College Avenue, Oakland, California 94618, 1977. $3.25. First in a series for organizing samples of your work. Others to follow are Batik, Natural Dyes, Synthetic Dyes and Weaving.

Quilt Reading List #2. By Charlotte Tufts. 531 Gaylord Drive, Burbank, California 91505.

Weaving, Spinning and Dyeing. By Lavonne Brady Axford. Libraries Unlimited, 1975. Spare-time guide: information for hobbies and recreation. Bibliography.

Funding for Crafts

by Bette London

If not many craftspeople are seeking grants these days, it may be for a good reason. Most important, of course, is the fact that there isn't very much money available—and there is especially little for individuals.

Most grant-making institutions, public and private, fund only nonprofit organizations. Craftspeople should be aware of these limitations before setting their hopes on the Great Grant. One way of dealing with the problem is for individuals to form their own nonprofit organizations. Still, it should be understood that, even for nonprofit crafts organizations, the options are limited.

Furthermore, very few funding institutions will pay craftspeople simply to pursue their work. Most fund specific projects and these projects are judged for their wide-ranging significance. In addition, most grants are only short-term, at best maybe a year or two. All told, they are a temporary, highly uncertain—though valid—solution to the economic problems facing craftspeople.

I have not, however, limited this article to discussing only fellowships and grants. Rather, I have also included programs that offer loans, contracts, employment opportunities and, in some cases, technical and managerial assistance. This broader coverage should provide a more realistic perspective on the funding sources available to craftspeople.

This study is by no means exhaustive. It is not a handbook with step-by-step instructions for obtaining grants; nor will it replace the many standard reference works already on the market. It is instead designed as a reader's guide to the appropriate sources of information.

Federal

National Endowment for the Arts

The NEA is one of the few funding sources that allocates monies specifically for crafts. Its Visual Arts Program has several categories of funding, including fellowships for individual craftspersons and matching grants for nonprofit, tax-exempt crafts organizations. The following is a brief summary of the NEA's crafts programs.

• *Craftsmen's Fellowships.* Unlike most grants, these fellowships do not require that you work on a special project in order to qualify for funding. They are designed to help exceptionally talented craftsmen advance their careers by enabling them to purchase materials and set aside more time for their work. Grant amount: $7,500.

• *Craftsmen Apprenticeship.* This program enables master craftsmen in such media as glass, textiles and wood to engage an apprentice. An individual master craftsman may apply for only one apprentice; nonprofit, tax-exempt organizations, for up to five apprentices. Matching funds are required for organizations. Grant amounts: $3,500 per apprentice.

• *Crafts Exhibition Aid.* Nonprofit organizations, including universities and community art centers, may apply for aid to bring crafts exhibitions of contemporary or historical importance to the public. Grant amounts: major exhibitions, matching grants up to $15,000; other projects, matching grants up to $7,500.

• *Crafts Workshops.* These workshops are designed to assist the production of new work by craftsmen of exceptional talent. The program encourages artists to test ideas and media, and to devise modes of working together. In general, the workshops are intensive, short-term experiences with a specific project. Grant amount: matching grants up to $15,000.

• *Craftsmen in Residence.* This program enables art schools and other institutions to invite craftsmen of their choice for short-term teaching assignments. Grant amounts: matching grants up to $1,500.

• *Services to the Field.* This program assists organizations, artists' groups and individuals who provide services to other artists. Projects that might be funded under this category include alternative publications and information services in such areas as legal problems and health and safety practices. Grant amounts: up to $10,000.

• *Art Critics' Fellowships.* This grant is open to art, crafts, photography and experimental film critics who are published regularly. Smaller fellowships for travel are also available. Grant amounts: $5,000 for specific projects; $1,000 for travel.

• *Works of Art in Public Places.* This program provides monies to non-federal government units, universities, nonprofit, tax-exempt private groups and state arts councils to commission works by American artists of regional or national significance. Proposals will be considered for art in plazas, airports, subways and other public places. Works of art may be in any one of the following media: sculpture, painting and photography murals, and crafts (ceramic murals and works in fiber). Matching funds are required for all projects.

For deadlines and complete information on these programs, consult the Visual Arts Application Guidelines available from the National Endowment for the Arts, Washington, D.C. 20506. For a complete listing of all NEA programs, consult the National Endowment for the Arts' Guide to Programs.

Also available from NEA is the *Cultural Post*, a bimonthly publication reporting current events, application deadlines and items of general interest in the arts. Free by writing Cultural Post Subscriptions, Program Information, National Endowment for the Arts, Washington, D.C. 20506.

Other Federal Aid

Two reference sources are extremely valuable in identifying other federal programs that fund craft activities.

The *Cultural Directory* describes more than 250 programs that offer assistance to individuals, groups and cultural institutions. It has an alphabetical listing of all programs arranged by federal agency and a comprehensive subject index. Listings include funds for research and training, fellowships, employment opportunities and technical assistance. Examples are given of how programs have been used in the past.

The *Cultural Directory* was published in 1975, so not all information is currently applicable. The book should be used in conjunction with more recent program information. It may be ordered from ACA Publications, 1564 Broadway, New York, New York 10036 for $4.

The *Catalog of Federal Domestic Assistance*, published by the Office of Management and Budget, describes over 850 federal benefits programs and activities. It includes information on grants, loans and scholarships; technical assistance, counseling and training; and statistical information.

The *Catalog* is published each spring and updated with a fall supplement. It may be ordered from the Superintendent of Documents, U.S. Government Printing Office, Washington, D.C. 20402 for $16.

In seeking federal assistance it may be necessary to reorient one's thinking patterns. Outside the NEA, craftspeople are not likely to find support if they think of themselves only as artists. To qualify for assistance, the individual craftsperson might have to consider himself as a member of some particular group. A crafts organization might have to represent itself as a source for preserving cultural heritage or as a center for vocational training.

The following is a brief survey of some of the federal programs of interest. They range from highly specialized research grants to broad programs of economic development.

At the most specialized end, the Smithsonian Institution offers fellowships for research on any subject for which material is available in the Smithsonian collections (including ceramics). Fellowships are available for postdoctoral research, dissertation research and directed graduate study.

The Small Business Administration offers guaranteed/insured loans and direct loans to small businesses which are independently owned and operated and are not dominant in their field. This is one program where profit-making potential is an advantage.

The SBA offers workshops for prospective business owners, management counseling and marketing information. For a list of available publications, ask for "Free Management Assistance Publications" (SBA 115A) and "For-Sale Booklets" (SBA 115B). For more information, contact your local SBA office or write to the Small Business Administration, Washington, D.C. 20416.

The Comprehensive Employment Training Act (CETA), a program of the Department of Labor's Manpower Administration, provides job training and employment opportunities for unemployed, underemployed and economically disadvantaged persons. Artists have been using this program with increasing success as a source of employment.

There are two major types of CETA programs. One, the Employability Development Program, uses CETA Title I funds. This program is of special interest to craftspeople seeking jobs or crafts organizations seeking subsidized employment.

Under the Employability Development Program's work experience program,

CETA subsidizes the full cost of positions in nonprofit agencies for a limited time, with the understanding that the agency will then hire the employee.

Under its on-the-job-training program, CETA pays half the salary for a specified training period in private industry. The business then contracts to take on the employee full-time at the end of that period.

The second major CETA program is the Public Service Employment Program, which uses CETA Title II and Title VI funds. This program gives money to local manpower agencies for direct public employment in jobs which are not "basic services." At the end of the allotted time the agency then hires the CETA employee.

CETA money is allocated to government bodies in areas with populations of 100,000 or more, which serve as prime sponsors. Organizations seeking subsidized manpower should apply to the prime sponsors in their area. Governors' offices, chief elected city and county officials and regional Manpower Administration offices can supply names and addresses of prime sponsors.

The Department of Agriculture has several programs that might be of help to craftspeople living in rural areas. In general, applicants for these programs must prove economic viability and be unable to obtain necessary credit elsewhere.

The Farmers Home Administration has three loan and loan-guarantee programs that secure funding for community, business and industrial development. Interested craftspeople should also consider Farm Operating Loans, Business and Industrial Loans and Community Facility Loans. All are administered through local FmHA county offices. General information is available from the Information Staff, Farmers Home Administration, Department of Agriculture, Washington, D.C. 20250.

The Federal Assistance Programs Retrieval System helps rural community leaders find federal programs for specific needs, including crafts. FAPRS is a quick, inexpensive computer operation. It scans a bank of over 600 federal programs and provides a printout of those programs that best suit the applicant's needs.

FAPRS is available to legitimate organizations with compatible computer equipment, at the federal, state or local level. For information, contact Rural Development Service, Department of Agriculture, Washington, D.C. 20250.

Groups interested in promoting crafts as a means of economic development in their areas might consider regional development programs. The Appalachian Regional Commission, for example, has grants for research and programs for concerted economic and social development in that area. Other regional commissions include those of the Upper Great Lakes, the Pacific Northwest and the Ozarks.

A project is considered in terms of the population and area it will serve, the financial resources of that area and the employment opportunities the project promises. Monies are allocated directly to the states within the region and then through the states to public bodies and nonprofit organizations.

The Community Services Administration helps support craft projects that are part of the economic development of an area. Many craft cooperatives have been funded by this program in the past.

Crafts-related projects that are part of larger programs may be considered for support. For further information, contact your local Community Action Agency or the Community Services Administration, 1200 Nineteenth Street NW, Washington, D.C. 20506.

At the "services" end of the spectrum, the Department of Health, Education and Welfare has a number of funding programs. The Office of Education sponsors several crafts-related activities. Projects funded include curriculum development for supplemental educational programs and educational assistance for Native Americans. While craft organizations may not be eligible for funding to develop their own projects in all of these programs, the programs can provide craftspeople with jobs as teachers and demonstrators.

The Office of Education also dispenses formula grants for the support of training programs to develop nonprofessional skills, crafts included. Institutions, agencies and facilities which have such programs may apply directly to their state board of vocational education for funding. Preference is given to facilities that can provide training for five or more occupations.

HEW also allocates monies to state vocational rehabilitation agencies and related nonprofit organizations to expand and improve rehabilitation services. Funds are available through the Rehabilitation Services Administration. They support projects that aid mentally and physically handicapped and/or aged persons by preparing them for gainful employment. Craft training programs may be included in this category. The program offers matching project grants and research contracts.

HEW's Office of Human Development funds community-based organizations with programs for the elderly. Several ACTION programs, including Foster Grandparents, SCORE (Service Corps of Retired Executives) and RSVP (Retired Senior Volunteer Program) also provide grants for establishing volunteer employment opportunities for elderly persons. These programs may involve teaching crafts, running a crafts workshop or organizing a crafts store.

Other ACTION programs utilize craftspeople. Peace Corps and VISTA volunteers teach classes in craft techniques and organize craft cooperatives for production and marketing of crafts. For information on ACTION programs, contact a regional office for the specific program or the Office of Domestic Operations, ACTION, 806 Connecticut Avenue NW, Washington, D.C. 20525.

Another public-service opportunity for craftspeople is in prison art programs. All federal prisons have recreation programs which generally include crafts. Craftspeople who want to work in federal prisons should contact the warden of the particular prison in which they are interested.

State & Local

All states have official state arts councils which administer funds to artists and craftspeople through grant and fellowship programs. Several states have grants for individuals. A complete list of state arts councils is provided in the Reference Section of this Catalog. In addition, most states publish guides to their state programs.

Many federal programs are administered at the state or local level, so craftspeople interested in various programs should contact appropriate regional, state or local offices. A number of federal/state programs, such as general revenue sharing and emergency job programs, have potential as arts projects—and to this date have not been sufficiently tapped. It is also worth noting that most recipients of federal funds may transfer all or part of their entitlements to "secondary recipients." This may include arts councils, museums and other arts organizations.

Private

Foundations—private, nonprofit philanthropic institutions—are the primary source of private funding. Finding a private institution compatible with your particular needs, however, is a painstaking process since information regarding all but the richest foundations is difficult to come by.

The Tax Reform Act of 1969 eliminated many of the tax benefits for private foundations. As a result, many foundations now tend to give only to other nonprofit organizations. And very few offer grants to individuals. In addition, many foundations regularly give grants to the same beneficiaries year after year and are not likely to be open to new requests.

One last warning: you should recognize the fact that your chances of landing a grant are slim. But if your determination has yet to be dampened by these disheartening facts, read on. The information that follows should be of help in your quest.

Reference Sources

Probably the single most important reference work is *The Foundation Directory*, fifth edition, edited by Marianna O. Lewis (Columbia University Press, 1975). It includes information on the 2,533 largest foundations, all of which have assets greater than $1,000,000 or grants of more than $500,000. These foundations account for about 90 percent of all foundation assets and 80 percent of all grants made in this country. The book costs $30 and can be found in all national and regional foundation center collections and in many libraries.

The Foundation Grants Index appears as a separate section in the bimonthly publication *Foundation News*. It details currently reported foundation grants of $5,000 or more and includes a recipient and key-word subject index. This information is cumulated annually and published in a single volume, *Foundation Grants Index*. Subscriptions to *Foundation News* cost $20 and may be ordered from the Council on Foundations, Inc., Box 783, Old Chelsea Station, New York, New York 10011. Annual volumes of the *Foundation Grants Index* cost $15 and are available from the Foundation Center, 888 Seventh Avenue, New York, New York 10019.

Following is a small sampling of the crafts-related projects that have recently received funds from some of the larger foundations: The Mary Duke Biddle Foundation of New York awarded $8,612 to the Duke University Art Department for arts and crafts workshops; the Robert Sterling Clark Foundation of New York awarded $20,000 to the American Crafts Council for the exhibit of crafts related to ''The Art of Personal Adornment''; the Lilly Endowment of Indiana awarded $25,000 to the World Crafts Council to conduct a report on crafts industry in the Middle East and North Africa; the Eloise and Richard Webber Foundation awarded $150,000 to the Society of Arts and Crafts of Detroit toward construction of a Center for Creative Studies.

Another important reference book is *The Foundation Center Source Book*, Volumes 1 and 2, edited by Terry-Diane Beck and Alexis Teitz Gersumky, (Columbia University Press, 1975/76). This publication provides comprehensive profiles on 227 of the country's largest foundations—whose assets are generally greater than $7 million. The *Source Book* costs $65.

The Annual Register of Grant Support (published by Marquis Academic Media, Marquis Who's Who, Inc.) provides information on the grant-support programs of government agencies, public and private foundations, business and industry, unions and special-interest organizations.

The Grants Register 1975-77, edited by Roland Turner (St. Martin's Press, New York), is primarily intended for graduate students, academic staff and people requiring advanced vocational training. It includes exchange opportunities, vacation stay awards, competitions, prizes and professional and vocational awards. The information covers Canada, Great Britain, Ireland, Australia, New Zealand and South Africa, as well as the United States.

Ocular is a quarterly directory for the visual arts. Its regular features include lists of grants and fellowships, competitions, exhibits, symposia, lectures, films and workshops. Articles and interviews also appear. No special listings are made for crafts, so interested persons will have to cull this information from the more general arts listings. Subscriptions cost $14 per year and are available from *Ocular*, 1549 Platte Street, Denver, Colorado 80202.

A search through all these reference works will not reveal many sources with funds earmarked especially for crafts. Examination of the major reference works is only the first step. Once you have found a program that particularly suits your needs, you will want to familiarize yourself with the policies and personality of the foundation that offers that program.

A good source is the Internal Revenue Service. The Tax Reform Act of 1969 requires all private foundations to file a 990-AR information return with the IRS. This form is available for public inspection. It contains the names and addresses of all principal officers of the foundation, total assets and investments of the foundation, and a complete listing of every grant made during the year. All published annual reports and IRS forms are on record at the National Foundation Center Headquarters. Records for foundations within the immediate state or region are available at regional Foundation Centers.

The major foundation reference books list only the largest foundations. But there are more than 23,000 smaller family or community foundations with assets of less than $1 million. It is these foundations that will be more likely to fund small-scale projects.

To help fund seekers identify these smaller foundations, a number of states have published directories to foundations in their state. An updated bibliography of state foundation directories, with complete ordering information, is available from the Foundation Center, 888 Seventh Avenue, New York, New York 10019.

Grantsmanship and the Resource Centers

The art of getting a grant has become so complex that a special term has been coined to describe it—''grantsmanship.'' Books, of course, are always available for patient research. Computers, too, can be set to work isolating potential funding sources. Workshops in fund seeking and proposal writing are offered in many community centers and schools and by profit-making institutions. Even professional grant hounds can be hired to ferret out special foundations. Grant seeking itself has become Big Business.

The following is a brief description of some of the resource centers that have devoted themselves exclusively to the problems and concerns of fund seekers.

The Foundation Center, 888 Seventh Avenue, New York, New York 10019. The Foundation Center is a nonprofit organization which gathers and disseminates factual information on philanthropic foundations. It operates national library collections in New York and Washington, D.C., that provide free public access to information about foundations. The Center has also established regional collections of foundation information within host libraries throughout the country.

There are currently fifty-seven such collections in forty-four states, Puerto Rico and Mexico. The regional collections each have multiple copies of all Foundation Center publications, as well as information—such as IRS information returns—for foundations within their state or region. A listing of locations for Foundation Center libraries is available on request from the New York Foundation Center office.

The Center maintains computerized files of foundation grants information. Associates pay an annual fee of $200. This entitles them to reference service by telephone and mail, custom searches of computer files and a library research service. Computer printouts of recent grants arranged by broad subject areas are sold to the general public. A number of publications and bibliographies are also available.

The Grantsmanship Center, 1015 West Olympic Boulevard, Los Angeles, California 90015. This nonprofit, educational institution provides services to other private nonprofit and governmental organizations. The program includes small-group training workshops in many cities across the country. These workshops are designed to improve the participants' funding and program-planning skills.

The Center also publishes a bi-monthly magazine, *Grantsmanship Center News*, which sells for $15 a year. It provides in-depth information and instruction about both public and private funding. Reprints of individual articles are available.

Public Service Materials Center, 355 Lexington Avenue, New York, New York 10017. This center provides information on fund-raising development. It publishes a number of works, including the following: *The Complete Fund Raising Guide* by Howard R. Mirkin, *America's Most Successful Fund Raising Letters* edited by Joseph Dermer, *The 1976-77 Survey of Grant-Making Foundations* and *How to Get Your Fair Share of Foundation Grants.*

American Crafts Council

The American Crafts Council is a national, nonprofit cultural and educational organization serving craftspeople and the public. Since its founding in 1943, ACC has played a significant role in the resurgence of crafts in the United States.

The ACC's magazine, *Craft Horizons*, is free to members. Its regular features include articles on crafts, extensive photography, exhibition reviews, a national calendar and special reports on developments in crafts throughout the United States.

The Museum of Contemporary Crafts, which was established in 1957 as part of the ACC building in New York City, covers all craft media. In addition, the museum operates a consultancy program to assist other institutions in planning and organizing craft exhibitions.

The Council-sponsored Research Library is a unique resource center. It features an extensive collection of current and historical craft books, exhibition catalogs, craft periodicals and slide archives. In addition, it keeps an indexed portfolio system of biographical and pictorial data on practicing American craftspeople.

ACC membership is open to all, with benefits accruing according to a sliding rate scale. A "Subscribing" membership costs $18 for one year and includes six issues of *Craft Horizons*; free admission to the Museum of Contemporary Crafts; eligibility for group insurance and member rates for all ACC events and publications.

A "Sponsoring" membership costs $100 and includes free admission to the Museum for all guests of the Sponsor; invitations to special functions and previews; a vote in ACC elections; and complimentary copies of Museum catalogs and all ACC publications.

Through its "Portable Museum" program ACC makes audiovisual material on over 100 of its exhibitions available for rental or purchase. The organization also supports a Regional and International program. For further information contact the American Crafts Council, 44 West Fifty-third Street, New York, New York 10019.

Crafts Organizations

Research compiled by Arlene Noble.

This list has been compiled through questionnaires sent out over the last year. If your organization has been overlooked, please send us information for inclusion in the next Catalog.

National

Advocates for the Arts, 570 Seventh Avenue, New York City, NY 10018. Tel. (212) 354-6655. *Dues:* $15. *Services:* Legal, economic, and political advocate group for the arts. *Publications:* Newsletters and memoranda.

American Needlepoint Guild, P.O. Box 4322, Charlotte, NC 28211.

Artist Blacksmiths of North America, R.R. #2, Box 1211, Valley Branch Road, Nashville, IN 47448. *Publications:* Newsletter.

Center for the History of Needlework (C.H.A.N.), P.O. Box 8162, Pittsburgh, PA 15217. Tel. (412) 422-8749. *Founded:* 1974. Organizing collections for exhibitions, developing oral history activities of needle artists, maintaining conferences & developing a registry for teachers and lecturers. *Publications:* C.H.A.N. Newsletter.

Embroiders Guild of America, Inc., 6 East 45th Street, Room 1501, New York, NY 10017. Tel. (212) 986-0460. *Services:* Workshops. *Publications:* Magazine.

Glass Art Society, Toledo Museum of Art, Toledo, OH 43609. *Publications:* Newsletter.

Handweavers Guild of America, Inc., 998 Farmington Avenue, West Hartford, CT 06107. Tel. (203) 233-7136. *Dues:* $12.50. *Publications:* Shuttle, Spindle & Dyepot. Quarterly. Directories.

Multinational Guild of Candle Artisans, 2000 First Street, Kearney, NE 68847. Tel. (308) 237-2800.

International Guild of Craft Journalists, Authors and Photographers, 1529 East 19th Street, Brooklyn, NY 11230. *Director:* Michael Scott. *Membership:* 75. *Founded:* 1976. *Dues:* $10. *Services:* Sharing information, publishing opportunities, techniques, etc. *Publications:* Guild Bulletin.

International Old Lacers, 2141 West 29th Street, Long Beach, CA 90810. *Publications:* Newsletter.

Iranian Brotherhood of Rugweavers, 1123 Broadway, Suite 1018, New York, NY 10010. Tel. (212) 691-3128. *Director:* R. Ghermezian.

National Ceramic Association, Box 39, Glen Burnie, MD 21061. Tel. (301) 987-1718. *Membership Director:* Olivia Higgs.

National Crafts Clearinghouse and Complaint Center, 2719 O Street, Northwest, Washington, DC 20007. *President:* Caroline Ramsay. *Services:* Forum for ideas from craftspeople, artists, designers, government representatives and business experts; advising on production, quality control, marketing, distribution, shipping; studies, papers, catalogs; referrals for specialized assistance; complaint center for payment problems; legal assistance.

National Council on Education for the Ceramic Arts, Indiana State University Art Department, Terre Haute, IN 47809. Tel. (812) 232-6311.

National Crafts Council, 517 South Lee Street, Marriett, IN 46738. Tel. (219) 357-3076.

National Crafts Foundation, Silver Dollar City, MO 65616. Tel. (417) 338-2611. *Executive Vice President:* Harry J. Brabec.

National Guild of Decoupeurs, Box 688, Fort Smith, AR 72901.

National Quilting Association, Inc., P.O. Box 62, Greenbelt, MD 20770. *President:* Gladys H. Dill. *Membership:* 1200. *Founded:* 1972. *Dues:* $5-regular; $3-Senior Citizens. *Services:* 41 Chapters throughout U.S.; instruction at meetings; exhibitions; annual judged show. *Publications:* Patchwork Patter. Quarterly.

National Institute of American Doll Artists, 5717 Elder Place, Madison, WI 53705. Tel. (608) 233-1645. *President:* Will Paulson.

National Standards Council of American Embroiderers, 826 Lincoln Avenue, Winnetka, IL 60093.

National Wood Carvers Association, 7424 Miami Avenue, Cincinnati, OH 45243. Tel. (513) 561-9051. *President:* Edward F. Gallenstein. *Membership:* 11,285. *Founded:* 1953. *Dues:* $5. *Services:* Promotes area exhibitions; exchange for information. *Publications:* Chip Chats; Bi-monthly.

Society of Batik Artists, c/o Astrith Deyrud, 395 Riverside Drive, New York, NY 10025.

Society of North American Goldsmiths, P.O. Box 247 University Station, Boston, MA. *Publications:* Newsletter.

Stained Glass Association of America, 1125 Wilmington Avenue, St. Louis, MO 63111. Tel. (314) 353-5683. *Publications:* Newsletter.

Surface Design Association, c/o Sara Edmiston, School of Art, Design Dept., E. Carolina Univ., Box 2704, Greenville, NC 27834. *President:* E. Sreevivasam. *Editor:* Stephen Blumrich. *Dues:* $15. *Services:* Seeks to stimulate, promote, improve, and encourage members and their work; has a store of technical, business and career information on textiles, dyes etc. *Publications:* Surface Design.

U.S. Potters Association, P.O. Box 63, East Liverpool, OH 43920.

Local

ALABAMA

Alabama Craftsmen's Council, P.O. Box 1168, Auburn, AL 36830.

Alabama Designer Craftsman, 3472 Birchtree Drive, Birmingham, AL 35226.

American Needlepoint Guild, Mountain Brook Chapter, 2512 Country Club Circle, Birmingham, AL 35223.

American Needlepoint Guild, Mountain Brook Chapter, 2512 Country Club Circle, Birmingham, AL 35223.

Azalea City Ceramic Association, 217 Maple Avenue, Satsuma, AL 36572.

Butler Ceramics Club, Butler, AL 36904.

Centrala Crafters, P.O. Box 6125, Montgomery, AL 36106.

Cloverdale Arts & Crafts Association, 2312 East Fourth, Montgomery, AL 36106.

Elberta Arts & Crafts Club, Route 1, Elberta, AL 36530.

Foothills Arts & Crafts Guild, 1469 Finley Curve, Montgomery, AL 36106.

Geneva County Arts & Crafts Association, Box 62, Samson, AL 36477.

Maxwells Officers Wives Clay Club, Box 5720 CMR, Maxwell Air Force Base, Montgomery, AL 36113.

Needle Art Club, 9 Wood Manor, Tuscaloosa, AL 35401.

Needle Art Club of Mobile, 327 Brawood Drive, Mobile, AL 36608.

Needlework Club, 1600 Birmingham Avenue, Jasper, AL 35501.

Northeast Alabama Craftsman's Association, P.O. Box 1113, Huntsville, AL 35807.

Port City Craftsmen, P.O. Box 1028, University of South Alabama, Mobile, AL 36608.

Prattville Arts & Crafts Guild, 431 Water Street, Prattville, AL 36067.

Tennessee Valley Ceramic Arts & Crafts Guild, 511 Cleveland Avenue, Florence, AL 35630.

ALASKA

Anchorage Weavers Guild, 2126 Dawson Street, Anchorage, AK 99503.

Bering Straits Eskimo Arts & Crafts Cooperative, C/O Kawerak, Inc., Box 505, Nome, AK 99762. *Services:* Marketing Native American arts and crafts. Non-profit.

Juneau Weavers Guild, 1109 C Street, Juneau, AK 99801.

Musk Ox Producers' Cooperative, 'Oomingmak', Box 80-291, College, AK 99701. *Services:* Marketing Native American arts and crafts.

Toksook Bay Arts & Crafts Cooperative, Toksook Bay, AK 99637. *Services:* Marketing Native American arts and crafts.

ARKANSAS

Arkansas Arts Center, MacArthur Park, Little Rock, AR 72202. Tel. (501) 376-3671. *Founded:* 1938.

Arts Center Of The Ozarks, 216 West Grove, Box 725, Springdale, AR 72764. Tel. (501) 751-5441. *Director:* Geneva Powers. *Membership:* 1,500. *Founded:* 1967. *Dues:* $10 and up. *Services:* Theatre productions; concerts; workshops; art fairs and festivals. *Publications:* Arts Center Newsletter. Bi-monthly. Sample copies.

Central Arkansas Weaver's Guild, 34 Scenic Boulevard, Little Rock, AR 72207. Tel. (501) 666-7958. *Founded:* 1970.

Community Arts Of Conway, 1838 College Avenue, Conway, AR 72032. Tel. (501) 329-3853. *Founded:* 1973.

Designer Craftsmen of Arkansas, c/o R. Fischer, Arkansas Arts Center, MacArthur Park, Little Rock, AR 72203. Tel. (501) 376-3671.

Eureka Brotherhood Co-op, Inc., 12 ½ First Street, Eureka Springs, AR 72632. Tel. (501) 253-9925. *Founded:* 1971.

Folk Cultural Center, Mountain View, AR 72560. *Founded:* 1973.

Fort Smith Art Center, 423 North Sixth Street, Fort Smith, AR 72901. Tel. (501(782-6371. *Founded:* 1949.

Hot Springs Ceramic Association, Route 4, Box 288-A, Hot Springs, AR 71901. Tel. (501) 767-3622. *Founded:* 1963.

Ozark Arts & Crafts Fair Association, War Eagle Mills, Hindsville, AR 72738. Tel. (501) 789-2540. *Founded:* 1954.

Ozark Foothills Crafts Guild, 908 Sugar Loaf, Heber Springs, AR 72543. Tel. (501) 362-2826. *Founded:* 1962.

Rogers Art Guild, Route 3, Rogers, AR 72756. *Founded:* 1972.

South Arkansas Arts Center, 110 East Fifth Street, El Dorado, AR 71730. Tel. (501) 862-6121. *Founded:* 1961.

ARIZONA

Apache Arts & Crafts Bead Association, Box 1026, Whiteriver, AZ 85941. *Services:* Marketing Native American arts and crafts. Non-profit.

Arizona Designer-Craftsmen, 8219 East Indianola, Tempe, AZ 85251. Tel. (602) 945-6464. *State President*: Ray Graves. *Founded*: 1959. *Dues*: Associate members - $5. *Services*: Special programs, shows around the state, information on state and out-of-state crafts activities. *Publications*: Newsletter and membership booklet.

Canyon De Chelly Arts & Crafts Association, Box 935, Chinle, AZ 86503. Tel. (602) 674-3411. *Services*: Marketing Native American arts and crafts.

Gila River Arts & Crafts Center, Box 457, Sacaton, AZ 85247. *Services*: Marketing Native American arts and crafts.

Hopi Silvercraft & Arts & Crafts Cooperative Guild, Box 37, Second Mesa, AZ 86043. Tel. (602) 734-2463.

Papago Arts & Crafts Cooperative Guild, Box 837, Sells, AZ 85634. Tel. (602) 383-2221, ext. 78. *Services*: Marketing Native American arts and crafts.

Splinter Brothers & Sisters Warehouse, 911 North 13th Avenue, Tucson, AZ 85705. Tel. (602) 622-9093. *Services*: Sharing tools and techniques with fellow craftsmen; gallery. Non-profit.

Tucson Art Center Craft Guild, 235 West Alameda, Tucson, AZ 85701. Tel. (602) 793-2916 (Janet Burner). *Services*: Sale of work at Tucson Art Museum.

Tucson Handweavers Guild, c/o Open Studio Gift Shoppe, 2458 North Pantano, Tucson, AZ 85715. Tel. (602) 296-6324. *Founded*: 1973. *Services*: Workshops; self-help study groups; sales; exhibits; books; slides; yarn samples; discounts on yarn; monthly meetings September through June. *Publications*: Newsletter.

Womankraft Corporation, c/o 1311 Duke Drive, Tucson, AZ 85719. Tel. (602) 793-1085. *Founded*: 1974. *Services*: Promotion and sale of work of artist-craftswomen; sharing of technical knowledge, marketing and business skills. Non-profit.

CALIFORNIA

Art Co-op, 1652 Shattuck Avenue, Berkeley, CA 94709. Tel. (415) 843-2527. *Membership*: 2,000. *Founded*: 1959. *Dues*: $7 to join; $10 annual gallery fee. *Services*: Display and sale of juried members work; monthly special shows; workshops. *Publications*: Art Co-op Newsletter. Quarterly.

Center for the Visual Arts, City Center, 1333 Broadway, Oakland, CA 94612. Tel. (415) 451-6300. *Membership*: 500. *Dues*: Artists $10; Public $20. *Services*: Exhibit and demonstration area; slide registry; seminars and lectures on legal and business aspects of art; information center. *Publications*: Center for the Visual Arts Newsletter. Bi-monthly.

Council For the Arts/Palo Alto & Mid-peninsula Area, P.O. Box 11564, Palo Alto, CA 94306. Tel. (415) 329-2651. *Services*: Information on area art events. *Publication*: Cultural Events Calendar. Quarterly.

Creative Arts League of Sacramento Inc., 6298 South Land Park Drive, Sacramento, CA 95831.

Craft & Folk Art Museum, 5814 Wilshire Boulevard, Los Angeles, CA 90036. Tel. (213) 937-5544. *Director*: Edith R. Wyle (programs. Administrative Director: Patrick H. Ela. *Services*: Exhibits, lectures, concerts, slide shows, demonstration, workshops, film series, theater performances. *Publications*: Exhibits; catalogs, three newsletters. Quarterly.

The Guild Store, 1131 12th Street, Sacramento, CA. Tel. (916) 446-2395. *Membership*: 15. *Founded*: 1972. *Dues*: 15% of gross sales. *Ser-*

vices: Co-operative crafts store for sale of members work.

The Mill Valley Arts Guild, 158 East Blithedale, Mill Valley, CA 94941. Tel. (415) 383-3630 or (415) 332-2635. *Director*: Shirely Banks. *Dues*: $15/year — exhibiting artist; $10-$25 — associate; $25-$50 — supporting. *Services*: Gallery for display and sale; classes; critique.

Mill Valley Quilt Authority, P.O. Box 270, Mill Valley, CA 94941. *Services*: Annual exhibit. *Publications*: Quilter's Calendar.

Monterey Peninsula Museum of Art, 559 Pacific Street, Monterey, CA 93940. Tel. (408) 372-5477. *Director*: June Braucht. *Membership*: 1,644. *Services*: Permanent and temporary exhibitions; lectures; Museum-on-Wheels program; workshops. *Publications*: Monterey Peninsula Museum of Art Courier. Monthly. *Books*: Yesterday's Artists on the Monterey Peninsula. Helen Spangenburg.

Mountain Weavers Guild, 9 Brookwood Drive, Susanville, CA 96103. Tel. (916) 257-3801. *Director*: Mary Beuchat. *Memberships*: 16. *Founded*: 1972. *Dues*: $5. *Services*: Workshops; annual exhibit at Northern California Conference of Handweavers.

Santa Clara County Quilt Association, 15305 Elm Park, Monte Sereno, CA 95030. *Dues*: $12. *Founded*: 1975. *Services*: Fairs, monthly meetings, museum, books. *Publications*: Santa Clara Valley Quilt Association Newsletter. Monthly. (Available for $3 to non-members.)

Santa Cruz Association of Artists and Craftspeople, 1250 Capitola Road, Santa Cruz, CA 95062. Tel. (408) 429-1537. *Founded*: 1975. *Dues*: $5/year — general member; sustaining member $50; $150 — patron member. *Services*: Co-operative gallery, Open Market; Art in Public Places; Slide Portfolio Index. *Publication*: Santa Cruz Association of Artists and Craftspeople Newsletter.

Southern California Designer-Crafts, 731 South Curson Avenue, Los Angeles, CA 90036. *Director*: Lee Erlin Show. *Membership*: 250. *Founded*: 1957. *Dues*: $12.50 active & sustaining; $8 student. *Services*: Exhibitions, workshops, seminars, liason with public and other craft organizations. *Publications*: SCDC Newsletter.

Davis Art Center, 1221 Fourth Street, Davis CA 95616. Tel. (916) 756-4100. *Director*: Marian Hamilton. *Membership*: 350. *Founded*: 1959. *Services*: Classes; workshops; art tours; gallery facilities; art festival; Christmas sale.

Enamel Guild: West, Box 721, La Jolla, CA 92038. Tel. (714) 454-0595. *Membership*: 200. *Founded*: 1976. *Dues*: $15. *Services*: Co-sponser of International Festival of Enamels; revolving exhibitions; workshops; group purchasing; information. *Publications*: Enamel Guild: West Newsletter. Bi-monthly.

Felton Guild, 5455 Highway Nine, Felton, CA 95018. Tel. (408) 335-3464. *Membership*: 30. *Services*: Gallery for display and sale; studio space; co-operative instruction. *Publications*: Information brochure.

COLORADO

Boulder Weavers, 1909 Spruce, Boulder, CO 80302.

Colorado Artist and Craftsmen, 1912 Mohawk, Fort Collins, CO 80521.

Colorado Potters, 1541 South Pearl, Denver, CO 80210.

Pueblo Weavers, 730 West Orman, Pueblo, CO 81004.

Southern Ute Arts and Crafts, Box 277, Ignacio, CO 81137. Tel. (303) 563-4531 or 563-4649. *Services*: Marketing Native American arts and crafts.

Northern Colorado Weavers, 2409 West Mulberry, Fort Collins, CO 80521.

CONNECTICUT

Guilford Handcraft Center, P.O. Box 221, Guilford, CT 06437. Tel. (203) 453-5947. *Director*: Beth Parrett. *Membership*: 950. *Founded*: 1957. *Dues*: 10-Family; $5-Individual; $3-Student. *Services*: Studio courses for children, teens, and adults; sponsers Guilford Handcraft Exposition.

New England Artists & Craftsmen's Guild, P.O. Box 142, Enfield, CT 06082. *President*: Ron Seagrave. *Dues*: $12. *Services*: Info service. *Publications*: NEACG, Inc., Newsletter. Monthly.

Wesleyan Potters Inc., 350 South Main Street, Middletown, CT 06457. *Membership*: 70. *Founded*: 1948. *Services*: Non-profit craft guild; classes, exhibits and sale held Nov.-early Dec. for 10 days.

Andover Arts and Crafts League, 44 Lakeside Drive, Andover, CT 06232.

Arts and Crafts Association of Meriden, P.O. Box 348, Meriden, CT 06450. Tel. (205) 235-4240.

Avon Arts & Crafts, 26 Laurel Lane, Simsbury, CT 06070. Tel. (203) 658-6982.

Connecticut Folk Arts Center, Route #7, Ridgefield, CT. Tel. (203) 438-9084.

Connecticut Guild of Craftsmen, Inc., P.O. Box 374, Bloomfield, CT 06002. Tel. (203) 232-1116. *Director*: Rudy Kowalczyk. *Membership*: 900. *Founded*: 1970. *Dues*: $12/year. *Services*: Craft shows; wholesale fair. *Publications*: CGC Newsletter (send self-addressed, stamped, legal-size envelope). Monthly.

Connecticut River Arts & Crafts, Inc., Norwich Road, Route #82, East Haddam, CT 06423. Tel. (203) 873-9443.

Farmington Valley Arts Center, Inc., P.O. Box 220, Avon Park North, Avon, CT 06001. Tel. (203) 678-1867.

Greenwhich Art Barn, Lower Cross Road, Greenwhich, CT 068300. Tel. (203) 661-9048. *Director*: Rebecca Bernstein. *Membership*: 400. *Founded*: 1962. *Dues*: $15/year. *Services*: Workshops; gallery, shop, annual invitational craft fair.

Guilford Handcrafts, Inc., P.O. Box 221, Guilford, CT 06437. Tel. (203) 453-5947.

HandweaversGuild of America — CT Chapter, 34 Forest Hill Drive, Simsbury, CT 06070.

New England Artist & Craftsmen Guild, Inc., P.O. Box 142, Enfield, CT. Tel. (203) 623-0520.

New Haven Paint and Clay Club, John Slade Ely House, 51 Trumbull Street, New Hven, CT 06510. Tel. (203) 624-8055.

Society of Connecticut Craftsmen, Inc., Box 37, Deep River, CT 06417. Tel. (203) 526-5812.

Southington Arts and Crafts Association, C/O Andrew Dignazio, President, 230 High Tower Road, Southington, CT 06489. Tel. (203) 621-0347.

DELAWARE

Brandywine Arts Festival, 1307 Orange Street, Wilmington, DE 19801.

Council Delaware Craftsmen, 342 Paper Mill Road, Newark, DE 19711.

Delaware Art Center, 2301 Kentmere Parkway, Wilmington, DE 19806.

Delaware Art Society, 2600 West 19th Street, Wilmington, DE 19806.

Delaware Crafts Council, 1007 Graylyn Road, Wilmington, DE 19830.

Harmony Weavers Guild, C/O Mrs. David Grant, 108 Barbury Drive, Wilmington, DE 19803.

Harmony Weavers, RD #3 Lamatan, Newark, DE 19711.

WASHINGTON, D.C.

The Embroiders' Guild, Congressional Branch,

C/O Ilene Joyce, Corresponding Secretary, 3003 Van Ness Street, Northwest, #W-94, Washington, D.C. 2008. Tel. (202) 244-5973. *President:* Mrs. Johanne T. Paine. *Membership:* 70. *Founded:* 1968. *Dues:* $15. *Services:* Workshops, exhibitions, library. *Publications:* The Embroiders' Guild, Congressional Branch Newsletter. Monthly, $2/year.

FLORIDA

Ceramic League of Miami, Inc., 8873 Southwest 129th Street, Miami, FL 33176. Tel. (305) 235-9732. *President:* Jean Waldberg. *Membership:* 250. *Founded:* 1950. *Dues:* $20 for members, juried by Board of Directors. *Services:* Sponsor visiting artists; studio facilities; Annual Membership Exhibition; Annual Fair. *Publications:* Newsletter. Monthly.

Miccosukee Arts and Crafts Center, Box 440021, Tamaimi Station, Miami, FL 33144. Tel. (305) 223-8380. *Services:* Marketing Native American Arts and Crafts.

Seminole Indian Village and Crafts Center, 6073 Stirling Road, Hollwood, FL 33024. Tel. (305) 583-7111. *Services: Marketing Native American arts and crafts.*

Tropical Weavers Guild, 2900 North Pine Hills Road, Apt. #62, Orlando, FL 32808.

GEORGIA

Camp Crafts Program, P.O. Box 1219, Moultrie, GA 31768.

Craft Career Center, P.O. Box 368, Main Street, Lilburn, GA 30247. Tel. (404) 921-2353. *Director:* Ella Wilkerson. *Dues:* $125 for class; $1,500 for Master Program. *Services:* Master Degree of Arts and Crafts.

Georgia Designer Craftsmen, C/O Chastain Arts and Crafts Center, 135 West Wieuca Road, Northwest, Atalant, GA 30342. Tel. (404) 252-2927. *President:* Jerry L. Chappelle. *Membership:* 200. *Founded:* late 60's. *Dues:* $10-singles; $15-husband/wife; $25-patron. *Services:* Workshops, demonstrations; exhibitions; lectures. *Publications:* GDC Newsletter. Annual.

Georgia Mountain Arts Products, P.O. Box 67, Tallulah Falls, GA 30573.

Happy Valley Pottery, Route #1, Farmington, GA 30638.

IDAHO

Citizens Council for Arts, P.O. Box 901, Coeur D'Alene, ID 83814.

Handweavers Guild of Boise, 1102 Drall, Boise, ID 83702.

Kamiah Arts and Crafts, Box 623, Kamiah, ID 83536.

Magic Weavers Guild, Route #1, Twin Falls, ID 83334. *Director:* Mrs. C.C. Blickenstaff.

Nez Perce Arts and Crafts Guild, Box 205, Lapwai, ID 83540. *Services:* Marketing Native American arts and crafts.

Palouse Hills Weavers, 532 North Moore, Moscow, ID 83843.

ILLINOIS

American Society of Artists, 700 North Michigan Avenue — Suite 205, Chicago, IL 60611. *President:* Nancy J. Fregin. *Membership:* 450. *Founded:* 1971. *Dues:* $30/year — $10 initiation fee. *Services:* Exhibition and sales gallery; festivals; discounts on supplies; lectures; demonstrations. *Publications:* Local art fair bulletin (national scope).

Artists League of the Midwest, Inc., 5555 Sheridan Road, Chicago, IL 60640. *President:* Irene Smoller. *Dues:* $15. *Services:* Listings of profes-

sional job opporunities, teaching positions; financial and investment ideas; art and craft exhibits and an artist assistance fund. *Publication:* Newsletter.

Illinois Ozarks Craft Guild, Inc., P.O. Box 3101, Carbondale, IL 62901. *President:* John Loyd. *Membership:* 50. *Founded:* 1975. *Dues:* $20-craftsperson; $10-friend. *Services:* Develop handicrafts; study and teach marketing; annual exhibition; seeking grants for low-income craftspeople. *Publication:* Illinois Ozarks Newsletter.

Mayor's Office For Senior Citizens, 330 South Wells Street, Chicago, IL 60606.

Southern Illinios Arts & Crafts Guild, 610 North Victor Street, Christopher, IL 62822.

Midwest Selling Crafts, 789 Vernon Avenue, Glencoe, IL 60022.

INDIANA

Designer Craftsmen Guild, 5209 Westbreeze Terrace, Fort Wayne, IN 46804.

Designer/Craftsmen Guild, 10220 Circlewood, Fort Wayne, IN 46804.

Eagle Creek Crafts Center, West 56 Wilson Road, Indianapolis, IN 46208.

Fort Wayne Shuttlecraft Guild, C/O M.A. Entwisle RR #3, Auburn, IN 46706. Tel. (219) 925-4637. *President:* Mary Anna Entwisle. *Membership:* 35. *Founded:* 1947. *Dues:* $2/year. *Services:* Workshops; annual exhibit.

Wabash Weavers Guild, 40 Elkton Court, Lafayette, IN 47905.

Indianapolis Weavers, 2633 East Kessler Boulevard, Indianapolis, IN 46220.

IOWA

Iowa Arts & Crafts, P.O. Box 23, Audabon, IA 50025.

Iowa City Craft Guild, 15 Montrose Avenue, Iowa City, IA 52240.

Iowa Federation of Handweavers, 306 Mullin Avenue, Iowa City, IA 52240.

Inland Artist & Craftsmen, 808 Connell Street, Dysart, IA 52224. *President:* Judith Griffin. *Founded:* 1972. *Services:* Workshops. *Publication:* Newsletter.

Northeast Iowa Weavers and Spinners, 518 Hillcrest Road, Waterloo, IA 50701.

Omaha Weavers Guild, Route #3 Box 203, Missouri Valley, IA 51555.

KENTUCKY

Art Center Association, 1622 Story Avenue, Louisville, KY 40206. Tel. (502) 583-6300. *Director:* Lynn Landis. *Membership:* 680. *Founded:* 1929. *Dues:* $10-individual; $5-student; $15-family; $25-patron; $50-sponsoser. *Services:* Workshops; exhibits; seminars. *Publications:* Focus.

Greenup Old Fashioned Days Art and Crafts Show, C/O Greenup Woman's Club, 203 Harrison Street, Greenup, KY 41144. *President:* Mrs. Clifford Enyart. *Membership:* 20. *Founded:* 1932. *Dues:* $7. *Services:* Civic organization for women; annual painting and crafts show. *Publications:* Greenup Woman's Club Newsletter.

Hobby Weavers of the Ohio Valley, 4815 South Sixth Street, Louisville, KY 40214. Tel. (502) 363-2770. *Director:* Amelia DeBusman. *Membership:* 28. *Founded:* 1956. *Dues:* $3. *Services:* Share weaving ideas.

Kentucky Guild of Artists and Craftsmen, Inc., Box 291 (213 Chestnut Street), Berea, KY 40403. Tel. (606) 986-3192. *Director:* Gary Barker. *Membership:* 450. *Founded:* 1961. *Dues:* $7.50-individual; $15-group. *Services:* Fairs; shop;

workshops; group insurance. *Publication:* The Guild Record. Bi-monthly.

Mountain Toymakers, Box 106, McKee, KY 40447.

Weavers of Ohio River Valley, 4815 South Sixth Street, Louisville, KY 40214.

LOUISIANA

Acadiana Weavers and Spinners Guild, Lafayette Natural History Museum and Planetarium, Lafayette, LA 70501. *President:* Audrey Bernard. *Membership:* 55. *Founded:* 1971. *Dues:* $5. *Services:* Promotes handloom weaving, spinning, high warp tapestry and vegetable dyeing.

Alternatives, 714 Cublin Street, New Orleans, LA 70118. Tel. (504) 866-6606. *Directors:* Nina Liv and Mary Crawford. *Founded:* 1971. *Services:* Crafts gallery; workshops.

Chetimacha Craft Association, Route #2, Box 224, Jeanerette, LA 70544. Tel. (318) 923-7547. *Services:* Marketing Native American arts and crafts. (Non-profit organization.)

Coushatta Cultural Center, Box 216, Elton, LA 70532. Tel. (318) 584-9905. *Services:* Marketing Native American arts and crafts.

Feliciana Crafts, Box 280, St. Francisville, LA 70775.

Louisiana Crafts Council, 139 Broadway, New Orleans, LA 70118. Tel. (504) 861-8267. *President:* Shirley Usinger. *Manager:* Lynne Higbee. *Membership:* 1007. *Founded:* 1961. *Dues:* $7.50-craftsmen; $6-non-craftsmen. *Services:* Gallery; shop; classes; workshops; lectures. *Publication:* Newsletter. Bi-monthly.

MAINE

Directions Fund, Inc., P.O. Box 4136, Station A, Portland, ME 04021. Tel. (207) 967-5553. *President:* John Platt. *Membership:* 80. *Founded:* 1975. *Dues:* $35 and up. *Services:* Exhibitions; fairs; wholesale events; helps in the display of crafts in government buildings. *Publication:* Directions in Maine Living; $3.

Franklin County Arts and Crafts, North Jay, ME 04262.

H.O.M.E., Box 408, Orland, ME 04472. Tel. (207) 469-7961. *Director:* Sr. Lucy Poulin. *Membership:* 450. *Founded:* 1970. *Dues:* $2. *Services:* Co-operative marketing outlet; craft and life-coping skills classes; social services including child care, home repair, counseling. *Publication:* Newspaper.

Hilltop Community Craft Center, University of Maine, Orono, ME 04473. Tel. (207) 581-7300. *Director:* Barbara Rogers Bridges. *Membership:* 800. *Founded:* 1970. *Dues:* $2. *Services:* Classes, workshops, walk-in facilities.

United Maine Craftsmen, RFD #2, Litchfield, ME 04350. Tel. (207) 666-3447. *Executive Secretary:* Joan P. Acord. *Membership:* 1000. *Founded:* 1969. *Dues:* Residents of Maine: $5-active; $7-family; $1.50-under 18; $2.50-seasonal resident. Non-resident contributing members: $15. *Services:* Fairs; workshops; publishes Annual Membership Directory. *Publication:* The Craft Tradesman. Quarterly.

MARYLAND

Bethesda Guild Potters, 7304 Western Avenue, Chevy Chase, MD 20015.

The Craftspeople's Guild Of Frederick County, P.O. Box 163, Buckeystown, MD 21717. Tel. (301) 874-5782. *President:* Nancy Bodmer. *Membership:* 28. *Founded:* 1972. *Dues:* $10. *Services:* Guest speakers; shows. *Publication:* Newsletter, monthly.

Creative Crafts Council, 1102 Brantford Avenue, Silver Spring, MD 20904. *Chairperson:* Jacqualine P. Voell. *Funded:* 1952. *Services:* Biennial exhibit. Composed of local Maryland crafts guilds.

Enamelist Guild, 14600 Homecrest Road, Silver Spring, MD 20906.

Maryland Arts and Crafts, Mt. Carmel Road, Parkton, MD 21120.

Washington Kiln Club, 7760 Lindy Lane, West Bethesda, MD 20034. *Founded:* 1946. *Services:* Retail shop; workshop and annual members exhibition. *Publication:* Newsletter.

The Takoma Weavers, 7326 Willow Avenue, Takoma Park, MD 20012. Tel. (301) 270-5494. *Librarian:* Neal Bozarth. *Founded:* 1972. *Services:* Study history and practice of selected techniques in the fiber arts; one-of-a-kind items produced for exhibitions and on commission.

MASSACHUSETTS

Box 64, Shutesbury, MA 01072. *Directors:* Michael Cohen and Aletta Schaap. *Membership:* 15 studios. *Founded:* 1977. *Services:* Coordinates sales to wholesalers; group buying; apprentice co-ordination program; group fair appearances. *Publications:* Information brochure on member studios.

Boston Area Spinners, 14 Edinboro Place, Newtonville, MA 02160.

Craft Center, 25 Sagamore Road, Worcester, MA 01605.

Hoosuck Guild, The Windsor Mill, North Adams, MA 01247. Tel. (413) 664-6382. *Services:* General education and professional training; business center for environmental art; endorses nonmember artisans' high quality work.

Lerverett Craftsmen and Artists, Inc., Leverett Center, MA 01054. Tel. (413) 549-6871. *Director:* Ann Connolly McMurray. *Membership:* 550. *Founded:* 1966. *Dues:* $10. *Services:* Classes; exhibitions; workshops; salesroom and exhibition gallery.

Lexington Arts and Crafts Society, Waltham Street, Lexington, MA 02173.

Massachusetts Association of Craftsmen, 9 Glen Avenue, Arlington, MA 02174.

Mohawk Trail Arts and Crafts Co-operative, Route #2, East Claremont, MA 01370. *President:* Barbarann Burger. *Membership:* 26. *Founded:* 1973. *Dues:* $3 plus 25% commission on sales. *Services:* Sales outlet; special exhibits; demonstrations of craft skills.

New England Weavers Seminar, 68 Sweetwater Avenue, Bedford, MA 01730.

Petersham Craft Center and Shop, Route #32, Petersham, MA 01366. Tel. (617) 724-3415. *Membership*: 350. *Founded:* 1954. *Dues:* $5-family; $4-single; $2-under 18; $2-consignor fee. *Services:* Classes; workshops; exhibits. *Publications:* Newsletter. 3 issues/year.

The Society of Arts and Crafts, 175 Newbury Street, Boston, MA 02116. Tel. (617) 266-1810. *Director:* Cyrus D. Lipsitt. *Membership:* 450. *Founded:* 1879. *Dues:* $10, $20 or $100. *Services:* Retail gallery; challenge exhibition gallery; library; slide and photo collection; fair listings; supplies sources; crafts historic data; craftsmen referral service for jobs; special commissions and workshops.

MICHIGAN

Birmingham Bloomfield Art Association, 1516 South Cranbrook Road, Birmingham, MI 48009. Tel. (313) 644-0866. *Founded:* 1956. *Dues:* $20-individual, $35-family, $50-patron, $500 life. *Services:* Open studios, workshops, classes, scholarship program, gallery, traveling exhibits, art objects for rent, speaker's bureau, volunteers in schools, exhibitions.

Detroit Handweavers and Spinners, C/O Mrs. Richard S. Richard. 1994 Progress Street, Lincoln Park, MI 48146. Tel. (313) 382-8896. *Director:* Elsie Bentley. *Membership:* 39. *Founded:* 1950. *Dues:* $5. *Services:* Workshops on weaving on loom, off loom and fiber techniques. *Publications:* Newsletter.

Michigan League of Handweavers, 2140 Martin Street, Grand Rapids, MI 49507.

National Guild of Decoupeurs, P.O. Box 5119, Grosse Pointe, MI 48236. Tel. (313) 882-0682. *Executive Director:* Ann Standish. *Membership:* 400. *Founded:* 1971. *Dues:* $25-entry fee; $12-annual dues. *Services:* Exhibitions; workshops; research. *Publications:* Decoupage Dialogue. Monthly. Information brochure.

"Yarnwinders" in Heritage Crafts, 606 Pine, Marquette, MI 49855. Tel. (906) 226-8807. *Coordinator:* Anita E. Meyland. *Membership:* 30. *Founded:* 1970. *Services:* Workshops, exhibits, demonstrations. *Publication:* The Yarnwinder.

Upper Peninsula Craft Council of Michigan, Box 246A Route #1, Sault Sainte Marie, MI 49783.

MINNESOTA

Minnesota Crafts Council, P.O. Box 1182, Minneapolis, MN 55440. Tel. (507) 289-3684. *President:* Judy Onofrio. *Membership:* 500. 400 subscribers. *Founded:* 1974 (re-founded). *Dues:* $10-membership; $3-subscription. *Services:* Workshop, annual show; summer fair. *Publication:* Craft Connection. Bi-monthly.

Up North Handcrafts/Lady Slipper Designs, 314 Houston Avenue, Croodston, MN 56716. Tel. (218) 281-3720. *Director:* James C. Shortridge, Jr. *Membership:* 120. *Founded:* 1972. *Services:* Design consulting and wholesale and retail marketing services for rural craftspeople; home-sewing cottage industry program.

Chief Ojibway Original Products, Box 97, Cass Lake, MN 56633. *Services:* Marketing Native American arts and crafts.

Pipestone Indian Shrine Association, C/O Pipestone National Monument, Box 727, Pipestone, MN 56164. Tel. (507) 825-5463. *Services:* Marketing Native American arts and crafts. (Non-profit organization.)

Red Lake Tribal Council, Red Lake, MN 56671. Tel. (218) 679-3341. *Services:* Marketing Native American arts and crafts.

MISSISSIPPI

Choctaw Craft Association, Philadelphia, MS 39350. Tel. (601) 656-6213. *Services:* Marketing Native American arts and crafts.

Craftsmen's Guild of Mississippi, Inc., Box 1341, Jackson, MS 39205. Tel. (601) 354-7336. *Director:* Dan Overly. *Membership:* 500. *Founded:* 1973. *Dues:* $6. *Services:* Craft fairs and exhibitions; statewide Crafts Center; workshops; marketing assistance. *Publication:* Crafts in Mississippi.

Gulf Coast Crafts Center, 4710 Kendell Avenue, Gulf Port, MS 39501.

Mississippi Gulf Coast Craftsmen's Guild, P.O. Box 58, Gulfport, MS 39501. *President:* Isabelle Keating. *Membership:* 150. *Founded:* 1973. *Dues:* $6-single; $6-first family member; $4-each additional member. *Services:* Exhibitions; convention programs; instruction. *Publication:* Mississippi GCCG Newsletter. Monthly.

MISSOURI

Shepherd of the Hills Weavers, C/O Tri-Lakes Adult Community Center, 105 South Fourth Street, Branson, MO 65616.

Ozarks Whittlers & Woodcarvers, 1625 South Broadway, Springfield, MO 65807. Tel. (417) 865-7705. *Dues:* $2.00. *Services:* Monthly meetings, instruction, demonstrations, nonprofit.

MONTANA

Blackfeet Art Foundation, Box 207, Browning, MT 59417. Tel. (406) 338-4075. *Services:* Marketing Native American arts and crafts. (Non-profit organization.)

Blackfeet Crafts Association, Box326, Browning, MT 59417. *Services:* Marketing Native American arts and crafts.

Chippewa Cree Crafts, Courthouse, Havre, MT 59501. Tel. (406) 265-5481, ext. 52 or Tribal Building, Rocky Boy, MT Tel. (406) 395-4478. *Services:* Marketing Native American arts and crafts.

Montana Craftsmen's Co-op, C/O Stephen Reichbach, Elk Creek Weavers, Heron, MT 59844.

Montana Institute of the Arts, 1800 Ninth Avenue, Helena, MT 59601. Tel. (406) 442-1128 or 442-1740. *President:* Mark Browning. *Membership:* 900. *Founded:* 1948. *Dues:* $10. *Services:* Annual Festival; SHARE program; workshops. *Publications:* Montana Arts Magazine; current issues $1; back issues $2.

Northern Cheyenne Arts and Crafts Association, Lame Deer, MT 59043. *Services:* Marketing Native American arts and crafts.

Northern Plains Indian Crafts Association, Box E, Browning, MT 59417. Tel. (406) 338-3911. *Services:* Marketing Native American arts and crafts.

The Warehouse, Artist Co-op and Gallery, 725 West Alder, Missoula, MT 59801.

NEBRASKA

Eaglefeather Crafts, Inc., Box 746, Chadron, NE 69337. Tel. (308) 432-3393. *Services:* Marketing Native American arts and crafts. (Non-profit organization)

Handweavers of Lincoln, 1638 Harwood Street, Lincoln, NE 68502.

Inter-Tribal Artist Guild, P.O. Box 238, Winnebago, NE 68071.

Old Market Craftmens Guild, 511 South 11th Street, Omaha, NE 68102.

Omaha Weaver Spinner, 151 North 41st Street, #208, Omaha, NE 68131.

River County Arts and Crafts, 820 12th Avenue, Nebraska City, NE 68410.

NEVADA

Arts and Crafts Guild of Nevada, 2615 East Charleston, Las Vegas, NV 89104.

Nevada Clay Arts Guild, Box 428, Reno, NV 89504.

Northern Nevada Spinners and Weavers, 3255 Elaine Way, Sparks, NV 89431.

Tuscarora Pottery School, Box 74, Tuscarora, NV 89834.

Wa-Pai-Shone Craftsmen, Inc., Schurz, NV 89427. *Services:* Marketing Native American arts and crafts.

NEW HAMPSHIRE

Kitterly Art Association, 29 Walnut Street, Rochester, NH 03867.

League of New Hampshire Craftsmen, 205 North Main Street, Concord, NH 03301. Tel. (603) 224-3375. *Director:* Merle D. Waler. *Membership:* 4,500. *Founded:* 1932. *Dues:* Varies, up to $7. *Services:* Wholesale gallery; annual fair; permanent and rotating exhibits; library; marketing program; file of sources for bulk fiber purchases; seminars; public school demonstrations; workshops. *Publications:* Newsletter; information brochures.

New Hampshire Weavers Guild, 35 North Mast Road, Goffstown, NH 03045.

Saffron & Indigo Guild, 41 Dunkoee Street, Concord, NH 03301.

NEW JERSEY

Artists & Craftsmens Guild, 17 Eastman Street, Cranford, NJ 07016.

First Mountain Crafters, 650 Prospect Avenue, West Orange, NJ 07052.

New Jersey Designer Craftsman, Inc., Dept. of Art, Glassboro State College, Glassboro, NJ 08028. Tel. (609) 445-7365. *Director:* Dr. John Ottiano. *Membership:* 300. *Founded:* 1956. *Dues:* $5 to $18, student to organization. *Services:* Workshops; exhibitions; annual fairs; lectures; entries to galleries and exhibitions. *Publications:* New Jersey Designer Craftsman Newsletter. Monthly.

Peters Valley Craftsmen, Layton, New Jersey 07851. Tel. (201) 948-5200. *Director:* Ned Foss. *Membership:* 600. *Founded:* 1970. *Dues:* $10 regular; $12 juried craftsmen; $50 plus patron. *Services:* Workshops, internships; extensive summer school; crafts store and gallery; open studios; ACC Regional Assembly Conference; NEA grantees. *Publications:* Newsletter.

Princeton Weavers Guild, Montgomery Road, Skillman, NJ 08558.

The Salem Craftsmen's Guild, 3 Alvin Place, Upper Montclair, NJ 07043. Tel. 746-8828. *Services:* School, gallery, distribute craft supplies & equipment.

NEW MEXICO

Crownpoint Rug Weavers' Association, Inc., Box 328, Crownpoint, NM 87313. Tel. (505) 786-5319. *Services:* Marketing Native American arts and crafts. (Non-profit organization)

Four Corners Navajo Arts and Crafts Cooperative, Box 1356, Shiprock, NM 87420. Tel. (505) 368-4473. *Director:* Eleanor M. Light. *Membership:* 250. *Founded:* 1970. *Services:* Cooperative sale of Navajo crafts.

Institute of American Indian Arts, Museum Sales, IAIA, Bureau of Indian Affairs, U.S. Department of the Interior, Cerrillos Road, Santa Fe, NM 87501. Tel. (505) 476-1281. *Services:* Marketing Native American arts and crafts.

Jicarilla Arts and Crafts Shop, Box 147, Dulce, NM 87528. Tel. (505) 759-3362. *Services:* Marketing Native American arts and crafts.

Las Cruces Designer Craftsmen, Art Building, New Mexico State University, Las Cruces, NM 88001. *President:* Ms. Lee Richards. *Membership:* 25. *Founded:* 1969. *Dues:* $10. *Services:* Joint juried crafts show with El Paso County, Texas.

Northern Pueblo Indian Artisans' Guild, P.O. Box 1079, San Juan Pueblo, NM 87566. Tel. (505) 872-2381. *Director:* Mrs. Michael E. Hamilton. *Membership:* 250. *Founded:* 1975. *Dues:* $1. *Services:* Aids Northern Pueblo Indians in marketing their crafts; sells raw materials; annual show. *Publication:* Artisans Guild Newsletter. Monthly.

Oke Oweenge Arts and Crafts, Box 925, San Juan Pueblo, NM 87566. Tel. (505) 852-2372. *Services:* Marketing Native American arts and crafts.

Taos Pueblo Craftsmen's Project, Inc., Box 1315, Taos, NM 87571. *Services:* Marketing Native American arts and crafts.

The Zuni Craftsmen's Cooperative Association, Box 426, Zuni, NM 87327. Tel. (505) 782-4425. *Director:* Terrell Piechowski. *Services:* The Craftsmen's Market Place; maintaining the Zuni way of life.

NEW YORK

Arachne Weavers, The Art Center, New Scotland Road, Albany, NY 12208. *Director:* Linda Richer.

Allegany Indian Arts and Crafts Cooperative, Haley Building, Jimersontown, Salamanca, NY 14779. Tel. (716) 945-1790. *Services:* Marketing Native American arts and crafts.

Artist-Craftsmen of New York, Inc., 149-47 Powells Cove Boulevard, Whitestone, NY 11357. Tel. (212) 767-6709.

Binghamton Handweavers' Guild, 45 Hawthorne Road, Binghamton, NY 13903. Tel. (607) 722-3590.

Buffalo Craftsmen, 203 Delaware Avenue, Buffalo, NY 14202. Tel. (716) 847-0236. *President:* Chuck Frank. *Membership:* 300. *Founded:* 1956. *Dues:* $10. *Services:* Workshops; monthly exhibitions, gallery and gallery shop; field trips; contact meetings; speakers' guide. *Publications:* Buffalo Craftsmen Inc.

Chautaqua County Weavers, 3854 Westman Road, Bemus Point, NY 14712. Tel. (716) 386-3644. *Membership:* 65. *Founded:* 1954. *Dues:* $6. *Services:* Meetings, programs, workshops. *Publications:* The Newsletter — Chautaqua County Weavers Guild. Bi-monthly.

Designer Crafts Council of the Schenectady Museum, Nott Terrace Heights, Schenectady, NY 12308. Tel. (518) 372-3386.

The Elder Craftsmen, 850 Lexington Avenue, New York City, NY 10021. Tel. (212) 260-2100. *Founded:* 1955. *Services:* Shop; workshops; design advice; craft instruction for the elderly homebound. *Publication:* Class schedule.

Embroiderers' Guild of the Southern Tier, 15 Spurr Avenue, Binghamton, NY 13903. Tel. (607) 724-0896.

Glass Masters Guild, 621 Avenue of the Americas, New York, NY 10011. Tel. (212) 924-2868. *Services:* Information on classes and instructors.

The Genessee Guild, 73 Wilmarth Road, Pittsford, NY 14534. Tel. (716) 381-0090.

Genessee Valley Craft Council, Inc., 8991 Main Street, Rushford, NY 14777. Tel. (716) 437-5316. *Director:* Mrs. Oliver J. Williams. *Membership:* 53. *Founded:* 1974. *Dues:* $2. *Services:* Craft classes; shows and sales.

Greene County Arts & Crafts Guild, C/O Chast RD 1, Athens, NY 12015. Tel. (518) 945-1026. *President:* Dorothy Chast.

Greenwhich House Potters & Sculptors, 16 Jones Street, New York, NY 10014. Tel. (212) 242-4106.

Lake County Craftsmen, Inc., P.O. Box 1477, Rochester, NY 14603. Tel. (716) 621-5352.

Long Island Craftsmen's Guild, Inc., Hofstra University Craft Center, 808 Fulton Avenue, Hempstead, NY 11550. Tel. (516) 560-3568.

Made in Brooklyn, 580 Marlborough Road, Brooklyn, NY 11230. Tel. (212) 462-6619.

Mission Crafts, Inc., Box 565, Hughsonville, NY 12537. Tel. (914) 297-7101.

Mohawk Crafts Fund, 101 East Main Street, Malone NY 12953. Tel. (518) 483-4550. *Director:* Jeff Bailey. *Membership:* 70. *Founded:* 1973. *Services:* Crafts marketing organization; encourages continuation of Indian crafts. *Publications:* Catalog.

Native American Center for the Living Arts, Inc., 466 Third Street, Niagra Falls, NY 14301. Tel. (716) 284-2427. *Services:* Marketing Native American arts and crafts. (Non-profit organization)

New York State Craftsmen, Inc., 27 West 53rd Street, New York, NY 10019. Tel. (212) 586-0026. *Director:* Harry Dennis, Jr. *Membership:* 1,300. *Founded:* 1953. *Dues:* $15 individual, $25 couple, $10 student, $5 children 10-17, $35-$100 patron. *Services:* Sponsors International Craft Show, Craft Fair Ithaca, and the International Craft Film Festival; workshops; seminars; discounts on supplies and books. *Publications:* Crafts Bulletin & Newsletter. Monthly. Crafts Annual Magazine.

North Country Yarn Crafters, 37 Draper Avenue, Plattsburgh, NY 12901. Tel. (518) 563-2870.

Northern Adirondack Crafts Guild, Inc., Market Street, Postdam, NY 13676. *Director:* Ann Mason. *Membership:* 125. *Founded:* 1972. *Dues:* $5. *Services:* Outlet for Northern NY craftspeople; occasional demonstrations. *Publication:* The Newsletter.

Northeast Craft Fair, 12 North Chestnut Street, New Paltz, NY 12561.

The Palisades Guild of Spinners & Weavers, P.O. Box 176, Pearl River, NY 10965. Tel. (914) 735-2735.

Rochester Folk Art Guild, Box 10, RD 1, Middlesex, NY 14507. Tel. (315) 548-3539. *President:* Merlin Dailey. *Membership:* 75. *Founded:* 1957. *Services:* Full-time workshops in ceramics, wood, weaving, glass-blowing, iron, graphics, clothing design. All work done anonymously in the Guild's name.

Seven Valley Weavers Guild, Inc., 37 Tompkins Street, Cortland, NY 13045. *President:* Mrs. Ed Swart. *Membership:* 55. *Founded:* 1959. *Dues:* $4. *Services:* Workshops; exhibits; special interest groups for technical areas; shows. *Publications:* Natural Dye Booklet ($3.50). Book on coverlets; area weavers; antique patternbook.

Studio-Workshop, 3 West 18 Street, New York City, NY 10011. Tel. (212) 242-9615. *Director:* Richard Rapaport. *Services:* Workshops, classes.

Sugar Loaf Crafts Guild, Sugar Loaf, NY 10981. Tel. (914) 469-4963. *President:* Dick Manley. *Membership:* 22. *Founded:* 1970. *Dues:* $100. *Services:* Village where craftspeople live, work and sell; several craft events each year.

Syracuse Ceramic Guild, RD 2, Lafayette, NY 13084. Tel. (315) 677-3724.

Thistledown Handspinners Guild, C/O Jean Travers, P.O. Box 606, Norwich, NY 13815. Tel. (607) 334-5918. *President:* Jean L. Travers. *Memberships:* 80. *Founded:* 1973. *Dues:* $4. *Services:* Workshops, seminars, Wool Day. *Publication:* Newsletter.

Tompkins County Quilter's Guild, 100 West Seneca Street, Ithaca, NY 14850. Tel. (607) 272-6713.

Village Artists & Craftsmen, P.O. Box 292, Hamilton, NY 13346. Tel. (315) 824-1343. *President:* Mrs. Phyllis Charles. *Membership:* 60. *Founded:* 1975. *Dues:* $5 single; $7.50 couple. *Services:* Two annaul arts and crafts fairs; sales outlets for members; exhibits, special programs, scholarship for high-school senior. *Publications:* VAC Newsletter.

Village Weaving Center, Inc., 434 Sixth Avenue, New York, NY 10011. Tel. (212) 260-2100. *Services:* Shop, classes, seminars. *Publication:* Class schedule.

Weavers Guild of Buffalo, YMCA, 161 Darwin Drive, Buffalo, NY 14226.

Weavers' Guild of Rochester, C/O Memorial Art Gallery, 490 University Avenue, Rochester, NY 14607. *President:* Joyce Fisher Robards. *Membership:* 140. *Founded:* 1946. *Dues:* $12. *Services:* Looms available; library; workshops; annual exhibit; demonstrations; volunteer services. *Publications:* The Yarn. Newsletter. $4 subscription.

Woodstock Guild of Craftsmen, Inc., 34 Tinker Street, Woodstock, NY 12498. Tel. (914) 679-2815. *Director:* K. Wangler. *Membership:* 200. *Founded:* 1951. *Dues:* $8 consignor; other memberships $3-$50. *Services:* Classes in various craft media; special craft exhibition in October; consignor's shop; home base for weaver's guild.

NORTH CAROLINA

Carolina Designer Craftsmen, P.O. Box 30132, Raleigh, NoC 27612. *President:* Helen Pratt. *Membership:* 215. *Founded:* 1970. *Dues:* $15 exhibiting craftsman; $10 craftsman; $7.50 associate. *Services:* Annual juried fair; workshops; lectures. *Publication:* Newsletter.

Haliwa Arts and Crafts Center, Haliwa Indian Center, Route #1, Box 329, Hollister, NC. *Director:* Arnold Richardson.

Maco Crafts, Route #2, Box 1345, Franklin, NC 28734. *Director:* Betty Jo Warstler.

Mass Crafts, Inc., Route #2, Box 1345, Franklin, NC 28734. Tel. (704) 524p7878. *President:* Margaret Ramsey. *Membership:* 350. *Founded:* 1969. *Dues:* $4. *Services:* Craft Co-op. *Publications:* Brochures of items for sale.

Piedmont Craftsmen, Inc., 300 South Main Street, Winston-Salem, NC 27101. *Director:* Lida Lowrey. *Membership:* 425. *Founded:* 1964. *Dues:* $10 associates; $25 patron; $15 exhibiting. *Services:* Shop; annual fair; workshops; lectures; library; exhibitions. *Publication:* Crafts. Bi-monthly.

Qualla Arts and Crafts Mutual, Inc., Box 277, Cherokee, NC 28719. Tel. (704) 497-3103. *Services:* Marketing Native American arts and crafts.

Southern Highland Handicraft Guild, 15 Reddick Road, P.O. Box 9145, Asheville, NC 28805. Tel. (704) 289-7928. *Director:* Robert W. Gray. *Membership:* 585. *Founded:* 1930. *Dues:* $6. *Services:* Workshops; seminars; 4 shops; fairs; wholesale department. *Publications:* Highland Highlights. $1/issue; $10/annual subscription.

NORTH DAKOTA

Artist-Craftsmen of North Dakota, C/O Ellen Rose-Auyong, P.O. Box 8134, University of North Dakota, Grand Forks, ND 58202. Tel. (701) 777-2257 or 777-2258. *Chairman of the Board:* Don Duda. *Membership:* 120. *Founded:* 1971. *Dues:* $25-patron; $5-designer/craftsman; $2-amateur/hobbyist; $2-student. *Services:* Annual show and sale; demonstrations; workshops; speaker's bureau; juried, traveling exhibit. *Publication:* Artist-Craftsmen of North Dakota.

Arts and Crafts Association, 905 Park Avenue, Dickinson, ND 58601.

Lake Region Art Association, Box 11, Devil's Lake, ND 58301. *Co-chairpersons:* Isabelle Suidal and Ben Jordan. *Membership:* 43. *Founded:* 1963. *Dues:* $2. *Service:* Annual show; monthly meetings. *Publication:* Newsletter.

North Dakota Artisan/Crats Council,. *President:* Don L. Duda. *Publication:* Newsletter. Quarterly.

Standing Rock Sioux Arts and Crafts, Fort Yates, ND 58358. Tel. (701) 584-2561. *Services:* Marketing Native American arts and crafts.

Three Affiliated Tribes Museum, Arts and Crafts Division, New Town, ND 58763. Tel. (701) 627-4477. *Services:* Marketing Native American arts and crafts. (Non-profit organization)

OHIO

Baycrafters Inc., 28975 Lake Road, Bay Village, OH 44140. Tel. (216) 871-6543. *Director:* Sally Irwin Price. *Membership:* 1,200. *Founded:* 1948. *Dues:* $10 family. *Services:* Classes; exhibitions; annual juried show; gallery; shop; scholarships for high school and junior high. *Publication:* Seasonal bulletin.

Canal Fulton Arts & Crafts Guild, 424 Chippewa Street, Canal Fulton, OH 44614. Tel. (216) 854-2920. *Chairman:* Mr. Russell Sherhag.

Central Ohio Weavers' Guild, 4187 Olentangy Boulevard, Columbus, OH 43214. *President:* Gillian Bull. *Membership:* 275. *Dues:* $6. *Services:* Workshops with outside artists; interest groups; spinning and dyeing group; library; looms and spinning wheel for rent. *Publications:* Thrums. Bi-monthly.

Ceramic Education Council, 65 Ceramic Drive, Columbus, OH 43214. Tel. (614) 268-8647. *Executive Director:* Frank P. Reid.

Cleveland Embroiderer's Guild, 26601 Normandy Road, Bay Village, OH 4414.

The Craft Guild of Greater Cincinnati, 933 Avondale Avenue, Cincinnati, OH 45229. Tel. (513) 281-8042. *President:* Joan Kay. *Membership:* 400. *Founded:* 1966. *Dues:* $5. *Services:* Workshops; annual juried show and sale. *Publication:* Newsletter.

Monroe Arts & Crafts Guild, 106 Olin Drive, Woodsfield, OH 43793.

NOVA — New Organization for the Visual Arts, 1240 Huron Road Mall, Cleveland, OH 44115. Tel. (216) 621-1844. *Director:* Cornelia Spring. *Membership:* 400. *Founded:* 1972. *Dues:* $15 individual; $50 sponsor. *Services:* Gallery; traveling exhibitions; juried shows; exhibitions and community projects; workshops; studios; slide registry for sale and rental of members' works. *Publication:* NOVA Newsletter. Monthly.

The Ohio Arts and Crafts Guild, Box 26, Cambridge, OH 43725. Tel. (614) 498-8439. *President:* Alta Lemasters. *Membership:* 600. *Founded:* 1962. *Dues:* $7.50. *Services:* To preserve, promote and develop fine arts, performing arts and crafts indigenous to Ohio. *Publication:* Newsletter.

Ohio Arts & Crafts Guild, East State Street, Newcomerstown, OH 43832. Tel. (614) 498-8439.

Ohio Designer Craftsmen, 65 Emmet Street, Dayton, OH 45405. Tel. (513) 222-4943.

Toledo Potters' Guild, 5403 Elmer Drive, Toledo, OH 43615. Tel. (419) 535-6937. *Director:* Jo Busick. *Membership:* 35. *Founded:* 1951. *Services:* Classes; workshops; studio.

Tri-County Weavers & Spinners Guild, 732 South Detroit, Xenia, OH 45385. Tel. (513) 372-5406.

Tuscarawas County Arts & Crafts Association, C/O The Schoolhouse Gallery, 111 East 14th Street, Dover, OH 44622.

Weavers Guild of Greater Cincinnati, 3218 Anniston Drive, Cincinnati, OH 45211. Tel. (513) 922-5239. *Membership:* 240. *Founded:* 1947. *Dues:* $5. *Services:* Nationally known speakers; workshops. *Publication:* The Weaver Bird News.

Weavers Guild of Miami Valley, 1545 Langdon Drive, Dayton, OH 95459. Tel. (513) 435-3562. *Director:* Ann Globe. *Membership:* 65. *Founded:* 1949. *Dues:* $6. *Services:* Monthly study groups; workshops. *Publication:* Newsletter.

OKLAHOMA

Ardmore Indian Arts & Crafts, 1429 Fourth Northwest, Ardmore, OK 73401.

Buffalo Heritage Arts & Crafts, P.O. Box 433, Buffalo, OK 73834.

Chahta Indian Arts & Crafts Association, Box 371, Idabel, OK 74745. *Services:* Marketing Native American arts and crafts.

Cherokee Crafts Center, Box 807, Tahlequah, OK 74464. Tel. (918) 456-6031. *Services:* Marketing Native American arts and crafts.

Oklahoma Designer-Craftsmen, 716 East Eufaula, Norman, OK 73071. Tel. (405) 360-2779. *President:* John Atlee. *Membership:* 214. *Founded:* 1965. *Dues:* $10 Associate; $15 Active. *Services:* Workshops; invitationals; annual exhibition. *Publications:* Oklahoma Designer Craftsmen Newsletter. Bi-monthly.

Oklahoma Indian Artists and Craftsmen's Guild, 832 North Warren, Oklahoma City, OK 73107. Tel. (405) 946-9589. *Services:* Marketing Native American arts and crafts.

Oklahoma Indian Arts and Crafts Cooperative Association, Box 966, Andarko, OK 73005.

Southwestern Oklahoma Indian Arts and Crafts, Inc., Box 309, Anadarko, OK 73005. Tel. (405) 247-5184. *Services:* Marketing Native American arts and crafts. (Non-profit organization)

Tribes of the Arbuckles Arts and Crafts Center, 1517 West Broadway, Sulphur, OK 73086. *Services:* Marketing Native American arts and crafts.

Wewoka Trading Post, 524 South Wewoka Avenue, Wewoka, OK 74884. Tel. (405) 257-5580. *Services:* Marketing Native American arts and crafts. (Non-profit organization)

OREGON

Contemporary Crafts Association, 3934 Southwest Corbett Avenue, Portland, OR 97201. Tel. (503) 223-2654. *Director:* Jan de Vries. *Membership:* 1,000. *Founded:* 1938. *Dues:* $10-$50. *Services:* Exhibitions; workshops; school programs. *Publication:* Contemporary Crafts News.

Eugene Spinners, 455 Kourt Drive, Eugene, OR 97404. Tel. (503) 689-4179. *Membership:* 20. *Founded:* 1954. *Services:* Informational and technique sharing meetings.

Maude Kerns Art Center, 1910 East 15th Avenue, Eugene, OR 97403. Tel. (502) 345-1126. *Director:* Callum MacColl. *Membership:* 850. *Founded:* 1956. *Dues:* $5 children/teen; $10 adult; $15 family. *Services:* Classes; gallery; shop. *Publications:* Maude Kerns Newsletter; class schedules and show announcements.

National Quilt Registry, Box 1645, Eugene, OR 87401.

Oregon Designer Craftsmen Guild, Box 2052, Portland, OR 97202. *Director:* Judge Needham. *Founded:* 1972. *Dues:* $15-individual; $25-couple; $5-associate. *Services:* Monthly meeting; slide shows; guest speakers; crafts people selected by jury twice a year. *Publication:* Oregon Designer Craftsmen Newsletter.

Pacific Northwest Weavers Guild, 135 Northwest 32nd Street, Corvallis, OR 97330.

PENNSYLVANIA

The Arts and Crafts Center of Pittsburgh, Fifth and Shady Avenues, Pittsburgh, PA 15232. Tel. (412) 361-0873. *Director:* Audrey Bethel. *Membership:* 1,600. *Founded:* 1944. *Services:* 17 member groups or guilds;

school serving 4,000 students a year; exhibitions; workshops. *Publication:* Quidnunc. Bi-monthly.

Bucks County Guild of Craftsmen, 111 Chapel Road, New Hope, PA 18938. Tel. (215) 862-2374. *Director:* Emil W. Peters. *Membership:* 100-150. *Dues:* $10-$25. *Services:* Bi-annual juried fairs; demonstrations; membership in the Pennsylvania Guild of Craftsmen.

Erie Guild Craftsmen, 1167 West Gore Road, Erie, PA 16509.

Manchester Craftsmen's Guild, 1718 Buena Vista, Pittsburgh, PA 15212.

Pennsylvania Guild of Craftsmen, 227 West Beaver Avenue, State College, PA 16801. Tel. (814) 234-0833. *Director:* Mildred T. Lynch. *Membership:* 1200. *Founded:* 1944. *Dues:* $10 plus Charter dues. *Services:* 19 Chapter members; annual State Craft Fair; seminars; workshops; demonstrations; membership in Craft Artsits of Pennsylvania. *Publication:* The Pennsylvania Craftsman. Monthly.

The Philadelphia Guild of Handweavers, Inc., 314 Exeter Road, Devon, PA 19333. Tel. (215) 688-2274. *President:* Mary Schlegel. *Membership:* 300. *Founded:* 1952. *Dues:* $12. *Services:* Lectures; workshops; classes; annual juried exhibition. *Publications:* Members' Directory of Activity.

South Shore Weaver's Guild, 568 Turnpike Road, Corry, PA 16402.

SOUTH CAROLINA

Foothill Arts and Crafts Guild, Box 1042, Clemson, SC 29631.

Guild of South Carolina Artists, 1112 Bull Street, Columbia, SC 29201.

Palmetto State Craftsmen, Chemistry Dept., University of South Carolina, Columbia, SC 29208. Tel. (803) 777-2295. *Director:* William Caldwell. *Membership:* 30. *Founded:* 1972. *Services:* Group of working craftsmen doing shows and sales; distributes mailing list.

South Carolina Craftsmen, 291 Middlesex Road, Columbia, SC 29210.

Waccamaw Arts & Crafts Guild, Box 1595, Myrtle Beach, SC 29577.

SOUTH DAKOTA

Dakota Crafts Association, 3140 Elmwood, Sioux Falls, SD 57100.

Sigangu Arts and Crafts Cooperative, Box 68, Rosebud, SD 57570. Tel. (605) 747-2404. *Director:* Dorothy Crane. *Membership:* 325. *Founded:* 1970. *Dues:* $1. *Services:* Cooperative of Sioux Indian craftspeople and artists.

Taopi Cikala Crafts Coop, Kyle SD 57752.

Tipi Shop, Inc., Box 1542, Rapid City, SD 57701. Tel. (605) 343-7851. *Services:* Marketing Native American arts and crafts. (Non-profit organization)

TENNESSEE

Cumberland Mountain Craft Association, Route #9, Holiday Hills, Crossville, TN 38555.

East Tennessee Crafts Council, P.O. Box 273, Oak Ridge, TN 37830.

East Tennessee Handcraft Guild, 3702 Taliwa Gardens, Knoxville, TN 37920.

Foothills Craft Guild, Inc., P.O. Box 99, Oak Ridge, TN 37830. *President:* Sam A. Thompson. *Membership:* 170. *Founded:* 1968. *Dues:* $5. *Services:* Juried membership; annual show and sale; scholarships and awards; participation in community cultural activities. *Publication:* Newsletter.

Smokey Mountain Crafts Coop, P.O. Box 1218, Morriston, TN 37814.

Tri-County Guild, Route #6, Box 294, Paris, TN 38570.

TEXAS

The Craft Guild of Dallas, 6923 Snider Plaza, Dallas, TX 75205. Tel. (214) 363-5480. *Director:* Mrs. Lois W. Isenberg. *Membership:* 225. *Founded:* 1948. *Dues:* $10, $15, $30. *Services:* Affiliate of the Dallas Museum of Fine Arts; classes; workshops; juried sho every 3 years. *Publication:* Newsletter.

Fort Worth Handweavers, 3716 Westcliff Road, Fort Worth, TX 76109.

Houston Designer & Craftsmen, 2214 McClendon, Houston, TX 77025.

Southwest Crafts Center, 420 Paseo Villita, San Antonio, TX 78205. *Services:* Legal, administrative and professional services; gallery.

Tribal Enterprise, Route #3, Box 640, Livingston, TX 77351. Tel. (713) 563-4391. *Services:* Marketing Native American arts and crafts.

Westbank Pottery, 901 West 10th, Austin, TX 78703. Tel. (512) 476-3137. *Services:* Classes, sale of clay; commission sales.

VERMONT

Craft Professionals of Vermont, Cambridge, VT 05444. Tel. (802) 644-5358.

Craftproducers Incorporated, Box 92, Readsboro, VT 05350. Tel. (802) 432-7692. *Directors:* Riki Moss, Charles Podley. *Membership:* 100-150. *Founded:* 1972. *Dues:* $10. *Services:* Juried shows. *Publication:* Newsletter.

Green Mountain Guild, Old Town Farm, White River Junction, VT 05001. Tel. (802) 295-7016.

Shelburne Spinners, Box 651, Burlington, VT 05401. Tel. (802) 862-7107. *Membership:* 12. *Founded:* 1972. *Services:* School to teach manufacture and marketing of handspun yarn; exhibits; fairs. *Publications:* Shelburne Spinners Newsletter. Bi-monthly. $3/year.

Vermont Artisans, Inc., On-the-Green, Strafford, VT 05072. Tel. (802) 765-9861. *Director:* Dorothy Swayze. *Membership:* 85. *Founded:* 1972. *Dues:* $10. *Services:* Shop; gallery; workshops; classes; pottery studio; summer festival; dances. *Publication:* Newsletter.

Vermont Arts & Crafts Service, State Dept. of Education, Montpelier, VT 05601.

Vermont Interagency Crafts Council, Dept. of Budget & Management, Pavilion Building, Montpelier, VT 05602. Tel. (802) 828-2376.

Vermont State Craft Center at Frog Hollow, Middlebury, VT 05753. Tel. (802) 388-4871. *Director:* Tricia Nolan. *Membership:* 200. *Founded:* 1971. *Dues:* $10 minimum contribution. *Services:* Consignment sales gallery; classes; information services system. *Publications:* Frog Hollow Information Services Bulletin. Bimonthly.

Windsor House Craft Center, Main Street, P.O. Box 110, Windsor, VT 05089. Tel. (802) 674-6729. *Membership:* 200. *Founded:* 1976. *Services:* State-designated craft center; retail consignment store, exhibition room, studios. *Publication:* Newsletter.

VIRGINIA

Aurora Stained Glass Guild, 11705 Bradley Forest Road, Manassas, VA 22110.

Ceramic Designers Association, 911 Gates Avenue, Norfolk, VA 23517.

Clinch Valley Handicraft Center, Dungannon, VA 24245.

Eastern Shore Arts & Crafts Guild, RFD, Parksley, VA 23421.

Enamelist Guild, C/O Gwen Anderson, 6250 Ivy Hill Drive, McLean, VA 22101.

Fairfax Weaver's Guild, C/O Mrs. Walter Johnson, Stubblefield, Sperryville, VA 22611.

Ferrum Craft Center, Ferrum, VA 24088.

The Folk Arts Cooperative, 1335 New Bridge Road, Virginia Beach, VA 23456.

Halifax County Artists & Craftsmen's Guild, C/O Ned Strange, P.O. Box 893, Halifax, VA 24558.

The Hand Work Shop, 316 North 24th Street, Richmond, VA 23219.

Helping Hands, Route #1, Box 166, Cartersville, VA 23027.

Highland County Crafts, Inc., Monterey, VA 24465.

Historic Appomattox Arts & Crafts Center, Route #1, Box 136, Appomattox, VA 24523.

Holston Mountain Arts and Crafts Cooperative, 279 East Main Street, Abingdon, VA 24210. Tel. (703) 628-7721. *Coop Manager:* Rees Shearer. *Membership:* 200. *Founded:* 1971. *Dues:* $4 plus 6 volunteer days or $10. *Services:* Shop; fairs; sampler catalog; design trainer; marketing and production assistance. *Publication:* HMAC Newsletter.

The Kiln Club of Washington D.C., C/O Scope Gallery, Torpedo Factory, 215 King Street, Alexandria, VA 22314.

McGuffey Art Center, Second Street, Charlottesville, VA 22901.

Northern Virginia Handcrafters Guild, P.O. Box 2221, Falls Church, VA 22042.

Northern VA Woodcarvers Association, C/O Don Early, 440 Olley Lane, Fairfax, VA 22030.

Pamunkey Pottery and Crafts, Route #1, King William, VA 23086. Tel. (804) 843-2851. *Services:* Marketing Native American arts and crafts.

Potomac Craftsmen, C/O Lois Sewell, 2840 North Harrison Street, Arlington, VA 22207.

The Potter's Co-op, McGuffey Art Center, Second Street, Charlotteville, VA 22901.

Quilters of America Unlimited, 1604 Palm Spring Drive, Vienna, VA 22180.

Richmond Craftsmen's Guild, Inc., P.O. Box 8594, Richmond, VA 23226. Tel. (804) 266-9628. *Membership:* 85. *Founded:* 1968. *Dues:* $8. *Services:* Workshops; exhibitions. *Publication:* Newsletter.

Richmond Weavers, C/O Tunnie Fox, 6423 Handy Lane, Richmond, VA 23226.

Richmond Weavers Co-op, C/O Carolyn Duckworth, 21 North Stafford Avenue, #1, Richmond, VA 23220.

Ridge Handicrafters, Route #1, Box 228, St. Paul, VA 24283.

Springtree Community Tinnery, Route #2, Box 50, A-1, Scottsville, VA 24590.

Tazewell County Artists and Craftsmen's Guild, P.O. Box 487, Tazewell, VA 24651.

Textile Designers Association, C/O Caroline McCartney, 5357 Marfield Drive, Norfolk, VA 23502.

Tidewater Craftsmen's Guild, C/O Susan DeLong, DeLong Studio, 204 16th Street, Virginia Beach, VA 23451.

Tidewater Weavers' Guild, C/O Mrs. T. Wayne Nowlan, 1551 West 49th Street, Norfolk, VA 23508.

Virginia Craft Council, C/O Dorothy Hassfeld, Route #2, Box 19-D, The Plains, VA 22171.

Virginia Mountain Crafts Guild, 777 Paragon Avenue, Salem, VA 24153. Tel. (703) 389-5551. *Director:* Dorothy R. Mahoney. *Membership:* 1,000. *Founded:* 1974. *Dues:* $12 per group. *Services:* Federation of mountain crafts groups; workshops; touring exhibition; publicity. *Publication:* Newsletter. Quarterly.

WASHINGTON

American Craftsmen Council, 4649 Sunnyside North, Seattle, WA 98103.

Artist and Craft Guild, 2108 Smith Tower, Seattle, WA 98104.

Lummi Indian Arts and Crafts, Marietta, WA 98268. Tel. (206) 734-8180. *Services:* Marketing Native American arts and crafts.

Needle Arts Guild of Puget Sound, C/O Mrs. C. William Funk, 4206 Beckonridge Drive West, Tacoma, WA 98466. Tel. (206) 564-7981. *President:* Miriam Innis. *Membership:* 206. *Founded:* 1973. *Dues:* $5. *Services:* Educational guild; works to raise and maintain standards for creative needlework. *Publication:* Puget Sound Sampler.

Northwest Designer Craftsmen, 5814-17th Street, Northeast, Seattle, WA 98105.

Pacific Northwest Arts and Crafts Association, 10310 Northeast Fourth, Bellevue, WA 98004. *Services:* Sponsors annual arts and crafts fair.

Seaview Weavers Guild, 8925-200 Street, Southwest, Edmonds, WA 98020.

WEST VIRGINIA

Cabin Creek Quilts, Box 383, Cabin Creek, WV 25035. Tel. (304) 595-3928. *Director:* McKinley Miles. *Membership:* 150. *Founded:* 1970. *Services:* Cooperative for sale and manufacture of quilts and patchwork items; instruction. *Publication:* Hands All Around.

Manongahela Arts and Crafts Association, P.O. Box 173, Fairmont, WV 26554.

McCorkle Craft Group, Box 524, Sod, WV 25564.

Mountain Artisans, 147 Summers Street, Charleston, WV 25301.

Mountain Weavers' Guild, C/O Olive Goodwin, Box 33, Valley Bend, WV 26293. *President:* Eleanor Hoult. *Membership:* 58. *Founded:* 1966. *Dues:* $2. *Services:* Information and skill sharing; classes; adult education classes.

Rural Arts and Crafts Association, 1333 Market Street, Parkersburg, WV 26101. *Director:* DeLoris Zech. *Membership:* 200. *Founded:* 1969. *Services:* Custom orders, classes in sewing; quality control, design, etc.; income supplement program. *Publication:* Brochure on products.

West Virginia Artists and Craftsmen's Guild, 337 Hawthorn Drive, Charleston, WV 25302. *President:* Philip Maxwell. *Membership:* 629. *Founded:* 1963. *Dues:* $7.50 individual; $10 family; $2 students. *Services:* Encourages arts and crafts in WV; classes; special programs. *Publication:* Guild Directory.

WISCONSIN

Community Crafts and Arts Coop, 118 North Carroll Street, Madison, WI 53703. Tel. (608) 257-4790. *Manager:* Sharon Friedland. *Membership:* 34. *Founded:* 1971. *Dues:* $10. *Services:* Coop for retail sales. *Publication:* Newsletter.

Door County Weavers, Route #1, Sister Bay, WI

Ojibwa Wigwam Corp., Route #2, Luck, WI 54583. Tel. (715) 857-5475. *Services:* Marketing Native American arts and crafts.

Potch-Chee-Nuck Cooperative, Route #2, Box 247A, Wittenberg, WI 54499. Tel. (715) 253-2928. *Services:* Marketing Native American arts and crafts.

Wauawtosa Weavers, 2206 North 68th Street, Wauwatosa, WI 53213.

Wisconsin Artist Association, 4061 South Taylor Avenue, Milwaukee, WI 53207.

Wisconsin Federation of Handweavers, C/O Mrs. Robert Scorgie, 11131 West Janesville Road, Hales Corners, WI 53130. Tel. (414) 425-0027. *Membership:* 448. *Founded:* 1950. *Dues:* $5. *Services:* Workshops; exhibitions; meetings. *Publication:* Wisconsin Federation Newsletter.

Government Arts Organizations

Research compiled by Bette London.

State Arts Councils

State arts councils are a good source for information on statewide cultural events, technical and managerial assistance, grants and fellowships for artists. For each entry we have tried to include information on operating budgets and specific monetary allocations for crafts. We have also included programs of special interest to craftspeople and arts council publications.

ALABAMA STATE COUNCIL ON THE ARTS & HUMANITIES, 449 South McDonough Street, Montgomery, AL 36130. Tel. (205) 832-6758. *Director*: M.J. Zakrzewski. *Funds*: 1976-77 Budget, $485,000. Grants available to craftspeople only through crafts organizations. *Programs*: Technical assistance; conference assistance; exhibit aid. *Publications*: Ala-Arts. Quarterly. Sample copy available.

ALASKA STATE COUNCIL ON THE ARTS, 619 Warehouse Avenue, Anchorage, AK 99501. Tel. (907) 279-1558. *Director*: Roy Helms. *Funds*: Grants available to non-profit arts organizations. *Programs*: Mini-workshops; Artists-in-Schools; Art Bank purchases from juried shows. *Publications*: The Arts in Alaska. Bi-monthly. Sample copy available.

AMERICAN SAMOA ARTS COUNCIL, Office of the Governor, Pago Pago, American Samoa 96799. *Chairman*: Palauni M. Tuiasosopo.

ARIZONA COMMISSION ON THE ARTS & HUMANITIES, 6330 North Seventh Street, Phoenix, AZ 85014. Tel. (602) 271-5882. *Director*: Louise C. Tester. *Funds*: 1976-77 Budget $98,400. $25,200 available to craftspeople in 1976-77; $25,200 in 1975-76. *Programs*: Arts Services; Artists-in-Schools. *Publications*: Newsletter. Monthly. Governor's Report. Annual. Limited supply of sample copies available.

ARKANSAS ARTS & HUMANITIES OFFICE, Suite 500, Continental Building, Little Rock, AR 72201. Tel. (501) 371-2539. *Director*: Sandra Perry. *Funds*: 1976-77 Budget $500,000. Grants available to non-profit, tax exempt cultural organizations. In 1975-76 approximately $16,000 in grants to organizations with craft programs. *Programs*: Artists-in-Schools; Artmobile; Visual Arts Workshops; craft festivals and shows. *Publications*: Art News/Comment. Monthly. The Arts are for Everyone. Sample copy available.

CALIFORNIA ARTS COUNCIL, 115 I Street, Dingley Spice Building, Sacramento, CA 95814. Tel. (415) 445-1530. *Director*: Clark Mitze. *Funds*: 1976-77 Budget about $1,000,000. Project and direct grants to non-profit arts organizations. *Programs*: Artists-in-Schools; Maestro-Apprentice Program; Cultural News Service. CNS (452 I Street, Sacramento, CA 95814) was created by the CAC. It provides comprehensive news and information services to artists and craftspeople statewide. *Publications*: State of the Arts. Monthly. Sample copy available.

COLORADO COUNCIL ON THE ARTS & HUMANITIES, 770 Pennsylvania Street, Denver, CO 80203. Tel. (303) 892-2617. *Director*: Robert N. Sheets. *Funds*: 1976-77 Grants Program $100,000. Grants available to craftspeople within programs; no grants to individuals. *Programs*: Artists-in-Schools; Chautauqua touring arts festival.

CONNECTICUT COMMISSION ON THE ARTS, 340 Capitol Avenue, Hartford, CT 06106. Tel. (203) 566-4770. *Director*: Anthony S. Keller. *Funds*: 1976-77 Budget $1,153,195. Grants available for individuals and organizations. 1975-76, $3,900 (4 grants) to individual craftspeople; $4,300 (4 grants) to craft organizations. *Programs*: Artists-in-School; Annual list of Arts Exhibitions, Shows, Festivals; Artist's Services Program: Workshops, VLA, Arts Jobs. *Publications*: Arts Calendar. Monthly. Subscription $3 per year. Limited supply of sample copies.

D.C. COMMISSION ON THE ARTS & HUMANITIES, 1329 E Street, NW, Washington, DC 20024. Tel. (202) 737-5334. *Director*: Larry Neal. *Services*: Sponsoring Craft-Art Expo. *Publications*: Newsletter. Sample copy available.

DELAWARE STATE ARTS COUNCIL, 1105 Market Street, Wilmington, DE 19801. Tel. (302) 571-3540. *Director*: Sophie Consagra. *Funds*: 1976-77 Budget $231,000. Grants available to arts organizations. *Programs*: Crafts festivals, shows, and workshops. *Publications*: Delaware Artline. Bi-monthly. Sample copy available for 25 cents.

FINE ARTS COUNCIL OF FLORIDA, Department of State, Division of Cultural Affairs, Tallahassee, FL 32304. Tel. (904) 487-2980. *Director*: John K. Urice. *Funds*: 1976-77 Budget $383,721. Grants available to individuals and non-profit organizations.

GEORGIA COUNCIL FOR THE ARTS & HUMANITIES, 225 Peachtree Street, NE, Suite 1610, Atlanta, GA 30303. Tel. (404) 656-3990. *Director*: John Bitterman. *Funds*: 1976-77 Budget $603,000. Grants available to non-profit, tax exempt organizations. *Programs*: Artists-in-Schools Residencies; Folk Art Project.

INSULAR ARTS COUNCIL OF GUAM, P.O. Box EK, University of Guam, Agana, Guam 96910. *Director*: Mrs. Louis Hotaling.

HAWAII STATE FOUNDATION ON CULTURE & THE ARTS, 250 South King Street, Honolulu, Hawaii 96817. Tel. (808) 548-4145. *Director*: Alfred Preis. *Funds*: Approximately $10,000 each year in 1975-76 and 1976-77 for statewide crafts programs. *Programs*: Artists-in-the-Schools. *Publications*: State Foundation on Culture and the Arts. Annual report. The Cultural Climate. Bi-monthly. Available through membership to The Hawaii Council for Culture and the Arts, P.O. Box 4263, Honolulu, Hawaii 96813. General membership, $10.

IDAHO COMMISSION ON THE ARTS AND HUMANITIES, Statehouse Mall, Boise, ID 83720. Tel. (208) 384-2119. *Director*: Suzanne D. Taylor. *Funds*: Grants available to non-profit, tax exempt cultural organizations. 1975-76 grants to Visual Arts and Crafts programs, $28,189. *Programs*: Artists-in-Schools. *Publications*: Annual Report. Sample copy available.

ILLINOIS ARTS COUNCIL, 111 North Wabash, Chicago, IL 60602. (312) 793-3520. *Director*: William Denton. *Funds*: 1976-77 Budget $1,990,408. $722,825 for grants. Grants available to non-profit organizations. *Programs*: Artists-in-Schools. *Publications*: Illinois Arts Council Newsletter. Bi-monthly. Sample copy available.

INDIANA ARTS COMMISSION, 155 East Market Street, Indianapolis, IN 46204. Tel. (317) 633-5649. *Director*: Janet I. Harris. *Funds*: 1976-77 Budget $1,170,673. Grants available through non-profit organizations. 1976-77, $13,356 for Crafts. 1975-76, $6,844 for Crafts. *Programs*: Artists-in-Schools; CETA. *Publications*: Indiana Arts Commission Newsletter. Quarterly. Sample copy available.

IOWA ARTS COUNCIL, State Capitol Building, Des Moines, IA 50319. Tel. (515) 281-4451. *Director*: Jack E. Olds. *Funds*: 1976-77 Budget $600,000. Grants available to incorporated and non-incorporated groups and individuals. Exhibits funded. *Programs*: Artists-in-Schools; Folk Artists-in-Schools, Solo Artists; Touring Art Exhibits; Consultant Services; Art-for-State Buildings. *Publications*: Iowa Arts News. Bi-monthly. The Outrider (newsletter for community arts organizations). Visual Arts Directory; Annual Calendar of Summer Art Fairs; Community Arts Handbook. Sample copies available.

KANSAS ARTS COMMISSION, 117 West Tenth Street, Topeka, KS 66612. Tel. (913) 296-3335. *Director*: John A. Reed. *Funds*: 1976-77 Budget $220,000. Grants available to non-profit organizations. 1975-76 awards to craftspeople, $854. *Programs*: Artists-in-Schools, consulting and resource services; textile workshops through Association of Community Arts Councils of Kansas (ACACK). *Publications*: Ensemble. Monthly. Published by ACACK. Free for state residents. $1 a year for out-of-state residents. Sample copies available.

KENTUCKY ARTS COMMISSION, 100 West Main Street, Frankfort, KY 40601. Tel. (502) 564-3757. *Director*: Miss Nash Cox. *Funds*: 1976-77 Budget approximately $1,000,000. Grants available to non-profit organizations. *Programs*: Artists-in-Schools; consultants; conferences; resource lists; technical assistance; workshops; traveling exhibitions. *Publications*: Kentucky Arts Commission Quarterly. Sample copy available.

LOUISIANA STATE ARTS COUNCIL, c/o Department of Education, State of Louisiana, P.O. Box 44064, Baton Rouge, LA 70804. Tel (505) 389-6991. *President*: Mrs E.H. Blum.

MAINE STATE COMMISSION ON THE ARTS & THE HUMANITIES, State House, Augusta, ME 04330. Tel. (207) 289-2724. *Director*: Alden C. Wilson.

MARYLAND ARTS COUNCIL, 15 West Mulberry, Baltimore, MD 21201. Tel. (301) 685-7470. *Director*: Kenneth Kahn.

MASSACHUSETTS COUNCIL ON THE ARTS & HUMANITIES, One Ashburton Place, Boston, MA 02108. Tel. (617) 727-3668. *Director*: Louise Tate. *Funds*: 1976-77 Budget $1,051,823. Grants available to incorporated, tax exempt cultural organizations. 1975-76 awards to craft organizations, $19,500. *Programs*: Technical Assistance; Artists in Residence (through Massachusetts Arts and Humanities Foundation).

MICHIGAN COUNCIL FOR THE ARTS, 1200 Sixth Avenue, Detroit, MI 48226. Tel. (313) 256-3731. *Director*: E. Ray Scott. *Funds*: Grants available to non-profit organizations. *Programs*: Michigan arts and crafts fairs and festivals directory.

MINNESOTA STATE ARTS BOARD, 314 Clifton Avenue, Minneapolis, MN 55403. Tel. (612) 874-1335. *Director*: Stephen Sell. *Funds*: 1976-77 Visual Arts Budget $56,500. Grants available to individual visual artists and to institutions and organizations for the preparation and/or mounting of art exhibits. In 1975-76, one grant of $1,000 was awarded to a craftsperson. *Programs*: Artists-in-Schools. *Publications*: MSAB Art News. Quarterly. Sample copy available.

MISSISSIPPI ARTS COMMISSION, P.O. Box 1341, Jackson, MS 39205. Tel. (601) 354-7336. *Director:* Lida Rogers. *Funds:* 1976-77 Budget approximately $400,000. $40,000 available to craftspeople for 1976-77. *Publications:* Arts in Mississippi. Monthly. Sample copy available.

MISSOURI ARTS COUNCIL, 111 South Bemiston, Suite 410, St. Louis, MO 63105. Tel. (314) 721-1672. *Director:* Donald Tapperson. *Funds:* 1976-77 Budget $1,885,433. Grants available to organizations. $10,230 allocated to crafts in 1976-77. *Programs:* Artists-in-Schools; Artists-in-Residence programs. *Publications:* MAC Newsletter. Quarterly. For state residents and state organizations only. Sample copy available.

MONTANA ARTS COUNCIL, 235 East Pine Street, Missoula, MT 59801. Tel. (406) 543-8286. *Director:* David E. Nelson. *Funds:* 1976-77 Budget $247,200. No grants to individual artists. *Programs:* Artists-in-Schools.

NEBRASKA ARTS COUNCIL, 8448 W. Center Road, Omaha, NB 68124. Tel. (402) 554-2122. *Director:* Gerald L. Ness. *Funds:* 1976-77 Budget $665,346. Grants available to non-profit, incorporated organizations. $5,000 available to craftspeople in 1976-77. $7,000 available in 1975-76. *Programs:* Artists' conferences; Artists-in-Schools. *Publications:* Arts in Nebraska. Bi-monthly. Sample copy available.

NEVADA STATE COUNCIL ON THE ARTS, 560 Mill Street, Reno, NV 89502. Tel. (702) 784-6231. *Director:* James D. Deere. *Funds:* 1976-77 Budget $325,000. *Programs:* Working on statewide listing of artists and craftspeople. Will sponsor statewide conference. *Publications:* Occasional publications available to state residents and organizations.

NEW HAMPSHIRE COMMISSION ON THE ARTS, 40 North Main Street, Phenix Hall, Concord, NH 03301. Tel. (603) 271-2789. *Director:* John G. Coe. *Funds:* 1976-77 Budget $190,000. Grants available to non-profit, tax-exempt organizations. *Publications:* Artsnews. Monthly. Sample copies available.

NEW JERSEY STATE COUNCIL ON THE ARTS, 27 West State Street, Trenton, NJ 08625. Tel. (609) 292-6130. *Director:* Al Kochka. *Funds:* 1976-77 Budget $210,000. Grants available to craftspeople. $9,900 (4 grants) to craftspeople in 1975-76. *Programs:* Artists-in-Schools. *Publications:* N.J.S.C.A. Newsletter. Quarterly. Limited supply of sample copies.

NEW MEXICO ARTS COMMISSION, Lew Wallace Building, Sante Fe, NM 87503. Tel. (505) 827-2061. *Director:* Bernard B. Lopez.

NEW YORK STATE COUNCIL ON THE ARTS, 80 Centre Street, New York, NY 10013. Tel. (212) 488-5222. *Director:* Kent Barwick. *Services:* The Center for Arts Information serves as a clearinghouse for information on the arts in New York State and provides arts groups with technical information.

NORTH CAROLINA ARTS COUNCIL, Department of Cultural Resources, Raleigh, NC 27611. Tel. (919) 733-7897. *Director:* Mary Brewer Regan. *Funds:* 1976-77 Budget $355,000. Grants available to non-profit organizations. Approximately 10 grants awarded to craftspeople in 1975-76. *Programs:* Visiting Artist Program; ThirdCentury Artist Program. *Publications:* State of the Arts. Quarterly. Sample copies available.

NORTH DAKOTA COUNCIL ON THE ARTS & HUMANITIES, Minard 320, North Dakota State University, Fargo, ND 58102. Tel. (701) 237-7143. *Director:* Glenn Scott. *Funds:* Grants available to tax-exempt organizations

for special projects, touring and technical assistance. *Publications:* The Arts Up Here. Sample copies available.

OHIO ARTS COUNCIL, 50 West Broad Street, Room 2840, Columbus, OH 43215. Tel. (614) 466-2613. *Director:* L. James Edgy, Jr. *Funds:* 1976-77 Budget $1,066,128. Grants available to non-profit organizations only. 1976-77, $250,653 in Visual Arts grants; 1975-76, $12,510 in grants to individual visual artists via organizations. *Programs:* Marketing conferences for craftspeople; Artists-in-Schools; Crafts Festivals and Competitive Show Calendar. *Publications:* Ohio Arts Council Newsletter. Monthly. Viewpoint. Quarterly. Sample copies available.

OKLAHOMA ARTS & HUMANITIES COUNCIL, Room 640, Jim Thorpe Building, Oklahoma City, OK 73105. Tel. (405) 521-2931. *Director:* Bill Jamison. *Funds:* 1976-77 Budget $190,000. Grants available to non-profit organizations. *Programs:* Artists-in-Schools. *Publications:* Newsletter. Bi-monthly. Sample copies available.

OREGON ARTS COMMISSION, 494 State Street, Salem, OR 97301. Tel. (503) 378-3625. *Director:* Peter Hero. *Funds:* 1976-77 budget $395,000. Grants available to non-profit, tax-exempt organizations. *Programs:* Seminars; workshops; marketing assistance; visiting craftsmen programs; Craftsmen-in-Schools. *Publications:* Oregon Arts Newsletter. Bi-monthly. Sample copy available.

COMMONWEALTH OF PENNSYLVANIA COUNCIL ON THE ARTS, 2001 North Front Street, Harrisburg, PA 17102. Tel. (717) 787-6883. *Director:* Otis B. Morse. *Funds:* 1976-77 budget about $7/800,000. Grants available to non-profit corporations. 1976-77, $66,000 to crafts organizations; 1975-76, $62,108 to crafts organizations. *Programs:* Artists-in-Schools; CETA.

INSTITUTE OF PUERTO RICAN CULTURE, Apartado 4184, San Juan, Puerto Rico 00905 Tel. (809) 724-6250. *Director:* Anibal Rodriguez Vera. *Programs:* Folk Arts Center. *Publications:* Boletin Artes Populares. Sample copy available.

RHODE ISLAND STATE COUNCIL ON THE ARTS, 4365 Post Road, East Greenwich, RI 02818. Tel. (401) 884-6410. *Funds:* Grants available to craftspeople. *Services:* Craftsperson-in-Residence; Crafts Specialists hired to work in Council programs (Arts in Education, Community Arts Programs, Art in Corrections). *Publications:* Rhode Island State Council on the Arts Newsletter. Sample copy available.

SOUTH CAROLINA ARTS COMMISSION, 829 Richland Street, Columbia, SC 29201. Tel. (803) 758-3442. *Director:* Rick George. *Funds:* 1976-77 Budget $1,800,000. Grants available to non-profit organizations and fellowships available to individual craftspeople. 1976-77, $2,500 (1 fellowship) to craftsperson; no set limits on grants. 1975-76, $12,000 (15 grants) to multi-arts activities which include crafts; no fellowships. *Programs:* Craft Truck. Charleston office to coordinate statewide crafts activities: SCAC Crafts Development Program, 16 Charlotte Street, Charleston, SC 29403. Tel. (803) 722-2759. *Director:* William W. Robinson. This office will work in three main areas: Promotion/information; education; marketing. *Publications:* Artifacts. Bi-monthly. Primarily for state organizations. Sample copy available.

SOUTH DAKOTA ARTS COUNCIL, 108 West 11th Street, Sioux Falls, South Dakota 57102. Tel. (605) 339-6646. *Director:* Charlotte Carver. *Funds:* 1976-77 Budget $398,000. Grants available to individuals and organizations. 1976-77, about $25,000 to projects

involving craftspeople; 1975-76, $20,000 to projects involving craftspeople (four grants to individual craftspeople). *Programs:* Artists-in-Schools; Visiting Arts Program. *Publications:* South Dakota Arts Council Newsletter. Bi-monthly. Sample copy available.

TENNESSEE ARTS COMMISSION, 274 Capitol Hill Building, Nashville, TN 37219. Tel. (615) 741-1701. *Director:* Lewis Snyder. *Funds:* Grants available to crafts organizations 1976-77, $33,000 to crafts groups. *Programs:* Crafts Division with staff of eleven. Director of Crafts, Crafts Training Coordinator; Crafts Marketing Coordinator; Research Center Coordinator; five Field Specialists; Accountant: Secretary.

TEXAS COMMISSION ON THE ARTS & HUMANITIES, P.O. Box 13406, Austin, TX 78711. Tel. (512(475-6593. *Director:* Maurice D. Coats. *Funds:* 1976-77 Budget about $275,000. Grants available to non-profit, tax-exempt organizations. *Programs:* Technical Assistance. *Publications:* Forum. Quarterly. Sample copy available.

UTAH STATE DIVISION OF FINE ARTS, 609 East South Temple Street, Salt Lake City, UT 84102. Tel. (801) 533-5895. *Director:* Ruth R. Draper. *Funds:* 1976-77 Budget $726,900. Grants available to non-profit, tax-exempt organizations. 1976-77, $8,600 (3 grants) to crafts organizations; 1975-76, $5,500 (2 grants) to crafts organizations. *Programs:* Artists-in-Schools; Artists-in-Residence. *Publications:* Utah Arts. Bi-monthly. Sample copy available.

VERMONT COUNCIL ON THE ARTS, 136 State Street, Montpelier, Vermont 05602. Tel. (802) 828-3291. *Director:* Ellen McCullochlovell. *Funds:* 1976-77 Grants-in-Aid Program $100,000. Grants available to non-profit organizations and individuals. 1976-1977, $3,400 to individual craftspeople; $12,600 to crafts organizations. 1975-76, $2,800 (3 grants) to individual craftspeople. *Programs:* Public Arts Program (employment for unemployed craftsmen); Craftsmen-in-the-Schools; Art in Public Places, technical assistance. *Publications:* Vermont Council on the arts newsletter. Monthly. $5 individual membership to Arts Council includes newsletter subscription. Sample copy available.

VIRGIN ISLANDS COUNCIL ON THE ARTS, Caravelle Arcade, Christiansted, St. Croix, U.S.V.I. 00820. Tel. (809) 773-3075. *Director:* Stephen J. Bostic. *Funds:* 1976-77 Budget $205,000. 1976-77, about $200,000 in grants to craftspeople. 1975-76, about $200,000 (30 grants) to craftspeople.

VIRGINIA COMMISSION OF THE ARTS AND HUMANITIES, 400 East Grace Street, Richmond, VA 23219. Tel. (804) 786-4492. *Director:* Jerry Haynie. *Funds:* Grants are available to craftspeople.

WASHINGTON STATE ARTS COMMISSION 1151 Black Lake Boulevard, Olympia, WA 98504. Tel. (206) 753-3860. *Director:* James L. Haseltine. *Funds:* 1976-77 Budget about $518,000. Grants available to non-profit, tax-exempt organizations. *Publications:* The Washington Arts. Sample copy available.

WEST VIRGINIA ARTS & HUMANITIES COUNCIL, Science and Culture Center, Capitol Complex, Charleston, WV 25305. Tel. (304) 348-3711. *Director:* James B. Andrews. *Programs:* Arts in the Community; Artists in Residence; WV Artists and Craftsmen's Directory. *Publications:* Goldenseal. Quarterly. Sample copy available.

WISCONSIN ARTS BOARD, 123 West Washington Avenue, Madison, WI 53702. Tel. (608) 266-0190. *Director:* Jerrold B. Rouby. *Funds:* 1976-77 Budget $195,000 (General Grant Program). Grants available to organizations and fellowships to individuals. 1976-77, $30,000 in grants in visual arts category. 1975-76, $30,000 (24 grants) to all visual artists. *Programs:* Artists-in-Schools; Community Arts Services; Volunteer Lawyers for the Arts; annual listing of arts and crafts fairs. *Publications:* Wisconsin Arts Board Quarterly. Sample copy available.

WYOMING COUNCIL ON THE ARTS, Cheyenne, WY 82002. Tel. (307) 777-7742. *Director:* John Buhler. *Funds:* 1976-77 Budget $190,000. Grants available to non-profit, tax-exempt organizations. 1976-77, $190,000 available to craftspeople. 1975-76, about $13,000 (16 grants) to craftspeople. *Services:* Artists-in-Schools. *Publications:* Art in Wyoming; Calendar of Art Events. Sample copy available.

Regional

MID-AMERICA ARTS ALLIANCE, G-50, Crown Center 3, 2440 Pershing, Kansas City, MO 64108. Tel. (816) 421-1338. *Director:* Henry Moran. *Serving:* Kansas, Missouri, Nebraska, Oklahoma.

WESTERN STATES ART FOUNDATION, 1517 Market Street, Denver, CO 80202. Tel. (303) 571-1561. *Director:* Richard Collins. *Serving:* Arizona, Colorado, Idaho, Montana, Nevada, New Mexico, Oregon, Washington, Wyoming.

AFFILIATED STATE ARTS AGENCIES OF THE UPPER MIDWEST, Butler Square, #349, 100 North Sixth Street, Minneapolis, MN 55403. Tel. (612) 338-1158. *Director:* Dean Myhr. *Serving:* Iowa, Minnesota, North Dakota, South Dakota, Wisconsin.

THE ARTS EXCHANGE, Regional Center, Wilson Hall, Hanover, NH 03755. Tel. (603) 646-2653. *Director:* Myra MacCuaig. *Serving:* New Hampshire, Vermont.

SOUTHERN FEDERATION OF STATE ARTS AGENCIES, 138 North Hawthorne Road, Winston-Salem, NC 27104. Tel. (919) 723-2523. *Director:* Howard R. Hall. *Serving:* Alabama, Arkansas, Florida, Georgia, Kentucky, Louisiana, Mississippi, North Carolina, South Carolina, Tennessee.

Federal

Many federal agencies offer services for craftspeople. Here are brief descriptions of just a few:

INTER AGENCY CRAFT COMMITTEE, Room 4004, Interior Building, Washington, D.C. 20240. *Chairman:* Robert G. Hart.

Established in 1969, the Committee was designed to provide the exchange of information and to strengthen communication between Federal agencies. Principal participants are government employees responsible for Federal programs concerning craftsmen and crafts products. Agencies represented include National Endowment for the Arts;

Smithsonian Institution; the departments of Agriculture, Commerce, Defense, Labor, Interior, and Health, Education and Welfare; Small Business Administration; ACTION; and Community Services Administration.

FARMER COOPERATIVE SERVICE, U.S. Department of Agriculture, Washington, D.C. 20250. *Craft Specialist:* Gerald Ely.

The Craft Program of the FCS is designed to improve the management capabilities of rural craftsmen. Research is geared toward identifying craft associations in the United States, evaluating the impact of crafts in a region, and gaining insight into the business activites of craftspeople.

Services: Assistance in developing regional craft federations and local craft associations; education and technical assistance on business skills for craftspeople and craft cooperatives; workshops on organizing craft cooperatives, marketing crafts, bookkeeping, and business procedures.

Publications: For detailed information on how to form cooperatives, write Publications, Farmer Cooperative Service, U.S. Department of Agriculture, Washington, D.C. 20250 for the following: *The Cooperative Approach to Crafts* — Program Aid 1001, William R. Seymour. *American Crafts: A Rich Heritage and a Rich Future* — Program Aid 1026, William R. Seymour. *The Cooperative Approach to Crafts for Senior Citizens* — Program Aid 1156, Gerald E. Ely. *What Are Cooperatives?* — FCS Information 67, C.H. Kirkman, Jr. *Is There a Co-op in Your Future?* — FCS Information 81, C.H. Kirkman, Jr. *How to Start a Cooperative* — Educational Circular 18, Irwin W. Rust. *List of Publications* — FCS Information 4, Marjorie B. Christie. *Economic Development through Cooperatives* — Program Aid 1088, Raymond Williams. *Accounting Exercise for Craft Cooperative Bookkeepers* — FCS Service Report 122, Francis P. Yager. *Guides to Co-op Bookkeeping* — FCS Information 89, Francis P. Yager. *Bookkeeping Forms Your Co-op Needs* — FCS Information 82, Francis P. Yager. *Kentuckians Fashion Better Living from Handcrafts* — "News" Reprint 387. *Cooperative Development in Rural Areas* — "News" Reprint 391.

INDIAN ARTS AND CRAFTS BOARD, Department of the Interior, Washington D.C. 20240. *General Manager:* Robert G. Hart.

Established in 1935, this Board promotes Indian arts and crafts. It serves Native Americans and the general public as an informational, promotional, and advisory clearinghouse on contemporary Indian, Eskimo, and Aleut arts in the United States. The Board does not make direct grants or fund projects or programs, but it does provide information to Native Americans about potential sources of funding. Its goal is to help Native Americans participate fully in the expanding contemporary art markets of the United States.

Services: Operation and development of three Indian museums and craft centers (The Sioux Indian Museum and Crafts Center in Rapid City, South Dakota; the Museum of the Plains Indian and Crafts Center in Browning, Montana; and the Southern Plains Indian Museum and Crafts Center in Anadarko,

Oklahoma; development and dissemination of technical and consumer information publications; assistance in planning and conducting demonstration workshops to improve craft skills; assistance for Native American groups in planning and establishing production and marketing operations.

Publications: Bibliography 1: Native American Arts and Crafts of the U.S.; Source Directory 1: Indian and Eskimo Organizations Marketing Native American Arts and Crafts.

AMERICAN FOLKLIFE CENTER, Library of Congress, Washington, D.C. 20540.

Established in 1976, the Center coordinates folklife activites within and outside the Federal government. "American Folklife" is defined as the traditional, expressive culture shared within the various familial, ethnic, occupational, religious, and regional groups in the United States. It includes custom, belief, technical skill, language, literature, art, architecture, music, play, drama, ritual, pageantry, and handicraft.

Services: Intiation and promotion of research, scholarship and training; performances, festivals, exhibitions, workshops, publications; establishing and maintaining a national archive of American folklife; collecting, preserving, and making available materials that represent or illustrate some aspect of American folklife. Services are performed by the Center staff and by outside contracts with individuals and groups.

Publications: The Center is developing a guide to Federal programs providing financial and technical assistance for folklife and folk culture.

EXTENSION SERVICE, Department of Agriculture, Washington, D.C. 20250.

The Extension Service, the educational branch of the Department of Agriculture, offers a variety of educational and technical assistance activities in crafts in cooperation with land grant universities and the Cooperative Extension Service.

Services: Classes, exhibits, and stores; sponsorship of local 4-H Youth Programs. For information, contact the local Extension Service office or the Extension Service Director at the nearest state land grant college or university.

ARMED FORCES RECREATION PROGRAMS, Department of Defense.

Army Arts and Crafts Program, Office of the Adjutant General, Attention DAAG-EMR-A, Washington, D.C. 20314.

Air Force, Directorate of Morale, Welfare and Recreation, AFMPC/DPMSOC, Randolph Air Force Base, Texas, 78148.

Department of the Navy, Bureau of Naval Personnel, Special Services (Pers 7211), Washington, D.C. 20370.

Marines, Recreation Section, Commandant of the Marine Corps, U.S. Marine Corps Headquarters, (Code MSMS-12), Washington, D.C. 20380.

Each of the Armed Forces Services provides a variety of arts and crafts recreational facilities for military personnel and their dependents and civilian personnel.

Services: Arts and crafts classes and workshops, hobby shops, lectures and demonstrations, exhibits, contests, and publications. Programs vary at each installation.

Schools

Research compiled by Avril Angevine and Arlene Noble.

The following is a list of schools, centers, guilds and people who teach craft skills. We have not included regular state and private colleges unless they offer unusually good, or just unusual crafts programs. They are, however, good places to find crafts courses. We also suggest that you investigate the adult education courses offered in local schools, "Y's" and community centers.

Where information has been available, we have included the type of crafts skills covered, degrees offered in crafts, special admission requirements and the names of the institution's major instructors.

Please remember that class schedules change every term. What you see here gives a general idea of an institution's coverage; it is not a definitive list.

For additional information, several reference books can direct a person interested in crafts to appropriate schools and courses. These include: American Artist Art School Directory, edited by Sheila Patterson, Billboard Publications, 1515 Broadway, New York, New York 10036; By Hand: A Guide to Schools and Careers in Crafts, by John Coyne and Tom Herbert, E. P. Dutton & Company, 200 Park Avenue South, New York, New York 10003; Contemporary Crafts Marketplace, compiled by the American Crafts Council, R. R. Bowker Company, 1180 Avenue of the Americas, New York, New York 10036; and Directory of Crafts Courses, American Crafts Council, Publications Department, 44 West Fifty-third Street, New York, New York 10019.

ALABAMA

Birmingham Museum of Art, Museum Art Education Council, Birmingham, AL 35203. Classes in ceramics, spinning, vegetable dyeing and weaving.

Owl and Olive Weavers, 704 29 Street South, Birmingham, AL 35233. Textile arts: batik, macrame, silkscreen, spinning, textile design, weaving and general textiles.

Zulphlus Studios, Box 271, Pelham, AL 35124. Ceramics.

ALASKA

Sheldon Jackson College, Fine Arts Department, Box 470, Sitka, AL 99835. Craft courses include Alaskan beadwork, ceramics, weaving and woodcarving.

ARKANSAS

Arkansas Arts Center, Education Department, MacArthur Park, Little Rock, AR 72203. Basic crafts courses, including glass blowing and enameling.

Arkansas College, Ozark Folklore Workshop, Ozark Folk Center, Batesville, AR 72501. The Summer program provides a rare opportunity to learn what's more American than motherhood and apple pie: Apple doll making, broom and candle making, chair caning, corn shuckery, fiddlemaking, hominy making, log cabin construction, lye soap making, basket weaving, and other craft skills.

Little Firehouse School, Art Department, 1516 Laurel, Pine Bluff, AR 71601. Ceramics, batik, enameling, macrame, print and dye, tie dye and general textile taught.

ARIZONA

Clay Pottery Workshop, 517 Sixth Avenue, Tucson, AZ 85705. Clay pottery of course!

Pendleton Fabric Craft School, The Pendleton Shop, Box 233, Sedona, AZ 86336. Tel. (602) 282-3671. Weaving, spinning, needlepoint, and other textile crafts.

Sedona Arts Center, Inc., Box 569, Sedona, AZ 86336. Ceramics and jewelry courses.

Tucson Art Center School, 179 Main Avenue, Tucson, AZ 85705. All craft media taught: batik, ceramics, jewelry, metalwork, spinning, weaving and woodworking.

CALIFORNIA

Academy of Art College, 625 Dutton, San Francisco, CA 94102. Craft courses include macrame, print and dye, general textiles, textile design and tie dye.

Academy of Art College, 625 Dutton, San Francisco, CA 94102. Craft courses include macrame, print and dye, general textiles, textile design and tie dye.

David Arnold Glass Studio, 1331 Kearney Street, San Francisco, CA 94133. Weekend workshops given in stained glass techniques.

Art in Architecture/Joseph Young, 1434 Spaulding Avenue, Los Angeles, CA 90019. General craft instruction including enameling, glass, plastics, silversmithing and textile design.

The Art School, Mar West and Esperanza, Tiburon, CA. A community art school open to beginners and advanced students. Professional teachers offer courses in jewelry, ceramics, weaving, and soapstone sculpture.

The Art School, Mill Valley Arts Guild, 158 East Blithdale, Mill Valley, CA 94941. Tel. (415) 383-3630. Weekly classes in the basic craft media: jewelry, ceramics, stained glass, fiber forms and weaving.

Barnsdall Art and Craft Center, 4800 Hollywood Boulevard, Los Angeles, CA 90027. Tel. (213) 661-6369. Classes in ceramics, copper enameling, glass blowing, stained glass, weaving and quilting.

The Batik Art Place, 530A Miller Avenue, Mill Valley, CA 94941. Tel. (415) 383-3848. Robin Grey gives day and evening courses in batik, along with workshops with guest batik artists.

Baulines Craftman's Guild, Box 305, Bolinas, CA 94924. Fabric, metalwork, enamel, woodworking and furniture, pottery, jewelry, leather, house construction. Individual Instruction Program for those students who wish to become independent, self-supporting craftspeople. Interdisciplinary Design program for an overall introduction to the various craft fields.

Big Creek Pottery, Davenport, CA 95017. Several two-week workshops and fall sessions in pottery and porcelain. Classes are taught by owner Bruce McDougal and visiting potters.

California College of Arts and Crafts, 5212 Broadway at College Avenue, Oakland, CA 94618. Tel. (415) 653-8118. The Crafts Division includes the ceramics, glass, metal arts and textiles departments. Each department has well-known artist-craftspersons among its faculty.

Clay in Mind, Ceramic Studio, 95 Mitchell Boulevard, San Rafael, CA 94903. Ceramics.

The Craft and Folk Art Museum, 5814 Wilshire Boulevard, Los Angeles, CA 90036. Classes taught by professional craftspeople available in levels of skill.

Creative Arts Group, 37 East Montecito Avenue, Sierra Madre, CA 91024. All the basics available, including plastic.

Roger D. Darricarrere Studio, Studio Workshop, 1937 San Fernando Road, Los Angeles, CA 90065. The glass business: glass casting, leaded and slab stained glass construction.

Evolution Art Institute, Inc., 6030 Robular Road, Petaluma, CA 94952. A variety of basic craft skills — blacksmithing, ceramics and kiln construction, furniture, glass, stitchery, wood and wood carving — are taught.

Fiberworks Center For The Textile Arts, 1940 Bonita Avenue, Berkeley, CA 94704. Tel. (415) 548-6030. Courses offered leading to B.F.A. and M.F.A. degrees; assistantships available. Courses and workshops include tapestry, embroidery, batik and resist dyeing.

The Fine Arts Museums of SF, Downtown Center, 651 Howard Street, San Francisco, CA 94105. Tel. (415) 543-0660. Classes are taught by professional artists who exhibit in the Bay Area. The crafts offerings include jewelry, ceramics and textiles, special classes for children.

Ida Grae Weaving Workshop, 424 Laverne, Mill Valley, CA 94941. Includes courses in crochet and basket making, as well as standard weaving skills.

Haillie's Alley Jewelry School, 13045 Ventura Boulevard, Studio City, CA 91604. Jewelry and silversmithing taught.

The Handweaver, 111 East Napa Street, Sonoma, CA 95476. A textile supply store that offers low-cost workshops on various fabric arts — natural dyeing, non-loom weaving, finishing and tatting.

Handweavers of Los Altos, 293 State Street, Los Altos, CA 94022. Tel. (415) 941-1815. Shows and classes given in the store, ranging from the basics of fiber technique to such unusual topics as basketry from garden weeds and soumak rug weaving.

The Hidden Village, 215 Yale Avenue, Claremont, CA 91711. Tel. (714) 626-2928. Darryl and Anne Herlow, noted for their expertise in spinning, batik and weaving techniques, give small classes in these areas as well as basketry, doll making and needlepoint.

Laguna Beach School of Art, 2222 Laguna Canyon Road, Laguna Beach, CA 92651. Tel. (714) 494-1520. Classes in design, enamel, jewelry, ceramics and photography. B.F.A. offered.

Loft Weaving School, 522 Ramona Street, Palo Alto, CA 94031. Macrame, weaving, spinning and textile design taught.

McGroarty Cultural Art Center, 7510 McGroarty Terrace, Tujunga, CA 91040. General courses offered in the standard craft media.

Mendocino Arts Center, 540 Little Lake, Mendocino, CA 95460. Batik, bookbinding, ceramics, enameling, glass, jewelry, macrame, print and dye, quilting, silversmithing, spinning, stained glass, stitchery and weaving.

Mill Valley Quilt Authority, Box 270, Mill Valley, CA 94941. Quilts, quilts, quilts!

Mollica Stained Glass, 1940-A Bonita Avenue, Berkeley, CA 94704. Stained Glass classes.

The Muddy Wheel, 12953 Ventura Boulevard, Studio City, CA 91604. Ceramics and spinning taught.

Nervo Leaded Art Stained Glass Works, 2027 Seventh Street, Berkeley, CA 94710. Courses given in a variety of glass construction techniques.

Otis Art Institute, Ceramics Department, 2401 Wilshire Boulevard, Los Angeles, CA 90057. Primarily for fine arts, but an M.F.A. in ceramics is offered.

Orion Craft Center, 1951 Abbot Street, San Diego, CA 92107. Ceramics and jewelry courses.

Pacific Basin Textile Arts, P.O. Box 7033, Berkeley, CA 94794. Tel. (415) 526-9836. Classes and workshops offered in a wide variety of fabric processes, from basketry, spinning and Navajo loom weaving to design, restoration of hand made rugs and photographic silkscreen techniques.

The Pot Farm, 2909 Santa Monica Boulevard, Santa Monica, CA. Tel. (213) 828-7071. A complete pottery workshop for beginning, occasional or serious potters. A wide range of classes are offered.

The Pot Shop, 324 Sunset Avenue, Venice, CA 90291. A combination of ceramics and weaving instruction under the same roof.

The Pottery, 5838 Perry Drive, Culver City, CA 90230. Ceramics instruction.

Richmond Art Center, 25th and Barrett, Richmond, CA 94804. Basic craft courses offered.

Riverside Art Center and Museum, 3425 Seventh Street, Riverside, CA 92501. Tel. (714) 684-7111. A large selection of craft classes, with special emphasis on ceramics and jewelry. Weaving, stained glass and tole painting are also taught.

San Francisco Art Institute, 800 Chestnut Street, San Francisco, CA 94133. Tel. (415) 771-7020. Ceramics, photography, printmaking and plastics.

San Francisco Museum of Art, Van Ness and McAllister, San Francisco, CA 94102. All kinds of craft courses taught, including lapidary, silversmithing and textile design.

San Francisco School of Fabric Arts, 417 14th Street, San Francisco, CA 94102. Tel. (415) 863-6115. The only school of its kind in San Francisco. The curriculum is designed for artists, professional trade and business persons who want to expand their range of expression through fabric art. Classes include photographic screen printing, indigenous costumes, batik, fabric dyeing and fabric painting.

Santa Barbara Art Institute, 14 State Street, Santa Barbara, CA 93101. Courses in general metalworking.

Rudolph Schaeffer School of Design, 2255 Mariposa, San Francisco, CA 94110. Mainly courses in textiles, but general glass technique is also taught.

Mary Sharp Enamels, 6219 Alviso Avenue, Los Angeles, CA 90043. Enameling.

Some Place Studio, 2990 Adeline, Berkeley, CA 94703. Instruction in general textiles, macrame and weaving, plus bobbin lace making.

Straw Into Gold, 5533 College Avenue, Oakland, CA 94618. Tel. (415) 652-SPIN. Large store with an extensive series of classes in weaving, spinning, dyeing, basketry, and various types of stitchery.

Studio West, 167 Saxony Road, Encinitas, CA 92024. General textiles, textile design, furniture construction and ceramics.

William Tapia Bindery, 7513 Melrose Avenue, Los Angeles, CA 90046. One of the few places that teaches bookbinding.

Textile Crafts, 3127-A Los Feliz Boulevard, Los Angeles, CA 90039. Batik, macrame, quilting, spinning, stitchery, textile design, tie dye and weaving.

Warp, Woof and Potpourri, 514 North Lake Avenue, Pasadena, CA 91101. Mostly warp and woof: batik, knit and crochet, macrame, quilting, spinning, stitchery and weaving.

Woman's Workshop, 17042 Devonshire Street, Suite 204, Balshire Square, Northridge, CA 91325. Tel. (213) 363-1112. A non-profit organization dedicated to self-expression. Classes in numerous craft fields are offered.

The Yarn Depot, Inc., 545 Sutter Street, San Francisco, CA 94102. Offers a number of courses in textile arts. Among the more unusual: bobbin lace, soft sculpture and sprang.

COLORADO

Anderson Ranch Arts Center, Box 2406E, Aspen, CO 81611. Tel. (303) 923-3181. One, two and three week sessions are held in ceramics, woodworking, fibers and mixed media.

Community Free School, 885 Arapahoe, Boulder, CO 80302. Ceramics, jewelry, leather, general metal, silversmithing, stained glass and weaving offered.

Dunconor Workshops, Box 2000, Crested Butte, CO 81224. Summer Program brings craftspeople together to refine existing practices, and to learn efficient methods of designing and constructing metal forms. Taught by Harold O'Connor.

Halcyon — The Weaver's Friend, 1121 California, Denver, CO 80204. Batik, quilting, spinning, textile design, and weaving instruction.

Leman's Quilts and Other Comforts, 5315 West 38 Avenue, Denver, CO 80212. Instruction given in skills demanded by the superior quilt: applique, needlepoint and patchwork.

Opus Foundation, Star Route #2, Box 12A, Sedalia, CO 80135. Classes include ceramics, glass blowing, blacksmithing, kiln construction and glass forming.

Sangre de Cristo Arts and Conference Center, Art Workshops, 210 North Santa Fe, Pueblo, CO 81003. Ceramics, jewelry, print and dye, and stitchery.

Summervail Art Workshop, Box 1114, Vail, CO 81657. Tel. (303) 476-4040. Three week courses in a variety of crafts.

The Weaving Shop, 1708 Walnut Street, Boulder, CO 80302. Everything textile.

CONNECTICUT

Brookfield Craft Center, Box 122, Route 25, Brookfield, CT 06804. Tel. (203) 775-4526. Classes given in all craft disciplines. Setting is a restored grist mill. Facilities include separate weaving studio.

Carrie Weaves Studio, 20 Dyer Avenue, Collinsville, CT 06022. Courses in weaving and woven textile design.

Creative Arts Center, 1240 Farmington Ave., Berlin, CT 06037. Craft offerings include ceramics, caning, jewelry, lapidary, needlepoint, plastics, rugmaking and stained glass.

Edgerton's Handcrafts, 210 W. Town Street, Norwich, CT 06360. The handcrafts concerned are spinning and weaving.

Guilford Handcrafts Center, Route #77, Box 221, Guilford, CT 06437. All kinds of crafts taught, especially strong in textile arts.

Hartford Art School at the University of Hartford, 200 Bloomfield Avenue, West Hartford, CT 06117. A B.F.A. in ceramics is available.

Moon Street Pottery, 1344 East State Street, Westport, CT 06880. Ceramics.

Pulpit Rock Community, Inc., Pulpit Rock Road, Box 100, Woodstock, CT 06281. Tel. (203) 928-2046. Established in 1968 to give young artists of promise a place to work with other artists. Crafts artists of a fine arts level are accepted.

The Rag Doll, 859 Post Road, Darien, CT 06820. This fabric shop gives classes in quilting and stitchery.

Silvermine Guild School of the Arts, 1037 Silvermine Road, New Canaan, CT 06840. All the basics are offered.

Society of Connecticut Craftsmen, Box 467, Farmington Valley Center, Avon, CT 06001. Basketry, batik, ceramics, jewelry, macrame, natural dye, quilting, stained glass and weaving.

Stamford Museum and Nature Center, Art Department, 39 Scofieldtown Road, Stamford, CT 06903. Batik, ceramics, embroidery, quilting, stitchery, tie dye and on-loom weaving.

Wesleyan Potters, 350 South Main Street, Middletown, CT 06457. Tel. (203) 347-5925. Offering classes in pottery, jewelry, weaving, quilting, pewter hollow-ware and other special topics.

DELAWARE

Delaware Art Museum, 2301 Kentmere Parkway, Wilmington, DE 19806. Tel. (302) 655-2720. Classes for adults and children in pottery, silversmithing, needle art, weaving and ceramics.

WASHINGTON, DISTRICT OF COLUMBIA

The Corcoran School of Art, Seventeenth Street and New York Avenue, Northwest, Washington, DC 20006. Tel. (202) 638-3211. Connected with the Corcoran Gallery of Art, this school offers instruction in the Fine Arts, including printmaking, photography and ceramics. Saturday courses for non-students are also available.

The Silver Shuttle, Studio Shop, 1301-35 Street Northwest, Washington, DC 20007. Regular classes available in spinning and weaving, with workshops in bobbin lace and natural dyeing offered periodically.

Smithsonian Institute, Smithsonian Associates, Washington, DC 20560. Classes in ceramics, enameling, fiber, stained glass and stitchery given.

FLORIDA

Ceramic League of Miami Inc., School of Crafts, 8873 Southwest 129 Street, Miami, FL 33156. Ceramics.

Craft House, 1091 North Military Trail, West Palm Beach, FL 33406. Jewelry construction taught.

Florida Gulf Coast Art Center, 227 Ponce de Leon Boulevard, Bellair, FL 33511. Ceramics, enameling, jewelry, metal, stitchery, and wood carving taught.

Colson School of Art, 1666 Hillview Street, Sarasota, FL 33579. The curriculum includes ceramics.

Franklin Art and Craft Center, 1623 Southeast Fort King Street, Ocala, FL 32670. Ceramics, jewelry and silversmithing.

Grove House, Inc., Arts and Craft Center, 3496 Main Highway, Miami, FL 33133. Ceramics, jewelry, metal, silversmithing, stitchery, and weaving.

Lafayette Arts and Crafts Center, Recreation Department, City Hall, Tallahassee, FL 32304. Basketry, batik, ceramics, jewelry, leather, macrame, quilting, textile design, spinning and tie dye.

Lemoyne Art Workshop, 125 North Gadsden, Tallahassee, FL 32301. General craft instruction, heavy on textiles.

Longboat Key Art Center, Box 151, Longboat Key, FL 33548. All craft media taught, including enameling and silversmithing.

Norton Gallery and School of Art, 1451 South Olive Street, West Palm Beach, FL 33401. Ceramics, metal and wood carving.

Spider Web Unique Yarns, 803 South Fort Harrison, Clearwater, FL 33516. Macrame, spinning, weaving, and fiber manipulations.

GEORGIA

Chastain Arts and Crafts Center, 135 West Wieuca Road Northwest, Atlanta, Georgia 30342. Tel. 252-2927. Classes and special workshops for adults and children, beginners and advanced craftspeople alike. All craft media available.

Fiberforms, 898 Monroe Circle, Atlanta, GA 30308. Weaving.

Georgia College, Milledgeville, GA 31061. Degree offered in Art Marketing. Prepares students in the area of craft merchandising and marketing, and helps them acquire a general knowledge of art, good design, quality production and sound business practices.

Rising Fawn Pottery Workshop, Route 2, Rising Fawn, GA 30738. Tel. (404) 657-4444. Six week instruction with students working in a real production studio, the philosophy being that this is the best learning method.

HAWAII

Brigham Young University, Hawaii Campus, Fine Art Department, Kulanui Street, Laie, HI 96762. Classes are offered in ceramics and Polynesian crafts.

Foundry Art Center, 899 Waimanu Street, Honolulu, HI 96813. Offers everything from metal construction to glass blowing and wood carving.

IDAHO

Sun Valley Center for the Arts and Humanities, Box 656, Sun Valley, ID 83353. Tel. (208) 622-9371. Workshop and class programs with visiting artists and teachers. College credit is available through Idaho State University. Crafts courses include ceramics, photography, fiber arts and graphic arts.

ILLINOIS

Countryside Art Center, 414 North Vail, Arlington Heights, IL 60004. Unusual offerings include workshops in soft sculpture and clay jewelry.

Columbia College of Chicago, 540 North Lake Shore Drive, Chicago, IL 60611. Courses in general crafts and craft history.

Evanston Art Center, 2603 Sheridan Road, Evanston, IL 60201. Batik, ceramics, jewelry, metal sculpture, silkscreen, tie dye, weaving and wood sculpture.

Looms and Lessons, 6014 Osage Avenue, Downers Grove, IL 60515. Weaving.

North Shore Art League, 620 Lincoln, Winnetka, IL 60093. Ceramics, stitchery, embroidery, jewelry and kiln construction.

The School of the Art Institute of Chicago, Michigan Avenue at Adams Street, Chicago, IL 60603. Tel. (303) 443-3718. Studio concentration and elective courses in fiber, clay, and fabric.

Weaving Workshop, 3352 North Halstead, Chicago, IL 60657. Tel. (312) 929-5776. Spinning, natural dyes, and rug weaving plus beginning, intermediate and advanced courses in weaving techniques.

INDIANA

The Art Center Inc., 121 North Lafayette Boulevard, South Bend, IN 46601. Ceramics, jewelry, textiles.

Evansville Museum of Arts and Science, 411 Southeast Riverside, Evansville, IN 47713. Classes taught in needlepoint and crewel design, quilting and stained glass.

Fort Wayne Art Institute Inc., 1026 West Barry, Fort Wayne, IN 46804. Offers B.F.A. in ceramics, jewelry, silversmithing and weaving.

Indianapolis Museum of Art, 1200 West 38 Street, Indianapolis, IN 46220. Craft courses include batik, ceramics, enameling, jewelry, silversmithing, stitchery and tie dye. B.S. degree available in enameling, silversmithing and stitchery; Masters in batik, tie dye, enameling, jewelry, silversmithing and stitchery. May be the only place in the world to get an M.A. in tie dye.

The Naguib School of Sculpture, Inc., Box 615,

Beverly Shores, IN 46301. Instruction provided in bronze casting and ceramic and bronze kiln construction.

IOWA

Craft Center, Iowa Memorial Union, University of Iowa, Iowa City, IA 52242. Ceramics, knit and crochet, macrame, general metal, quilting, off-loom weaving and wood carving.

Davenport Municipal Art Gallery, 1737 West 12 Street, Davenport, IA 52804. A slim schedule of ceramics, knitting and crochet.

Des Moines Art Center, Greenwood Park, IA 50312. Ceramics, jewelry, silversmithing, textiles and weaving.

Memorial Union Crafts Center, Iowa State University Campus, Ames, IA 50010. Classes include bookbinding, glass blowing, leather, lapidary, spinning and wood carving plus all the basics.

The Octagon Art Center, 232½ Main, Ames, IA 50010. Batik, ceramics, print and dye, spinning, stitchery and tie dye.

Sioux City Art Center, 513 Nebraska Street, Sioux City, IA 51101. Batik, ceramics, jewelry, metal and weaving.

South Bear School, Rural Route 5, Decorah, IA 52101. Classes in pottery, spinning, dyeing and weaving. "The environment invites creativity and aesthetic romance."

The Weaving Studio, 812 Summit Street, Iowa City, IA 52240. They teach you to weave.

KANSAS

Fredonia Arts Council Inc., Recreation Department, 327 North Seventh Street, Fredonia, KS 66736. Ceramics, glass and wood courses offered.

School of the Wichita Art Association, Inc., 9112 East Central, Wichita, KS 67201. Ceramics, enameling, macrame, silversmithing, spinning, stitchery, textile design, and weaving.

KENTUCKY

The Louisville School of Art, 100 Park Road, Anchorage, KT 40223. Tel. (502) 245-8836. Craft specialties include ceramics, metalsmithing and textiles. B.F.A. degree offered as well as instruction for part-time, non-degree students.

LOUISIANA

Alternatives Gallery, 714 Dublin, New Orleans, LA 70118. Tel. (504) 866-6606. Classes for adults and children include pottery, batik, jewelry and silkscreen.

The Blanchet School, RFD Route #4, Box 397, Abbeville, LA 70510. General crafts courses with emphasis on fabric skills: knit and crochet, quilting, stitchery and weaving.

Louisiana Crafts Council, 139 Broadway, New Orleans, LA 70811. Ceramics, chair caning, embroidery, jewelry, knit and crochet, macrame, needlepoint, quilting, silkscreen and stitchery.

Weavers Workshop, 716 Dublin Street, New Orleans, LA 70118. Weaving.

MAINE

Brunswick Craft Center, Three Cedar Street, Brunswick, ME 04011. Ceramics, jewelry, silversmithing, and weaving.

Crafts Center, University of Maine at Orano, Orano, ME. Tel. (207) 581-7300. Open to the university community and general public. Craft facilities include jewelry, leather, pottery, weaving, quilting, stained glass, woodwork, batik, macrame, silkscreen and enamel.

Craftschool, 11 Lisbon Street, Lewiston, ME 04240. Tel. (207) 783-9711. A non-profit organization that offers instruction in contemporary crafts

to people of all ages: weaving, applique and stitchery, jewelry, woodworking, stained glass and pottery. Special features include craft supplies, scholarships, free workshop time, and Gallery.

Crow Hill Pottery, Abbot Village, ME 04406. Ceramics courses.

Haystack Mountain School of Crafts, Deer Isle, ME 04627. A small number of teachers and students from the international crafts community come together for short periods to concentrate on work and the considerations of group living. Summer courses are offered in all major craft media.

The Hinckley Summer School of Crafts, Box N, Hinckley, ME 04944. Tel. (207) 453-7893. Three week summer courses in ceramics, weaving, jewelry, batik, foundry and stained glass.

Portland School of Art, 97 Spring Street, Portland, ME 04101. Tel. (207) 775-3052. The oldest professional art school in Northern New England and the only one to offer a B.F.A. Fully equipped studios for ceramics, graphic design, jewelry, silversmithing and printmaking.

Professional Maine Craftsmen's Association Inc., Franklin Building, 108 State Street, Bangor, ME 04401. Wood Carving.

MARYLAND

The Baltimore Museum of Art, Art Museum Drive, Baltimore, MD 21218. Ceramics courses.

The Maryland Institute, College of Art, 1300 West Mount Royal Avenue, Baltimore, MD 21217. Designer-Craftsman Department with courses in ceramics, jewelry and metal work, woodworking, furniture, puppetry, fibers and weaving. The program encourages approaches that involve individualized expression.

Maryland School of Art and Design, 640 University Boulevard, Silver Springs, MD 20901. Ceramics program.

The Weaver's Place, 2137 Glynn Oak Avenue, Baltimore, MD 21207. All kinds of textile classes, including rugmaking and on- and off-loom weaving.

MASSACHUSSETTS

Amherst Potters Supply, Pottery Workshop, 44 McClellan Street, Amherst, MA 01002. Ceramics.

The Art Institute of Boston, 700 Beacon Street, Boston, MA 02215. B.F.A. degrees are available in batik, ceramics, metal and wood carving.

Attleboro Museum Inc., Art Department, Capron Park, Attleboro, MA 02067. Weaving courses.

Boston Center for Adult Education, 5 Commonwealth Avenue, Boston, MA 02116. Classes in the craft standards.

Boston University, Program in Artisanry, 121 Bay State Road, Boston, MA 02215. Ceramics, textiles, metal and wood. This innovative and important program prepares students for professional careers as designer-artisans qualified to establish their own businesses. Degrees awarded are Associate of Applied Arts, Bachelor of Applied Arts and Certificate of Mastery.

Boston YWCA, Workshops in Creative Arts, 140 Clarendon Street, Boston, MA 02116. Classes in tapestry plus standard offerings.

Cambridge Center for Adult Education, 42 Brattle Street, Cambridge, MA 02138. A full range of craft classes, including leather, basketry, furniture, rugmaking and silversmithing.

Community Art Workshop, 21 Dudley, Roxbury, MA 02119. Ceramics and silkscreen.

Craft Center, 25 Sagamore Road, Worcester, MA 01605. Tel. (617) 753-8183. Courses in ceramics, jewelry design, woodworking, enameling, furniture refinishing, weaving, stained glass and needlework are offered at the 25-year old Craft Center.

De Cordova Museum, School of Art, Lincoln, MA 01773. Lots of basic unusual crafts offerings: bookbinding, lapidary, leather, spinning, textile design.

Gertrude's Weaving Studio, 269 The Great Road, Bedford, MA 01730. Weaving.

The Great Barrington Pottery, Route #41, Housatonic, MA 01236. Japanese methods of pottery are taught.

High Hedges, 992 Tremont Street, Duxbury, MA 02332. For fabrics: printing and dyeing, spinning, textile design and weaving.

Hill Institute, 83 Pine Street, Florence, MA 01060. Mainly textile crafts, plus woodworking and furniture construction.

The Hoosuck Institute, North Adams State College, North Adams, MA 01247. Tel. (413) 664-4511. Taught by professional master craftsmen, classes include some unusual offerings, such as bobbin lace, guitar and dulcimer making, and contemporary tapestry weaving.

Hudson Institute, Farm Craft School, Hosmer Street, Hudson, MA 01749. Ceramics, metal, macrame, stained glass, stitchery and wood.

Massachusetts College of Art, 364 Brookline Avenue, Boston, MA 02215. Tel. (617) 731-2340. The Fine Arts Department offers programs in ceramics, weaving, glass blowing and jewelry.

Mudflat, 196 Broadway, Cambridge, MA 02139. Ceramics.

The Nantucket School of Needlery, Nantucket Island, MA 02554. Needle handling, plus macrame, quilting and spinning.

Needham Arts and Crafts, 1404 Highland Avenue, Needham, MA 02192. General crafts instruction includes enameling, jewelry, needlepoint and stained glass.

The New England Craftsmanship Center, 5 Bridge Street, Box 47, Watertown, MA 02172. Classes in various media, especially wood techniques.

The Old Schwamb Mill, 17 Mill Lane, Arlington, MA 02174. Craft classes available in all the basic skills.

Petersham Craft Center, North Main Street, Route #32, Petersham, MA 01366. Chair caning, embroidery, jewelry, leather, needlepoint, quilting, spinning, stained glass, on loom weaving and wood carving.

Polyarts-Cambridge Crafts Center, Crafts School 861 Main Street, Cambridge, MA 02139. Batik, ceramics, dyeing, stitchery and weaving.

Powell and Tierney, 209 Main Street, Northampton, MA 01060. An intern program is available in furniture and cabinetmaking.

Project, Inc., 141 Huron Avenue, Cambridge, MA 02138. Tel. (617) 491-0187. Organized 12 years ago by a group of parents to supplement their children's education in the visual arts, Project has expanded to include classes in art, ceramics and photography for adults as well as students.

School of the Museum of Fine Arts, 230 the Fenway, Boston, MA 02115. Tel (617) 267-9300. Full-time and part-time instruction in ceramics, jewelry, metalsmithing, welding and stained glass.

The Stained Glass Workshop, Concord Road, Lincoln, MA 01773. Stained glass.

Truro Center for the Arts, Castle Road, Truro, Cape Cod, MA 02666. Tel. (617) 349-3714. Weaving, ceramics, jewelry, silversmithing, blacksmithing and woodcarving. Morning, afternoon and evening classes, plus intensive workshops.

MICHIGAN

Ann Arbor Potters Guild, 201 Hill Street, Ann Arbor, MI 48104. Ceramics.

Art School of the Society of Arts & Crafts, Crafts Department, 245 East Kirby, Detroit, MI 48282. A four year college offering part-time day and evening classes in furniture and cabinetmaking, carpentry and industrial design.

Birmingham Bloomfield Art Association, 1516 South Cranbrook Road, Birmingham, MI 48009. Tel. (313) 644-0866. A broad range of classes in fine arts and crafts are offered, including papermaking, batik, and stained glass as well as the basics of ceramics, fiber and metal techniques.

Center for Creative Studies — College of Art and Design, 245 Kirby, Detroit, MI 48202. Tel. (313) 872-3118. A non-profit, private, undergraduate art college granting a B.F.A. degree in ceramics, fabric design, glass, graphic arts, metal and jewelry, and photography. Evening, Saturday and special classes open to non-students.

Cranbrook Academy of Art, 500 Lone Pine Road, Bloomfield Hills, MI 48013. Tel. (313) 645-3300. Classes available in ceramics, fiber, metalsmithing, and woodworking.

Greenfield Village and Henry Ford Museum, Adult Education Division, Dearborn, MI 48123. Courses include bobbin lace making, chair caning, crochet and glass blowing.

Kalamazoo Institute of Arts, 314 South Park Street, Kalamazoo, MI 49006. Ceramics, jewelry and weaving.

Lamb's End, 165 West Nine Mile Road, Ferndale, MI 48220. Knit and crochet, macrame, natural dyeing, spinning and weaving.

Northwood Institute, Fine Art Department, Midland, MI 48604. Ceramics, jewelry, macrame, metalsmithing, and weaving.

Pontiac Creative Arts Center, 47 Williams Street, Pontiac, MI 48053. Batik, bronze casting, ceramics, jewelry, knit and crochet, macrame, silversmithing, textile design and construction, tie dye, weaving and wood carving.

Rockford School of Weaving, 11 Squires Street Square, Rockford, MI 49341. Knots, loops, warp and woof.

MINNESOTA

Chris Effrem's Woodcarving School, 3112 West 28 Street, Minneapolis, MN 55416. One, two and seven week summer courses are available in wood sculpture and carving.

Gail Kristenses Ceramics, 1775 Hillcrest, St. Paul, MN 55116. Ceramics instruction.

Minneapolis College of Art and Design, 200 East 25 Strret, Minneapolis, MN 55404. Tel. (612) 870-3316. Innovative summer workshops in clay, fiber, wood and metal, emphasizing the development of an experimental attitude toward the media. Papermaking, blacksmithing, furniture and enamel are among the topics offered.

Minnesota Museum of Art, Art School, 30 East Tenth Street, St. Paul, MN 55101. Ceramics, enameling, jewelry, macrame, metal, silversmithing and weaving.

Rochester Art Center, 320 East Center Street, Rochester, MN 55901. Batik, ceramics, jewelry, print and dye, spinning, tie dye, weaving.

Weavers Guild of Minnesota, 2232 Carter Avenue, St. Paul, MN 55108. All sorts of fabric instruction, from general fiber knowledge to basketry, bobbin lace and natural dyeing.

MISSOURI

Craft Alliance, 6640-44 Delmar, St. Louis, MO 63130. Classes, seminars, lectures and children's classes. Subjects range from the basics to color and design theory, papermaking, chair caning and funky crochet.

Essayons Studio Inc., 8725 Big Bend Blvd., St. Louis, MO 63119. Full range of courses: batik, ceramics, enameling, glass, knit and crochet, macrame, needlepoint, print and dye,

spinning, silversmithing, stitchery and textile design, tie dye and weaving.

Kansas City Art Institute, 4415 Warwick Boulevard, Kansas City, MO 64111. Tel. (816) 561-4852. The Crafts Department offers specialized study in ceramics and fiber. Ceramics instruction includes construction of kilns, preparing clay, handbuilding, slab and coil pinch, pitfiring, woodfiring and raku. The fiber program includes printing and dyeing processes. Studio facilities include several multi-harness looms.

MONTANA

Archie Bray Foundation, 2915 Country Club Avenue, Helena, MT 59601. Ceramics and glass blowing taught.

Council Grove Art School, Route #2, Missoula, MT 59801. Tel. (406) 728-1846. Two and three week summer sessions feature professional instruction in ceramics, fabric, enameling, wood, blacksmithing, puppetry and pewtersmithing.

Yellowstone Art Center, 401 North 27 Street, Billings, MT 59101. Ceramics, jewelry, quilting.

NEBRASKA

Haymarket Art Gallery Inc., 119 S. Ninth Street, Lincoln, NE 68508. Teaches American Indian Crafts as well as batik, ceramics, jewelry, macrame and weaving.

Lincoln YWCA, Art Department, 1432 N Street, Lincoln, NE 68508. All basic craft skills taught.

Old Market Craftsmen Guild, 511 South 11th Street, Omaha, NE 68102. All standard craft courses available, including on and off-loom weaving.

NEVADA

Tuscarora Pottery School, Tuscarora, Nevada 89834. Two week summer workshops include such subjects as raku, salt and high temperature firing, firing with oil and clay aesthetics. The studio is always open.

NEW HAMPSHIRE

Arts and Science Center, 14 Court Street, Nashua, NH 03060. Ceramics, textiles and quilting.

League of New Hampshire Craftsmen, 205 North Main Street, Concord, NH 03301. Classes in batik, ceramics, enameling, jewelry, macrame, quilting, rug braiding and hooking, stitchery, weaving, woodworking and wood carving.

Manchester Institute of Arts and Sciences, 148 Concord Street, Manchester, NH 03104. The institute, established in 1898, offers courses in a variety of craft fields, including blacksmithing. College credit for courses available through Notre Dame College and the University of New Hampshire.

Sharon Arts Center, RD 2, Box 361, Peterborough, NH 03458. Tel (603) 924-7256. A non-profit creative center offering expert instruction in the serious pursuit of handcrafting and designing in wood, metals, paint, pottery and fabrics.

NEW JERSEY

Artisans Workshop, 18 East Mount Pleasant Street, Livingston, NJ 07039. Ceramics, metal sculpture, furniture, jewelry, stitchery.

Artist and Craftsmen Guild, 17 Eastman Street, Cranford, NJ 07016. General crafts courses offered.

The Beautiful Things Factory, Inc., 1838 East Second Street, Scotch Plains, NJ 07078. The beautiful things are macrame and jewelry.

Candles Created by Martin, 680 Leigh Terrace, Westwood, NJ 07675. Martin will teach you how to create candles too.

Craft Concepts, Inc., 41 Hudson Street, Ridgewood, NJ 07450. Mainly textiles, but ceramics and jewelry courses offered too.

Du Cret School of the Arts, 559 Trout 22, North Plainfield, NJ 07060. Ceramics and textiles skills taught, as well as ceramic kiln construction.

Earth and Fire Ceramic Studio and Gallery, 20 Morris Street, Morristown, NJ 07960. Ceramics.

Guild Craft Fair and Supplies, 260 Woodbridge Center, Woodbridge, NJ 07095. Textile crafts, jewelry, ceramics and plastics.

Long Beach Island Foundation of the Arts and Sciences, Long Beach Boulevard, Loveladies, NJ 08008. Ceramics and weaving available.

Medina Lowden Studio, 3700 Long Beach Boulevard, Brant Beach, NJ 08008. Craft courses given in batik, enameling and macrame.

Montclair Art Museum Art School, 3 South Mountain Avenue, Montclair, NJ 07042. Weaving and quilting courses.

Newark Museum Arts Workshop Department, 43-49 Washington Street, Newark, NJ 07101. Ceramics and weaving taught.

Old Church Cultural Center, 561 Piermont Road, Demarest, NJ 07627. Tel. 767-7160. Classes are offered in all media, along with seminars and workshops in blacksmithing, raku and origami.

Peters Valley Craftsmen, Layton, NJ 07851. A year round crafts community offering a curriculum of workshops during spring and fall weekends, and an eight week intensive summer session. Six craft studios are open to the public. Internship program in blacksmithing, ceramics, jewelry, textiles, and woodworking.

Quincy Hall Crafts Shop and Studio, 410 Maple Street, Kearny, NJ 07032. All crafts offered including metalsmithing and rugmaking.

The Salem Craftsmens Guild, 1042 Salem Road, Union, NJ 07083. Ceramics Classes.

The Salem Craftsmens Guild, Three Alvin Place, Upper Montclair, NJ 07043. All general craft media taught.

Studio for the Lapidary Arts, 49 Drum Hill Road, Summit, NJ 07901. Jewelry and lapidary courses.

Summit Art Center, 68 Elm Street, Summit, NJ 07901. Ceramics, jewelry, weaving and woven sculpture.

Weiss Studio and Craft Workshop, 161 Culbertson Road, Basking Ridge, NJ 07920. Tel. (201) 766-1323. Nadine Weiss, a full-time craftsperson, whose studio has been in operation since 1948, offers day and evening classes in pottery, stitchery, rug hooking, loom and non-loom weaving, glass, and copper enameling.

NEW MEXICO

American Stained Glass Institute, P.O. Box 4605 AC, Santa Fe, New Mexico 87501. Maurice Loriaux, director of the school, says that the aim of the school is to rekindle the wonderful and exciting art of stained glass. Each student leaves the school with a full, well-rounded knowledge of this ancient art.

Carrizo Lodge Art and Craft Courses, Drawer A, Ruidoso, NM 88345. Jewelry instruction given.

Mary Lou Cook Workshops, Box 428, Tesuque, NM 87574. Stitchery techniques and basket making.

Gallery One, 3500 Central Southeast, Albuquerque, NM 87106. Weaving classes offered.

Taos Mountain Workshop, The Thunderbird Lodge, Taos Ski Valley, NM 87571. Summer courses in ceramics, leather, silversmithing and textiles.

Textile Workshop, Inc., 320 Artist Road #51, Santa Fe, NM 87501.

Turley Forge, P.O.Box 2051, Santa Fe, NM 87501. Tel. (505) 983-6986. Frank Turley offers instruction in the arts of blacksmithing and horseshoeing. His emphasis is on the forging of hardware and tools. Horseshoeing lectures feature demonstrations in trimming hoofs, fitting shoes, and nailing them on.

NEW YORK

Abbey School of Jewelry and Art Metal Design, 116 West 29 Street, NYC, New York City, NY 10001. A variety of jewelry and metal skills taught.

Abracheff School of Art, 410 West 110; Street, New York, NY. Ceramics, jewelry, textile and wood skills.

Accord Art Center, Box 101, Accord, NY 12404. All Craft media.

Adirondack Lakes Center for the Arts, Blue Mountain Lake, NY 12812. Tel. (518) 352-7715.

Alfred University, State University College of Ceramics, Alfred, NY 14802. Tel. (607) 871-2111. B.F.A. and M.F.A. degrees offered in ceramics and glass blowing.

Arnot Art Museum, 235 Lake Street, Elmira, NY 14901. All basic craft skills.

Art Life Craft Studios, 1384 Third Avenue, New York, NY 10021. All crafts taught.

Arts and Crafts at Riverside Church, 490 Riverside Drive, New York, NY 10027. Tel. (212) 749-8140. Arts and crafts courses.

The Arts Center, Holy Names Campus, 1069 New Scotland Road, Albany, NY 12208. Tel. (518) 438-7895. Classes in early American design, quilting, weaving, jewelry, enameling, rug-braiding, spinning, chair caning and basketry. Special workshops and exhibits.

Baldwin Pottery, School of Ceramics, 540 La Guardia Place, New York, NY 10012. Tel. (212) 475-7236. Daily classes are now offered to adults and children.

The Brooklyn Museum Art School, 188 Eastern Parkway, Brooklyn, NY 11238. Tel. (212) 638-4486. Courses of study include woodworking, jewelry, ceramics, stained glass and textiles. One, three or five days a week classes.

Buffalo Craftsmen Inc., 641 Delaware Avenue, Buffalo, NY 14202. Just jewelry.

Clay Crafts Community, 222 West 79 Street, New York, NY 10024. Ceramics.

Coulter Studios, 118 East 59 Street, New York, NY 10022. Tel. (212) 421-8085. Year round courses in all sorts of textile techniques — weaving, basketry, knitting and crochet — plus Saturday workshops in specialized areas such as tatting, soft basketry, natural dyeing and Obijawa twining.

The Craft Workshop Inc., 214 Caroline Street, Ogdensburg, NY 13669. All basic crafts, plus basketry, leather and spinning.

Craftsmen Unlimited, 16 Main Street, Bedford Hills, NY 10507. Various textile skills offered.

The Crafts Students League, YWCA, 610 Lexington Avenue at 53rd Street, New York, NY 10022. Tel. (212) 755-4500. Classes in everything from basketry and bookbinding to whittling and woodcarving; special workshops; and trips to country craft studios and New York area craft fairs.

Durham Studios, 115 East 18 Street, New York, NY 10003. Stained glass.

Educational Alliance Art School, 197 East Broadway, New York, NY 10002. Batik, ceramics, enamel and metalsmithing, stitchery and tie dye.

Everson Museum of Art, 401 Harrison Street, Syracuse, NY 13210. Ceramics and weaving.

Fashion Institute of Technology, 227 West 27 Street, New York, NY 10001. Tel. (212) 760-7647. A part of the New York State University System.

Offers associate degrees in jewelry design and textile design. The social sciences department has a program in the history of American crafts.

Garrison Art Center, Depot Square, Garrison, NY 10524. All kinds of crafts.

Glass Master's Guild, 621 Avenue of the Americas, New York, NY 10011. Tel. (212) 924-2868. Free demonstrations of various facets of the glassmaster's art are given during the summer in stained glass, lamp making, and the basic skills.

Greenwich House Pottery, 16 Jones Street, New York, NY 10014. Ceramics.

Haber School of Sculpture and Pottery, 1170 Old Northern Boulevard, Roslyn, NY 11576. Instruction in sculptable materials: clay, metal, plastic, fiber and wood.

John Harra Studio, Inc., 39 West 19 Street, New York, NY 10010. Five and ten week courses in wood and related areas: carpentry, furniture making and crafts.

Henry Street Settlement School of Art and Pottery, 265 Henry Street, New York, NY 10002. Ceramics plus some textile media.

Hofstra University, Division of Continuing Education, Hempstead, Long Island, NY 11550. Tel. (516) 560-3568. Under the direction of the Long Island Craftsmen's Guild, a complete selection of courses is offered to students, craftspeople and the general public. Classes in weaving, basketry, batik, leather, jewelry, enamel, ceramics and glass taught by professional craftspeople.

Kirkland Art Center, On the Park, Clinton, NY 13323. Ceramics and quilting.

Kulicke Academy of Jewelry Art, 2231 Broadway, New York, NY 10024. Intricate and advanced techniques of jewelry construction.

Lake Placid School of Art, Center for Music, Drama and Art, Saranac Avenue at Fawn Ridge, Lake Placid, NY 12946. Ceramics.

Lighthouse School of Art, 654 Route 9W, Upper Grandview, NY 10960. Ceramics, jewelry and weaving.

Malone Extension Center, North Country Community College, 101 East Main Street, Malone, NY 12953. Crafts Management offered in both day and evening classes. Both crafts production — stressing the traditional rural crafts, weaving, woodcarving, pottery and blacksmithing — and managing a crafts business will be taught.

Mavros Workshop, , 49 West 28 Street, New York, NY 10011. Tel. (212) 689-1097. Instruction in the many facets of clay working. Studio environment. The director and principal instructor is Donal Mavros.

Memorial Art Gallery, Creative Workshop, 490 University Avenue, Rochester, NY 14607. Batik, ceramics, jewelry, spinning, stitchery and weaving.

Museum of American Folk Art, 49 West 53 Street, New York, NY 10019. Tel. (212) 581-2474. Classes in subjects such as early needlepoint, rug hooking, quilting, basketry and rug braiding.

Museums at Stony Brook, Craft Center, Christian Avenue, Stony Brook, NY 11790. Tel (516) 751-0444. Daytime and evening courses in a wide range of subjects. Where else could you learn scrimshaw and manuscript writing? Less exotic classes are given as well: fiber techniques, silversmithing, leathercraft, woodworking and doll making.

Naples Mill School of Arts and Crafts, P.O.Box 567, Naples, NY 14512. Tel (716) 374-6386. A facility providing an intensive learning experience in the visual and performing arts. Designed to fill public and individual needs not catered to by other educational institutions. All craft disciplines are offered including bookbinding, knifemaking, stained glass, and sculptural fiber.

New Muse-Community Museum of Brooklyn,

1530 Bedford Avenue, Brooklyn, NY 11216. All craft media taught.

The New School for Social Research, 66 West 12th Street, New York, NY 10011. Tel. (212) 741-5630. Especially strong in textile arts. Glass, leather, enamel and ceramics are also offered, plus courses in craft marketing.

Niddy-Noddy, 416 Albany Post Road, Croton-on-Hudson, NY 10520. Fabric crafts.

North Country Arts Center, Box 231 Main Street, Warrensburg, NY 12885. All craft subjects.

Northeast County Neighborhood Craft Center, 117 East Manlius Street, East Syracuse, NY 13057. Thursday morning classes in ceramics. Students produce canal boat models, reminiscent of those on the Erie Canal, which are marketed by mail or craft fairs.

171 Cedar Inc., 171 Cedar Street, Corning, NY 14830. Fibers, printing, spinning, dyeing, stained glass and weaving.

Parsons School of Design, Crafts Department, 66 Fifth Avenue, New York, NY 10011. Tel. (212) 741-8910.

The Potter's Workshop, 186 West 4 Street, New York, NY 10012. Ceramics.

Pratt-New York Phoenix School of Design, 160 Lexington Avenue, New York, NY 10016. Tel. (212) 685-2973. The complete school of design. Offers program in textile design with basic instruction in flower drawing and painting, drawing from antique designs and life, historic ornamentation and rendering designs in printed textiles.

The Riverside Church, 490 Riverside Drive, New York, NY 10027. Tel. (212) 749-8140. Operating for over forty years, with extensive course offerings on everything from Chinese painting to macrame.

Roberson Center for the Arts and Sciences, 30 Front Street, Binghamton, NY 13905. Ceramics, jewelry, stained glass and textiles.

Rochester Institute of Technology, Office of Admission, One Lomb Memorial Drive, Rochester, NY 14623. Tel. (716) 464-2234. The School for American Craftsmen prepares craftspeople to operate their own studios and shops as self-employed professionals, and to work in business and industry as artists and designers. Major areas of concentration are ceramics, metal and jewelry, woodworking and furniture, weaving and textile design, and glassblowing.

Rochester Museum and Science Center, School of Sciences and Man, 657 East Avenue, Rochester, NY 14603. Blacksmithing, tinsmithing, knit and crochet, lapidary, macrame, quilting, textiles and weaving.

Rockland Center for the Arts, 27 Old Greenbush Road, West Nyack, NY 10994. Tel. (914) 358-0877. Weaving, stained glass, jewelry, graphics, calligraphy and ceramics for adults, teenagers and children. Exhibitions and special workshops.

Rome Art and Community Center, 308 Bloomfield, Rome, NY 13440. All the basic craft skills.

Saratoga Arts and Workshop Center, 119 Phila Street, Saratoga Springs, NY 12866. A variety of sewing craft skills plus ceramics.

School of Visual Arts, 209 East 23 Street, New York, NY 10010. Everything available in crafts.

Six Summer Art Program, Skidmore College, Saratoga Springs, NY 12866. An intensive learning program giving participants a special opportunity to explore and develop ideas in depth. Craft courses in ceramics, weaving and jewelry. The courses are taught by resident faculty with workshops and critiques given by visiting artists.

Spencer Depas Studio, 227 Cumberland Street, Brooklyn, NY 11205. Macrame, weaving and wood carving.

Studio Workshop, 3 West 18 Street, New York, NY 10011. Tel. (212) 242-9615. Richard Rapaport has

developed a unique method of teaching the basics of pottery in less than half the time required by traditional methods. The studio is open 24 hours a day with continuous instruction. Jewelry and fine art courses also offered.

Synechia Arts Center Inc., 150 N Street, Middletown, NY 10940. All craft media.

Takako Studio, 347 West Broadway, New York, NY 10013. Batik instruction.

Thousands Islands Museum Craft School, 314 John Street, Clayton, NY 13624. Tel. (315) 686-4123. Art courses, including early American decoration, plus courses in pottery, wood and textiles.

Threadbare Unlimited, 20 Cornelia Street, New York, NY 10014. All the fabric skills available, including vegetable dyeing.

A touch of Whimsy, 1054 Lexington Avenue, New York, NY 10021. Ceramics, decoupage, enameling, knit and crochet, macrame, quilting, spinning, stained glass, stitchery and weaving.

Village Weaving Center, 434 Sixth Avenue, New York, NY 10011. Tel. (212) 260-2100. Weaving classes plus fiber basketry, crochet and knotting. Workshops on special topics and some free Saturday seminars.

Visual Arts Center, 209 Sullivan Street, New York, NY 10012. Ceramics, enameling, furniture and other work with wood.

The Weaver's Loft, 29 West 19 Street, New York, NY 10011. Tel. (212) 255- 1886. Individual instruction on loom controlled weaves up to 20 harness.

Westchester Art Workshop, County Center Building, Tarrytown Road, White Plains, NY 10606. Tel. (914) 682-2481. Adult classes are given in ceramics, calligraphy, design, jewelry, silversmithing, enamel, weaving, macrame, quilting and patchwork, with special offerings for teenagers and children.

The Woodsmith's Studio, 457 3rd Avenue, New York, NY 10016. Tel. (212) 889-5678. A woodworking school for amateurs run by men who know the woodworker's craft. Ten week course with small weekly classes.

NORTH CAROLINA

Arts and Crafts Association, Inc., Community Center, 610 Coliseum Drive, Winston-Salem, NC 27106. Tel. (919) 723-7395. A non-profit instructional group offering classes for children and adults on a quarterly basis. Subjects include ceramics, jewelry, weaving, batik and photography.

The John C. Campbell Folk School, Brasstown, NC 28902. Tel. (704) 837-2775. Two week courses during the spring, summer and fall in several craft media. Field trips to visit the many accomplished traditional craftspeople in the area.

Jugtown Pottery, Route 2, Seagrove, NC 27341. Jugtown is a 50-year old pottery employing traditional production processes and tools. Two to four apprentices are in training at most periods of the year. Jugtown is dedicated to the continuation of folk art as one of the mainstreams of American cultural achievement.

Kelishek Workshop, Brasstown, NC 28902. Tel. (704) 837-5833. Master Violin Maker George Kelishek offers professional training in instrument making. A small number of talented and determined young people are accepted each year to study for nine months. Four week summer workshops are open to all.

Mint Museum of Art, 501 Hempstead Place, Charlotte, NC 28207. Stitchery classes.

Penland School of Crafts, Penland, NC 28765. Summer courses at one of the country's best known craft communities. Ceramics, enameling, glass, metal, wood and weaving.

Summer Workshops, Southern Highland Handicraft Guild, Box 9145, Asheville, NC 28805.

Summer courses in quilting, wood design, pottery, dollmaking, basket making, chair bottoming, cornhusk crafts and conework, and crafts business skills.

OHIO

Baycrafters, Gallery House, Huntington Park Reservation, 28795 Lake Road, Bay Village, OH 44140. Tel. (216) 871-6543. Classes in weaving, needlework, enameling, glass, ceramics and macrame.

Cleveland Institute of Art, 11141 East Blvd., Cleveland, OH 44106. B.A. available in ceramics, enameling, glass blowing, jewelry, silversmithing, textile design and weaving.

College of Dayton Art Institute, Ceramics Department, 445 Belmont Park North, Dayton, OH 45405. Offers a B.F.A. in ceramics.

The Crafty Weaver, 12912 Woodland Avenue, Cleveland, OH 44120.

Finnish Weaving Workshop, Corinne Whitesell, Box 107-King's Yard, Yellow Springs, OH 45387. A two week concentrated program of traditional and modern Finnish weaving taught by an instructor from the Varpapuu Summer Weaving School in Finland. Instruction in all levels of experience, theory and practice courses in techniques such as raanu, ryija, Finnweave, Kuvikas and transparent weave.

The Lake Erie Islands Workshop, Catawba Avenue, P.O.Box 293, Put-in-Bay, Oh 43456. The workshop provides working space, facilities, living quarters and sales opportunities for producing artists. Each person is responsible for all the operations of his craft — potters, for example, make their own clay, fire kilns and sell their pots. Resident craftspersons are available for assistance.

Riverbend Art Center, 142 Riverbend, Dayton, OH 45405. Everything available, including bookbinding and metal casting.

The Toledo Museum of Art, School of Design, Monroe at Scottwodd, Toledo, OH 43601. Ceramics, glass blowing, metal and silversmithing.

Wooster Art Center, East University Street, Wooster, Oh 44691. Ceramics, enameling, furniture construction, on-loom weaving and woodworking.

The Working Hand Craft Center, 515 Conneaut, Bowling Green, OH 43402. Jewelry.

Zanesville Art Center, 1145 Maple Street, Zanesville, OH 43701. Ceramics and macrame taught.

OKLAHOMA

Contemporary Handicrafts, 2927 The Paseo, Oklahoma City, OK 73103. Textile crafts.

Firehouse Art Station, 444 South Flood, Norman, OK 73069. Ceramics and kiln construction, furniture jewelry, stained glass and weaving.

Philbrook Art Center, 2727 South Rockford Road, Tulsa, OK 74114. All the regular craft offerings.

OREGON

Coos Art Museum, 515 Market Street, Coos Bay, OR 97420. Basic craft classes.

Corvallis Art Center, 700 Southwest Madison, Corvallis, OR 97330. Ceramics, plastics, stained glass and weaving.

Damascus Pioneer Craft School, 14711 Southeast Anderson Road, Clackamas, OR 97015. Tel. (503) 658-2704. Fall, winter and spring terms have classes in spinning, quilting, knitting and stitchery, weaving Navajo weaving and lace making.

Maude Kerns Art Center, 15 Avenue and Villard, Eugene, OR 97403. A wide variety of craft skills are offered.

Marylhurst Education Center, Marylhurst, OR 97036. According to our research, the only place to teach bookbinding in Oregon! Ceramics, fiber, spinning and weaving offered also.

Menucha Creative Arts Community, P.O.Box 8887, Portland, OR 97208. Tel. (503) 281-7101. One or two week summer workshops offer wide range of disciplines taught by outstanding Northwest artists. Guest artists make evening appearances. Participants work in one or two disciplines including calligraphy, fiber forms, jewelry, pottery and wood sculpture.

Museum Art School, Southwest Park and Madison Streets, Portland, OR 97205. Ceramics program teaches traditional methods of making tableware as a means of acquiring fundamental throwing skills.

Hal Painter Summer Workshops, Star Route, Chiloquin, OR 97624. Cardweaving, spinning and Navajo style weaving.

The School of Arts and Crafts, 616 Northwest 18th, Portland, OR 97209. Tel. (503) 228-4741. One of the oldest cultural institutions in Portland, housing a library, slide collection and gallery. Courses are available in ceramics, calligraphy, metal arts, textiles, weaving, woodcarving and stained glass.

PENNSYLVANIA

Arts and Crafts Center of Pittsburgh, 1047 Shady Avenue, Pittsburgh, PA 15232. Basic craft offerings.

Cheltenham Art Center, 439 Ashbourne Road, Cheltenham, PA 19012. The basic craft courses.

Fringe and Frame Inc., 732 Filbert Street, Pittsburgh, PA 15232. Lots of textile crafts, plus ceramics.

Lenos Handcrafts, 2037 Walnut Street, Philadelphia, PA 19103. Spinning and weaving.

The Mannings Handweaving School, Route #2, East Berlin, PA 17316. Basic textile skills.

Moore College of Art, 20th and Race Streets, Philadelphia, PA 19103. Tel. (215) 568-4515. The only women's art college in the country. The Fine Arts division offers majors in ceramic design, jewelry and metalsmithing, and printmaking; the Professional Arts division offers a textile arts major.

The Pottery Shed, 1125 West Main Street, Stroudsburg, PA 18360. Tel. (717) 421-4818. Myra Kyle gives classes for adults and children in all phases of ceramics — techniques of handbuilding, introduction to the potter's wheel, kiln firing and mold making.

The Silver Shop at the Barn Shops, Box 198, Chadds Ford, PA 19307. Enameling, jewelry and silversmithing in a very artistic town!

RHODE ISLAND

Chin's Pottery and Craft Center, 511 Warwick Avenue, Warwick, RI 02888. Ceramics only.

Rhode Island School of Design, 2 College Street, Providence, RI 02903. Tel. (401) 331-3511. The division of Fine Arts, in an attempt to increase the interrelationship of all creative activities, now includes courses in apparel design, textile design, light metal, ceramics and glass blowing.

SOUTH CAROLINA

Columbia Museum of Art, Richland Art Workshop, 1112 Bull Street, Columbia, SC 29201. Ceramics and enameling.

Gibbs Art Gallery, Dudley Vaill Memorial Bindery, 135 Meeting Street, Charleston, SC 29401, Bookbinding.

Museum School of Art of Greenville County, 420 College Street, Greenville, SC 29609. Associate degrees offered in a number of craft fields.

TENNESSEE

Arrowmont School of Crafts, Box 567, Gatlinburg, TN 37738. Tel. (615) 436-5860. Arrowmont began as a Settlement School and grew to be the largest Cottage Weaving Industry in the U.S. There are now seven studios at the School, offering a full range of craft courses, from jewelry and enameling to textile and dyeing techniques. College credit is available through the University of Tennessee.

The Memphis Academy of Arts, Overton Park, Memphis, TN 38112. Tel. (901) 726-4085. Offers majors in metal arts, pottery, printmaking and textiles.

TEXAS

Craft Guild of Dallas, Dallas Museum of Fine Arts, Fair Park, Dallas, TX 75226. Batik, bookbinding, ceramics, jewelry and silversmithing, stitchery, weaving and tapestry.

Hill Country Art Foundation, Box 176, Ingram, TX 79409. Ceramics and stitchery.

The Museum of Fine Arts-Houston, School of Art, 3815 Garrott, Houston, TX 77006. Ceramics, jewelry and printmaking.

PM Limited Inc., 2708 Southwest Freeway, Houston, TX 77006. Jewelry, lapidary and silversmithing.

The Southwest Craft Center, 300 Augusta Street at Old Ursuline, San Antonio, TX 78205. Provides training in a variety of craft media to people of all ages. A special two-year program has been developed for those who seek professional art careers. Subjects include ceramics, metal, textile design and fiber, and graphics.

UTAH

Pioneer Craft House Inc., 3271 South Fifth E, Salt Lake City, UT 84106. All kinds of craft classes, from basketry to wood carving.

Salt Lake Art Center School, 54 Finch Lane, Salt Lake City, UT 84102. Batik, ceramics, enameling, jewelry, spinning, stitchery, tie dye and weaving.

VERMONT

Creative Education, South Main Street, Northfield, VT 05663. Ceramics, jewelry, knit and crochet, macrame, quilting, spinning and stitchery.

Fletcher Farm Craft School, Ludlow, VT 05149. Sponsored by the Society of Vermont Craftsmen. A variety of two week craft classes are offered in the spring, summer and fall terms. Everything from weaving, pottery and spinning to rosemaling, raku and the construction and decoration of paper lampshades.

Judy Fox, East Warren Road, Waitsfield, VT 05673. Tel. (802) 496-2402. Judy's weaving classes run throughout the summer in one week sessions. Only four students are accepted at a time. The studio was once a barn; the farm setting and outdoor work — gathering plants for dyeing classes — are unusual aspects of the program. Bring your own loom if you have a favorite.

Shelburne Craft School, Harbor Road, Shelburne, VT 05482. Ceramics, dyeing, furniture construction, jewelry, weaving and woodworking.

Vermont Artisans, Box 26, Strafford, VT. Tel. (802) 765-9861. Courses are aimed at both adults and children, and include craft subjects as well as guitar and recorder instruction.

Vermont State Craft Center, Frog Hollow, Middlebury, VT. Tel. (802) 388-4871. Classes are given year round for adults and children, featuring block printing, calligraphy, patchwork, quilting, applique and trapunto, pottery, silversmithing and weaving.

Russ Zimmerman, Box 76, Underhill Center, VT

05490. Two day courses in woodturning.

VIRGINIA

Hand Work Shop, 316 North 24 Street, Richmond, VA 23223. Ceramics and weaving.

Strasburg Museum, East King Street, Strasburg, VA 22657. Ceramics instruction.

Vaten School of Crafts, Sullins College, Glenway Avenue, Bristol, VA 24201. Basketry, chair caning, ceramics, macrame, needlepoint, quilting, spinning, stitchery, wood carving.

Virginia Museum, Boulevard and Grove Avenue, Richmond, VA 23221. Ceramics and weaving.

Yarns Etcetera, 215 King Street, Alexandria, VA 22314. The Etcetera is basketry!

WASHINGTON

Carnegie Center of the Arts, 109 South Palouse, Walla Walla, WA 99362. Ceramics, jewelry, spinning, stained glass, stitchery and weaving.

Cornish School of Allied Arts, 710 East Roy Street, Seattle, WA 98102. Ceramics and jewelry techniques — enamel, metal and silversmithing.

The Factory of Visual Art, 4649 Sunnyside North, Seattle, WA 98103. Tel. (206) 632-8177. Offers a complete visual art program to anyone seriously interested in the art experience. Classes can be taken for credit or non-credit. Three and four year certificate programs in ceramics, metal design and textiles.

Loom and Leather, South 123 Wall Street, Spokane, WA 99204. Weaving.

WEST VIRGINIA

Augusta Heritage Arts Workshop, 135 Buffalo Street, Elkins, WV 26241. Tel. (304) 636-1467. A varied program of folk arts, music, folklore and history taught by Appalachian craftsmen and other artisans. Students either stay at Davis and Elkins College or camp out in the Monongahela National Forest. Craft classes include pottery, basketry, quilting, spinning, natural dyeing, weaving and musical instrument construction.

Cedar Lakes Craft Center, Ripley, WV 25271. Tel. (304) 372-6263. Spring and summer courses are offered to the public, sponsored by the West Virginia Department of Education. The courses stress design as well as technique. Typical classes include rug braiding fundamentals, honeysuckle basketry, spinning, and folk art design and painting.

Huntington Galleries, Park Hills, Huntington, WV 25701. Wide range of craft courses.

Oglebay Institute Downtown Center, 841½ National Road, Wheeling, WV 26003. Basic craft classes.

WISCONSIN

Country Crafts, Route #2, Plymouth, WI 57073. Ceramic, chair caning, needlepoint, rosemaling, stained glass and off-loom weaving.

Foxfire at Alpine Valley, P.O. Box 615, East Troy, WI 53120. Tel. (414) 642-3900. The Workshop/Gallery houses 60-70 artists and craftspeople who create, teach, demonstrate and sell their work to visitors to the center.

John Michael Kohler Arts Center, 608 New York Avenue, Sheboygan, WI 53081. A variety of courses, workshops and lectures. Take a look at their newsletter—everything sounds like fun.

WYOMING

Gallery 323, 323 South David, Casper, WY 82601. Macrame, spinning and weaving.

Publications

Research compiled by Arlene Noble.

ACA Reports. Associated Councils of the Arts, 570 Seventh Avenue, New York, NY 10018. Monthly, includes membership.

ACA Word from Washington. Associated Councils of the Arts, 570 Seventh Avenue, New York, NY 10018. Monthly, $30. News-magazine for arts organizations. Covers fund raising, legal matters affecting the arts, government support, arts in education.

ACC Outlook, American Crafts Council, 44 West 53rd Street, New York, NY 10019. Bi-monthly, $18.50. Small, attractive newsletter dealing mainly with American Crafts Council business and Museum of Contemporary Crafts shows. Good information about publications, grants, exhibitions and current craft production.

ACC Northeast Gazette. 222 West Twenty-third Street, New York, NY 10011. Quarterly. Chapter news.

American Artist. 1 Astor Plaza, New York, NY 10036. Monthly, $13. For practicing visual artists. Paintings, prints, drawings, illustrations, sculpture and creative visual crafts.

Advocates for the Arts. *See* the Arts Advocate.

American Ceramic Society Journal. American Ceramic Society, 65 Ceramic Drive, Columbus, OH 43214. Bi-monthly, $45.

American Ceramic Society Bulletin. American Ceramic Society, 65 Ceramic Drive, Columbus, OH 43214. Bi-monthly, $20.

American Fabrics. Doris Publishing Company, 24 East Thirty-eighth Street, New York, NY 10016. Quarterly, $24. Swatches, news, and articles on dyeing techniques.

American Folklife. RD 2, Oley, PA 19547.

American Indian Art Magazine. 7045 Third Avenue, Scottsdale, AZ 85251. Indian arts and crafts.

American Artists Business Letter. 1515 Broadway, New York, NY 10036. Ten issues per year, $15; $3 single issue. Subscriptions: 2160 Patterson Street, Cincinnati, OH 45214. Legal and financial news pertaining to the professional artist.

Art and the Law. Volunteer Lawyers for the Arts, 36 West Forty-fourth Street, New York, NY 10036.

Art Educators of Iowa Message. *See* Message.

Art Letter. 150 East Fifty-eighth Street, New York, NY 10022. Twelve issues per year, $28.

Artisan. Canadian Crafts Council, 46 Elgin Street, Suite 16, Ottawa, Canada K1P 5K6. Bi-monthly, $25 includes membership, $2 single issue for non-members. Supercedes the Newsletter of the Canadian Crafts Council. Covers such topics as safety and legal rights, development of crafts in the third world. Listing of events throughout Canada.

Artists-Blacksmiths Association of North America (ABANA). Newsletter. The Forge and Anvil, 3271 Roswell Road, Atlanta, GA 30305.

Artists League of the Midwest, Inc. Newsletter 555 Sheridan Road, Chicago, IL 60640. Exhibitions; art and craft fairs; classified job opportunities; teaching positions; and grants.

Artists's Market (California). Box 2203, Capistrano Beach, CA 92624. Bi-monthly, $5. California arts and crafts shows and competitions.

Artist's Market (Ohio). 9933 Alliance Road, Cincinnati, OH 45242.

The Arts Advocate. C/O Associated Councils of the Arts, 570 Seventh Avenue, New York, NY 10018. Quarterly, $15 includes minimum membership fee.

Arts and Crafts Newsletter. 131 Sunset Drive, Burlington, VT 05401. Quarterly. Listing of craft shows and fairs in New England, new books and films.

Arts and Crafts Society News. 616 Northwest Eighteenth Avenue, Portland, OR 97209. $8 and up includes membership.

Arts, Inc. Newsletter for Job Referral in the Visual and Performing Arts. Box 32382, Washington, DC 20007. Monthly, $15. Nationwide clearinghouse for job opportunities in the arts. Information on current opportunities in the areas of employment, exhibitions, galleries and freelance assignments.

The Arts Journal. 324 Charlotte Street, Asheville, NC 28801. Monthly, $3, 25 cents single issue. Covers Western North Carolina's arts and crafts with news on exhibitions, fairs and workshops.

Artweek, West Coast News. 1305 Franklin Street, Oakland, CA 94612. Forty-four issues per year, $14. Exhibition reviews, calendar and competition listings; emphasis is on California and the West.

Art Workers News. 220 Fifth Avenue, New York, NY 10001. Subscription with membership $10, subscription only $7, institutions $12. Coverage concerns art and politics, both in New York City and on a national level.

The Bead Journal. Box 24 C 47, Los Angeles, CA 90024. Quarterly, $12. Features articles on ancient, ethnic and contemporary jewelry. For serious professional jewelers.

Bittersweet. Bittersweet, Inc., Special Class at Lebanon High School, 777 Brice Street, Lebanon, MO 65536. Quarterly, $6. Articles feature craftspeople of the Ozark area of the U.S.

Black Sheep Newsletter. Route 2, Box 123-D, Monroe, OR 97456. Quarterly, $2. Serves growers of black sheep, spinners and weavers throughout the U.S., Canada and Australia. Focus is on such topics as buying fleeces, raising black sheep and testing tensile strength.

CGC Newsletter. Connecticut Guild of Craftsmen, Inc., P.O. Box 374, Bloomfield, CT 06002. Monthly, $10 and up including membership. Connecticut crafts happenings plus national exhibitions.

CHAN Newsletter. Center for the History of American Needlework, 2216 Murray Avenue, Pittsburgh, PA 15217. Quarterly, $10 includes membership. Organizational focus, news about all areas of needlework and stitchery.

Canada Crafts. G.P. Page Publications Ltd., 380 Wellington Street West, Toronto, Ontario, Canada M5V 1E3. Bi-monthly, $15. Canadian craft activities, events and exhibitions.

Canada Quilts. Conroyal Publications, 360 Stewart Drive, Sudbury, Ontario, Canada P3E 2R8. Five issues per year, $4.45.

Canadian Crafts Council Newsletter. *See* Artisan (Canadain Crafts Council).

Casting and Jewelry Craft. Alian Publications Inc., 507 Fifth Avenue, New York, NY 10017. Bi-monthly, $7.50. An illustrated magazine containing technical information, pertinent articles by prominent jewelers and a new products section.

Center for the History of American Needlework. *See* CHAN Newsletter.

Center for the Visual Arts Newsletter. City Center, 1333 Broadway, Oakland, CA 94612. Bi-monthly, $15 artist membership, $20 and up non-artist membership.

Ceramic Scope. 6363 Wilshire Boulevard, Los Angeles, CA 90048. Monthly, $5. For dealers, distributors and teachers in the ceramic hobby industry. Articles cover all phases of studio management as well as teaching projects and case histories of studio operation.

Ceramics Industry. Cahners Publishing Co., 270 St. Paul Street, Denver, CO 80206. $8. Primarily a trade magazine for industrial ceramic companies. Contains useful information for the studio potter.

Ceramics Monthly. P.O. Box 12448, Columbus, OH 43212. Monthly, $8. Includes features on ceramists, instructional articles, exhibition reviews and calendar.

Chicago Artists Coalition Newsletter. C/O CAC, Margalit Matso, 4146 Clarendon, Chicago, IL 60613. Subscription with membership $12, subscription only $3.

The China Decorator. Box 575, Shingle Springs, CA 95682. Monthly, $7.

Chip Chats. National Woodcarvers Association, 7424 Miami Avenue, Cincinnati, OH 45243. Bi-monthly, $5 includes membership. Woodcarving and whittling.

Cobblestone, The Art Newspaper for Southern California. Fragments West, Box 1128, Los Alamitos, CA 90720. Monthly, $5.

Colorado Art Show News. Colorado Art Shows, Inc., Box 609, Littleton, CO 80120. Quarterly, $10. Listings of fine art and craft shows in Colorado and adjacent states.

Congressional Branch, Embroiders Guild Newsletter. C/O Fran Winston, 3917 Leisure Drive, Temple Hills, MD 20031.

Counted Thread Society of America Newsletter. 3305 South Newport Street, Denver, CO 80224. $3.

Craft and Folk Art Museum Newsletter and Calender of Events. 5814 Wilshire Boulevard, Los Angeles, CA 90036. Quarterly, $25 and up including membership. News of the Museum's events, classes, exhibitions and publications.

Craft Connection. Minnesota Crafts Council, P.O. Box 1182, Minneapolis, MN 55440. Bi-monthly, subscription with membership $10, subscription only $6. Written for and about the Midwestern crafts community.

Craft Dimensions/Artisanale. Canadian Guild of Crafts, 29 Prince Arthur Avenue, Toronto, Ontario, Canada M5R1B2. Bi-monthly, $10, $2 single issue.

Craft Horizons. American Crafts Council, 44 West Fifty-third Street, New York, NY 10019. Bi-monthly, $18 includes membership. Covers all craft media on an international basis. Calendar, exhibition, film and book reviews and feature articles.

Craft Midwest. *See* Working Craftsman.

Craft Model and Hobby Industry. Hobby Publications, 225 West Thirty-fourth Street, New York, NY 10001. Monthly, $5. Trade magazine. Emphasis on product promotion and company stories.

Craft News. Mass Craft, Box 858, Laveratt, MA 01054. Monthly. Published by Western Massachusetts Craft Marketing Project.

Craft News. Ontario Crafts Council, 346 Dundas Street West, Toronto, Ontario, Canada M5T 1G5. Bi-monthly.

Craft Ontario. Ontario Craft Foundation, 8 York Street, Toronto, Ontario, Canada M5J 1R2. Ceramics, fiber arts.

The Craft Tradesman. United Maine Craftsmen, RFD 2, Litchfield, ME 04350. $5 includes active membership, $7 includes family membership. Maine fairs listings. National coverage on suppliers, feature articles.

Crafts. Piedmont Craftsmen, Inc., 300 South Main Street, Winston-Salem, NC 27101.

Bi-monthly, $10 includes associate membership, $15 exhibiting membership, $25 patron.

Crafts Annual. New York State Craftsmen, Inc., 27 West Fifty-third Street, New York, NY 10019. Annual, $1.50 single issue. Directories of craft resources such as shops, books, organizations, films and courses, with an emphasis on New York State.

Crafts Bulletin. New York State Craftsmen, Inc., 27 West Fifty-third Street, New York, NY 10019. Monthly, $20 includes membership. A guide to craft events, jobs, grants, competitions, and other opportunities for the craftsperson living in New York State.

The Crafts Fair Guide. P.O. Box 262, Mill Valley, CA 94941. Quarterly with monthly supplements, $10 for two issues.

The Crafts Report. 1529 East Nineteenth Street, Brooklyn, NY 11230. Monthly, $13.50. Crafts marketing, merchandising techniques, selling opportunities, legal and accounting problems, and other business subjects.

Craftsman. Ontario Crafts Council, 346 Dundas Street West, Toronto, Ontario, Canada M5T 1G5. Bi-monthly, $10 includes membership. Excellent photographs and interviews.

The Craftsman's Gallery. The Guild of American Craftsmen, Box 645, Rockville, MD 20851. Quarterly, $8. Profiles of craftspeople and their work.

Craftspirit '76. Artisan Crafts, P.O. Box 398, Libertyville, IL 60048. Three issues per year, $6. Published as a Bicentennial special with articles on crafts in all media.

Creative Crafts. P.O. Box 700, Newton, NJ 07860. Bi-monthly, $4.50. Instructional magazine for the serious hobbyist.

The Creative Needle: A newsletter for Needlework Lovers. Erica Wilson's Creative Needlework Society, 717 Madison Avenue, New York, NY 10021. Quarterly, $3 includes membership.

The Cultural Post. National Endowment for the Arts, Program Information, Mail Stop 550, Washington, DC 20506. Bi-monthly, free.

Decorating and Craft Ideas. Southern Living, Inc., 1303 Foch Street, Ft. Worth, TX 76107. Ten issues per year, $8. The magazine for the creative woman. Good mass market magazine. Contains lots of projects.

Design: The Magazine of Creative Art for Teachers, Artists and Craftsmen. The Saturday Evening Post Co., 1110 Waterway Blvd., Indianapolis, IN 46202. Bi-monthly, $7.

The Dulcimer Players News. P.O. Box 157, Front Royal, VA 22630.

The Dumb Ox. A Quarterly Art Journal. c/o James Hugunin, 18521 Dearborn, #304, Northridge, CA 91324. Quarterly, $4.

Early American Life. Robert Miner, Publisher, P.O. Box 1831, Harrisburg, PA 17105. $6 per year. Articles on the arts, crafts and social history of early America.

Enamel Guild West Newsletter. Box 721, La Jolla, CA 92038.

Family Craft Ideas. 363 Seventh Avenue, New York, NY 1001. Bi-monthly, $5.

Federal Art Patronage Notes. 250 East 73rd Street, #11C, New York, NY 10021. $10 per year.

Feminist Art Journal. Feminist Art Journal, Inc., 41 Montgomery Place, Brooklyn, NY 11215. Quarterly, $7 individuals; $14 institutions.

Fiber News. Illinois Legion/Handweavers Guild of America, Center of Visual Arts/College of Fine Arts, Illinois State University, Normal, IL 61761. Quarterly. Membership includes conferences, exhibitions, workshops, classes, fairs, sales, and reference outline with guilds, publications, sources and other useful information.

Fiber Digest of North Carolina. 3 Dogwood Acres Drive, Chapel Hill, NC 27514. Quarterly.

Fiberarts. 3717 Fourth Northwest, Albuquerque, NM 87107. Bi-monthly, $9.

Fine Woodworking. Taunton Press, Box 355, Newton, CT 06470. Quarterly, $8.

The Flying Needle. 1265 Southwest 300th Place, Federal Way, Washington, DC 98003. Quarterly, $10. Journal of the National Standards Council of American Embroiderers, 826 Lincoln Avenue, Winnetka, IL 60093. Instructional articles accompanied by line drawings; calendar, Council news.

Gems & Minerals. Germac Corp., P.O. Box 687, Mentone, CA 92359. Monthly, $6.50. Tel. (714) 794-1843. Book reviews; features; new product news; technical features.

Gems & Minerals Merchandiser. P.O. Box 808, Mentone, CA 92359. Monthly, free. Trade paper for people who buy gems.

Glass. Evergreen Publishing Corp., 7830 Southwest 40th Avenue, Portland, OR 97219. Monthly, $20. A color illustrated magazine about contemporary stained glass. Features include consumer reports on supplies and tools for stained glass, interviews with artists, art consultants and architects. Formerly Glass Art.

Glass Art Magazine. Oakland, CA. See Glass (Portland, OR).

Glass Art Society (GAS). C/O Tom McGlauchlin, Toledo Museum of Art, Toledo, OH 43609. Newsletter.

The Glass Workshop. Stained Glass Club, P.O. Box 244, Norwood, NJ 07648. Bi-monthly, $4.

Gold Dust. Society of North American Goldsmiths (SNAG), 591 Washington Street, Wellesley, MA 02181. Bi-monthly, includes membership.

Goodfellow Review of Crafts. Box 4520, Berkeley, CA 94704. Monthly, $8. A journal promoting high quality handcrafts and containing articles of special interest to artisans in all fields.

Guild of Book Workers Journal. Guild of Book Workers, 1059 Third Avenue, New York, NY 10021. 3 issues a year, $36, includes Guild membership. Guild news and feature articles on individual bookbinders and techniques.

The Guild Record. The Kentucky Guild of Artists and Craftsmen, Inc., 213 Chestnut Street, Box 291 Berea, KY 40403. Bi-monthly, $7.50 individual membership; $15 group membership to Guild.

Handcrafters' News. 608 High Mountain Road, Franklin Lakes, NJ 07417. Monthly, $18. Exclusive, money-making, money-saving opportunities for the professional craftsperson.

Handcrafts. Handicraft Center, P.O. Box 2147, Halifax, Nova Scotia. Quarterly.

Handweavers' Guild of America. See Shuttle, Spindle and Dyepot.

Handweaving with Robert and Roberta. Ayottes Designery, Center Sandwich, NH 03227. Quarterly, $15. The Ayottes share their knowledge and experience as professional handweavers and designers with technical information plus tips on pricing and selling.

Highland Highlights. Southern Highland Handicraft Guild, 15 Reddick Road, P.O. Box 9145, Asheville, NC 28805. Monthly, $10. News about members and articles of general interest on crafts. Lists national craft fairs.

Indian America. P.O. Box 52038, Tulsa, OK 74152. Quarterly, $8. Indian crafts and culture.

International Guild of Craft Journalists. Authors & Photographers. Guild Bulletin, 1529 East 19th Street, Brooklyn, NY 11230. $5 individual membership; $10 institutions.

International Old Lacers. Newsletter: C/O Muriel Perz, 2141 West 29th Street, Long Beach, CA 90810.

International Wood Collectors Society. Eleanor Frost, 148 Summer Street, Lansboro, MA 01237. Bulletin.

Interweave. 2938 North Country Road 13, Loveland, CO 80537. Quarterly, $8. Technical and feature articles for fiber craftspersons with an emphasis on the West.

The Journal of Contemporary Metalcraft, Casting and Related Arts. Magic Circle Corp., 622 Western Avenue, Seattle, WA 98104. Quarterly, $5.50.

Journal of Glass Studies. Corning Museum of Glass, Corning Glass Center, Corning, NY 14830. Scholarly articles on the art and history of glass, lists of important acquisitions by private and public collections throughout the world, and check lists of recent publications.

Kentucky Guild of Art and Craftsmen. See the Guild Record.

La Mamelle. Box 3123, San Francisco, CA 94119. 8 issues for $12.

The Lace Magazine of the World. Muriel Perz, 2141 West 29th Street, Long Beach, CA 90810.

Ladies Circle Patchwork Quilts. Lopez Publications, 21 West 26th Street, New York, NY 10010. Quarterly, $1.25/issue.

Lapidary Journal. Lapidary Journal, Inc., Box 80937, San Diego, CA 92138. Monthly, $7. Articles include gem collecting, gem cutting, jewelry making, and gemology for the hobbyist.

Lapidary Reporter. P.O. Box 80937, San Diego, CA 92138. Monthly.

League of New Hampshire Craftsmen Newsletter. 205 North Main Street, Concrod, NH 03301. Bi-monthly, $7 includes membership. Current and national news, book reviews, news of Guilds' activities and exhibits.

Lily Weaving Suggestions Quarterly. Belding Lily Co., P.O. Box 88, Shelby, NC 28150. Quarterly. Fresh ideas about use of yarn from one of the largest yarn suppliers.

The Looming Arts. The Pendleton Shop Handweaving Studio, Box 233, 407 Jordan Road, Sedona, AZ 86336. Bi-monthly, $5.50. A bulletin containing supply sources, instructional articles and patterns accompanied by swatches and yarn samples.

Lynn Brooks Needlework. Rostam Publishing Co., P.O. Box 1374, New York, NY 10022. Quarterly, $4. Mass market; knitting, needlework and crochet projects.

McCall's Creative Handcraft. McCall Pattern Company, 230 Park Avenue, New York, NY 10017. Annual, $1. A how-to magazine featuring step-by-step directions for making handcraft and needlework designs.

McCall's Needlework Crafts. McCall Pattern Co., 230 Park Avenue, New York, NY 10017. Quarterly, $6. Subscriptions: P.O. Box 2650 Boulder, CO 80302.

McCall's Christmas Make-It Ideas. McCall Pattern Co., 230 Park Avenue, New York, NY 10017. Annual, $1.50.

Make It With Leather. Leathercraftsman Inc., Box 1386, Fort Worth, TX 76101. Bi-monthly, $6.

The Mallet. National Carvers Museum Foundation, 14960 Woodcarver Road, Monument, CO 89132. Monthly, for woodcarvers.

Marin Needlepeople. Chapter of Embroiderers Guild of America, C/O Blanche Drury, 90 Del Casa Drive, Mill Valley, CA 94941. Monthly, $12 includes membership.

Master Weaver. Z-Handicrafts, Fulford, Quebec, Canada. Quarterly, $5.50. Bulletin for handweavers. Deals with practical problems of handweaving designing, drafting, weaves, equipment, projects, yarns, exhibitions and marketing.

Message. Art Educators of Iowa, 1307 Muscatine Avenue, Iowa City, Iowa 52240. 3 issues per year,

$2.50 student membership; $7 active membership; $10 commercial.

Midwest Art. 2025 East Fernwood, Box 17419, Milwaukee, WI 53207. 10 issues per year, $5.

The Miniature Magazine. Carslens Publications Inc., P.O. Box 700, Newton, NJ 07860. $1/issue. For those interested in miniature doll and furniture making and collecting.

National Calendar of Indoor and Outdoor Art Fairs. Henry Niles, 5423 New Haven Avenue, Fort Wayne, IN 46803. Quarterly, $10.

National Calendar of Open Competitive Art Exhibitions. 5423 New Haven Avenue, Fort Wayne, IN 46803. Quarterly, $10. Listings of exhibitions by date with information on entry requirements and fees.

National Carvers Review. 7821 South Reilly, Chicago, IL 60652. Quarterly, $5. How-to's, patterns, suggestions and hints for the novice and accomplished carver.

National Council on Education for the Ceramic Arts (NCECA). C/O Dick Hay, Indiana State University, Art Department, Terre Haute, IN 47809.

National Needlepoint News. 171 Guadalupe, Sonoma, CA 95476. Quarterly, $3.50. Trade News; product information.

National Quilting Association, P.O. Box 62, Greenbelt, MD 20770. Quarterly, $5. Provides information on quilting on a broader level than most localized publications.

National Standards Council of American Embroiderers. See the Flying Needle.

National Wood Carvers Association. See Chip Chats!

N.E.A.C.G., Inc. New England Artists & Craftsmen's Guild, P.O. Box 142, Enfield, CT 06082. Monthly, $12. Shows, feature articles, local and national coverage.

Needle Arts. Embroiderers Guild of America, Inc., 6 East 45th Street, New York, NY 10017. Quarterly, $12 includes Guild membership. Instructional and feature articles on contemporary and historical needlework.

Needlepoint Bulletin. 50 South U.S. 1, Suite 200, Jupiter, FL 33458. Bi-monthly, $12. Projects, book reviews, and news on needlepoint.

Needlepoint News. Box 668, Evanston, IL 60204. Bi-monthly, $7. An illustrated magazine containing information, techniques and designs for needlepoint.

The New Art Examiner. 230 East Ohio, Chicago, IL 60611. 10 issues per year, $6.

New England Weavers Seminar. C/O Mrs. Robert Barrett, 68 Sweetwater Avenue, Bedford, MA 01730.

New York State Craftsmen, Inc. See Crafts Annual; Crafts Bulletin.

Newsletter on the Arts. 2968 Dona Susana Drive, Studio City, CA 91604. Bi-monthly, $6. Features, shows, exhibitions.

Northwest Designer Craftsmen, Inc. C/O Luella Simpson, 1440 Southwest 158th Street, Seattle, WA 98166.

Nova Newsletter. New Organization for the Visual Arts, 1240 Huron Road, Cleveland, OH 44115. 11 issues per year, $5.

Ocular. 1549 Platte Street, Denver, CO 80202. Monthly, $12. Current listings of gallery and competitive exhibits, instruction, grants and fellowship opportunities.

Olde Time Needlework, Patterns & Design. Tower Press Inc., Box 428, Seabrook, NH 03874. Bi-monthly, $3.50.

Ontario Handweavers and Spinners Quarterly Bulletin. C/O Ms. Pauline Fanning, 207 Crescent Street, Petersborough, Ontario, Canada KGJ2G5. Quarterly, $5. News articles and swatches.

Open Chain: Monthly Newsletter for Threadben-

ders. 632 Bay Road, Menlo Park, CA 94052. Monthly, $5. Includes crewel, stitchery, embroidery, needlepoint, applique, and quilting. Resource lists, book reviews, and features.

The Original Art Report. See T.O.A.R.

The Ozarks Mountaineer, Star Route 4, Box 10, Forsyth, MO 65653.

Pennsylvania Craftsman. Penn. Guild of Craftsmen, 227 West Beaver Avenue, State College, PA 16801.

Pennsylvania Folklife. 717 Swarthmore Avenue, Swarthmore, PA 19081.

Piedmont Craftsmen, Inc. See Crafts.

Popular Ceramics. Popular Ceramics Publications, Inc. 6011 Santa Monica Boulevard, Los Angeles, CA 90038. Monthly, $9.50. Instructional articles by prominent writers and experts in ceramics, mosaics, glass, china, painting, sculpture and related crafts.

Popular Handcraft & Hobbies: For Fun and Profit. Rower Press, Inc., Box 428, Seabrook, NH 03874. Bi-monthly, $4.50.

Popular Needlework and Craft. Tower Press, Inc., Box 428, Seabrook, NH 03874. Bi-monthly, $3.50.

Pottery Collectors Newsletter. Box 446, Asheville, NC 28802. 10 issues per year, $7.50.

Profitable Craft Merchandising. PJS Publications, Inc., News Plaza, Peoria, IL 61601. Monthly, $5. Helps the craft retailer make or save money. Lots of craft advertising.

Quilt World. The House of White Birches, Inc., Box 337, Seabrook, NH 03874. B-monthly, $3.50. Covers quilts, appliques and people. Includes quilt patterns.

Quilter's Calendar. (Mill Valley Quilt Authority), P.O. Box 270, Mill Valley, CA 94941. Quarterly, $2.50. For the serious quilt-maker and collector; a listing of monthly West Coast quilt shows plus exhibitions, tours, books and classes.

Quilter's Newsletter. Leman Publications, Inc., Box 394, Wheat Ridge, CO 80033. Monthly, $7. Articles, information and instructions on quilting.

The Quilting Bee Newsletter. 209 State Street, Los Altos, CA 94022. Free. Shop newsletter.

Quiltmakers Time. 521 Orkney Road, Baltimore, MD 21212. $1.50/issue.

Red Herring. C.I.F. Inc., P.O. Box 557, Canal Street Station, New York, NY 10013. 3 issues per year, $6 individual; $9 institution. Funded by the National Endowment for the Arts and New York State Council on the Arts. News on laws effecting artists, museum news, and feature news articles with national coverage.

Regional Art Fair List, Box 136, RR #1, Stockholm, WI 54769. Quarterly, $8.

A Report. Center for Folk Art and Contemporary Crafts, 2721 Hyde Street, San Francisco, CA 94109. Bi-monthly, $10 and up, includes membership. Notes about the Center's activities, a calendar of exhibits in the Bay Area and in depth article about current exhibit.

Rock and Gem. Behn-Miller Publications, Inc., 16001 Ventura Boulevard, Encino, CA 91436. Monthly, $9. Reports on the lapidary, gem and mineral hobbies, with an emphasis on how-to-do-it jewelry making.

The Rug Hooker, News and Views. W. Cushing & Co., North Street, Kennebunkport, ME 04046. Bi-monthly, $7. Instructional articles on hooking, designing and hand-dyeing.

Santa Clara Valley Quilt Association. 15305 Elm Park, Monte Sereno, CA 95030. Monthly, $12 includes membership; $3 subscription. A calendar of local events, news of publications and quilt patterns.

S.C.A.N. Southern Crafts and Arts News, Route #14, Box 571, Cullman, AL 35055. Bi-monthly, $7. $1.50/issue.

Sew Business. Wilsir Publications, 1271 Avenue of the Americas, Suite 3560, New York, NY 10020. Monthly, $3.50. Mainly concerned with sewing and fabric news. Also marketing ideas and articles.

Shelburne Spinners. Box 651, Burlington, VT 05401. Bi-annual, $2.

Shuttle, Spindle and Dyepot. Handweavers Guild og America, 998 Farmington Avenue, West Hartford, CT 06107. Quarterly, $12.50 includes mebership. A full color magazine reporting on all aspects of the fiber arts including feature and instructional articles, calendar and reports of new equipment.

Society of North American Goldsmiths (SNAG). See Gold dust.

Southern Crafts and Arts News. See S.C.A.N.

Southern Highland Handicraft Guild. See Highland Highlights.

Spin-offs. Maine Guild of Spinners and Weavers, C/O Norma Ballew, RR #1, Box 392, Yarmouth, ME 04096.

Stained Glass. Stained Glass Association of America, 1125 Willmington Avenue, St. Louis, MO 63111. Quarterly, $10. A magazine containing descriptive articles on contemporary and historical stained glass.

Straw Into Gold Review and Trade Journal. Straw Into Gold, 5533 College Avenue, Oakland, CA 94618. Quarterly, $3. Newsletter which focuses on fibers, dyes, weaving, spinning. Classifieds, reviews, events, store specials.

Straw Notes. 5533 College Avenue, Oakland, CA 94618. Quarterly, $1.95/issue. Vignettes on different subjects.

Studio Potter. Daniel Clark Foundation, Box 172, Warner, NH 03278. Semi-annual, $7.50. Profiles of potters, detailed technical articles on ceramic studio problems, feature articles on historical and contemporary ceramics.

Sunshine Artists, U.S.A. Sun Country Enterprises Inc., P.O. Box 426, Fern Park, FL 32730. Monthly, $10. Lists, reviews, and ratings of arts and crafts shows and fairs.

Surface Design. Surface Design Association, C/O Sara Edmiston, School of Art, Dept. of Design, East Carolina University, Box 2704, Greenville, NC 27834. Technical, business and career information on textiles, dyes and related areas.

Tactile. Canadian Guild of Potters, 100 Avenue Road, Toronto, Ont. M5R2H3, Canada. Bi-monthly, $10.

Textile Museum Journal. The Textile Museum, 2320 S Street, Northwest, Washington, DC 20008. Annual, $15 includes museum membership.

T.O.A.R. (The Original Art Report). P.O. Box 1641, Chicago, IL 60690. Monthly, $11.

Treasure Chest. The Egger's Journal, 87A Lewis Street, Phillipsburg, NJ 08865. Quarterly, $5. News of egg decorating, egg artists, shows, books, etc.

Untitled: A mid-South Quarterly Review of the Visual Arts. Mid-South Independent Artists Association, P.O. Box 82282, Memphis, TN 38152. Quarterly, $5 includes membership.

Village Artists and Craftsmen Newsletter. Box 292, Hamilton, NY 13346. Monthly.

Warp and Weft. Robin and Russ Handweavers, 533 North Adams Street, McMinnville, OR 97128. Monthly, $8.00. Includes woven samples for 4-harness loom, threading and tie-up drafts, book reviews, supplies information, news, and classified and R & R news.

The Washington International Arts Letter. Allied Business Consultants, Inc., Townhouse Four, Harbour Square, 1321 Fourth Street, Southwest, Washington, DC 20024. 10 issues per year, $6 individual; $32 institutions.

Washington Kiln Club. C/O Jane Shenker, 7700 Lindy Lane, West Bethesda, MD 20034.

Weavers Jounral. Rink Building, Suite 125, 1722 14th Street, Boulder, CO 80302. Quarterly, $8.

Weavers Newsletter. Box 259, Homer, NY 13077. 9 issues per year, $6. Information on supplies, exhibitions, grants, competitions, trends, and book and film reviews.

West Art: West Coast Art News Scene. Box 1396, Auburn, CA 95603. Bi-weekly, $6. West Coast competitions, fairs, festivals, pictures, exhibit and book reviews.

Women Artists Newsletter. Box 3304, Grand Central Station, New York City, NY 10017. 10 issues per year, $5.

Women's Day. Granny Square, Fawcett Publications, Inc., Fawcett Building, Greenwich, CT 06830.

Wool Gathering. Babock, WI 54413. Bi-annual, $1/issue.

Wood Burning Quarterly. 8009 34th Avenue, South, Minneapolis, MN 55420. Quarterly, $5.

Workbasket. Modern Handcraft Inc., 4251 Pennsylvania Avenue, Kansas City, MO 64111. Monthly, $2.50. Patterns and directions to knit, tat and crochet.

Workbench. Modern Handcraft Inc., 4251 Pennsylvania Avenue, Kansas City, MO 64111. Bi-monthly, $3. Tested plans for homeworkshop projects, guidance in home remodeling, repairs, shop tips, refinishing clinic, sources for tools and materials.

World Crafts Council. 29 West 53 Street, New York, NY 10019.

The Working Craftsman. Box 42, Northbrook, IL 60062. 5 issues per year, $9. Focuses on how and where to sell crafts. Formerly Crafts/Midwest.

Index of Crafts

Index of Craftspeople

Photo Credits

Adame, Susan 139, (Middle)
Adame, Tom 139, (Bottom)
Anderson, Robert 185
Arteaga Photo 270
Ayre, Bob 224
Axner, Howard 134, 135
Baca, Lorenzo 313
Barad, Dorothy 61
Bedford, Jane 333
Blair, Richard P. 49
Bletsch, Frank 308
Bloom, William 142, 143
Bloomberg, Bob 28
Bonar, Mark 44 (Bottom)
Boye, David 204, 205
Brashear, Wayne 265
Brier, Andrew 340 (Bottom)
Brousseau, Andre 189
Brown, Robin 6, 7
Brunner Studio 73
Buck, Norman 123
Buck, Shelley 52
Burlingame, Craig 74
Burns, Gary 325 (Top)
Caldwell, Margie 281
Castaneo, Wilfred 103
Clayton, John 97
Coatsworth, Josephine 234, 235 (Bottom)
Cohen, Jane 286, 287
Conde, Clemente 284
Cooper, Ron 162, 163
Cougar Photography 218, 219
Crutcher, Kerry 171
Davidoff, Michael 24
Davis, Clark 253 (Bottom)
Debye, Jan 155
DeHaven, Janet 188
Dobbins, Peter 10, 11
Dunagin, Dr. Jack A. 330 (Bottom)
Dobranski, Michael 299
Dougherty, Katherine 261 (Bottom)
Drower, Sara 175 (Bottom)
Easley, Dale 209
Edwards, Barbara 332 (Bottom)
Eksted, Christina 271
Emmons, Mush 150
Evans, James 242 (Top)
Ferry, James 152
Fleischmann, Crista 54, 55
Fox, Carol 260
Francia, Vicente 148, 149
Freeman, Robin 334 (Top)
Freeman, Stephen 304
Frizzell, Charles 283
Galt, Elizabeth 318
Gamble, Russell 288 (Bottom)
Gill, Robert 335 (Bottom)
Glass, Dan 29

Green, Murray 58
Harding, Goodwin 115
Harper, Rick 238, 239
Hawkins, Paul 267
Haywood, Robert 80 (Bottom)
Hellman, Almut 65
Hensel, Herbert 151, 202, 203
Herrera, Rogelio 212, 213
Hess, Panna 228, 229
Hillmann, Robert 88
Hodgkins, Fred 338
Holland, Nina 14, 15
Hooper, Jamie 90
Hotelling, James 85
Hunt, Randall 174
Hussy, David 176
Jeffers, Kathy 94, 95
Jones, Phyllis 254
Indian Images 324
Kahn, Herbert 340 (Top)
Kaufman, Michael 100
Kinzie, Huey 38
Kintzing, Chuck 328 (Bottom), 329
Kitchey, Kyle 136, 137
Kloperstein, David M. 291
Larson, Ninette 67
Lehrman, Don 330 (Top)
Leni Studio 76, 77
Liberty Studios 194, 195
Librizzi, Joel 331
Loffler, Gary 128, 129
Lommassen, Jim 2, 3
Long, Douglas 320 (Top)
Lynch, Gene 46, 47
MacSwain, Duncan 217
Maione, Michael 291 (Top Left)
Mann, Sally 230, 325 (Bottom)
Mariana, Nicholas 309
Marsico, Dennis 220, 221
Matthew, Curt 140
McCarthy, David 286, 287
McCarty Studio 321
McKay, David 78
Melious, Larry 112
Merchant, Weldon 206, 207
Milens, Sanders 200, 201
Milligan, Jeanne 30
Mitchell, Stan 314, 315
Moon, Anna Kaufman 346 (Bottom) 347
Moorer, Andy 290
Morris, Helen 297
Murray 198, 199
Myers, David 26, 27
Nathan, Kathleen Dillon 278
National Collection of Fine Arts 82, 83
Nielsen, James 118, 119
Novic, Barry 292
O'Neil, Jim 289
Optic Axis Photography 62, 63
Orser, Owen 320 (Bottom)
Palko, Sandor 274, 275
Patrick, Vernon, 110, 111
Perlman, Martin 344
Pirtle, Paul 282
Porter, Dorothy 328 (Top)
Price, Dean 122
Rehm, Jordan 106, 107

Rittberg, Barry 96
Ritter, Dave 322
Rockhill, Morgan 32, 33
Rosenblum, Maureen 113
Rosenbluth, Bill 300, 301
Ross, Fisher 331 (Bottom Left)
Rubin, Julius 18, 19
Samaras Photography 156, 157 246, 247
Sargent, Richard 164
Schipper, Jan 171 (Top)
Schwarz, Jonathan 53
Scott, Ed 244, 245
Semington, Craig 105
Sherman, Garry 20
Simola, Robert 79
Sitts, Ron 68, 69 70, 71
Smith, David 268, 269
Smith, Jack 121 (Top)
Smith, William E. 196, 197
Stanley, Bob 168, 169, 323 (Bottom)
Steir, Merle 226, 227
Stevens, Mike 43
Stokes, Rip 230 (Bottom)
Strayer, John 234 (Top), 235 (Top)
Streetman, Don 246
Sultan, Larry 319
Surving, Sagrina 346 (Top, Middle), 347
Swanson, Tim 130 (Top)
Takeuchi, Vincent 56, 57
Taylor, Kenneth, 316
Teis, Dan 108
Teller, Henry 263
Thomas, Wesley 86, 87
Thompson, Gary 24, 252
Thurston, Bill 285 (Top)
Tondra, Joan 261 (Top)
Tonelli, Karla 170
Trottier, Charles 153 (Top)
Valley Portraits 303 (Bottom)
Valley Studio 44 (Top Left)
Whipple, Andy 177
Winters, Lynne 67 (Bottom Right)
Wolter, Don E. 145
Young, Dave 124
Yuen, Simon 180, 181
Zimmerman, Robert 22, 23

The Goodfellow Photography Service

Bob Knickerbocker and Bill Netzer, 12, 16, 31, 34, 35, 36, 37, 59, 75, 80, 89, 98, 99, 104, 109, 124, 125, 126 (Top), 127, 153 (Bottom), 166, 249, 294 (Top), 297, 334 (Bottom)

Bill Netzer, 1, 25 (Bottom), 48, 66 (Top),100, 101, 102, 154 (Bottom), 158, 182 (Bottom), 184, 208 (Top), 210 (Top), 211, 214 (Bottom), 215, 222, 225, 232, 237 (Top), 240, 241, 255 (Top), 262 (Top), 264, 266 (Top), 266 (Bottom), 285 (Bottom), 294 (Bottom), 306, 324 (Top), 345, 348